D1030880

THE NEW MIDDLE AGES

BONNIE WHEELER, *Series Editor*

The New Middle Ages is a series dedicated to transdisciplinary studies of medieval cultures, with particular emphasis on recuperating women's history and on feminist and gender analyses. This peer-reviewed series includes both scholarly monographs and essay collections. The following books have all been published by Palgrave:

Women in the Medieval Islamic World: Power, Patronage, and Piety
edited by Gavin R. G. Hambly

The Ethics of Nature in the Middle Ages: On Boccaccio's Poetaphysics
by Gregory B. Stone

Presence and Presentation: Women in the Chinese Literati Tradition
by Sherry J. Mou

The Lost Love Letters of Heloise and Abelard: Perceptions of Dialogue in Twelfth-Century France
by Constant J. Mews

Understanding Scholastic Thought with Foucault
by Philipp W. Rosemann

For Her Good Estate: The Life of Elizabeth de Burgh
by Frances A. Underhill

Constructions of Widowhood and Virginity in the Middle Ages
edited by Cindy L. Carlson and Angela Jane Weisl

Motherhood and Mothering in Anglo-Saxon England
by Mary Dockray-Miller

Listening to Heloise: The Voice of a Twelfth-Century Woman
edited by Bonnie Wheeler

The Postcolonial Middle Ages
edited by Jeffrey Jerome Cohen

Chaucer's Pardoner and Gender Theory: Bodies of Discourse
by Robert S. Sturges

Crossing the Bridge: Comparative Essays on Medieval European and Heian Japanese Women Writers
edited by Barbara Stevenson and Cynthia Ho

Engaging Words: The Culture of Reading in the Later Middle Ages
by Laurel Amtower

Robes and Honor: The Medieval World of Investiture
edited by Stewart Gordon

Representing Rape in Medieval and Early Modern Literature
edited by Elizabeth Robertson and Christine M. Rose

Same Sex Love and Desire Among Women in the Middle Ages
edited by Francesca Canadé Sautman and Pamela Sheingorn

Sight and Embodiment in the Middle Ages: Ocular Desires
by Suzannah Biernoff

Listen, Daughter: The Speculum Virginum and the Formation of Religious Women in the Middle Ages
edited by Constant J. Mews

Science, the Singular, and the Question of Theology
by Richard A. Lee, Jr.

Gender in Debate from the Early Middle Ages to the Renaissance
edited by Thelma S. Fenster and Clare A. Lees

Maloryís Morte Darthur: Remaking Arthurian Tradition
by Catherine Batt

The Vernacular Spirit: Essays on Medieval Religious Literature
edited by Renate Blumenfeld-Kosinski, Duncan Robertson, and Nancy Warren

Popular Piety and Art in the Late Middle Ages: Image Worship and Idolatry in England 1350–1500
by Kathleen Kamerick

Absent Narratives, Manuscript Textuality, and Literary Structure in Late Medieval England
by Elizabeth Scala

Creating Community with Food and Drink in Merovingian Gaul
by Bonnie Effros

Representations of Early Byzantine Empresses: Image and Empire
by Anne McClanan

Encountering Medieval Textiles and Dress: Objects, Texts, Images
edited by Désirée G. Koslin and Janet Snyder

Eleanor of Aquitaine: Lord and Lady
edited by Bonnie Wheeler and John Carmi Parsons

Isabel La Católica, Queen of Castile: Critical Essays
edited by David A. Boruchoff

Homoeroticism and Chivalry: Discourses of Male Same-Sex Desire in the Fourteenth Century
by Richard Zeikowitz

Portraits of Medieval Women: Family, Marriage, and Politics in England 1225–1350
by Linda E. Mitchell

Eloquent Virgins: From Thecla to Joan of Arc
by Maud Burnett McInerney

The Persistence of Medievalism: Narrative Adventures in Contemporary Culture
by Angela Jane Weisl

Capetian Women
edited by Kathleen Nolan

Joan of Arc and Spirituality
edited by Ann W. Astell and Bonnie Wheeler

The Texture of Society: Medieval Women in the Southern Low Countries
edited by Ellen E. Kittell and Mary A. Suydam

Charlemagne's Mustache: And Other Cultural Clusters of a Dark Age
by Paul Edward Dutton

Troubled Vision: Gender, Sexuality, and Sight in Medieval Text and Image
edited by Emma Campbell and Robert Mills

Queering Medieval Genres
by Tison Pugh

Sacred Place in Early Medieval Neoplatonism
by L. Michael Harrington

The Middle Ages at Work
edited by Kellie Robertson and Michael Uebel

Chaucer's Jobs
by David R. Carlson

Medievalism and Orientalism: Three Essays on Literature, Architecture and Cultural Identity
by John M. Ganim

Queer Love in the Middle Ages
by Anna Klosowska Roberts

Performing Women: Sex, Gender and the Medieval Iberian Lyric
by Denise K. Filios

Necessary Conjunctions: The Social Self in Medieval England
by David Gary Shaw

Visual Culture and the German Middle Ages
edited by Kathryn Starkey and Horst Wenzel

Medieval Paradigms: Essays in Honor of Jeremy duQuesnay Adams, Volumes 1 and 2
edited by Stephanie Hayes-Healy

False Fables and Exemplary Truth: Poetics and Reception of a Medieval Mode
by Elizabeth Allen

Ecstatic Transformation
by Michael Uebel

Sacred and Secular in Medieval and Early Modern Cultures
edited by Lawrence Besserman

Tolkein's Modern Middle Ages
edited by Jane Chance and Alfred Siewers

Representing Righteous Heathens in Late Medieval England
by Frank Grady

Byzantine Dress
by Jennifer Ball

The Laborer's Two Bodies
by Kellie Robertson

The Dogaressa of Venice, 1200–1500: Wife and Icon
by Holly S. Hurlburt

Medieval Theology of Work: The Contributions of Peter Damian and the Medieval Movement
by Patricia Ranft

On the Purification of Women: Churching in Northern France, 1100–1500
Paula Rieder

Logic, Theology, and Poetry in Boethius, Abelard, and Alan of Lille: Words in the Absence of Things
by Eileen Sweeney

Voices from the Bench: The Narratives of Lesser Folk in Medieval Trials
by Michael E. Goodich

VOICES FROM THE BENCH: THE NARRATIVES OF LESSER FOLK IN MEDIEVAL TRIALS

Edited by

Michael Goodich

VOICES FROM THE BENCH: THE NARRATIVES OF LESSER FOLK IN MEDIEVAL TRIALS
© Michael Goodich, 2006.

First published in 2006 by   Cak
PALGRAVE MACMILLAN™
175 Fifth Avenue, New York, N.Y. 10010 and
Houndmills, Basingstoke, Hampshire, England RG21 6XS
Companies and representatives throughout the world.

PALGRAVE MACMILLAN is the global academic imprint of the Palgrave Macmillan division of St. Martin's Press, LLC and of Palgrave Macmillan Ltd. Macmillan® is a registered trademark in the United States, United Kingdom and other countries. Palgrave is a registered trademark in the European Union and other countries.

ISBN 1–4039–6691–5

Library of Congress Cataloging-in-Publication Data

Goodich, Michael, 1944–
    Voices from the bench : the narratives of lesser folk in medieval trials / Michael Goodich.
        p. cm.
    Includes bibliographical references and index.
    ISBN 1–4039–6691–5 (alk. paper)
    1. Working class—History. 2. Peasantry—History. 3. Europe—Social conditions. 4. Court records—Europe. I. Title.

HD4847.G66 2000
305.5'60940902—dc22   2005044600

A catalogue record for this book is available from the British Library.

Design by Newgen Imaging Systems (P) Ltd., Chennai, India.

First edition: April 2006

10 9 8 7 6 5 4 3 2 1

Printed in the United States of America.

To Maya and Gali

CONTENTS

Acknowledgments   ix

Introduction   1
Michael Goodich

1. Arnaud Sicre: Spy   15
   James Given

2. The World of Witnesses and the Holy Tribunal: Fifteenth-
   Century Trials of Castilian Judaizers   43
   Renée Levine Melammed

3. The Inquisitorial Perspectives of an Unmarried Mulatta
   Woman in Mid-Seventeenth-Century Mexico   67
   Amos Megged

4. The Multiple Miseries of Dulcia of St. Chartier (1266)
   and Cristina of Wellington (1294)   99
   Michael Goodich

5. The Toddler in the Ditch: A Case of Parental Neglect?   127
   Ronald C. Finucane

6. A Case of Demonic Possession in Fifteenth-Century Brittany:
   Perrin Hervé and the Nascent Cult of Vincent Ferrer   149
   Laura Ackerman Smoller

7. Single Women, Work, and Family: The Chancery
   Dispute of Jane Wynde and Margaret Clerk   177
   Cordelia Beattie

8. "...et examinatus dicit...": Oral and Personal History in the
   Records of English Ecclesiastical Courts   203
   Robert N. Swanson

9. Witness programs in Medieval Marseille   227
      Daniel Lord Smail

10. A Rape Trial in Saint Eloi: Sex, Seduction, and Justice in the
      Seigneurial Courts of Medieval Paris   251
      Edna Ruth Yahil

List of Contributors   273

Index   275

ACKNOWLEDGMENTS

The number of people and institutions deserving thanks for this volume is innumerable. Each of these papers is based on primary sources whose access depends on the goodwill and cooperation of scholars and libraries in Europe, North America, and the Middle East. Such libraries as the Bibliothèque nationale (Paris), the British Library (London), the Staffordshire Record Office (Stafford), the Bodleian and Exeter College Libraries (Oxford), the Biblioteca Angelica (Rome), the Archives nationales (Paris), the Vatican Library, Archives Départementales des Bouches-du-Rhône (Marseille), Archives Départementales du Morbihan (Vannes), National Archives (London), University of Pennsylvania Special Collections, Biblioteca Nacional (Madrid), Archivo Histórico Judicial, Institúto nacional de antrologiá e historia (Puebla), the Public Records Office (London), the Borthwick Institute of Historical Research (York), and the West Yorkshire Archive Service (Bradford) have allowed the contributors to this volume to make use of their manuscript collections. Thanks is due to the Masters of the Bench of the Inner Temple (London) for permission to use the Court of Chancery illumination, R.00-6-21; and to the Archivo General de la Nación (Mexico City) for permission to use AGN, Inquisición, volumen 1136, fc. [foliación corrida] 215.

Burrowing in these artifacts of the past, we have all had the exhilarating experience of unearthing the testimony of hitherto forgotten people who have helped bring history alive. To this distinguished list of archives and libraries must be added the large number of other universities and academic institutions that have provided the necessary support and hospitality needed to complete these papers. In addition, each of the fine scholars who have contributed to the volume has enjoyed the intellectual stimulation and assistance of a host of professional colleagues. My wife Marian has provided continuing encouragement. A debt of gratitude must also be extended to the anonymous reader and the editorial staff of Palgrave/Macmillan who assisted in bringing this volume to fruition.

Michael Goodich
Haifa, 2005

INTRODUCTION

Michael Goodich

Following in the footsteps of such historians as Michelet, Bloch, and Febvre to write "history from below" the aim of this volume is to chronicle the traumas, life changes, personal prejudices, and legal struggles of formerly anonymous folk drawn from the urban and peasant classes, who had been marginalized in earlier works.[1] The focus is on those whose lives have not stood at the center of the traditional historical narrative.[2] In recent years, the contributions and identity of such groups as the disabled, gays, ethnic minorities, and others have come to the forefront of historical inquiry.[3] Medieval history has ceased to be the narrative of the political, ideological, and economic victories of the governing classes. Medievalists have thus begun to raise doubts about the myth of a uniform, faith-oriented society that had so long held sway.[4] Such journals as *Quaderni storici*, *History Workshop*, *Annales, Économies, Sociétés, Civilisations, and Past* and *Present*, have focused their attention on the experiences of the peasantry and urban folk. The feminist movement has likewise encouraged the reexamination of women in medieval society, becoming a major dynamic force in medieval studies and the impetus for the study of other formerly neglected groups.[5] This has more recently been joined by works on the study of masculinity, and by queer studies, all of which might be subsumed under the broader rubric of gender studies.[6] Medievalists associated with the *Annales* school such as Jean-Claude Schmitt and Emmanuel Le Roy Ladurie, influenced by anthropology and other social sciences, have likewise studied marginal groups such as the poor, shepherds, and children; themes such as death, dreams, and ritual have also received greater attention.[7]

In many respects, as a historical period the Middle Ages itself has remained the epitome of "otherness," remote, mysterious, foreign, inexplicable and thus, perhaps more intriguing and attractive than the modern age and more amenable to a variety of interpretations and approaches.[8] Traditional historical periodization—ancient, medieval, modern—has likewise broken down, revealing the persistence of modes of behavior and beliefs over the long term (*la longue durée*).[9] Medievalists have begun to follow the path of early modernists, such as Natalie Davis, Judith Brown, and Carlo Ginzburg, for example, who have undertaken the microhistorical study of one person, family, or community rather than the accumulation of undifferentiated raw data or the survey of ideologically laden primary sources as a more authentic way of appreciating the past.[10]

This attempt to focus on a particular event, such as a battle or ritual, for example, or on one person's experience in order to discover clues to an understanding of the wider society has recently been adopted by a number of historians of medieval Europe concerned with the history of women, heretics, the peasantry, and other formerly neglected groups. As in the exact sciences, it is hoped that through an analysis of a small part of society it will be possible to shed light on the whole, that the microcosm can illuminate the macrocosm. Through the sharpened prism of one person, his or her family, or community, it is often easier to clarify the textured dynamics of society than through the perspective of theory or high politics.[11] Medieval society was in many ways a tapestry of localized communities, perhaps best understood on a "micro-local" level. The metanarrative that underlays so much historical inquiry can thus be best tested against individual cases.[12]

Perhaps the most fruitful sources for reconstructing the world of such otherwise inaccessible folk are the surviving medieval trial protocols recorded by both secular and church courts. These documents give voice to the experiences of the members of all social classes, male and female, rural and urban. Even the concerns of the clergy and nobility may be better reflected in such sources. As Edward Muir remarked:

> If documents generated by the forces of authority systematically distort the social reality of the subaltern classes, then an exceptional document, especially one that records the exact words of a lower-class witness or defendant, could be much more revealing than a stereotypical source.[13]

In the absence of sources produced directly by the "subaltern classes" themselves, criminal and civil trials, canonization hearings, and inquisition records may inform us about the lives of the unlettered and how the underlying themes of medieval culture impacted on the individual. The reading of such sources is accompanied by one central caveat. Because they were employed by the state or church the records kept by the court personnel, that is, the notaries, lawyers, judges, procurators, translators, and others may perhaps be suspect. Their reports are often summarized, rather than recorded verbatim, the translations from the local tongue may be inaccurate, and the documents necessarily circumscribed by the legal forms in which they were cast. Cordelia Beattie and Ronald Finucane, for example, in their essays in this volume thus warn the reader to be cognizant of the intervention of such persons in the narrative. We may often be painfully aware of their presence, functioning almost as hidden puppeteers, controlling both the subject of our inquiry, and even guiding our own analysis. These unseen actors have often laid down the rules for our historical encounter and have set the stage of the drama, in which the historian simply plays the role of another actor. Nevertheless, the probing questions of the court officials may allow us to recreate the lost private worlds of a host of otherwise silent denizens of our historical imagination.

The courtroom serves as a fit setting in which the convergence and sometimes conflict of private and public worlds is played out. Through a careful reading of the dialogue between deponents and their questioners, it may be possible to recreate a more textured portrayal of their lives and their social context. Witnesses and court personnel often present differing, or even conflicting portraits of the same events, thus freeing us from the hegemonic views found in formal legal treatises or commentaries.[14] The Middle Ages represent a particularly fruitful field for the historian. Conflicting and divided jurisdictions created a large number of legal fora for adjudication. Even a metropolis such as Paris contained several, sometimes overlapping judicial authorities—royal, municipal, seigneurial, and ecclesiastical (as is here pointed out by Edna Ruth Yahil). The chief liability for microhistorians is that prior to the thirteenth century, it is difficult to find continuous, reliable court records. England is probably best served with a welter of suitable primary sources. These include manorial and probate records, inquisitions postmortem, chancery proceedings, muster, tax, subsidy, mayor's court, and king's bench court rolls, courts of common pleas, deeds, county surveys, hundred rolls, pipe rolls, rolls of justices in eyre, of the peace, gaol deliveries, assizes, oyer and terminer, and coroners' rolls, along with a host of other legal records which may well serve the microhistorian (as reflected in the contributions by Swanson and Beattie in this collection). Medieval France is likewise well documented (see the articles by Smail and Yahil).

Some historians of heresy, sainthood, and religious minorities, such as Sharon Farmer, John Arnold, and David Nirenberg have already undertaken the use of court records in order to shed light on the social history of single women, heretics, and religious minorities.[15] The present volume contains a series of essays focusing on witnesses at such trials during the later Middle Ages (from the thirteenth to the fifteenth centuries). Two essays (Melammed and Megged) demonstrate the persistence and institutional continuity of medieval legal traditions into Spain and the New World (Megged). The processes of conquest, settlement, Crusade, and the imposition of religious conformity, born in the Middle Ages, continued into the Iberian peninsula and the Spanish colonies. Conducted under royal auspices, all of the features of the medieval inquisition were likewise established throughout the Spanish Empire. As Alan Watson has pointed out, "to an enormous extent law develops by borrowing from another place and even from another time. . .within the legal tradition there exists a strong predisposition in favor of borrowing."[16] This continuity of medieval traditions is perhaps nowhere more apparent than in Spain and the New World, where inquisitorial tribunals followed the precedents, investigative methods, procedures, and raison d'être of their predecessors. The inclusion of these two essays in this volume expands our definition of the Middle Ages, and provides fresh and compelling evidence of its persistence beyond its traditional chronological boundaries.[17]

The aim is to employ the individual case studies revealed through a reading of such court records as a means of learning about the wider society and about some specific themes which may otherwise elude the historian. An effort has been made to provide the reader with a wide variety of legal contexts, including the so-called inquisition (Melammed, Megged, and Given), canonization trials (Goodich, Smoller, and Finucane), local ecclesiastical (Swanson), seigneurial (Yahil), urban (Smail) and chancery courts (Beattie). We may profitably exploit these trials as a rich source for the mundane environment of the deponents, learning about such issues as how time and distance were measured, the geographical limits of the deponent's experience, collective and individual memory, the medical knowledge of the peasantry, the dynamic relationships among members of the family, friends, and neighbors and the daily struggle for economic survival. It is perhaps not surprising that a majority of the essays in this volume focus on women, since legal sources most readily lend themselves to the microhistorical study of their lives. Jewish women hauled before the Castilian Inquisition (Melammed), a brewer contesting her mistress' will (Beattie), a woman accused of stealing a pig and subsequently transported to Ireland (Goodich), and a mulatta healer and midwife in New Spain whose clients included members of the local aristocracy (Megged), are some of those formerly invisible persons whose stories are revealed here.

These trials also uncover a complex dialogue with the governing authorities and their servants, the officers of the court, and how various strategies might be employed to circumvent their intrusion into the lives of the witnesses. Such a study sheds more light on the role of the dominant ideology in the lives of individuals than one may acquire through a reading of philosophical or theological tracts, secular law codes or a host of other official documents produced by state, church, and university. Grand historical narratives such as the conflict of church and state, the rise of constitutional

government, or the feudal system are placed within a specific context.
For example, Yahil's contribution analyzes a case of rape in fifteenth-century
Paris, which provides us with a specific graphic example to complement
more general studies in the history of sexuality. Her paper reveals that
despite the severe penalties enacted for rape, prosecutions were extremely
rare, thus providing us with another example of the wide gap between
ideology, law, and praxis so widespread in the Middle Ages.

Such microhistorical reconstructions may help liberate us from the
stereotypical and return us to the complex, concrete environment of those
too often left out of the historical narrative.[18] Broader, more theoretical
approaches to history often overlook the specific cases upon which
observation of historical trends are based. A detailed reading of these cases
becomes the prism through which wider issues may be reflected.[19]
Each article in this collection contains an introduction to the sources (who
produced them and under what circumstances), an examination of the
authenticity or reliability of the evidence, a narrative reconstruction of
the events recorded in the testimony, and a discussion of the conclusions to
be drawn about both the immediate environment of the deponents and
their interlocutors and the wider historical context.

The contributions of Given, Melammed and Megged, which span a
period of four hundred years, deal with cases that appeared before inquisitorial tribunals. Historians now reject the notion of "the Inquisition" as a con-
tinual formal body with extraordinary power, but rather stress that this was
a form of inquiry established initially under papal auspices in order to investigate the dangerous spread of heresy in southern France and Italy.[20] This
trial method was applied to other crimes. The first papal bull which prefig-
ures the establishment of a new procedure, the "inquisition of heretical
depravity," was issued by Pope Lucius III in 1184, aimed at encouraging
local bishops to identify and bring to trial suspected heretics. Special investigators were appointed, and the legal trial method of *inquisitio* was adopted
(replacing *accusatio*) in the early thirteenth century under Innocent III. The
activities of the inquisitor spread very early to northern Europe, where
both heresy and witchcraft fell under investigation. The Spanish Inquisition
was established in the fifteenth century in order to deal with the special
circumstances of a region with large numbers of recently converted (albeit
often forcibly) Jews and Muslims who continued to practice their old faiths
in secret. Its activity was given a new lease on life by its extension to the
New World, where newly converted peoples often continued their prior
practices and beliefs or created a syncretistic faith that was frowned upon
by the authorities. Those found guilty of heresy might be forced to wear
an identifying sign on their outer clothing, undergo penance, take part in
a penitential procession, suffer loss of property, civil rights, expulsion,

imprisonment, or, ultimately, execution. Despite the zeal of the inquisitors, corroborating evidence was required, and we have thus been left an important legacy of testimony concerning the beliefs and mores of a broad segment of the population, both heretical and orthodox. The persistence of heresy in many areas suggests the occasional assistance of the local population in sheltering heretics and an animus toward the interference of the inquisitors, some of whom, like Peter Martyr of Milan, were assassinated. Isabel de Montoya (whose highly detailed case is presented here by Amos Megged) was brought before the inquisition in New Spain, moving about from place to place during her long career as a healer. Her clients included leading political figures, and she was tried several times before she was confined and her successful career curtailed. The cooperation of the local secular authorities was clearly a sine qua non for the prosecution of such cases. The deponents therefore devised a number of strategies to escape the tribunal, which are discussed in the essays in this volume.

The inquisition also represents the trial form applied to the papal canonization of saints. Although there is evidence of the testimony of witnesses and the weighing of evidence in earlier cases, in the thirteenth century all bulls of canonization were preceded by a formal inquiry in the course of which witnesses testified before a papally appointed commission concerning the candidate's life and miracles. Goodich, Finucane, and Smoller attempt to draw out the social history underlying such inquiries, which have been increasingly recognized as an effective means of reaching otherwise inaccessible persons. Popular versus elite views of the supernatural, the organization of the campaign for canonization, the genres of miracle in which the subaltern classes were involved, hearsay and eyewitness testimony, family life in rural society, and the distinction between magic and miracle, are just some of the themes developed through a reading of the testimony at these trials.

Among the holy persons whose files are examined in this volume are Vincent Ferrer and Thomas of Hereford, whose cults spanned a wide geographical area involving deponents of all social classes; and Philip of Bourges, whose cult was more geographically restricted. The focus here, however, is on certain select posthumous miracles attributed to the saint in which lesser folk appeared as witnesses and through which wider issues can be fruitfully perceived. The wide participation of women in particular, as in heresy trials, provides invaluable evidence which contemporary treatises (produced by men) and saints' lives, cannot supply. The clerical authorities directed these trials and the deponents were not given full rein to report their personal experiences of the sacred, but were required to adhere to a prepared list of questions. Nevertheless, the peasants and urban folk, young and old, male and female who testified are given a rare opportunity to provide their own versions of the alleged intervention of the supernatural in their lives, albeit via the filter of the prevailing ideology. The case presented by Ronald Finucane deals with a toddler who recovered miraculously from what appeared to be a fatal fall at Castle Conway in Wales, during Edward I's wars of conquest and colonization. It graphically illustrates the social and familial ambience at a military fortress built in recently subdued Welsh territory in the late thirteenth century. Finucane's treatment approaches that of a detective, provided with several conflicting versions of the same event, reported by different persons at different times (both immediately after the event and four years later), filtered through the reading/censorship of both church and civil authorities. Was the child's death the result of parental neglect? Was his mother drunk, and therefore in no condition to think of her child's welfare? Whose version of the events is more accurate? How much collusion was there among witnesses in order to enhance the putative saint's reputation? Finucane uses this case as the opportunity to reflect on social life and family ties in the border regions in the late thirteenth century.

Laura Smoller suggests how a case of possession in fifteenth-century Brittany could serve as the focal miracle in the canonization case of Vincent Ferrer and reveal to us the network of family, patronage, and friendship in the ducal household. The encouragement of this cult enhanced the position of the Montfort dynasty and countered cults associated with its predecessor. The exorcism of Perrin Hervé at the site of Vincent's tomb at Vannes ignited interest in the nascent cult. This was especially due to the large number of witnesses, the position of the *miraculé* as a client of the duke, the high status of the event's participants, and the importance of this particular miracle as a spur to other miracles experienced by the witnesses. Hervé's case thus serves as a prism through which we can view the dynamics of cult-creation and the formation of its constituency in the Middle Ages, revealing a complex web of familial, neighborly, and social ties which lay at the basis of the cult. In the same way, Goodich's paper provides a face to several rural women involved in the formation of the episcopal cults of Philip of Bourges and Thomas of Hereford. Dulcia of St. Chartier had suffered from possession, apparently brought on by being poisoned by her husband and his paramour with the assistance of a local witch. The various versions of her tale suggest how church authorities pared and censored cases which appeared suspicious. Cristina of Wellington had been found guilty of stealing a pig and was miraculously saved after being hanged for her crime. Due to the alleged posthumous intervention of Thomas of Hereford, her punishment was commuted and she was transported to Ireland. Her case represents a rare example of the convergence of the earthly and heavenly. The graphic testimony, complemented by our knowledge of the social, legal, and economic history of Herefordshire permit us to reconstruct the site and circumstances of Cristina's life.

A second series of papers deals with the milieu of heresy and its prosecution. James Given's contribution focuses on the well-known series of trials of heretics conducted by Jacques Fournier, bishop of Pamiers (later Pope Benedict XII) in 1320–23.[21] Arnaud Sicre, whose mother had been a Cathar heretic (married to a Catholic), cooperated with the inquisition as an informer in the hope of regaining his family's confiscated goods. He traveled across the Pyrenees in order to locate renegade heretics in their safe havens and lure them into the hands of the authorities. The account of his duplicitous journey as reported to the court provides a unique portrait of the lives of members of a dissident religious community in the process of disintegration, after its leadership and organization had been decimated following years of persecution. Arnaud's subterfuges managed to bring some of the Cathar faithful back into dangerous territory and eventually led to mass arrests and the virtual dissolution of the last remnants of the Cathar community. His motives appear to have been a combination of personal, venal, and ideological, recalling other medieval and modern cases of betrayal. This paper illuminates the marriage practices, social and familial ties, superstitions, and geography of the heretic community in the early fourteenth century.

The inquisition in Castile and New Spain are the venues for the trials against religious nonconformists presented by Renée Levine Melammed and Amos Megged. Despite the gap of two hundred years which separate these two papers, the contours of the two trials are very similar: one is directed against New Christians (*conversos*) accused of persisting in their Jewish faith in 1483–94; the other against a woman who made use of pre-Christian healing practices to assist persons of all social classes in seventeenth century Mexico. Both cases paint a far more textured and conflicted portrait of the transition from old to new faith than can be conveyed in traditional narrative or theological texts. The role of friends, employees, coreligionists, clients, house servants, spouses, and other close family members as informers in cases tried before inquisitorial courts and the intrusion of the public into the private is no more evident than in these cases. Six trials are examined by Melammed. The defendants and other witnesses at Ciudad Real provide testimony about the daily lives, religious rituals, and beliefs of the secret Jews, and reveal the strategies of subterfuge necessarily employed by those caught in the ideological conflicts of fifteenth-century Spain. In the case presented by Amos Megged, due to the extraordinarily rich documentation of the inquisition in New Spain and the fact that the chief defendant was tried several times in the course of thirteen years, we are able to reconstruct a veritable family and life history for Isabel de Montoya. An otherwise invisible figure comes alive, whose personal experiences are intertwined with the broad themes of early colonial society. Her knowledge of medicinal plants and the healing arts brought her into contact with all levels of Mexican society.

A third group of papers deals with the solution of disputes in the courts, both lay and clerical. Cordelia Beattie examines a case which was brought before the English court of chancery in the late fifteenth century by a woman asking to be recognized in the bequest of her former employer, a relatively wealthy brewer. This case reflects on women's position in the law. The file contains two versions of the relationship between the two women and the circumstances of the employment arrangement between them. The petitioner had understood that she would be treated as her employer's daughter and heir and was joined by her husband in the suit. Among the themes discussed are the nature of women's work, the relationships between employers and their apprentices and servants, and the terms of service and remuneration. The role of family and kin in the world of work is revealed.

Robert N. Swanson presents several cases adjudicated in the ecclesiastical court at York, which may be "the closest it is possible to get to medieval English oral history." The church housed a welter of courts and judicial authorities, all of which were subsumed under papal auspices. Many of the cases are formulaic and were necessarily edited as a result of the need to provide a Latin translation, and subornation, prompting, and collusion may have tainted the reliability of the testimony. Nevertheless, the examples analyzed by Swanson indicate how the witnesses were concerned to prove that their own version of events conformed to the *publica fama* prevalent in the region. One case relates to an attempt to impede the execution of a will. A second, more detailed case, involves a man who attempted to prove that his father's second marriage had been invalid due to consanguinity, thus canceling his "stepmother's" right to dower. Several alternative narratives were presented by the deponents. The third case pitted whole villages against each other in a dispute concerning the rights and identity of a subsidiary settlement within a larger parish seeking to claim certain traditional rights, such as the provision for a local chaplain. Many of the witnesses appealed to collective and individual memory in pleading their cases.

The issue of *fama* is likewise a central theme in Daniel Lord Smail's essay on marriage and dowry cases in the courts of Marseille in the fourteenth century. He argues that the boilerplate testimony characteristic of so much legal testimony in the Middle Ages is deceptive. The aim of witness programs and strategy was to create an overall impression rather than simply relate a series of facts, aimed at enhancing or impugning the *fama* or reputation of a deponent. He focuses on a case of dotal retrocession, in which a woman's father attempts to regain a dowry which appears to have been swallowed up in the debts incurred by the insolvent estate of her husband and father-in-law. A culture of vengeance and recrimination characterizes this ten-month-long lawsuit. Whatever the facts of the case, the accumulation of testimony raising doubts about a defendant's *fama* could be enough to impeach his or her case. Thus, much of the testimony appears scripted (a feature of nearly all the trials examined in this volume) and the heavy hand of the lawyers and court personnel is apparent. Nevertheless, this case provides us with valuable evidence concerning the status and economic condition of some of the urban peasantry of the Marseille region and the "rhythms of everyday drinking habits," among other themes.

The case analyzed by Edna Ruth Yahil is drawn from the seigneurial court of St. Eloi in Paris in the late fifteenth century. It concerns a young Parisian dressmaker accused of raping and "deflowering" a servant-girl, despite his allegations that full penetration had not occurred and that, in any case, she was, if not a prostitute, at least highly complicit to his advances. This unusual case, by its very rarity, indicates the gap between the master historical narrative and the evidence provided by microhistorical research. Late medieval customary and legal texts prescribe severe punishment for rape. The absence of other documented accusations of rape, and the fact that in this case the young girl's defenders were more concerned with the family's honor and reputation and forcing him to wed her, indicates the chasm separating rhetoric and reality in medieval culture. This paper exposes us to the youth culture of late medieval Paris, populated by recent immigrants, apprentices, unemployed youth, and servants.

The essays in this volume invariably go beyond the testimony of the witnesses or the specific legal cases in which they were involved. Rather, such cases can be read as a microcosm of the political and intellectual history of the Middle Ages and beyond. A wider portrait is often revealed of the social ambience, ideology, and material conditions in which one person, family, village, community, or whole class of people, dwelled. Rather than the cultural and institutional history of the elite classes, the court records discussed in this volume have allowed us to rescue from oblivion a wide range of persons, including apprentices, peasants, the urban poor, litigious neighbors and kin, children, widows, laborers, renegades, religious nonconformists, and others. These papers draw us away from the political center into the margins and back again, focusing on the concrete rather than the abstract. Georg Iggers has pointed out some of the pitfalls of this approach: (1) the narrative of the microhistorian can too easily degenerate into "anecdotes and antiquarianism"; (2) past cultures may be romanticized; and (3) politics, still regarded by many as the skeleton on which history rests, is disregarded.[22] These caveats have been more than adequately addressed in the essays included in this volume.

Notes

1. See e.g., André Burguière, "The New *Annales*: A Redefinition of the Late 1960s," reprinted in Stuart Clark, ed., *The Annales School. Critical Assessments*, 4 vols. (London: Routledge, 1999), 2:35–46.

2. Eileen Power, *Medieval People*, 10th edn. (New York: Barnes and Noble, 1963); George G. Coulton, ed. and trans., *Life in the Middle Ages*, 4 vols. (Cambridge: Cambridge University Press, 1967), for two influential works that focused on less conventional sources.

3. Among the few discussions of this are Robert Bartlett, "Medieval and Modern Concepts of Race and Ethnicity," *Journal of Medieval and Early Modern Studies*, 31 (2001): 39–56; William C. Jordan, "Why 'Race'?" *Journal of Medieval and Early Modern Studies*, 31 (2001): 165–73; David Brakke, "Ethiopian Demons: Male Sexuality, the Black-Skinned Other, and the Monastic Self," *Journal of the History of Sexuality*, 10 (2001): 501–35.

4. The methodological problem of how "Christian" the Middle Ages was is discussed in John Van Engen, "The Christian Middle Ages as a Historiographical Problem," *American Historical Review*, 91 (1986): 519–52.

5. For a summary see Judith M. Bennett, "Medievalism and Feminism," *Speculum*, 68 (1993): 309–331.

6. See the case of a London transvestite working as a prostitute, in addition to his other occupations uncovered in David Lorenzo Boyd and Ruth Karras, "The Interrogation of a London Transvestite Prostitute in Fourteenth-Century London," *GLQ*, 1 (1995): 459–65.

7. Jean-Claude Schmitt, *The Holy Greyhound. Guinefort, Healer of Children since the Thirteenth Century*, trans. Martin Thom (Cambridge: Cambridge University Press, 1983); Emmanuel Le Roy Ladurie, *Montaillou, the Promised Land of Error*, trans. Barbara Bray (New York, 1978); Alain Boureau, *The Myth of Pope Joan*, trans. Lydia G. Cochrane (Chicago: University of Chicago Press, 2001); Malcolm Gaskill, *Crime and Mentalities in Early Modern England* (Cambridge: Cambridge University Press, 2000). For a collection of essays from the *Annales* school of historians see Jacques Revel and Lynn Hunt, eds., *Histories. French Constructions of the Past*, trans. Arthur Goldhammer et al. (New York: The New Press, 1995).

8. Paul Freedman and Gabrielle Spiegel, "Medievalisms Old and New: The Rediscovery of Alterity in North American Medieval Studies," *The American Historical Review*, 103 (1998): 677–704.

9. See Caroline Walker Bynum, "The Presence of Objects. Medieval Anti-Judaism in Modern Germany," *Common Knowledge*, 10 (2004): 1–32.

10. Edward Muir and Guido Ruggiero, eds., *Microhistory and the Lost Peoples of Europe*, trans. Eren Branch (Baltimore: Johns Hopkins University Press, 1991) contains articles taken from the *Quaderni storici* written by microhistorians,

along with a valuable introduction by Muir entitled "Observing Trifles" (pp. vii–xxviii); see also Carlo Ginzburg, *The Cheese and the Worms*, trans. John and Anne Tedeschi (Baltimore: Johns Hopkins University Press, 1980); Natalie Z. Davis, *Women on the Margins* (Cambridge, MA: Harvard University Press, 1995); Natalie Z. Davis, *The Return of Martin Guerre* (Cambridge, MA: Harvard University Press, 1983); Judith C. Brown, *Immodest Acts: the Life of a Lesbian Nun in Renaissance Italy* (New York: Oxford University Press, 1986); Edward Muir, *Mad Blood Stirring: Vendetta in Renaissance Italy* (Baltimore: Johns Hopkins University Press, 1998); Giovanni Levi, *Inheriting Power: The Story of an Exorcist*, trans. Lydia G. Cochrane (Chicago: University of Chicago Press, 1988); Richard L. Kagan, *Lucrecia's Dream. Politics and Prophecy in Sixteenth-Century Spain* (Berkeley: University of California Press, 1990); Jacques Revel, "Micro-analyse et construction du social," in *Jeux d'échelles. La micro-analyse à l'expérience*, ed. Jacques Revel (Paris: Gallimard, 1996), pp. 15–36. Some caveats in reading such works are suggested in Jill Lepore, "Historians who Love Too Much: Reflections on Microhistory and Biography," *The Journal of American History*, 88 (2001): 129–44.

11. Peter Brown has spoken of "micro-Christendoms" in his *The Rise of Western Christendom, Triumph and Diversity, A.D. 200–1000* (Oxford: Blackwell, 2003).

12. Sigurdur Gylfi Magnusson, "The Singularization of History. Social History and Microhistory within the Postmodern State of Knowledge," *Journal of Social History*, 36 (2003): 701–735.

13. Muir, *Microhistory and the Lost Peoples of Europe*, p. xvi.

14. Edward Muir and Guido Ruggiero, "Introduction: The Crime of History," in *History from Crime*, trans. Corrada Biazzo Curry et al. (Baltimore: Johns Hopkins University Press, 1994), pp. vii–xviii.

15. John H. Arnold, *Inquisition and Power. Catharism and the Confessing Subject in Medieval Languedoc* (Philadelphia: University of Pennsylvania Press, 2001); Sharon Farmer, *Surviving Poverty in Medieval Paris. Gender, Ideology and Daily Lives of the Poor* (Ithaca: Cornell University Press, 2002); David Nirenberg, *Communities of Violence. Persecution of Minorities in the Middle Ages* (Princeton: Princeton University Press, 1996).

16. Alan Watson, *The Evolution of Law* (Baltimore: Johns Hopkins University Press, 1985), p. 118.

17. This continuing history of the inquisition has often been told. See e.g., Edward Peters, *Inquisition* (Berkeley: University of California Press, 1989), pp. 75–104; Richard E. Greenleaf, *Inquisicion y sociedad en el Mexico colonial* (Madrid: Ediciones Jose Porrua Turanzas, 1985), 1–25; Francisco Bethencourt, *L'Inquisition à l'Époque moderne. Espagne, Italie, Portugal xve–xix siècle* (Paris: Fayard, 1995), pp. 17–34.

18. Carlo Ginzburg, "Morelli, Freud and Sherlock Holmes: Clues and Scientific Method," *History Workshop*, 9 (1980): 15–16.

19. Carlo Ginzburg, "Microhistory: Two or Three Things that I Know About It," *Critical Inquiry*, 20 (1993): 10–35; Barry Reay, *Microhistories: Demography, Society and Culture in Rural England, 1800–1930* (New York: Cambridge University Press, 1996), p. 260.

20. Henry Ansgar Kelly, "Inquisition and the Prosecution of Heresy: Misconceptions and Abuses," in *Inquisitions and Other Trial Procedures in the Medieval West*, Variorum Collected Series Studies CS708 (Aldershot, UK: Ashgate, 2001), 1:439–51; Winfrid Trusen, "Der Inquisitionsprozess: Seine historischen Grundlagen und frühen Formen," *Zeitschrift der Savigny Stiftung für Rechtsgeschichte. Kanonistische Abteilung*, 74 (1988): 168–230; see also Adhémar Esmein, *A History of Continental Criminal Procedure with Special Reference to France*, trans. John Simpson (South Hackensack, NJ: Rothman Reprints, 1968).

21. For a translation of the testimony of three of the leading witnesses at this trial, see Michael Goodich, ed. and trans., *Other Middle Ages. Witnesses at the Margins of Medieval Society* (Philadelphia: University of Pennsylvania Press, 1998), pp. 39–51, 117–43, 201–15.

22. Georg G. Iggers, *Historiography in the Twentieth Century. From Scientific Objectivity to Postmodern Challenge* (Hanover, NH: Wesleyan University Press, 1997), pp. 103–115.

CHAPTER 1

ARNAUD SICRE: SPY

James Given

The following is the story of one of the more unusual characters to emerge from the pages of the records of the inquisitors of early fourteenth-century Languedoc. Arnaud Sicre, the child of a woman executed for heresy, worked as a spy for the inquisitors in the hopes of regaining the property confiscated from her mother. The inquisitorial registers are full of stories of double agents, impostors, and traitors, but Sicre is unusual in the initiative he took in approaching the inquisitors, and in the success he enjoyed in penetrating and betraying the underworld of fugitives suspected of involvement with the heresy known, at least to modern historians, as Catharism.

It is tempting to think of the medieval inquisitors as all-knowing, all-seeing policemen whose inquiries penetrated into the most secret nooks and crannies of the lives of those they investigated. There is a grain of truth in this perception. The inquisitors were capable of extracting information from even the most obdurate of suspects.[1] But to picture them as comprising something like a modern secret police is surely wide off the mark. The inquisitorial apparatus in the south of France and its neighboring regions was not very substantial. To be sure, there were Dominican inquisitors installed in Toulouse, Carcassonne, and in the kingdom of Aragon. Some enterprising bishops, such as Jacques Fournier, bishop of Pamiers, established their own inquisitorial apparatus, but inquisitors were always few on the ground, their tribunals tended to lack institutional continuity,[2] and cooperation between them was often fraught with difficulties. The tribunals in Toulouse and Carcassonne had the most institutional continuity, but their staffs were very small. In the middle of the thirteenth century, for example, the inquisitors of Toulouse were served by about twenty-seven individuals, including four "masters," a sergeant, a cook, a doorkeeper, eleven messengers, and three jailers.[3]

To extirpate heresy the inquisitors needed the help of outsiders. Temporal and ecclesiastical lords were required to assist the inquisitors, but that assistance could be feeble and grudging. Parish priests were probably the most effective source of information, but many were more interested in getting along with their parishioners than in ferreting out heretics. Acquiring information was thus a formidable challenge to the inquisitors. Arnaud Sicre's adventures allow us a glimpse of at least one of the ways in which the inquisitors were able to penetrate the shadowy world of fugitive heretics and their sympathizers.

Sicre first enters the inquisitorial records not long before Christmas 1320, when he presented himself to Jacques Fournier's inquisitorial tribunal in Pamiers.[4] Fournier, who would eventually become Pope Benedict XII, had been operating his own inquisitorial tribunal from 1318, in conjunction with the inquisitor of Carcassonne.[5] What Sicre had come to offer the bishop was the alluring possibility of securing the arrest of a Cathar Good Man.

To understand the context in which Sicre approached the bishop, we need to go back almost a generation, to the end of the thirteenth and the beginning of the fourteenth centuries, at which time the inquisitors were engaged in eradicating the last significant cells of Cathar heretics in the south of France. Catharism was a dualist sect.[6] The Cathars believed that this world and everything in it was the creation of Satan (variously interpreted as either a fallen angel or an evil god co-eternal with the good god who had created heaven). The world was also a prison in which Satan kept confined those angels whom he had lured out of the good god's heaven. To make these spirits forget their heavenly origins, Satan had shut them up in human bodies. When an individual died, his soul, his angelic self, left the body, to be harried through the air by demons until it took refuge in the womb of the first pregnant creature it happened upon, whether human or animal.

To redeem these captive souls, the good god sent one of his angels, whom the Cathars identified with the Jesus of the New Testament, into the world to reveal to them their true nature. Unlike the Christ of the Catholic Church, this savior figure was not God himself, nor did he assume a human body, nor actually die on the cross. The Cathar savior bequeathed his followers the power to perform the central ritual of the Cathar faith, the *consolamentum*. This was a baptism of the Holy Spirit, conferred by the laying on of hands. Those who received it were freed of the taint of sin; when they died, their souls were not reincarnated but instead returned to heaven.

The sect was divided into two groups, which the inquisitors referred to as the "perfect" (*perfecti*, fem. pl.: *perfectae*) and the "believers" (*credentes*;

sing.: *credens*). The *perfecti*, whom the Cathars themselves called Good Christians or Good Men and Good Women, were individuals who, after a period of probation, had received the *consolamentum*. They devoted their lives to strict asceticism and to preaching and performing the *consolamentum* on those who were about to die, thus liberating them from the prison of this world.[7]

The *credentes* were, strictly speaking, not members of the Cathar church at all. Not having received the *consolamentum*, they remained mired in this world of sin and were condemned to reincarnation. What made them believers was the fact that they had agreed that when their final hour came they would receive from the hands of the Good Men the salvation-conferring *consolamentum*. This adhesion to the sect was figured in the ritual known as the *melioramentum* (which the inquisitors understood as an act of "adoration"), in which the believer prostrated himself before a Good Man, exchanged kisses with him, and called on him to intercede on his behalf with God.

This heresy had gained widespread support in the south of France in the late twelfth and early thirteenth centuries. Over the course of the thirteenth century it provoked a major campaign of repression by the church. The Albigensian crusades at the beginning of the thirteenth century brought the region under the effective control of the kings of France and drove the Cathar church underground. The fall of the Cathar strongholds of Montségur and Quéribus in the 1240s and 1250s convinced most of the local nobility that it was not in their interests to protect the heretics. The implantation of the Franciscan and Dominican friars brought the energies of these dynamic new orders to bear on the faithful of Languedoc. And the inquisitors of heretical depravity made the south of France uncomfortably hot for Good Men and their supporters.[8] The result had been a steady stream of Good Men and their believers across the Alps from Languedoc to the cities of Lombardy, where conditions remained for a time more favorable.

By the 1290s the Cathar sect seemed all but extinct in the south of France. But around Lent of 1298 or 1299 there arrived in Languedoc from Lombardy two Good Men whose initiative would spur the last efflorescence of Catharism in the south of France.[9] These men were the brothers Pierre and Guillaume Autier. Both had been notaries in the town of Tarascon in the county of Foix in the eastern Pyrenees. In 1296 or 1297 they experienced a spiritual crisis. They decided to abandon their homes and their old lives and go to Lombardy seeking salvation.[10] There they made contact with a Cathar exile community, gained instruction in the tenets of the religion, and ultimately received the *consolamentum*.

In Lent of 1298 or 1299 they returned to Foix.[11] They gathered about themselves a group of other Good Men, including Pierre's son Jacques.

This group embarked on its task of preserving the spirits of the remaining believers and seeking new converts at an unusually favorable moment. The inquisitors of Carcassonne and Toulouse were distracted by quarrels with the people of Albi and Carcassonne, who at times managed to secure the intervention of the pope and the king of France.[12] Looking back at these unhappy years, the inquisitor Bernard Gui would later note, "During this persecution of the inquisitors and interference with their office, many heretics came together, and their numbers began to multiply and heresies sprouted up and infected many people. . ."[13] For almost a decade the Autiers and their companions were able to crisscross Languedoc, preaching to secret gatherings of believers, and conferring the *consolamentum* on the dying.

Ultimately, however, the inquisitors overcame their problems and tracked down the Autiers and their colleagues. In 1309 Pierre Autier, lured by a traitor to Limoux on the pretext of performing a *consolamentum* for a dying believer, was arrested. On April 9, 1310, he was burned.[14] Almost all of Pierre's colleagues followed him either to the stake or into the prisons of the inquisitors.

Arnaud Sicre's family had been deeply involved in the affairs of these Cathar heretics, and deeply divided by them. Arnaud's mother, Sibille den Baille, was a fervent believer, renowned for her piety. Her husband, Arnaud Sicre, however, was hostile to the heretics. Therefore Sibille threw him out of her house, and forced him to move back to his native town of Tarascon. Subsequently, Arnaud became an inquisitorial agent, searching out fugitive heretics.[15] Sibille's religious beliefs also led to the scattering of her children. Sibille had three sons and a daughter. When she began to become deeply involved in heresy, the eldest, Bernard, was old enough to understand his mother's beliefs, and to keep his mouth shut about them. Indeed, Bernard eventually became a Good Man. Unlike most of his comrades, Bernard avoided the stake, escaping south over the Pyrenees into exile. Sibille's two younger sons, Arnaud and Pierre, experienced different fates. When Sibille became a believer, they were old enough to talk, but not old enough to understand what was going on. Sibille, fearing that their childish babble might betray her, sent them away. Arnaud went to Tarascon to be raised by his father. Pierre was sent to Sibille's sister, Alazaïs, in the Seo d'Urgel.[16] Ultimately, Sibille herself went to the stake and her property was confiscated.[17]

The confiscation of Sibille's property was the crucial factor that impelled Arnaud Sicre into the arms of the inquisitors. Of Arnaud's adult life before he set off on his quest to arrest a Good Man, we know almost nothing. His deposition indicates that he had mastered the trade of cobbler, but beyond that almost everything is blank. We pick up his story when he paid

a visit to his brother Pierre in the Seo d'Urgel, probably in the spring of
1319. There he sought Pierre's counsel on how he might recover their
mother's property. Pierre thought that the only way Arnaud could possibly
do this was to arrange the arrest of a vested heretic, that is, a Good Man.[18]
This Arnaud resolved to do. Aware that Cathars and their sympathizers
had fled into Catalonia and the kingdom of Aragon, he set off across the
Pyrenees to look for them. The search did not go well. Although he
scoured Aragon, he could find no trace of the fugitives. Finally, almost
exhausted, he arrived in the town of San Mateo, where he found employment making shoes in the shop of one Jayme Vital. One day, as he was
working on a pair of shoes, he heard a woman in the street crying out,
"Any grain for grinding?" Another man in the workshop, said to Sicre,
"Eh, Arnaud, here is a *gannana* [i.e., female worker] from your country."
Sicre went out into the street and asked the woman where she was from.
She told him that she came from Saverdun. Pierre, however, recognized
her dialect as being in actuality that of either Prades d'Alion or Montaillou,
two villages high in the Pyrenees and deeply involved with heresy. In fact,
as he was to discover, she was Guillemette Maury, a fugitive from
Montaillou in the Sabarthès. Sicre asked her where she was really from.
She replied, "And you, where are you from?" Arnaud said that he was from
Ax, and was the son of Sibille den Baille. Hearing this, Guillemette said
that Sibille had been "a very upright woman." Arnaud inquired if she knew
the whereabouts of his brother, Bernard, who was going under the name
of Jean. Guillemette sighed, "Oh me, so many friends of God are wandering through the world, not recognizing one another." Then she asked,
"Do you have understanding of the 'good'?" This was a crucial question,
since "understanding of the good" was a codeword for Cathar belief. To
this, Arnaud replied that, yes, he had an understanding of everything good,
if God willed it. Guillemette, observing that they could see one another on
Sundays and feast days, left.[19] A few days later, on San Mateo's market day,
Guillemette came to the workshop, accompanied by one of her sons, and
the Good Man, Guillaume Bélibaste.[20]

Bélibaste was from the village of Cubières, in the Capcir. His parents
had been warm supporters of the Autiers and their fellow Good Men.
By trade, Guillaume had been a shepherd. At some point he had killed
another shepherd, and fled to the town of Rabastens to escape punishment.[21]
The killing did not prevent him from later becoming a Good Man. During
the inquisitorial sweep of the Autiers and their colleagues, Guillaume had
been arrested and imprisoned in the *mur* at Carcassonne. But he and
another Good Man, Philippe d'Alayrac, had escaped. After spending a
night hiding in a stream near Carcassonne, they had made their way into
Catalonia. Philippe had eventually gone back across the Pyrenees, to be

arrested again at Roquefort in the Fenouillèdes. Guillaume's less than charitable comment on his companion's fate was that it was his own fault for having returned to a country where he knew persecution was raging.[22] Bélibaste himself made sure to keep the Pyrenees between himself and the inquisitors. Sometimes going by the name Pierre Bélibaste, sometimes by the name Pierre Penchenier, he supported himself at times by making reeds or sleys for weavers' looms,[23] at times by hiring himself out as a shepherd. Eventually, around 1315, he settled in the town of Morella, in the kingdom of Valencia.[24]

The initial meeting between Guillaume and Sicre did not go too well. Guillaume stared at Arnaud for a time, and then left the shop without saying a word. Guillemette, evidently vexed, said to Arnaud, "Act, act, my lord, in the name of the Lord!"[25] Despite this awkward beginning, a few days later Guillemette invited Sicre to visit her at home. There Sicre encountered Guillemette, her sons, Jean and Arnaud, and her brother, Pierre. As they were drinking, Guillemette took Arnaud's hand and led him out into the courtyard. There she asked him, "Would you not give thanks to God if the 'good' were shown to you?" Sicre replied, "What kind of 'good' are you talking about?" Guillemette said that it was the good that his mother and maternal grandfather had possessed, but not his father, on account of which his father had been expelled from his mother's house. Arnaud, showing a gift for deviousness, said that he had no desire to see that "good," since he and his father's family had suffered a great deal because of the heretics. Flustered, Guillemette replied that she had not been talking about the heretics, and changed the subject.[26]

Two weeks later Sicre decided it was time to make his opening move. He went back to Guillemette's house, took her by the hand, led her out into the courtyard, and asked, "That which you said the other day about showing me the good, were you joking?" Guillemette replied, "Why do you ask? Do you have the understanding of the 'good'?" Arnaud replied that he did, and that he had seen Pierre and Jacques Autier. Guillemette, impressed by his acquaintance with these charismatic figures, told him that she would arrange for him to meet the friends and companions of the Autiers, and asked him to return the following night.[27]

When Sicre did so, he found Guillemette, her sons, her brother, and Bélibaste all standing by the fire. Arnaud sent out for some wine, and as they sat talking, Bélibaste asked about his parentage. When he learned that Arnaud was the son of Sibille den Baille, he said, "You are the son of a person who was a good woman; if all the women from here to there were like her, they would be much more honest than they are." He added, "God still wants you to be a good man." To which Arnaud, said, "Amen." Guillemette interrupted, "My lord, the son of such a good woman cannot help but make a good end!" Bélibaste agreed, saying, "I know that if he wants to be like his mother, he can do only good."[28] Sicre then asked Bélibaste where he lived. When he found out that Bélibaste was dwelling in Morella, he asked whether the heretic planned to return home the following day. When Bélibaste said that his plans were uncertain, Arnaud offered to provide him with dinner the next day.

On the one hand, this meeting with the heretic seemed to go swimmingly. However, Sicre's ignorance of Cathar ways led him into some potentially damaging missteps. After Bélibaste agreed to eat with Arnaud if he were still in San Mateo on the following day, Arnaud took Guillemette aside and told her that he would send her some mutton to cook for them. Guillemette, amused, pointed out to Sicre what any good Cathar believer should have known, namely, that Good Men did not eat meat, but only bread, vegetables, and fish. Although Guillemette's suspicions were apparently not aroused by this, Bélibaste was less certain of Arnaud's good intentions. At least later, after Sicre had arranged his arrest, Bélibaste said to him, "O Judas! When you first came to me, I immediately realized that you were lying when you told Guillemette that you had seen the good *barbes* Pierre and Jacques Autier. If you had met them, they would have taught you to do a *melioramentum* when you met us."[29]

Despite his fears, Bélibaste continued to meet Sicre. The next night Arnaud, provided fish as instructed and dined with Bélibaste at Guillemette's. This time Bélibaste formally blessed the bread they were about to eat, and distributed it to those present, who received it in order, according to how long they had been believers. On receiving the bread, each believer said, "A blessing, my lord," to which Bélibaste replied, "May God bless you." After dinner, Bélibaste preached on how Saul was converted from a persecutor of the Good Men into the Good Man Paul, and on the greed of the Catholic clergy.[30]

The next day Bélibaste returned to Morella. A few days later another exile, Guillemette's cousin, Pierre Maury, a native of Montaillou, arrived at Guillemette's house. Maury, a shepherd by trade, had long been a devout Cathar believer.[31] When Pierre learned that Sicre was in San Mateo, he sent Guillemette to summon him. When they met, Pierre told Sicre that he had known him as a nursing infant. Indeed, he explained why Arnaud and his brother Pierre had been sent away by their mother. "You and your brother Pierre did not have the understanding of the 'good,' because at that time, when your mother began to be a believer, you two were little. But because you could talk, we feared that you would reveal us. Therefore your mother sent you to Tarascon, and your brother Pierre to her sister Alazaïs, who lived in the Seo d'Urgel. But because Bernard [Sibille's eldest son] had attained the age of reason and was beginning to have understanding of the 'good,' your mother kept him with her and he became one of the best believers in the county of Foix."[32] In the course of this conversation it developed that Pierre, despite his devotion to Bélibaste, did not hold him in the highest regard. At one point he asked Sicre, "Have you seen the lord of Morella?" When Arnaud said that he had, Pierre sighed, "Who sees the good that there now is, and saw what it once was, ought to burst, because the lord of Morella does not know how to preach. But he who heard the lords Peter and Jacques Autier, that was glorious; they knew how to preach well."[33]

Arnaud treated Pierre to some wine, and the two went out into Guillemette's courtyard, where they could talk frankly. There Pierre asked Arnaud why he had come to San Mateo. Sicre answered that his mother's condemnation for heresy had made it difficult for him to live in his own country. He had therefore come to Aragon to look for his maternal aunt, Alazaïs, who was rich, in hopes of being able to live with her. He was also searching for his brother Bernard, so that they could both live with their aunt.[34] After this conversation, Pierre returned to his flocks.

As the weeks passed, Arnaud was gradually instructed in Cathar belief and practice. He also learned a good deal about how the Good Men and their believers tried to conceal themselves. For example, Bélibaste made a practice of keeping with him a woman, Raimonde de Junac. This woman, although married to Arnaud Picquier of Tarascon, posed as Bélibaste's wife.[35] From Pierre Maury of Montaillou Arnaud learned how Cathar believers posed as good Catholics. Pierre told Arnaud that confessing to priests was worthless, since they were whoremongers. Indeed, confessing to a priest was like a sheep confessing to a wolf. Just as wolves kill and eat sheep, priests wanted "to eat us both alive and dead." Nevertheless, to keep up the pretense that they were good Catholics, believers should confess regularly to priests, taking care not to reveal their secret sins, which they should instead confess to a Good Man.[36]

Bélibaste also told Sicre how he feigned the outward marks of catholicity. He signed himself with the sign of the cross, observing that this was as good a way as any to shoo away flies.[37] Similarly, when his former companion and fellow Good Man Raimond de Toulouse lay deathly ill in Tortosa, Guillaume summoned a priest to his comrade's bedside to give him communion. When the priest asked Raimond if he believed that the consecrated host he was about to receive was the body of his savior Jesus Christ, conceived by the holy sprit and born of the Virgin Mary, Guillaume replied that he believed as a Good Man should, which is to say, not at all. When queried on the other articles of faith, he gave the same answer. Then he received the host from the priest. When Sicre asked Bélibaste if either he or Guillaume believed that the host was truly the body of Christ, Guillaume replied, "Of course not! But he would not have much of an appetite who could not eat such a tiny piece of bread!"[38] At Raimond's funeral, Bélibaste continued his mummery, sprinkling holy water on those in attendance. As he remarked later, three or four drops of water certainly didn't hurt anyone, especially considering that people on the road endured worse.[39]

Arnaud's experiences also provide insight into the problems confronted by the Cathar church in its last days. Central to the religion was the charismatic purity of its adepts, the Good Men. In the early days of the church, there had been extensive mechanisms to ensure the indoctrination and discipline of the Good Men, and at times Good Women. The church had been organized into dioceses, each with its own bishop. The bishop was assisted by two elected assistants, the "elder" and "younger son," and a number of deacons. Aspirants to the status of Good Man often spent a year of probation engaged in fasting and religious instruction before receiving the *consolamentum*. Discipline was maintained by the monthly *apparellamentum*, a collective confession of faults, presided over either by deacons or the bishop. And, to settle major questions, synods were held.[40] But when the Cathar church was driven underground, this organization melted away. The Autiers and their colleagues had been little more than independent entrepreneurs. And Guillaume Bélibaste reveals clearly that the caliber of person recruited as Good Man had declined.

For one thing, Bélibaste found it very difficult to live up to the strict code of sexual conduct required of the Good Men. His companion, Raimonde, seems at times to have been more than that. This emerges from the strange hugger-mugger of Pierre Maury's "marriage" to Raimonde. One day as Bélibaste and Maury were walking from Morella to San Mateo, Bélibaste tried to persuade Maury to marry someone who was a Cathar believer. If he did so, he would have someone to look after him in his old age. If he had children, they would be able to care for him in his illnesses. Finally, if he were married to a fellow believer, he would be able to fetch a Good Man to his deathbed to perform the *consolamentum*. Pierre's initial reply was that he did not want to get married since he had enough trouble as it was supporting himself. When Bélibaste continued to insist that he marry, Pierre asked the heretic's opinion as to whom he should wed. Bélibaste immediately suggested his companion. Pierre saw an obvious objection to this: Raimonde was already married. To this Bélibaste replied that he doubted that Raimonde's husband was still alive. Even if he was, Bélibaste thought that he would not come looking for them.

When they reached Guillemette Maury's house in San Mateo, they continued to discuss the matter. Pierre finally yielded to Bélibaste's entreaties, and asked him to speak to Raimonde about the match. He also asked that Bélibaste speak to his uncle, Guillemette's brother, also named Pierre Maury. The heretic's response was that they should not discuss the matter with anyone until after the marriage. Pierre should have realized that this was a sign of impending difficulties.

When they returned to Morella, Bélibaste spoke apart with Raimonde. A Cathar marriage presented something of a theological problem, since the Cathars regarded all sexual relations as sinful, serving to create new bodies in which the angels fallen from heaven were imprisoned. Nevertheless, Bélibaste had Raimonde and Pierre stand next to the fire, and made a little speech explaining his position on marriage. He stated that Good Men played no role in the wedding of believers, except to make a few remarks. If the two believers then agreed in the presence of the Good Man to get married, this was pleasing to the Good Man. This was the total extent of his involvement in the ceremony. Bélibaste then asked Raimonde if she wanted to take Pierre as her husband. When she said that she did, Bélibaste smiled and said that they had done well. And that was that.

After a wedding supper of eels, the newlyweds retired to bed. The next morning Bélibaste showed signs of regret. He refused to go to the market. Instead, Pierre did the marketing, buying some mutton for himself and Raimonde. When he returned to Bélibaste's house, he found the heretic sad and pensive. When he asked him what was wrong, Bélibaste said, "Nothing." Raimonde cooked the mutton for herself and her new husband, and some eels for the heretic. After they had eaten, Bélibaste was unable to work. Throwing himself on his bed, he put himself in the *endura*, refusing all nourishment.[41] For three days he lay in this state. Eventually he got out of bed, and Pierre Maury came home to find him arguing with Raimonde. Bélibaste complained that Raimonde was now speaking haughtily to him. When Pierre asked what they were arguing about, Bélibaste fell silent. Pierre, steeped in the patriarchal culture of his day, remarked that one should not attach any weight to the disputes of women. This prompted Bélibaste to say, "Alas, and it is for women's quarrels that I have labored! I see that I cannot stay here any longer!"[42] He started packing up his tools. Pierre asked him to stop and suggested that they all eat. Bélibaste and Raimonde, however, refused to eat for the rest of the day; Pierre ended up dining alone with Raimonde's daughter, Guillemette.

After eating, Pierre went out and did not come home until late. He found that during his absence Bélibaste and Raimonde had patched up their quarrel. All three sat down to eat, with Bélibaste blessing the bread. Bélibaste then proceeded to complain about the way he had been treated. To Raimonde he said that there had been a time when Pierre would have beaten her for speaking to him as she had, since, if a man is not the master of his wife, he is worth nothing. Addressing himself to Pierre, he said that

Pierre had taken Raimonde's side in the quarrel, and said that he was involved in the quarrels of women. Pierre replied that he had not meant to say this, but merely that the argument between Bélibaste and Raimonde had been like a quarrel between women. Bélibaste replied that he had understood Pierre's remarks in the first sense, not the second. Raimonde then asked the heretic to pardon Pierre, which he did.

The next morning Pierre and Guillaume took a walk outside of town. Bélibaste said that he regretted having arranged the marriage between Raimonde and Pierre. If Pierre were willing, he would release him from his bond to Raimonde. If by chance Pierre had impregnated Raimonde, he would send Pierre the infant once it was born. Pierre agreed to this, and shortly thereafter left Morella, in such bitter cold that he almost perished in the hills.[43]

In due time, Raimonde produced a child, whom Pierre acknowledged as his. However, there is a distinct possibility that the real father was Bélibaste. At least in the past there had been strong suspicions that Bélibaste and Raimonde were having sexual relations. When Condors Marty, Raimonde's sister, learned of Pierre's brief marriage to Raimonde, she told Pierre that she, her sister, and Bélibaste had once all lived in the same house in the town of Prades. One day she happened to enter the bedroom and discovered Guillaume and Raimonde in bed, with Guillaume on his knees as though he were about to have, or had just finished having, intercourse with Raimonde. She exclaimed, "*A na malnada!*[44] You have thrown into disorder the entire Holy Church!"[45] There ensued a major argument. Henceforth, so Condors stated, she had no respect for the heretic. Emersende Marty, who was also taking part in the conversation, remarked, "Ho, ho, nephew! It is no wonder that, if the heretic and Raimonde duped you, they couldn't stand your presence."[46]

Bélibaste was also remarkably superstitious, even by the standards of his day. On one occasion he asked Sicre to visit a Muslim diviner who lived in the town of Calanda. From him Arnaud was to try to learn where his aunt was living. Guillemette Maury also had her own list of questions to put to the diviner. She wanted to know whether a marriage between Sicre and one Mathena, the daughter of Esperte Servel, another fugitive Cathar believer from the county of Foix, would be a good idea. Guillemette also wanted Arnaud to inquire if her house was under a spell and why she, her sons, and her cousin Pierre Maury were losing their animals, since no one else in San Mateo was having the same problem. When Sicre agreed to carry out this task, she gave him pieces of clothing belonging to herself, her sons, her brother, and her cousin.

On his way to Calanda, Arnaud spent the night in Morella with Bélibaste. Raimonde, Bélibaste's companion, was suffering from heart trouble, and gave him a piece of her clothing so that he could ask the diviner what to do about her illness. The next day Sicre, laden with pieces of cloth, arrived in Calanda. There a young boy guided him to the diviner's house. Arnaud apparently was less confident of the diviner's abilities than Bélibaste and the others. For the first thing he asked, after having greeted the diviner, was if the man knew why he had come. To this the Muslim replied, "Am I God?" Arnaud then pointed out, fairly reasonably, that he had been told that the diviner knew in advance what was wanted by those who sought him out.

Despite this less than auspicious start to the consultation, the two agreed on a price of two sous jacquins for the diviner's services. The man then placed a book, written in Arabic, on the floor of his house. He sat on one side of the book, and had Arnaud sit on the other. Arnaud was given a little square stick of wood about as long as an index finger. At one end the stick was marked with transverse lines.[47] The diviner took a piece of clothing belonging to the person about whom a question was to be asked and put it on the book. Instructing Sicre to hold the stick firmly over the book by its cord, he began to read. As he read, no matter how much Arnaud tried to keep the stick from moving, it jerked about. The diviner then told Sicre to drop the stick onto the book. Once again, no matter how gently Arnaud tried to let the stick fall, it bounced off the book, sometimes a palm's length, sometimes two or three palms' lengths. All of this, so Arnaud told Bishop Fournier, he found marvelous.

The diviner's answers, however, were less marvelous. He told Sicre that he was either married or affianced. When Arnaud said that he was neither, the diviner said that people were working to find him a wife. Arnaud replied that he knew nothing of this. As for Sicre's aunt and his sister, Raimonde, the diviner said they were well and living in the kingdom of Aragon, and that Raimonde was married. Guillemette Maury was losing her animals because envious people had cast a spell on them. However, if she remained in San Mateo, by the end of the year her affairs would turn out well. Guillemette's son, Jean, should marry. Her cousin, Pierre Maury, the shepherd from Montaillou, should not fear to remain in the country, since he would be safe from his persecutors if he stayed with his animals and avoided the market. As for Guillemette's son Arnaud, he would not marry during the year. Finally, the diviner predicted that Raimonde, Bélibaste's companion would continue to suffer from various illnesses. Sicre asked no questions about Bélibaste, since he had been told that the diviner, although he could see the future of those who lived in sin and error, could see nothing about a man like Bélibaste who followed the path of truth. All in all, Arnaud was not impressed. He paid the diviner only 20 pence, telling him rather sourly that of the questions he had asked only half had been answered truthfully.[48]

Arnaud's testimony reveals not only that Bélibaste was a rather unprepossessing Good Man, it also shows that living a life in exile in constant fear of arrest was creating a strain among this group of exiles. One of the fugitives from the county of Foix was Emersende Marty of Montaillou, who had fled with her daughter, Jeanne, to the village of Beceite in Catalonia. There Jeanne married Bernard Befayt, also a devotee of Catharism. In Montaillou Jeanne had been a good Cathar; but in Catalonia she became, if not a good Catholic, at least a good hater of Cathars. She came to loathe the sight of the Good Men. On one occasion, she drove Bélibaste out of her mother's house and told him that if he ever came back she would kill him.[49]

She harassed her mother, calling her "a little old heretic," and threatened to have her burned. On one occasion the two came to blows. One day Emersende and Jeanne argued during dinner and Jeanne began to beat her mother. Bernard Befayt was summoned to administer husbandly correction, which he did with great zest, throwing his wife down the stairs and out of the house, a commotion which brought the neighbors to watch.[50]

Eventually the exile community began to fear that Jeanne would betray them. They met to discuss how to prevent this. Among other things, it was proposed to take her to a distant town and abandon her there. Not surprisingly, this was judged to be an inadequate measure, as was returning her to Montaillou, since there would be nothing to prevent her from going to the inquisitors once she had been abandoned. Finally, it was decided that the best solution was murder.

Lengthy discussions then followed as to the best person and method to carry out the deed. The techniques considered included throwing Jeanne off various cliffs and bridges and stabbing her with an assortment of lances and swords. The plotters finally settled on poison as the best method. However, the apothecary from whom they tried to buy some poison (under the guise of treating sick donkeys) refused to sell it, suspecting the purpose for which it might be used; Jeanne thus escaped with her life.[51]

To return to the narrative after this digression about the problems plaguing the exile community, Sicre, on his way back to San Mateo after his visit to the Muslim diviner, stopped in Morella. After dinner he and Bélibaste spoke just outside the heretic's house. During this conversation Arnaud began to lay his trap. After repeating the diviner's words, he added, "Since my aunt and my sister are here in the kingdom of Aragon, I want, if it seems good to you, to go look for them and bring them here to stay with you."[52] Bélibaste thought this was a good idea. Certainly, Sicre's aunt would want to live close to a Good Man. And he hoped that Arnaud's sister would be willing to marry Guillemette Maury's son, Arnaud. Guillaume, however, urged Sicre to wait about a month. Since it was almost Christmas, the short days would make traveling difficult.

The next morning Sicre left for San Mateo. A month later Bélibaste came to visit the believers in San Mateo. He met with Sicre, Guillemette Maury's family, and Pierre Maury the shepherd. They agreed that Arnaud would leave as soon as possible to find his aunt and his sister, whom Sicre claimed were living in the mountains of Palhars. He was to bring them to either San Mateo or Morella, where Sicre's sister would marry Guillemette Maury's son, Arnaud.[53] Bélibaste also wanted Sicre to find out if his aunt knew where there was another Good Man, since Bélibaste was tired of living without a companion. Bélibaste also urged him to marry the daughter of Esperte Servel, who was living with her mother in Lérida. Bélibaste pointed out to Arnaud that it was good for believers to marry one another. That way they could discuss their faith, receive heretics in their home, and receive the *consolamentum* on their deathbed, all of which was difficult if one spouse was not a believer.[54]

When Arnaud set off, he went, of course, not to look for his aunt, but to inform Jacques Fournier of what he had discovered. On his journey, however, he found time to make some stops. Raimonde, Bélibaste's companion, asked him to recover some goods she had left with Gaillard, the lord of Junac, and his sister, Esclarmonde. Having reached Tarascon on his way to Pamiers, Sicre made the detour to Junac. There, he feigned a desire to buy some salted fish. While he was in the fish seller's house haggling over the price, Gaillard arrived. Arnaud drew him aside and greeted him on behalf of Raimonde. When Gaillard asked where she was, Arnaud said she was not far, and that she had sent him to recover her goods. The two went up to the castle, where they met Gaillard's sister, Esclarmonde. Gaillard and his sister agreed to bring Raimonde's things to Sicre in Tarascon on the following Tuesday. On the appointed day Gaillard met Arnaud in the plaza at Tarascon. But he did not bring Raimonde's things, fearing lest he be discovered. He urged Arnaud to bring Raimonde to visit him and his sister, but Arnaud told him that she was in Catalonia. Gaillard then tried to persuade him to bring her into the county of Foix via the Balamir pass. Ultimately, when Arnaud returned to Morella, he discovered that there was a good reason why he had not been able to obtain Raimonde's things. Raimonde had arranged with Gaillard and Esclarmonde that any messenger coming from Raimonde would have to present a small knife that belonged to her to prove that he indeed represented her. Raimonde had not sent this knife with Arnaud.[55]

Arnaud also tried to recover some of Raimonde's goods from a woman named La Gasca, who lived in Tarascon. Arnaud found her next to the cross below the town of Tarascon on the way to Ax, and asked her if she had Raimonde's belongings. When La Gasca asked if Raimonde was near, he said that she was. However, at that moment some people happened by, and La Gasca broke off the conversation out of fear that the passersby might think something sinister was going on.[56]

After these fruitless detours, Sicre finally arrived in Pamiers. There he revealed to Bishop Fournier and his Dominican colleague, Gaillard de Pomiès, all that he had discovered in Catalonia and Aragon. From Fournier he received permission to behave as though he were a Cathar believer, as well as money to use in an effort to lure Bélibaste into the county of Foix where he could be arrested.[57] With the bishop's blessing and cash, Sicre crossed the Pyrenees back into Catalonia. In Lérida he stopped to visit Esperte Servel. He told her that he had found his aunt and his sister, and that his aunt was very rich. However, she could not travel, due to age and gout. But she very much wanted to see Bélibaste, and she wanted Arnaud to return to her around Easter. When Esperte learned that Sicre had visited the Sabarthès, she asked, "Is that evil spirit [i.e., Bishop Fournier] still in Pamiers?" Arnaud said that he was, but "now he can't hurt our friends because he is busy with the books of the Jews." Esperte replied, "Oh, the evil devil! Why doesn't he fall off a cliff?"[58]

From Lérida Arnaud went to San Mateo, arriving about two weeks before Christmas 1320. There he repeated his story to Guillemette Maury. He also told her that his aunt wanted his sister to marry Guillemette's son, Arnaud. When Guillemette asked if "that devil," the bishop of Pamiers, was still alive, Arnaud said that he was, and he was treating their friends very badly, even summoning to appear before his tribunal those who had already received penances and making them confess again. "And he is so evil that, when I crossed the passes, the hair on my head stood on end out of fear!" To which Guillemette said, "Behold what the devil's shadow does! Surely Satan is incarnated in him. He has Satan in his heart, and seven evil spirits." Ten months later, when Arnaud repeated this story to Fournier, he noted, with some circumspection, that he voiced approval of Guillemette's comment and added a few nasty remarks of his own about the bishop's cruelty.[59]

A few days later Pierre Maury arrived. He brought with him the news that Bernard, the husband of the evil Jeanne, had been killed when a rock fell on him as he was digging a ditch. Sadly, Maury observed, he had been damned, since he had not received the *consolamentum* from Bélibaste. Maury also wanted to know if the "evil spirit," Jacques Fournier, was still in Pamiers. When Pierre found out that he was, he wanted to know if he had arrested Pierre Clergue, the priest of Montaillou. Clergue and his brother, Bernard, although sympathizers with the Cathar church, had been betraying their fellow believers to the inquisition. Sicre told him that the bishop had had the priest arrested. On hearing this, Guillemette rejoiced, saying, "See what has happened to this priest, who persecuted the Church

of God! There is no one who persecutes it who does not come to a bad
end. And God demonstrates this in this very world."[60] For, so she told
Pierre and Arnaud, when Geoffroy d'Ablis, the inquisitor of Carcassonne
had died, no one was with him. But when in the morning his body was
discovered, two black cats were seen sitting on either side of his bed; these,
according to Guillemette, were the two evil spirits who had kept him company
in life.[61]

Sicre told Pierre that he wanted to use some of the money his aunt had
given him to celebrate Christmas with Bélibaste. Pierre was enthusiastic
about this, and they agreed to split the holiday expenses fifty-fifty.
Together they set out for Morella. On the way, Maury taught Arnaud how
to perform the *melioramentum*. At Morella they found the heretic, his companion, Raimonde, and her sister, Condors. Sicre informed Bélibaste that
he had discovered his aunt and his sister living in a town close to Cerdagne.
His aunt was very rich, and had for some time maintained two Good Men.
She had rejoiced on learning that Arnaud had acquired an "understanding
of the good." She was eager to see Bélibaste, but was unable to travel due
to age and gout. She also approved of the projected marriage between
Sicre's sister and Guillemette's son, Arnaud. However, Sicre noted, his
sister had to take care of their aunt, and therefore she couldn't come to visit
them. "However, if you could go to her [i.e., Sicre's aunt], everything
would be as you desire, because, as she told me, she believes more in one
word of yours than in a hundred of mine. If you want to make the journey,
she gave me enough money to take care of your expenses and bring you to
her on horseback. Nevertheless, do what you think is best. My aunt told
me that if you want to come to her, you should wait until Lent, when you
and other people are eating the same type of food. Since you don't eat
meat, if you came at another time, you might be recognized." Not wishing
to appear too eager to persuade Bélibaste, Arnaud added, "Nevertheless,
take care that no harm can come to you, because it would be better for
you to stay home than make the journey and have harm come to you. You
should think about this, for whether you go or not, I will give you that
which my aunt gave me for you."[62]

Guillaume asked, "Are the evil spirits in those parts now persecuting our
friends?"[63] Arnaud replied that they were, and repeated his story about
being so afraid that his hair stood on end when he entered the county of
Foix. When Pierre Maury asked who was persecuting the Cathars, Arnaud
replied that it was the bishop of Pamiers. Bélibaste asked whether he was
conducting his own inquisition, or relying on the Dominicans. Sicre
replied that Fournier was making his own inquiries, but was acting in
conjunction with one Brother Gaillard. At this Condors burst out, "I know
this Brother Gaillard, and he is already an old man. Oh, how long has the

devil lived!" To this Bélibaste replied, "Let the demons do what they can against the flesh in this world, for we will have the upper hand in the next."[64] Arnaud added one final detail to the embroidery of his deceit, saying that his aunt wanted him to search for his brother Raimond, the perfected heretic, in the kingdom of Valencia, so that he could bring him as well as Bélibaste to Palhars, since his aunt could support both of them.[65] After a long discussion, they ate dinner.

The next day after breakfast Sicre showed Bélibaste and Pierre Maury a coin known as an *agnel d'or*. This, he said, he had gotten from his aunt, along with nine others. Two he had already spent, but he still had the other eight. These Bélibaste could take if he wished, since his aunt wanted no one else to pay for his expenses during the holiday season. To this the heretic replied, "May this be for the love of God, and may God save our friends, both male and female."[66]

Four days after Christmas Pierre Maury and Sicre set off to look for Arnaud's brother, Bernard, and a believer named Raimond Issaura. Their search brought them to Valencia. There they learned that Bernard had left a long time before to take part in the war then raging in Sicily. Empty handed, the two returned to Morella. There, they continued to make plans for their journey north. On two occasions Bélibaste visited San Mateo to discuss arrangements. Finally, two weeks after the beginning of Lent, Sicre, Pierre Maury, and Guillemette Maury's brother, Pierre, and her son, Arnaud, set off for Morella. On the way there, Pierre said to Sicre, "Arnaud, you should realize how much the lord of Morella and we trust you, since we are willing to let the lord go with you! He sent me to see Emersende [Marty] at Beceite, since she knows and has seen more of the 'good' than we, to ask her if it was a good idea for the lord to go with you to your aunt. She said that it wasn't, because she had seen many lords betrayed by false believers and that we couldn't yet trust you fully, since you had not yet been proven. And she said, 'It would be much better if you, Pierre, or Arnaud [Guillemette Maury's son] or some other one went first to Arnaud's aunt, to see if things are as Arnaud says they are. If they are, then the lord can go.'" Maury, however, had told the heretic that they didn't need to worry about Arnaud, since, if he were a traitor, he could already have easily arranged to have them arrested where they were living. Persuaded by the logic of this, Bélibaste had decided to ignore Emersende's advice.[67] When Sicre remarked that Pierre had certainly given better advice than Emersende, Pierre replied, "Arnaud, Arnaud, don't betray us, for your family has had other evil people and false traitors to the Church of God."[68]

That night they arrived in Morella. Bélibaste was clearly feeling uneasy about the journey. For he took Pierre Maury aside and told him the following story. Worried about what might happen to him, Bélibaste had consulted one of his neighbors, a diviner named Galia. Galia had proposed the following: he would take one of Bélibaste's shoes and use it to measure from the hearth of his house to the doorway. If, when he had finished measuring, the shoe, or the greater part of it, was outside the doorway, this would indicate that Bélibaste would not return. However, if the shoe, or the greater part of it, remained within the doorway, then he would come back. The results of the test augured ill for Bélibaste: his shoe wound up outside the doorway. As a control, the diviner also measured from the hearth to the doorway using Raimonde's shoe. Although Raimonde and Bélibaste had the same size shoe, Raimonde's shoe remained within the threshold.

Maury told Bélibaste that he shouldn't worry about such auguries, since they were worthless. Bélibaste agreed that the hugger-mugger with the shoes might mean nothing, but that his father had set much value on such things. To which Maury replied that if his heart was set against the voyage, he should not go. Bélibaste replied that since he had promised Arnaud, he would go, "adding that if God the Father wanted him, it was time for him to go to Him."[69]

The group then turned to discussing the details of the fictive marriage arrangement between Guillemette's son, Arnaud, and Sicre's sister. Arnaud Maury agreed that, if he married Sicre's sister, he would not ask for a dowry larger than 60 livres, excluding clothing and a mule to carry it. Arnaud swore to this in the heretic's hands. For, as Pierre Maury commented, an oath sworn in the hands of a heretic was worth more than one sworn on the Gospels. To this Bélibaste replied, "You could certainly say so."[70]

The next morning Bélibaste, Sicre, Pierre Maury, and Arnaud Maury, Guillemette's son, set off for the north. Their first objective was Beceite, where they wanted to visit Emersende Marty. However, they were afraid that her daughter Jeanne might reveal them. So they halted just outside Beceite and sent Pierre and Arnaud Maury into town to see if Jeanne was around. They found Jeanne with her mother. This meant that they could not risk staying with Emersende. They were forced to lodge in an inn on Beceite's plaza. However, after dinner, Emersende took to her bed feigning illness. This persuaded Jeanne to leave the house, and Pierre and Bélibaste were able to dine with her.[71] As Pierre Maury slept, Bélibaste and Emersende sat up talking until cockcrow. When Maury awoke, Emersende repeated her fears that Bélibaste might be betrayed. Maury offered the opinion that if Bélibaste's heart was against the journey, he should not go, but should remain in Beceite or go back to Morella. Once again Bélibaste replied that since he had promised to go, he would go, and "if God the Father wanted him, it was time for him to go to Him."[72]

At this point Sicre's testimony begins to diverge from that later given by Pierre Maury. According to Sicre, Guillemette's son Arnaud left them that morning. Sicre also stated that, once the party reached Lérida, Pierre Maury also left. Pierre's testimony, however, makes it clear that both he and Arnaud accompanied Sicre and Bélibaste every step of the way on their final journey.[73] Whatever its exact composition, the party eventually reached Asco. There, as Sicre put it, they found good wine.

Bélibaste and Maury, despite having ignored Emersende's advice about the advisability of checking out Arnaud's story, still had some lingering doubts. For, as Sicre told Bishop Fournier, his companions pressed the wine on him. He also saw Pierre secretly mixing two wines together with the goal of getting him drunk.

Arnaud played along. Pretending to be drunk, he collapsed next to the table. Pierre put him to bed. When Arnaud began to act like he was going to urinate at the head of the bed, Maury helped him out to the street. There Pierre whispered, "Arnaud, do you want to take this heretic to the Sabarthès and make fifty or a hundred livres tournois? We could live honorably off such a sum. This peasant speaks only evil." Carefully slurring his words, Arnaud replied, "O Pierre, you want to betray the lord? I didn't think you would be someone who would sell him." Pierre answered, "And I would never allow it." Muttering to himself, Arnaud went back to their room and threw himself on the bed. Pierre removed his shoes and undressed him, and covered him with a blanket. Arnaud then pretended to sleep. He listened to Pierre and Guillaume discuss what had just happened, and heard Pierre say, "I have certainly found him loyal; he will not play us false."[74]

The next morning Pierre asked Arnaud, "How did you sleep last night?" Arnaud said that he had slept well, since they had had good wine. Pierre then asked, "What did we talk about?" Arnaud said he couldn't remember. At this point Bélibaste chimed in and asked Arnaud if he knew who had put him in bed, taken off his shoes, and undressed him. To this Arnaud replied that he had done it all himself. Bélibaste's retort was, "Friend, you were very well prepared to do all that!"[75]

That day they got as far as Sarroca. The next day they made Lérida, and stayed with Esperte Servel and her daughter, Mathena. That night, to further the pretense that he was a good believer, Arnaud ate three eggs, although it was then the middle of Lent.[76] The next morning they set out for Agramunt. Bélibaste told Arnaud that if he wanted to get married, he should wed Mathena, Esperte Servel's daughter, since she had the understanding of the good. Pierre, perhaps remembering his brief "marriage" to Raimonde, took Arnaud aside and told him, out of Bélibaste's hearing, that he should not marry a woman unless she pleased him.[77]

According to Sicre, as they walked along, two cawing magpies flew across the road. They landed on a tree beside the road, flew back to the other side, and then crossed the road in front of them for a third time. Seeing this, Bélibaste sat down. Arnaud urged him to get up, but Bélibaste said that he was tired, and added, "Arnaud, may God will it that you lead me to a safe place!" Arnaud said that he was, and added, "If you think that I want to betray you, could I not do it here as well as elsewhere?" To which Bélibaste answered, "If my Father requires me, may his will be done."[78] Pierre Maury's account of this episode differs a little from Arnaud's. According to Pierre, only one magpie flew over the road three times. And when the heretic sat down on a rock, all anxious and sad about what he had just seen, it was Pierre who told him that it was the business of old women to worry about birds and other auguries. To which Bélibaste answered that his father had taught him that it was a bad sign when birds flew over the path one was following.

Whoever persuaded Bélibaste to start walking again, once the heretic was on his feet they went on to the town of Pons, where they ate. They then set out for Trago, where they spent the night. But, for the rest of the day, so Pierre Maury later testified, Guillaume frequently said to Sicre, "Arnaud, God will it that you lead us to a good place!" To which Arnaud replied, "Let's go, my lord; if God wills it, I will do so."[79] On the way they forded a river, with Pierre Maury carrying each of his companions across on his shoulders. From Trago they went to Castelbón, and from Castelbón to Tirvia. In Tirvia they were in the lands of the count of Foix. Arnaud decided the time had come to spring his trap.

He spoke to the *bayle* of the place, a man named Pinhana. Pierre Maury saw the two together, but the only words he could pick up were Arnaud's cryptic comment, "Everything will end in a good harbor."[80] The next morning the *bayle* came with Sicre and a multitude of men to the house where the travelers were staying, and arrested them. When they were taken to the *bayle*'s house, Sicre approached Pierre and told him that, in the name of God, he should leave. He informed Pierre that he bore him no ill will, but that he had lost his property on account of the heretics, and he had contrived Bélibaste's arrest so that he could recover it. In Pierre's hearing, he told the *bayle* of Tirvia that he had hired both Pierre and Arnaud Maury to accompany him. As a result, the two were allowed to leave the next morning, taking with them two sous jacquins that Bélibaste had given Pierre.[81]

Bélibaste put himself into the *endura*. Arnaud, fearing that Bélibaste was trying to kill himself, told him that he regretted having him arrested, and that he would yet help him escape from prison. As a result, Bélibaste began to eat again.[82] Both Arnaud and Guillaume were imprisoned at the top of the highest tower in Castelbón, shackled together by the feet. Bélibaste, evidently not wanting to give his persecutors the satisfaction of burning him at the stake, told Arnaud that it was not yet too late to atone for his treachery. "If a good spirit can still enter you, and you repent of what you have done to me, I will receive you. Then we will both jump from this tower, and immediately our souls will ascend to the heavenly Father, where now there are crowns and thrones prepared for us."[83]

Arnaud did not accept the offer. For the rest of the time they were together, Bélibaste reviled him as no son of Sibille den Baille, but rather a Judas, a Pharisee, a son of the devil, and a viper. He also told Arnaud that there were four great devils who ruled the world, the pope in Rome, who was the greatest, the king of France, the bishop of Pamiers, and the inquisitor of Carcassonne.[84]

Ultimately, Bélibaste was burned in the town of Villerouge on the order of the archbishop of Narbonne.[85] Bélibaste's arrest was shattering news for his followers. The first to learn of the catastrophe was Esperte Servel of Lérida, informed by Pierre and Arnaud Maury. Esperte and her daughter, Mathena, promptly fled to Juncosa.[86] There they were later joined by Jean Maury, who married Mathena.[87] Emersende Marty and her daughter Jeanne fled to Alcañiz, where they later died.[88] Bélibaste's companion, Raimonde, together with her sister, Condors, went to Caseras in Aragon. Pierre Maury went to Mallorca, but he did not like the island, and returned to the mainland, where he eventually settled around Tortosa.[89]

Arnaud's career as an inquisitorial agent did not end with the capture of Bélibaste. There were still fugitive heretics at large. With Guillaume Mathieu of Ax he journeyed to Ax, where they captured one Guillaume Maurs of Montaillou. Guillaume was turned over to the inquisitor of Aragon, and ultimately transferred to the custody of Jacques Fournier. On July 4, 1322, he was condemned to perpetual imprisonment in the *mur*, or inquisitorial prison, at Carcassonne. Sometime in the spring of 1323 it was the turn of Jean Maury, his wife Mathena, and his mother-in-law, Esperte Servel, who were seized by Arnaud in Casteldáns. Pierre Maury, whom Arnaud had earlier allowed to escape, fell into Sicre's hands sometime around the middle of May.

These last four were handed over to the inquisitor of Aragon, Bernard Puigcercós. From June through December 1323 he interrogated them in Lérida. What became of Mathena and Esperte we do not know. The Maury brothers were transferred to Fournier's custody sometime early in 1324. Both gave long and detailed depositions to the bishop. On August 12, 1324 they were sentenced to life imprisonment in the *mur*. As far as we know, they both died in prison.

Arnaud also tried to use his position as an agent of the inquisitors to engage in some extortion. Sometime after having conducted Bélibaste to prison in Carcassonne, he returned to Tarascon where he found Gaillard, the lord of Junac, from whom he had tried to get Raimonde's property. To Gaillard he said, "Now, won't you give me Raimonde's cape?" Gaillard fell silent. Arnaud amplified his comments, "Raimonde lived in the same house with the heretic, whom I arrested; I know now that you didn't give me her things because I did not bring with me the knife which you had arranged as a sign when she left. You would do well to give me those things; otherwise be aware that I will reveal all this to the lord bishop." Gaillard was finally prompted to speech. "Now we know that no one but you can reveal us." He then made off, saying in a menacing tone, "Eh, good man, your master will not live forever." When Arnaud asked if Gaillard was threatening him, Gaillard said no, but added, "We have not done you evil; therefore you should not do us evil."[90]

Did Arnaud ever get his property back? On January 14, 1322, in the city of Carcassonne Bishop Fournier, Bernard Gui, inquisitor of Toulouse, and Jean de Beaune, inquisitor of Carcassonne, issued letters in which they declared that Arnaud was to be quit of any suspicion he might have incurred in feigning adherence to the Cathars. They also declared that, thanks to his success in arranging the arrest of Guillaume Bélibaste, Arnaud had acquired their "special grace and favor."[91] Whether this special grace and favor enabled Arnaud to recover his mother's property, we do not know.

There is much in Arnaud's career as a spy on which to reflect. His testimony, and that of the people whom he entangled in his net, shed light on many things: life on the run for a fugitive Good Man, the problems of a fugitive exile community trying to make its way in a new environment, "popular" religious or magical practices, and even something on the nature of wage labor and the market.

Sicre's tale offers insight into some of the methods by which the inquisitors acquired the intelligence they needed. Sicre was on the edge of one of the most interesting phenomena to grow out of the inquisition, that is, a marginalized, stigmatized, and manipulable group, that of the penitent heretic or heretical sympathizer. The inquisitors operated a flexible system of punishments. For example, Bernard Gui, the famous inquisitor of Toulouse, sent only forty-one people to the stake during his decade and a half at Toulouse from 1307 to 1323. The vast majority of people he condemned for heresy suffered other punishments: imprisonment, loss of property, and disinheritance of their heirs.[92] Many were not even imprisoned but were required to perform penitential pilgrimages, or wear conspicuous yellow crosses on their clothing. If one proved contrite and cooperative enough, it was possible to have one's penalties relaxed, that is, be freed from prison or be allowed to lay aside his crosses. This flexible system of punishment was a powerful stimulus for condemned heretics to be cooperative.

Indeed, a number of the inquisitors' servants were recruited from the ranks of ex-heretics. Sicre himself had never been tried as a heretic. Nevertheless, he had felt the sting of the inquisition's lash in the form of the confiscation of his mother's land. As we have seen, it was Sicre's hopes of regaining his lost inheritance that gave him the idea of becoming a freelance heresy hunter.

Another phenomenon that Sicre's testimony casts light on is the way in which inquisitorial pressure could weaken the ordinary bonds of social solidarity. Sicre himself was the product of a marriage broken by heresy: his father evicted from his mother's home and he himself sent away for fear that childish prattle might betray the circle of heretical sympathizers around Sibille den Baille. This breaking of family ties under inquisitorial pressure drove Arnaud's father into the arms of the inquisitors and almost cost Jeanne Marty her life. Sicre's testimony is also full of the conflicts and tensions between Emersende Marty and her daughter Jeanne, which constantly threatened to destroy the little Cathar community south of the Pyrenees.

Sicre's career thus illuminates some of the factors that enabled the inquisitors, despite their small staffs, to enjoy as much success as they did in eradicating heresy from southern France. His career also illustrates how people operating on the fringes of the inquisition tried to use their special access to the tribunals in order to further their own interests. The story of Pierre Clergue, the priest of Montaillou, who used his position as the village priest not only to protect Good Men but to tyrannize over his fellow villagers by threatening to denounce them to the inquisitors, is well known,[93] as is that of Menet de Robécourt, notary of the inquisitor of Carcassonne in the early fourteenth century, who used his position to extort money and destroy his enemies.[94]

Arnaud did not occupy the crucial position of link and intermediary between the world of the village and outside, governing institutions that Clergue did, nor was he a formal servant of the inquisitors, knowledgeable about the ways in which they could be persuaded to act on false testimony. Arnaud's position as a spy offered less scope for manipulation. But, as we have seen, he did what he could. He tried to extort property from Gaillard, the lord of Junac. And he quite clearly allowed those heretical sympathizers whom he liked, such as Pierre Maury and Arnaud Maury, who accompanied him and Bélibaste on the fatal march to Tirvia, to escape.

We know tantalizingly little about Sicre. How he lived before he embarked on his career as a spy, how he fared after delivering Bélibaste and his followers to the inquisitors, and what other people in the county of Foix thought of all of this, we do not know. Despite the shadows that surround his brief career as a spy, his adventures open a small window into a new world that was taking shape in the thirteenth and fourteenth centuries. Everywhere across western Europe new institutions of governance were being forged by rulers of all sorts—kings, popes, and city governments. These new institutions, with their quasi-bureaucratic structures, their increasingly professionalized servants, and their records, marked a major advance in political organization. The inquisition, although never really an institution in the sense that, for example, the English Exchequer was, can be seen as an example of this process. These new institutions may have given rulers more effective tools with which to govern, but for the most part they remained small and their reach often limited. Much of their success depended on their ability to enlist the assistance of outsiders who fed them information and acted on their behalf. This shadowy world on the edge of institutionalized power is very hard to perceive. Arnaud Sicre's career has allowed us a brief glimpse into this important but largely unknowable world.

Notes

1. James Given, "The Inquisitors of Languedoc and the Medieval Technology of Power," *American Historical Review*, 94 (1989): 336–59 and James Given, *Inquisition and Medieval Society: Power, Discipline, and Resistance in Languedoc* (Ithaca: Cornell University Press, 1997), pp. 23–90.
2. See Richard Kieckhefer, "The Office of Inquisition and Medieval Heresy: The Transition from Personal to Institutional Jurisdiction," *Journal of Ecclesiastical History*, 46 (1995): 36–61.
3. Given, *Inquisition*, p. 195.
4. Jean Duvernoy, ed., *Le Registre d'inquisition de Jacques Fournier (1318–1325)*, 3 vols. (Toulouse: Édouard Privat, 1965), 2:67–68.
5. The best study of Fournier's activity remains that of Jean-Marie Vidal, *Le Tribunal d'inquisition de Pamiers* (Toulouse: Édouard Privat, 1906).
6. Introductions to this sect can be found in Malcolm Lambert, *Medieval Heresy: Popular Movements from the Gregorian Reform to the Reformation*, 3rd edn. (Oxford: Blackwell Publishers, 1992), pp. 105–146; Malcolm Lambert, *The Cathars* (Oxford: Blackwell Publishers, 1998); and Malcolm Barber, *The Cathars: Dualist Heretics in Languedoc in the High Middle Ages* (Harlow: Pearson Education Limited, 2000). See also Arno Borst, *Die Katharer*, Schriften der Monumenta Germaniae Historica 12 (Stuttgart: Hiersemann, 1953) and *Historiographie du Catharisme*, Cahiers de Fanjeaux 14 (Toulouse: Privat, 1979). For a rather different take on "Cathars" in early thirteenth-century Languedoc, see Mark Gregory Pegg, *The Corruption of Angels: The Great Inquisition of 1245–1246* (Princeton, NJ: Princeton University Press, 2001).
7. When the inquisitors used the term "heretic," they almost invariably meant the Cathar Good Men. Most of the people prosecuted and condemned by

the inquisitors were not "heretics" in this narrow sense. To describe this group the inquisitors employed a large vocabulary distinguishing different forms of aiding and abetting of the heretics proper. To avoid excessive circumlocution, I shall refer to all those who supported heresy of all types, whether Cathar Good Men or not, as "heretics."

8. On this process, see Walter L. Wakefield, *Heresy, Crusade and Inquisition in Southern France, 1100–1250* (Berkeley: University of California Press, 1974), and *Effacement du Catharisme? (XIIIe–XIVe s.)*, Cahiers de Fanjeaux 20 (Toulouse: Privat, 1985).

9. On their careers, see Jean-Marie Vidal, "Les Derniers ministres de l'albigéisme en Languedoc: leurs doctrines," *Revue des questions historiques*, 79 (1906): 57–107; Jean-Marie Vidal, "Doctrine et morale des derniers ministres albigeois," *Revue des questions historiques*, 85 (1909): 357–409; 86 (1909): 5–48; and Élie Griffe, *Le Languedoc cathare et l'inquisition (1229–1329)* (Paris: Letouzey et Ané, 1980), pp. 171–213.

10. Duvernoy, *Registre*, 2:403–404.

11. The date of the Autiers' arrival from Lombardy is that proposed in "Derniers ministres," 66.

12. On this, see Michel de Dmitrewski, "Fr. Bernard Délicieux, O.F.M., sa lutte contre l'inquisition de Carcassonne et d'Albi, son procès, 1297–1319," *Archivum franciscanum historicum*, 17 (1924): 183–218, 313–37, 457–88; 18 (1925): 3–32; and Alan Friedlander, *The Hammer of the Inquisitors: Brother Bernard Délicieux and the Struggle against the Inquisition in Fourteenth-Century France,* in *Cultures, Beliefs and Traditions* 9 (Leiden: Brill, 2000).

13. Bernard Gui, *De fundatione et prioribus conventuum provinciarum Tolosanae et Provinciae Ordinis Praedicatorum*, ed. P.A. Amargier, in *Monumenta Ordinis Fratrum Praedicatorum Historica* 24 (Rome: Institutum Historicum Fratrum Praedicatorum, 1961), p. 204.

14. Duvernoy, *Registre*, 2:393.

15. Duvernoy, *Registre*, 2:9, 28, 170–71. I find Duvernoy's argument (2:171 n299) that Arnaud did not take part in the mass arrest of the people of Montaillou unconvincing.

16. Duvernoy, *Registre*, 2:28.

17. Duvernoy, *Registre*, 2:9.

18. Duvernoy, *Registre*, 2:21.

19. Duvernoy, *Registre*, 2:22.

20. There is an extensive discussion of what is known of Bélibaste in Vidal, "Derniers ministres," 92–107.

21. Duvernoy, *Registre*, 3:155.

22. Duvernoy, *Registre*, 3:160.

23. Hence the name Penchenier.

24. See summary in Vidal, "Derniers ministres," 93–95.

25. Duvernoy, *Registre*, 2:22.

26. Duvernoy, *Registre*, 2:22.

27. Duvernoy, *Registre*, 2:23.

28. Duvernoy, *Registre*, 2:24.

29. Duvernoy, *Registre*, 2:23–24.

30. Duvernoy, *Registre*, 2:24–27.

31. See his deposition in Duvernoy, *Registre*, 3:110–252.

32. Duvernoy, *Registre*, 2:28.

33. Duvernoy, *Registre*, 2:28.

34. Duvernoy, *Registre*, 2:29.

35. Duvernoy, *Registre*, 2:31.

36. Duvernoy, *Registre*, 2:38–39.

37. Duvernoy, *Registre*, 2:53.

38. Duvernoy, *Registre*, 2:55.

39. Duvernoy, *Registre*, 2:55.

40. On Cathar organization in Languedoc in the early thirteenth century, see Wakefield, *Heresy, Crusade and Inquisition*, pp. 31–43, and Lambert, *The Cathars*, pp. 141–58.

41. This was the term that the inquisitors used to refer to the state of near total abstinence from food and drink that believers on their deathbeds entered after receiving the *consolamentum*. Wakefield, *Heresy, Crusade, and Inquisition*, pp. 40–41.

42. Duvernoy, *Registre*, 3:191.

43. Duvernoy, *Registre*, 3:188–92, 198.

44. Duvernoy suggests, "Madame la bâtarde!" as a translation. Jean Duvernoy, trans., *Le Registre d'inquisition de Jacques Fournier (évêque de Pamiers), 1318–1325*, 3 vols. (Paris: Mouton, 1978), 3:1029, n125.

45. Duvernoy, *Registre*, 3:198.

46. Duvernoy, *Registre*, 3:198.

47. In the original copy of Sicre's deposition the notary inserted a figure of this talisman. Unfortunately, this was not reproduced in the final register. Duvernoy, *Registre*, 2:40.

48. Duvernoy, *Registre*, 2:39–41.

49. Duvernoy, *Registre*, 2:63–64.

50. Duvernoy, *Registre*, 3:178.

51. Duvernoy, *Registre*, 2:55–57, 3:172–78, 247.

52. Duvernoy, *Registre*, 2:42.

53. Sicre and Maury had previously agreed that Arnaud Maury would receive a dowry of 60 livres. Duvernoy, *Registre*, 2:43.

54. Duvernoy, *Registre*, 2:43–44.

55. Duvernoy, *Registre*, 2:60–62.

56. Duvernoy, *Registre*, 2:62.

57. Duvernoy, *Registre*, 2:67–68.

58. Duvernoy, *Registre*, 2:68.

59. Duvernoy, *Registre*, 2:68.

60. Duvernoy, *Registre*, 2:69.

61. Duvernoy, *Registre*, 2:69.

62. Duvernoy, *Registre*, 2:70–71.

63. Duvernoy, *Registre*, 2:71.

64. Duvernoy, *Registre*, 2:71.

65. Duvernoy, *Registre*, 2:71.

66. Duvernoy, *Registre*, 2:72.

67. Duvernoy, *Registre*, 2:75.

68. Duvernoy, *Registre*, 2:75.

69. Duvernoy, *Registre*, 3:207–208.

70. Duvernoy, *Registre*, 2:75–76.

71. Duvernoy, *Registre*, 2:76.

72. Duvernoy, *Registre*, 3:208–209.

73. Duvernoy, *Registre*, 3:211.

74. Duvernoy, *Registre*, 2:76–77.

75. Duvernoy, *Registre*, 2:77.

76. Duvernoy, *Registre*, 2:78.

77. Duvernoy, *Registre*, 2:209–210.

78. Duvernoy, *Registre*, 2:78.

79. Duvernoy, *Registre*, 3:210.

80. Duvernoy, *Registre*, 2:211.

81. Duvernoy, *Registre*, 3:211.

82. Duvernoy, *Registre*, 2:78.

83. Duvernoy, *Registre*, 2:58.

84. Duvernoy, *Registre*, 2:78–79.

85. Duvernoy, *Registre*, 2:416. The historians have not been kind to him. Jean-Marie Vidal, who has given his career its most extensive treatment, characterized him as a "paysan grossier et cupide." (Vidal, "Derniers ministres," 96.) Le Roy Ladurie termed him a hypocrite. (Emmanuel Le Roy Ladurie, *Montaillou: village occitan de 1294 à 1324* (Paris: Gallimard, 1975), p. 149.) But, as Le Roy Ladurie also noted, he was a hypocrite willing to go to the stake a martyr for his religion.

86. Duvernoy, *Registre*, 3:116.

87. Duvernoy, *Registre*, 2:460, 487.

88. Duvernoy, *Registre*, 3:213–14.

89. Duvernoy, *Registre*, 3:116.

90. Duvernoy, *Registre*, 2:62.

91. Duvernoy, *Registre*, 2:81.

92. James Given, "A Medieval Inquisitor at Work: Bernard Gui, 3 March 1308 to 19 June 1323," in *Portraits of Medieval Living: Essays in Memory of David Herlihy*, ed. Samuel K. Cohn, Jr. and Steven Epstein (Ann Arbor: University of Michigan Press, 1996), pp. 207–232.

93. Le Roy Ladurie, *Montaillou*.

94. Jean-Marie Vidal, "Menet de Robécourt, commissaire de l'inquisition de Carcassonne," *Moyen Age*, 16 (1903): 425–49.

CHAPTER 2

THE WORLD OF WITNESSES AND THE HOLY TRIBUNAL: FIFTEENTH-CENTURY TRIALS OF CASTILIAN JUDAIZERS

Renée Levine Melammed

In 1478, a papal bull was issued which enabled the establishment of a Spanish Inquisition. The expectation was that the medieval guidelines laid down by papal inquisitors such as Bernard Gui[1] would be strictly followed. While the format and structure of the Holy Tribunal in Spain were indeed based on the medieval predecessor, it allowed itself to deviate from it at times despite distinct papal objections. Thus the Spanish tribunal accepted servants' testimonies, limited grace periods for confessions, and kept the identity of its witnesses secret.

As will be seen, reading an inquisition trial is, in many ways, like finding one's way though a maze of witness testimonies. In one single trial, there can be multiple lists of names ranging from witnesses for the prosecution to different categories of witnesses for the defense. If this is not confusing enough, some of the same names can appear on each of these lists as each side was working independently while the defense was not informed as to who was summoned by the prosecution. The fact that the Spanish Inquisition insisted on maintaining secrecy was by all means the determining factor here. As Beinart points out, "The Inquisition realized that without witnesses it could not operate, and it therefore took all possible measures to protect them. It kept secret the identity of those who testified for it, and concealed any detail that might have provided a clue as to who they were."[2] This was not an innovation, for secrecy was central to the workings of the medieval Papal Inquisition as well as the Spanish and

French secular courts. However, according to Beinart, what was a matter of principle was converted into a method that no one dared question.[3]

When a trial was about to begin, the prosecutor had to assess the situation before determining how to proceed. For example, if the defendant had disappeared or had died, the heirs were given thirty days in order to appear and defend the deceased; at that time the arraignment was presented along with witness testimonies. At the same time, because testimonies were often recorded years prior to any given trial, it was not always possible to abide by the rules and to summon each prosecution witness to verify his or her testimony; that witness might no longer be accessible or even among the living. When this was the case, the Book of Testimonies was relied upon in place of current or corroborated evidence.

In cases where the defendant was alive and well and available, the trial was more elaborate. On the whole, one discerns the willingness of the prosecution to accept testimony from anyone and everyone. As defense tactics became more sophisticated, this lack of selectivity on the part of the prosecution is, at times, almost embarrassing.[4] As a matter of fact, when the defense succeeded in pointing to the weaknesses of its adversary's witnesses, the prosecution never bothered to deny them.

Double standards ruled the day, for while the prosecution received lists of the witnesses for the defense, the defense was never awarded the same courtesy. As discussed further, because of this lack of reciprocity, the defendant and his or her lawyer had to grope in the dark in the hope that they would correctly guess the identity of all the witnesses for the prosecution. While the prosecution could choose to invoke the testimony of friends, family members and servants, the same family members were usually disqualified as defense witnesses. Whereas a Jew technically was not allowed to testify against a Christian,[5] there were nonetheless some Jews who testified during the first decade of inquisitorial activity.

Essentially, anyone who might possess knowledge of judaizing in any capacity was a potential witness. Thus Jews who sometimes had contact with judaizing conversos were considered to be an ideal source of information. At the same time, fellow conversos who judaized sometimes testified as well. In the long run, some of them became active informants for the prosecution, the equivalent of agents and professional denouncers. In the trials from Ciudad Real, one learns of a former rabbi with whom the judaizers had extensive contact; he later converted to Catholicism, enabling him to become one of the most effective informants possible. His testimony and that of others like him were incontestable; as a result, between 1483 and 1485, the series of trials in Ciudad Real were carried out extremely efficiently.[6]

Despite myriad rules and regulations, one can find differences as well as discrepancies in the records of trials from different locales; this might reflect the makeup of the court or the nature of the local population and its relations with the conversos. For instance, after analyzing the trials in Jaén, Luis Coronas Tejada is convinced that the witnesses for the prosecution there were motivated by greed and jealousy of the more powerful and wealthy conversos.[7] The fact that their identity remained secret proved extremely helpful in obtaining denunciations. Some assumed that if the conversos on trial would be convicted, then their confiscated property would be sold at affordable prices and therefore, it was worthwhile for fellow tradesmen and members of the middle class to turn them in.[8]

This scholar is also convinced that in Jaén, false testimony was abundant, in particular, testimony provided by slaves and servants. According to the defendants' court records from this locale, information was often obtained through coaxing or threats. Promises of freedom were dangled before these built-in witnesses along with an assurance that their masters would never learn that they had been involved.[9] In these trials, one also senses that some of the witnesses had become akin to "professional." Together with these individuals, there were also those who approached the stand as the result of more traditional motivation, that is to say, as stalwart Catholics who were making their statements as a matter of conscience.[10]

The refusal to reveal the names of the prosecution witnesses to the defendant and to his or her lawyer created serious obstacles when attempting to build a defense. The defense tactics, at least at the outset, consisted of two approaches. In the early years, the first tactic was to compile a questionnaire aimed to refute the list of charges and to prove the defendant's fidelity to the church. The appointed lawyer would consult with the defendant and his or her family regarding the questions or *indirectas* and the individuals to be summoned to respond to them. This list of *abono* witnesses was often rather lengthy, as the defense was anxious to prove that the accused was an upstanding member of the Catholic community. The responses would hopefully demonstrate that the witness knew the defendant well and for a reasonable amount of time, could attest to his or her good character and faithfulness to the church and to the fact that judaizing had not been part of his or her lifestyle. On the one hand, the respondents were restricted and could reply only to the questions asked by special examiners. On the other hand, the judges could take the liberty of posing questions that did not appear on the list![11] Interviewing all the individuals whose names appeared on the list of *abono* witnesses was often a lengthy and time-consuming process.

It should be noted that this tactic was more or less abandoned in the sixteenth century because the defense realized that it was not effective in convincing the court of the innocence of its client. Any successful crypto-Jew was able to maintain the façade of being a devout Catholic to the outside world while secretly observing Judaism, so proof of this sort was essentially meaningless. Even the most detailed and comprehensive questionnaires could not prove that the accused was not a judaizer, so eventually this method became obsolete. At the same time, because the names of the prosecution witnesses were not available to the defense, it might unknowingly list these very same people as appropriate to answer *indirectas* intended to support the defense.[12]

The second defense tactic, however, could actually succeed, both in theory and in practice. As has been stated, it was extremely difficult to undermine the case presented by the prosecution because it had concealed the names of its witnesses. Beinart assumes that anonymity was intended to deter the defense in its attempt to disqualify the witnesses by means of *tachas*. No doubt this task was formidable because the defense could only engage in guesswork regarding the identity of these witnesses. As a result, numerous lists of *tachas* were formulated in the hope of correctly naming those individuals who had indeed testified against the accused. These lists were sometimes overwhelming, but in actuality, the court only related to the correctly named witnesses for the prosecution, if indeed they appeared.

Moreover, it must be pointed out that it did not suffice to accurately guess the name of a hostile witness or even to supply a convincing reason why he or she might have been motivated to testify against the accused. In addition, the defense had to provide the names of two individuals who could corroborate this claim, namely, that the suspected witness had bad relations with or ill will toward the defendant and thus was unreliable. If these two witnesses successfully verified this contention, that particular testimony was then invalidated.[13] As is obvious, the defense was at a serious disadvantage without an actual list of names of bona fide prosecution witnesses. Consequently, it spent a great deal of time and energy compiling *tachas* despite the fact that the majority of the names on the potential enemy list were not relevant to the case. But even when they were, there was no guarantee that the persons named to corroborate their claims would indeed recall and confirm the defense's contention.[14]

It should be pointed out that, if the defendant managed to disqualify all the witnesses for the prosecution, the court might call for yet another type of witness, the compurgatory witness. These witnesses were asked to give statements quite similar to those requested of the defense witnesses (*abonos*); the intended goal was to have a good Christian swear to the fact that the defendant was indeed also a good Christian. In one trial, the defendant was asked to name eight such individuals, but after only two were suggested, the court was not quite satisfied.[15]

Every trial was different, had a different number of witnesses for the prosecution (if they were present), did or did not have witnesses for the defense whose number also varied, and might have *abonos* and *tachas* whose numbers would vary as well. Six trials of condemned judaizers from the end of the fifteenth century will be compared here. The first, the trial of Sancho de Ciudad and his wife, María Díaz, took place from November 14, 1483 until January 30, 1484; both defendants were absent at the time of the arraignment. The prosecutor was undaunted by their absence and method-ically provided thirty-two witnesses for the prosecution. The first of them was the converso Lope de Villa Real of Segovia who had lived with Sancho twenty years earlier. He considered Sancho and his family to be the equivalent of "pure Jews," for they not only prayed in a tower in their home, but kept the Sabbath as well. Besides, Sancho had supposedly informed him of his intention to return to the law of Moses.[16] As has already been intimated, it was not always safe to trust one's fellow Jew or converso and this witness testimony is clear proof of that.

Another converso who testified was Juan de Fez whose name appears in more than one of his brethren's trials. He and the defendant had traveled together, but when Friday night approached, Sancho refused to continue any further; he did not use money on the Sabbath and only ate meat that was slaughtered according to Jewish law. He had even tried to convince de Fez to join him;[17] this comment is rather odd as it emanates from a converso who had confessed during a grace period and was then tried simultaneously with Sancho. De Fez, a tax farmer, ultimately provided testimony in a number of trials in the hope of appearing relatively passive in comparison to his active cohorts. This ploy, however, was unsuccessful and he later confessed during his own trial under the threat of torture and was thus burned at the stake along with his wife in February 1484.[18]

The next witness was none other than the daughter of the defendant who described her parents' judaizing activities and how she herself observed Jewish law only while living with them during which time she was subject to their authority. Catalina de Ciudad confirmed the fact that her parents were absent from the trial because they had fled the inquisition.[19]

Most of the other witnesses provided additional details regarding the judaizing activities of Sancho and his wife. One referred to group observance of the Sabbath in their home;[20] another had accompanied her mistress there, but was sent home while she and various conversos engaged in prayer.[21] Others described these prayer sessions in detail, whether on the Sabbath or at other times: Sancho read from books that might well have been in Hebrew and sometimes read or prayed aloud.[22] One referred to a prayer over the wine, although it is not clear if it was said on Friday night or on Saturday night.[23] Other festivals seem to have been observed as well.[24] At the same time, Sancho apparently prayed in the vineyard and in other locations if he was unable to go to the tower.[25]

This extremely large number of witnesses leaves an overwhelming impression that would have been hard to refute. All of them had seen Sancho and his wife judaize; Beinart writes that he was circumcised in 1463 (at an undetermined age) and after that, he no longer hid (or could hide) his Jewish way of life.[26] Even after the defendants were found and tried, it would have been extremely difficult to have disproved the case of the prosecutor: the circumcision was an irreversible act that no defense could have withstood. Sancho may well have been the leader of the judaizers in Ciudad Real, and because he had not hidden his lifestyle, he had no recourse but to flee before his trial began. After his capture, he could not avoid the inevitable and was condemned a second time.

Other trials were similar to this one, although none had nearly as many prosecution witnesses. The second trial under discussion, beginning on the same day but concluding almost a month later, was that of (another) María Díaz, who was also absent at the time; consequently, there were no witnesses for the defense here either. Like Sancho de Ciudad, María Díaz had also been a leader in the converso community. Her sentence to be burned in effigy was read on the same day as Sancho's. The list of prosecution witnesses in her trial was smaller than his, comprising "only" thirteen individuals, although it should be pointed out that this number is actually a very substantial one and larger than that found in most trials. There was one witness who participated in both trials, namely, Juan de Fez, who himself had fled Ciudad Real to Daimiel, and as has been pointed out, once facing the tribunal, attempted to place the blame on other conversos rather than to take responsibility for his own observances. Here he related that she observed the Sabbath, ate meat during Lent, carried out all the Jewish ceremonies and only ate meat that had been ritually slaughtered. He knew all this because he had been in her home where he had participated in judaizing since he too was a converso.[27]

It was her misfortune that the prosecution also employed another converso, Fernán Falcón, who was mentioned above because his testimony appears in many trials. Falcón made a detailed confession of his own sins on November 3, 1483 during a grace period; then the domino effect took place, for his confession resulted in mass arrests of numerous conversos from Ciudad Real. "On that November day the die was cast: Fernán Falcón was chosen to serve the inquisition as chief witness in all the trials that were to be held against the New Christians of Ciudad Real and its environs."[28] In this trial, he reported seeing María and other conversos praying from a Jewish prayer book on the Sabbath.[29]

As if these two were not strong enough witnesses, Fernando de Trujillo, the former rabbi, also testified for the prosecution. He stated that about seven years prior, while in Palma (Cordova), he saw María observe the

Sabbath and holidays in precisely the same way that he himself did. He described her celebration of the first nights of Passover, when she ate lettuce and celery and (bitter) herbs, vinegar, and unleavened bread, performing a ceremony symbolizing bitterness while wearing clean clothes and eating in new vessels that had not come into contact with leavening; at this time, she prayed like a Jew. She also observed the Festival of Weeks and of the Booths and Hanukkah and the New Year with the appropriate prayers. He saw her observe Yom Kippur, fasting all day while remaining barefoot. This conversa also had a Hebrew name and only ate meat that had been ritually slaughtered. This witness saw her instruct many conversos and commented on the high level of her knowledge of Judaism. During the seven months that he was in contact with her, he never once saw her behave as would a Christian woman.[30] The former rabbi obviously spoke from experience and with great authority; the only enigma here is why so many other witnesses were necessary in order to incriminate her.

If only for the sake of comparison, a look at the statements of some of the other less seasoned witnesses can be taken. Catalina de Zamora had also fled to Palma and was tried later in 1484. She related that she had heard that while there, María and her daughter Constanza arranged a ritual bath for a conversa bride by going to a stream or river. However, when "Rabbi" Trujillo appeared with a glass of wine to wed the couple, Constanza's husband violently objected to his wife's participation and interrupted the ceremony.[31] The second witness, Juan de la Torre, was none other than María's son-in-law who related that he had seen how she lit candles and prepared food beforehand in honor of the Sabbath; María ate meat during Lent; in general, the meat she ate had been slaughtered ritually. As part of her holiday observance, she wore festive clothes. He never saw her make the sign of the cross and as far as he was concerned, she was a pure Jewess.[32] María Díaz had lived with the defendant for two years in the 1450s at which time the defendant and her three daughters observed the Sabbath fully, wearing clean holiday clothes, reading from a book all day, preparing food beforehand and lighting candles. The defendant sewed on Sundays, ate ritually slaughtered meat on Friday nights as well as during Lent and was joined at these meals by her husband and other conversos. She never made the sign of a true Catholic; in addition, this witness had overheard plans to travel to Constantinople in order to live openly as Jews.[33]

Juan de Merlo was the brother of the aforementioned second witness, María's anti-judaizing son-in-law. He detailed Sabbath and festival observance in addition to partaking of meat slaughtered according to Jewish law.[34] Antonia Gómez had lived with the family some eight years prior and knew that its members observed the Sabbath, especially by praying. They also observed other holidays, fasted once a week, and ate fowl slaughtered by the defendant's brother-in-law. On Passover, they baked unleavened bread and ate in new plates and bowls. They never went to mass, crossed themselves, or ate meat from the Christian slaughterhouse.[35]

The conversa Catalina González had been with her in Palma where she saw her and her daughter at prayer sessions[36] as did Gómez de Chinchilla, also a converso. He distinctly recalled that she would not interrupt her prayers in order to give him money for food. He also knew that she and her daughter Constanza were particular about the meat they would get, and would eat fish if they were not satisfied with the meat that was available. In addition, they dressed up elegantly on the Sabbath.[37]

Two additional women testified for the prosecution, namely, Marina Gutierrez and Catalina. The former approached one of María's maidservants who was carrying a pair of pigeons and who explained to Marina that they had to be beheaded in a certain way in order for them to be eaten.[38] The latter had lived near the defendant twenty-four years earlier and had seen her observe the Sabbath by wearing clean clothes, lighting candles, and preparing food in advance. She also knew that the family observed some holiday during Holy Week, fasted until nightfall and never made the proper Christian signs.[39]

The third trial, that of María González began twelve days later, on November 25 (and ended on February 23, 1484), but in this case, unlike the first two, the defendant was actually present. Although she had made a voluntary confession a month earlier during a grace period, the court was not satisfied with the information she offered it, especially since she attempted to place more emphasis upon her husband in the role of active judaizer.[40] Beinart maintains that her lawyer was not particularly zealous or effective during the trial.[41]

The names of seven defense witnesses are listed but only five are recorded; unlike most trials, in this one the defense testimonies were recorded a week prior to that of the prosecution. These witnesses were presented with *indirectas*, eight questions in all, which were formulated by María González herself. The questions began with whether or not he or she knew the defendant, if she had taught her children any of the doctrines of Catholicism, if she had done housework on the Sabbath since getting married and if she dressed differently on that day. In addition, the witnesses were asked if she always did her work on all the days of the year other than Sundays and church holidays, if she had made *hadas*[42] for any of her children, if she had observed Lent, and if she had behaved like a good Catholic or not.[43]

The first *abono* (character witness) was María de Pedrosa who knew the defendant for thirty years, but was unable to discuss the level of Catholic education in her household. She had never entered this home on Saturdays but had heard that the defendant used her spinning wheel on this day. She had not seen María dress differently on Saturdays nor had she seen her observe other holidays. However, she did see her attend mass on Sundays.[44] The second witness, Alonso García, knew María for only three years and had heard that she had trained her daughters to be devout Catholics. He never noticed different attire on Saturdays, had seen her observe Catholic holidays and Lent, and had seen her attend mass on Sundays and during the week as well.[45]

The three other witnesses were also male, but the fourth was considered to be especially valuable as he was a priest named Diego Sánchez, although in actuality he was not particularly helpful to the defense. After stating that he knew the defendant, he claimed to have no knowledge pertaining to anything on the list of questions except the last one, for he had seen her attend church the past two Lents and take communion like a good Catholic.[46] The next *abono*, Dicho de Lope Malara, had known the defendant for thirty years. He had no idea as to what took place inside her home on Saturdays but did see her go out to the vineyards to inspect the workers on that day. He saw her attend mass at church and knew no more than this.[47] The final recorded testimony for the defense was not very enlightening either. Juan de Villarreal, who knew María for three years, could not answer any but the final question. He stated that he had seen her attend church, mass, and the divine offices many times.[48] That was all he could offer.

Eight witnesses for the prosecution then testified. The first was none other than Fernán Falcón who simply stated that María and her husband were Jews and he had seen them observe the Sabbath.[49] The second, Alonso de la Serna, who had been a magistrate until 1478, made a blanket statement declaring that all the conversos of Ciudad Real were really Jews and that María's husband Juan was the converso butcher.[50] Three witnesses were sworn in on the following day, December 10, 1483. The first of them, Pascual, said that many conversos came to this household to obtain meat of animals that were beheaded in the Jewish style.[51] The second, María López, explained that her home had faced that of this couple; she stated that the entire family observed the Sabbath, wearing clean blouses and eating food prepared the day before.[52] The third, Antón Martínez Castellano, had also resided opposite this family for two years and had seen them observing the Sabbath, dressing up and lighting candles on Friday nights. It appeared to him that they engaged in work on Sundays as their spinning wheels looked ready for action; besides, María had supposedly claimed that she had to spin on Sundays because she needed additional money for food.[53]

The last three witnesses appeared on the following day. Diego de Poblete, like the second witness Alonso de la Serna, stated that all the conversos in town were Jews and that their butcher was María's husband.[54] The next witness attested to the fact that Juan González Panpan slaughtered beasts according to Jewish law.[55] María González testified that thirty years prior she had lived with this family for nine years. During that time, she saw them observe the Sabbath by dressing up, by preparing food including meat dishes beforehand, and by lighting clean wicks. They also celebrated festivals and fasts, ate matsah during Passover, ate meat during Lent, and did not eat rabbit or hare. Together with many other conversos, they prayed from Jewish books, especially on the Sabbath. Lastly, this built-in witness said that when their children were born, this couple organized *hadas* celebrations.[56]

The fourth trial, that of Juan González Pintado began three days after María's, but ended on the same day. While the prosecution began with leaders within the community, this converso had been prominent outside of it, for he had served as secretary to two kings. His son, rather than accepting a court-appointed lawyer, chose to organize his father's defense; thus there was a valiant effort made to exonerate the accused.

First, eleven *indirectas* were prepared to ask the witnesses for the defense. The first of nine witnesses was a monk who knew Juan for twenty years. He testified that he had never seen the defendant eat, but that he had seen him at mass and attending sermons, he had heard his confession and that Juan had fed twelve poor men in honor of the twelve apostles.[57] The second witness was a fellow royal secretary who had lived with the defendant for an entire year some twenty years earlier. Pedro de Arevalo stated that Juan ate the same food as did any Old Christian, including pork and that he went to Mass and gave alms to poor Christians. In addition, he had prayed in many churches and even purchased an image of the Virgin Mother for the monastery of Saint Domingo. He never saw him light special candles or dress up on Saturdays.[58]

The cleric, Juan de Soto, had seen Juan in church on Sundays and holy days, attending mass and the divine offices, and knew that he had confessed (in his presence) and taken communion during Lent on Holy Thursday.[59] The butcher, Alonso García, knew the defendant for thirty five years; Juan and his male servants often bought meat and legs of beef from him. The following witness, Juan de Pedrosa, who knew the accused for twenty-eight years, answered more questions than the others. His knowledge was based on the fact that they had once lived together; during this time, González Pintado brought pork and other meat home from the various butcher shops and ate these foods as well as food served to him elsewhere. His roommate saw him attend mass at court, both in and outside of the city; he likewise saw him buy an image and give alms to the poor. By contrast, he had never seen this converso light a special candle or prepare food for the Sabbath; on the contrary, he had seen him cook on that day. De Pedrosa himself often cooked and noted that the defendant ate whatever meat was served, whether it was brought home clean or dirty.[60]

Juana de Cadahalso, who knew the defendant for twenty years, had also seen him eat everything; she even saw him kill a pig at home. She knew that he had washed meat that was brought home but had no idea if he did anything else to it. She was certain he had attended services at churches and monasteries, heard mass and sermons and devotions, and went to confession; he had also made an altar and arranged for the poor to be fed. His daily attire was neat and clean without exception.[61] The next witness, Diego de Mazariegos, had known him for forty-five years and had seen him eat every kind of food wherever he went. The defendant had heard mass and sermons, had made an altar, gave alms, and generally behaved like a true Christian.[62] Mateo Sánchez had also lived with him at the court forty years earlier; at that time he saw him eat everything served there as well as when they dined at the confraternities. He had entered churches and been present at mass and sermons, although this witness had never personally seen him confess or take communion. Juan's servants had brought him fish and meat from the plaza, but Mateo did not see how it was prepared. However he had seen him eat roasted river eels. Mateo pointed out that Juan had fed the poor, especially on Good Friday when he gave them alms as well.[63] The ninth witness, Diego Sánchez, a priest, was the last to answer the queries. He knew Juan for thirty years and in his opinion, he always behaved like a good Catholic in and out of the court. He ate whatever other Catholics ate including meat from the butcher, although once when he was ill, this priest gave him permission to eat meat during Lent because his physicians claimed that it would help him recover.[64]

On the very same day, December 9, 1483, the nine prosecution witnesses also testified;[65] eight of these testimonies were procured from the Book of Testimonies recorded during the grace period that had taken place less than two months earlier in October. The first was Antonia, a servant, who stated that the defendant had frequented her master's home where Hebrew was being read; she herself had seen him pray like a Jew. In addition, her master Alonso de Herrera slaughtered meat which he then sent to Juan.[66] Catalina Sánchez, who had lived in Juan's house for eight or nine months some four years before, knew that the Sabbath was observed there. The defendant would wear clean and festive clothes, visit relatives and light candles on Friday nights. In this house, meat was eaten during Lent.[67] The third witness, María Sánchez, claimed to know that on Fridays, food that had been prepared in advance for the Sabbath was brought to Juan's house.[68] The fourth witness was Juan, the son of Gonzalo de Aguilar, who had lived with the defendant for a year; he had seen him eat eggs during Lent and prepare food for the Sabbath in advance.[69]

The next prosecution witness was María Ruíz who said that she saw laundry being hung out at the defendant's house on a Sunday.[70] The next witness was the notorious Fernán Falcón who explained that Juan's wife was his relative; he heard that she was "very Jewish" and believed it because her father was also "very Jewish"; she was probably taught by him. A few times when the defendant was not home, Falcón entered the house, only to discover his relative observing the Sabbath.[71] A worker who had lived with the family provided detailed information. Juan Martínez stated that this couple lit a lamp on Friday nights, prepared food in advance for the Sabbath, ate meat and eggs during Lent, ate meat that was specially slaughtered and treated, prayed something he did not understand, ate some white flat bread (probably matsah) on some occasion and also ate a spicy cooked dish called *adafina*.[72] The next witness, Juan Martínez Cepudo was only able to affirm the fact that the defendant had been reconciled to the church.[73] The final witness, María Alfonso, had lived for five years with this couple some forty years earlier. She recalled that Juan was rarely if ever at home, but that his wife observed the Sabbath by dressing in clean clothes, lighting clean wicks, and preparing food in advance. She saw her mistress fast until the stars emerged and knew that she kneaded matsah during Lent, although she did not know if Passover had been celebrated or not. She did, however, see her pray.[74]

After hearing the testimonies of these eighteen witnesses, nine for the defense and nine for the prosecution, Juan's son decided to proceed further with the defense of his father on January 19, and to present *tachas* in order to attempt to discredit all hostile witnesses. First he listed five individuals whom he suspected of testifying for the prosecution, all who appear to have been shady characters; yet none of them had actually testified. Three defense witnesses were brought in to confirm these facts but when these names do not appear on the actual list provided by the prosecution, this effort is completely in vain.[75] Interestingly enough, the third of the three new witnesses, Gonzalo de Aguilar, was directly related to the fourth prosecution witness; he was a barber whose son, Juan had lived with the defendant for a year and who said he saw him prepare food for the Sabbath and eat eggs during Lent. These final *tachas* do not further the cause of the accused because the defense has not correctly guessed the identities of the actual prosecution witnesses; as a result, they unfortunately serve little purpose in the long run.

The fifth trial at this time began on December 1, 1483 and ended on February 23, 1484, the same date the two previous trials concluded. Eight witnesses for the prosecution and ten for the defense appeared in the records of the trial of Juan González Daza, a notary, another important public figure. As in the third trial, the defendant had confessed beforehand but the tribunal considered the confession to be incomplete and thus opted to prosecute. During the first two weeks of December, the prosecution brought in its witnesses. As in the previous trial, all but the final witness had provided testimony during a grace period in October or November of 1483. Antonia Martínez was a day laborer in the home of Juan's son, and knew that on Yom Kippur, his wife was asked for forgiveness by others; she placed her hands on the heads of those making this request. Juan and his family observed the Sabbath, abstaining from work and visiting family, preparing food on Fridays, and lighting clean wicks in their lamps. They also observed Jewish festivals such as Passover.[76] The next witness, Leonor González made some nebulous statements that do not seem to provide very strong support for the prosecution[77] whereas the third witness had a more incriminating statement. The father of Paris de la Torres stored wine in the defendant's house and would send his son over there on Saturdays to obtain it; as a result, he saw the family observe the Jewish day of rest, nicely dressed, whereas they treated Sundays like ordinary days.[78]

Next was none other than Fernán Falcón who claimed to know that the couple observed the Sabbath fully, for Juan's wife was a serious Jewess who fulfilled Jewish ceremonies. He had not seen this himself but believed that they were Jews; he also mentioned that he had seen González Daza shaving on Fridays in preparation for the Sabbath.[79] The spice merchant, Pedro de Molina, recalled a conversation with the defendant's son who had come into his store on Easter eve. When he asked the boy what they had eaten, the reply was lamb or mutton liver, clearly in contradiction to church teachings.[80] Alonso Rodríguez, a pack-saddle maker, recounted entering a home in the neighborhood on a Friday night; among the many conversos reading there was Juan González Daza.[81]

The next testimony exposes the precarious position of the conversos whose home was no longer a private domain. One Friday, the worker Juan García Barva was repairing roof-tiles and needed to pass through the defendant's kitchen. As a result, he saw González Daza's mother there cooking what he suspected was meat in a pot. When she eventually left her charge in order to chat with some conversas, Juan uncovered the pot so as to ascertain that they had meat planned for that Friday night dinner.[82] The final prosecution witness was the only one who had not previously testified during a grace period; Elvira González entered the house of a converso named Fernando de Teva whom she had heard was "a great traitor rabbi." There in the kitchen, she discovered him reading, dressed like a priest in white. Together with Fernando was his mother as well as Juan's wife and mother, but, interestingly enough, the defendant was not present.[83]

As in the previous trial, the defendant's son took charge of the defense and provided seven questions and ten witnesses. Each witness was asked if Juan had been a faithful Catholic, if he had worked on Saturdays, lit oil lamps with one or two wicks every evening, lit fire in his house on

Saturdays and had eaten dinner Friday evening just as he did every other evening. Juan pointed out that when he had been sick, he might have eaten meat on forbidden days in order to recuperate.[84]

Juan González de Molina knew the defendant for thirty years; during this time, he had seen him at mass and sermons, working on Saturdays, and he knew that every night there were lamps consistently lit in his home.[85] Juan de Lievana knew him for forty years and always saw him behave as a proper Christian; he worked on Saturdays, always had two wicks lit at night, ate regular meals on Friday nights, and attended mass.[86] María González knew Juan for twenty years; she had seen him attend mass in two different churches and request candles for communion together with his wife. She had seen him work on Saturdays, knew that his house had lamps lit every night, and never saw him eat meat during Lent.[87] Pascuala Martínez, who also knew him for twenty years, saw him in church attending mass, never saw a Jewish ceremony enacted in his home, and considered him to be a man of good counsel.[88]

María García had lived in this household for four years about twenty years earlier. According to her testimony, the couple attended church, sermons and went to confession, had worked on Saturdays, and always had two lamps lit in the evening. In addition, Juan had taught his children the Pater Noster, the Ave Maria, the Credo, and the Salve Regina.[89] A thirty year acquaintance, Bartolomé, had seen the defendant attend mass and vespers and listen to sermons; there was no doubt in his mind that Juan had definitely worked in his office on Saturdays.[90] The parish priest, Fernando Alonso, had seen Juan behave like a good Christian during the ten years he knew him: he attended church and mass, especially during festival season, vespers and even sang from a music stand at times. He recalled that Juan went to confession during Lent and he was sure he had worked on Saturdays.[91] A second cleric, Pedro Ferrandes, who had known Juan for twice as long, said he always behaved like a good Christian, attending church, mass and sometimes vespers on Sundays and listening to sermons and to preaching; he was also sure that he worked as a scribe on Saturdays.[92]

A fellow scribe, Bartolomé González, knew Juan for fifteen years and had seen him at church, especially on Sundays at mass and sometimes even singing or reciting the Creed (Articles of Faith) with the clerics; he also listened to sermons. Although this witness did not know what Juan taught his children, he did know that he worked on Saturdays.[93] The final character witness, Alonso Martínez, was another cleric who knew Juan for twenty-five years and had seen him consistently attend church and mass on Sundays; he had definitely listened to sermons like all good Christians.[94]

The last trial under discussion, that of Marina González took place in 1494 and concerns a very different process because the defendant had been reconciled to the church ten years earlier after offering a confession in 1481. The prosecution presented five testimonies, including that of Marina's own husband, Francisco de Toledo, and of her cousin, Fernán Falcón, the converso informer and reformed judaizer whose presence always augured ill for the defendant.[95] The prosecutor was convinced that her original confession had not been genuine and that she had reverted to her previous lifestyle. His first witness was Pedro de Teva who was a close friend of Marina's husband, Francisco. Pedro recounted that whenever he joined Francisco for a meal at his house, if pork or drowned birds (and other non-kosher foods) were served, Marina refrained from joining them; she also refused to drink from her husband's cup. The rest of his testimony was based on hearsay, and was clearly less reliable.[96]

The second witness was none other than her husband, Francisco de Toledo, who explained that Marina refused to eat pork products despite her reconciliation to the church, supposedly for health-related reasons.[97] This was followed by Falcón's statement, the longest of them all, which began with a report that the house did not contain any proper Catholic images. He also claimed to have seen her dressed in finery on Saturdays and had overheard her husband say that she would not eat pork or cook with it. Falcón had the impression that there had been friction in the household because she did not want to go out on Saturdays. In addition, he had heard that she worked on Sundays.[98]

The fourth witness was her cousin who was also Falcón's sister-in-law and the source of the hearsay in the previous testimony. Juana de la Cadena had visited the couple in 1482 on a Friday when she noticed that they had washed various items of clothing (petticoat, head cover, etc.) which were then worn the following Saturday and on this day she did not see Marina engage in any work. On Sunday, however, she did see her work with linen, explaining that her husband Francisco was not well and that they needed the income in order to marry off their daughter.[99] The fifth witness, Gracia, said that during one of the three carnival days before Ash Wednesday, Marina refused to eat pork or pancakes made with lard; she did not cook with these foods at home either. Once when Marina was brought meat, she excused herself and removed a piece from the meat but Gracia did not know what it was because a hen quickly gobbled it up.[100] One can see that these accusations are not as incriminating as in the previous trial.

In these proceedings, eight witnesses were named by the defense, although only seven testified. Marina's lawyer prepared eight questions, beginning with references to her faithfulness to the church and encompassing her post-reconciliation period. The witnesses were asked if she observed Jewish or Catholic Sabbaths and holidays, ate pork and rabbit and the like as long as she was feeling well, and if, on the whole, she had violated the restrictions set for the reconciled, except for wearing one colorful skirt. The first witness answered some, but not all of the questions. The second, a neighbor, had seen her attend mass, do her chores on Saturdays, and had seen images such as crosses in her home. The third, also a female neighbor, had seen her at mass and confession and had not seen her do anything against the faith. On Saturdays, Marina had engaged in chores as well as spinning. Whereas the first three witnesses had known the defendant for only a year or two, the fourth, Leonor Fernández, was her cousin and thus they had known each other for over thirty years. She saw Marina at church on Sundays and holy days, working on Saturdays, eating the same foods as any Christian, and never saw her do anything against church doctrine except perhaps wearing the said skirt. The fifth testimony was similar to the first three whereas the sixth, also given by a neighbor, concerned attending mass, wearing a colorful skirt, and hearsay that she did not eat pork, rabbit, or octopus.[101]

Marina's husband, who had testified for the prosecution, is listed as a witness for the defense as well. No testimony appears in his name and he began to compile *tacha* lists the following month. His first suspected enemy was indeed a witness for the prosecution, none other than Juana de la Cadena, the wife of Diego Falcón who was both Fernán Falcón's brother and Marina's cousin. Francisco proceeded to relate an unpleasant encounter concerning Diego and Juana, his fiancée at the time, that had taken place in the couple's previous home in Almagro. He was convinced that since that time, Juana had been his wife's enemy.[102] Francisco proceeded to name fourteen other women whom he suspected of testifying against his wife, although only one of them had actually provided the prosecution with information.[103] This was Gracia de Espina, the fifth prosecution witness, who was also Marina's relative and had been castigated by the defendant so that she would desist in her evil ways, something Gracia's mother and brothers clearly knew about.[104] But there does not seem to be any testimony available which would serve to ascertain this claim and effectively disqualify her as a witness for the prosecution. Thus two names were correctly listed but the defense was unable to disqualify them as prosecution witnesses.

Interestingly enough, on the same day, after denying the accuracy of the accounts of the anonymous prosecution witnesses, Marina's barrister, Diego Tellez and Gutierrez de Palma who was his cohort and defense counsel, presented another list of *tachas*, which, Beinart points out, was crossed out by the scribe because the names were not pertinent.[105] On the other hand, when one studies the trial in its entirety along with the witnesses involved, these lists are indeed relevant. Eight more names appear here, five of them belonging to women. The list actually began with a neighbor named Torres who sold wine and had threatened the defendant when she also began to deal in wine, saying it would cost them dearly if they did not desist.[106] The second suspect was a woman with whom Marina had argued frequently, none other than the wife of the aforementioned Torres, and his brother was listed next due to business tensions with her son Diego.[107] The fourth was a woman, the wife of Taracena, who had sent her son over to threaten the defendant after they had had an altercation.[108] The fifth was a former maidservant named Mayor whom she had castigated and eventually fired.

The third male mentioned was none other than Fernán Falcón with whom Diego had also had unpleasant dealings in his store; the former dealt in wool while the latter dealt in silk.[109] It is not clear if this level of animosity was sufficient to discount Falcón's testimony. The seventh was another maidservant, the daughter of Payo Gómez, with whom she had quarreled.[110] Marina had also crossed paths with one of her father's maidservants.[111]

Essentially, Marina's husband had successfully named three of the five witnesses for the prosecution (Falcón, Juana de la Cadena, and Gracia de Espina), not to mention Francisco himself. At the same time, Francisco's testimony was used against Marina while he was struggling to disqualify the other prosecution witnesses, proof of a convoluted situation indeed.

At this point, the court decided to subject Marina to torture, and, unlike de Fez who succumbed and confessed when merely threatened with torture, she withstood a formidable amount of it without uttering a word. Finally, she stated that she had a neighbor who fasted some fasts, and added that she was referring to the wife of Gómez de Chinchilla. She was asked if these were Jewish or Christian fasts and she replied that they were Jewish fasts that had occurred about a year ago.[112] An interim verdict was recorded the following week in which the prosecutor was told that he had not completely proved his case.[113] As a result, a few weeks later, Marina was asked to name eight compurgatory witnesses; she named Bartolomé de Badajoz of Ciudad Real who had earlier been named as a witness for the defense and now was to be considered to be for the prosecution. The second name given was that of Antonio de Caracule of Almagro; despite a two-week extension, Marina did not add to or complete this list.

At this time, this conversa unexpectedly went on a hunger strike and the jailer, Pedro González, attested to the fact that a physician examined her and found her to be healthy. Interestingly enough, the jailer suddenly was serving as a witness to the state of mind of the defendant as well as to her behavior in the cell. This type of testimony is not included in any of the known categories but was obviously acceptable to the court. She was sure that she would be condemned to death and had nothing to confess.

When asked if she believed in the church, she said that if she had, she would not be there.

Just prior to sentencing, the prosecutor came forth with more witnesses, perhaps because Francisco had succeeded in invalidating two or three of them; he might have felt the need to strengthen his somewhat shaky case or to prove that her refusal to eat essentially incriminated her. The jailer's servant reported that she had fasted for ten or twelve days and refused to confess, later stating that no one took her for a Christian. A fellow female prisoner also attested to her refusal to eat because she was going to be killed and cut up into pieces anyway.[114]

Rarely does one see such a wide array of witnesses, beginning with the list provided by the prosecution and the character witnesses for the defense. Next one encounters the *tacha* lists, with names of witnesses to attest to the enmity between the suspected informer and the defendant. Compurgatory witnesses are requested and some are supplied. A jailer, his servant, and a fellow inmate provide more testimony as a last resort on the part of the prosecution to counter the partial success of the *tachas*. The majority of the recorded material consists of different witness testimonies from all levels of society; some have come forward voluntarily while others have been summoned. In the long run, the prosecution was more successful than the defense in proving its case, and Marina González was sentenced to be relaxed to the secular arm. The witnesses could then testify to her demise, and possibly, appear again in the court as witnesses in yet other trials of the inquisition.

By examining six different trials, one can see how witnesses were essential to the entire process. Both the defense and the prosecution relied upon them either to attest to the character of the defendants or to incriminate them. When the defendants were absent, as in the first two trials, the prosecution inundated the court with testimonies that were never contested. When the defendants were present, the numbers of prosecution versus defense witnesses seem to have been relatively balanced. However, once the *tachas* appeared, the defense could name an interminable number of potential witnesses to come to its aid.

One cannot ignore the fact that some of the prosecution witnesses were extremely effective, namely the former rabbi, Fernando de Trujillo, or the professional witness, Fernán Falcón. The vast and endless pool of witnesses included these men as well as family members, friends, neighbors, business associates, and servants. The last trial analyzed reveals a husband who is listed as a prosecution witness and then creates his own lists of *tachas* in an attempt to save his wife; because some of them were correct, he seems to have weakened the prosecutor's case. Thus Marina González is asked to name compurgatory witnesses, but she does not fully comply. By the end of the fifteenth century, the character witnesses disappear from the proceedings, but the defense will continue to compile *tacha* lists in the hope of discrediting the witnesses for the prosecution. As has been seen, while guidelines had been established by papal inquisitors concerning this medieval institution, Spain defiantly altered some of the rules to suit its own needs, especially regarding the identity and legitimacy of witnesses for the prosecution. Nevertheless, it is clear that the world of witnesses and the Holy Tribunal remain intertwined for as long as the inquisition continues to function in Spain.

Notes

A judaizer was a baptized Catholic accused of the heresy of observing Judaism. In Spain, the accused were converted Jews known as *conversos* or New Christians or their descendants, labeled in the same manner for generations.

1. See Yosef Hayim Yerushalmi, "The Inquisition and the Jews of France in the Time of Bernard Gui," *Harvard Theological Review* 63 (1970): 317–76.

2. Haim Beinart, *Conversos on Trial* (Jerusalem: Magnes Press, 1981), p. 127.

3. Beinart, *Conversos*, p. 130.

4. In Beinart's assessment, "the severity of the deeds for which the accused were on trial convinced the Inquisition that there was no need to examine its witnesses' credentials." Beinart, *Conversos*, p. 131.

5. See Henry Charles Lea, *A History of the Inquisition of Spain*, 4 vols. (New York: Macmillan, 1907), 2:537; see also Haim Beinart, "Jewish Witnesses for the Prosecution of the Spanish Inquisition," *Acta Juridica* (1976): 37–46.

6. Beinart, *Conversos*, pp. 133–35. For background on the judaizers and conversos, see I. S. Révah, "Les marranes," *Revue des études juives* 118 (1959–1960): 29–77; Yitzhak Baer, *A History of the Jews in Christian Spain*, vol. 2 (Philadelphia: Jewish Publication Society, 1966 and 1992); Haim Beinart, "The Converso Society in 15th Century Spain," in *The Sephardi Heritage*, ed. Richard D. Barnett (London: Vallentine, 1971), pp. 425–56; Simha Asaf, "The Marranos of Spain and Portugal in Responsa Literature" [Hebrew], *Me'assef Zion*, 5 (1932–33): 19–60; David M. Gitlitz, *Secrecy and Deceit: The Religion of the Crypto-Jews* (Philadelphia: Jewish Publication Society, 1996). Regarding the inquisition, see Bartolomé Bennassar, "L'Inquisition ou la pédagogie de la peur," in *L'Inquisition espagnole: XVe-siècles*, ed. Bartolomé Bennassar and Catherine Brault-Noble (Paris: Marabout, 1979), pp. 42–52; Jean-Pierre Dedieu, "Les quatre temps de l'Inquisition," in *L'Inquisition espagnole: XVe-XIXe siècles*, ed. Bartolomé Bennassar and Catherine Brault-Noble (Paris: Marabout, 1979), pp. 13–40; and Edward Peters, *Inquisition* (Berkeley: University of California, 1989).

7. Luis Coronas Tejada, *Conversos and Inquisition in Jaén* (Jerusalem: Magnes Press, 1988), p. 33.

8. Coronas Tejada, *Conversos*, p. 33.

9. Coronas Tejada, *Conversos*, pp. 34–35.

10. Coronas Tejada, *Conversos*, p. 34.

11. Beinart claims that this technique could enable the judge to turn the witness for the defense into a witness for the prosecution. Beinart, *Conversos*, p. 183.

12. Beinart speculates about what occurred in these situations and assumes that such witnesses were probably told to claim ignorance. Beinart, *Conversos*, p. 130.

13. Beinart contends that the defense hoped to turn the witness for the prosecution into a perjurer, but he points out that even if it did succeed in doing so, the "perjurer" was protected and never punished. Beinart, *Conversos*, p. 183.

14. While these lists and descriptions were not helpful to the defense, they are extremely interesting for the social historian. They reveal the social structure of converso society, the interactions between New and Old Christians, and much more. See Renée Levine Melammed, *Heretics or Daughters of Israel: The Crypto-Jewish Women of Castile* (New York: Oxford University Press, 1999), pp. 94–139, for analyses of three interrelated trials based on *tachas* and lists of names in appendix 1, pp. 175–88. See also Renée Levine Melammed, "Sixteenth Century Justice in Action: The Case of Isabel López," *Revue des études juives*, 145:1–2 (1986): 51–73, for an analysis of the manner in which the defense almost succeeded in invalidating all of the prosecution witnesses as unreliable.

15. See Haim Beinart, *Records of the Trials of the Spanish Inquisition in Ciudad Real*, 5 vols. (Jerusalem: The Israel Academy of Sciences and Humanities), 2:8–9.

16. See Beinart, *Records* 1:16–17.

17. See Beinart, *Records* 1:17.

18. Beinart, *Records* 1:182.

19. Beinart, *Records* 1:17. She and her husband were tried and reconciled to the church; see Beinart, *Records* 4:430.

20. See, for example, the testimony of Catalina Fernández; Beinart, *Records* 1:18.

21. This was Catalina, the servant; see Beinart, *Records* 1:18–19.

22. Juana de Jones [*sic*] heard him singing without understanding him. María Díaz went with her parents to a room in his home where Jewish prayers were recited and other observances took place. Elvira lived with Sancho's brother, visited the house often and had seen Sancho rise at midnight to pray. She also witnessed groups of conversa women arriving in twos and threes; from what she could surmise, these conversos entered a tower on Friday night and did not exit until Saturday night. Fernando de Mora claimed that Sancho stopped at sundown to pray for half an hour while María Díaz heard him reading just like a rabbi (at midnight), blessing and reading for about two hours. His neighbor, Teresa Núñez, saw him sitting at a table with a large book while reading and praying. See Beinart, *Records* 1:19–21. Others, such as Pedro de la Torre, Rodrigo de Santa Cruz, Mencia González, confirmed these reports. Beinart, *Records* 1:21–22. Juan de la Torre spoke of a book in the defendant's house (p. 23). Ferrando de

Toledo described a visit to the house when he saw conversos praying with their faces turned to the wall at which time he asked if it was a synagogue (p. 24). Juan de Herrera saw him reading a Hebrew book after mass (p. 25). Antonio de la Torre, a scribe, went over to investigate and determine if the books in the house were Hebrew or not (pp. 25–26). Pero Franco heard loud prayers in the house (p. 26); Pedro de Murcia also saw him praying the way that the Jews did (pp. 26–27).

23. This was a member of the order of Santo (Saint) Domingo, Fray Gómez Mexia, who came to do business and saw a prayer being made over wine at the end of a meal. Beinart, *Records* 1:22.

24. María Díaz saw fasts and holidays observed and matsah eaten (p. 19); Pedro de la Torre also mentioned holidays (p. 21). Mencia González reported observance of the Sabbath and holidays (p. 22) as did Theresa who also referred to going barefoot on Yom Kippur and to bathing on Friday afternoons (p. 24); Juana, who had lived with their son and daughter-in-law for twelve years, saw the Sabbath and festivals and "all" the ceremonies observed (p. 26).

25. Gonzalo de Mora saw him praying on a cart; Iohan Rico saw him dismount a mule and walk through a vineyard praying. See Beinart, *Records* 1:22–23.

26. See Beinart, *Records* 1:1.

27. Beinart, *Records* 1:56.

28. Beinart, *Conversos*, p. 95.

29. Beinart, *Records* 1:54–55.

30. Beinart, *Records* 1:57–58.

31. Beinart, *Records* 1:52–53.

32. Beinart, *Records* 1:53–54. This notary testified against many of the conversos of Ciudad Real; see Beinart, *Records* 4:515.

33. Beinart, *Records* 1:54.

34. Beinart, *Records* 1:55.

35. Beinart, *Records* 1:55–56.

36. Beinart, *Records* 1:56.

37. Beinart, *Records* 1:56–57.

38. Beinart, *Records* 1:57.

39. Beinart, *Records* 1:57.

40. This is not usually the case, as husbands often attempted to blame their wives for initiating judaizing while presenting themselves as the more passive participants.

41. Beinart, *Records* 1:70.

42. The *hadas* were usually held on the eighth night after the birth of a male or female infant. This was a medieval rite that was perpetuated only by the Spanish Jews. For further details, see Renée Levine Melammed, "Noticias Sobre Los Ritos de Los Nacimientos y de la Pureza de las Castellanas del Siglo XVI," *El Olivo*, 13 (1989): 235–43.

43. Beinart, *Records* 1:76–77.

44. Beinart, *Records* 1:78–79.

45. Beinart, *Records* 1:79.

46. Beinart, *Records* 1:80.
47. Beinart, *Records* 1:80.
48. Beinart, *Records* 1:81.
49. Beinart, *Records* 1:82.
50. Beinart, *Records* 1:82.
51. Beinart, *Records* 1:83. Pascual was a prosecution witness in three other trials as well; see Beinart, *Records* 4:495.
52. Beinart, *Records* 1:83.
53. Beinart, *Records* 1:83.
54. Beinart, *Records* 1:84.
55. Beinart, *Records* 1:84. This witness himself was tried and condemned in 1484.
56. Beinart, *Records* 1:84–85.
57. Beinart, *Records* 1:103.
58. Beinart, *Records* 1:104–105.
59. Beinart, *Records* 1:105.
60. Beinart, *Records* 1:106–107.
61. Beinart, *Records* 1:107–108.
62. Beinart, *Records* 1:108–109. For information on his activities, see Beinart, *Records* 4:483.
63. Beinart, *Records* 1:109–110.
64. Beinart, *Records* 1:110.
65. Beinart claims that the "interrogation of all these witnesses on the same day shows the urgency of the trial," *Records* 1:110.
66. Beinart, *Records* 1:111.
67. Beinart, *Records* 1:111–12. She also testified against the defendant's wife; see Beinart, *Records* 1:481–482.
68. Beinart, *Records* 1:112–113. She also testified against Juan de Fez and Catalina Gómez; see Beinart, *Records* 1:199.
69. Beinart, *Records* 1:113.
70. Beinart, *Records* 1:113–14.
71. Beinart, *Records* 1:114. The wife was indeed tried separately at a later date, in effect, posthumously; their son did not defend her as he had his father, perhaps because he knew she was such an active judaizer; see pp. 474–86.
72. Beinart, *Records* 1:114–15. *Adafinas* were stews prepared for the Sabbath, cooked slowly overnight and eaten on the Sabbath day.
73. Beinart, *Records* 1:116.
74. Beinart, *Records* 1:116–17.
75. See Beinart, *Records* 1:126–29.
76. Beinart, *Records* 1:147–48.
77. See Beinart, *Records* 1:148.
78. Beinart, *Records* 1:148–49.
79. Beinart, *Records* 1:149.
80. Beinart, *Records* 1:150.
81. Beinart, *Records* 1:150.

82. Beinart, *Records* 1:151.
83. Presumably he was wearing a prayer shawl (*tallit*). See Beinart, *Records* 1:152.
84. See Beinart, *Records* 1:138–39.
85. Beinart, *Records* 1:140–41.
86. Beinart, *Records* 1:141.
87. Beinart, *Records* 1:141–42.
88. Beinart, *Records* 1:142–43.
89. Beinart, *Records* 1:143.
90. Beinart, *Records* 1:144.
91. Beinart, *Records* 1:144–45. His name also appears in the trial of Sancho de Ciudad, p. 145.
92. Beinart, *Records* 1:145.
93. Beinart, *Records* 1:146.
94. Beinart, *Records* 1:146.
95. "And though various defendants succeeded in questioning his validity as a witness, his testimony was accepted by the court as reliable, and the defense was unable to refute it. In fact, in every trial in which Fernán Falcón testified the accused was found guilty." Beinart, *Conversos*, p. 134.
96. See Beinart, *Records* 2:21–22. He was a witness in a number of trials; see vol. 4, p. 514.
97. Beinart, *Records* 2:22.
98. Beinart, *Records* 2:22–23.
99. Beinart, *Records* 2:23–24.
100. Beinart, *Records* 2:24.
101. Beinart, *Records* 2:16–20. The questions appear on p. 16; the testimony of Alfonso de Zarza is on p. 17 (he appeared in a number of trials as a witness; see vol. 4, p. 524); the testimony of Marina Ruíz is on pp. 17–18; María Sánchez's testimony appears on p. 18; her cousin Leonor Fernández testified on pp. 18–19; Fernando de Madrid is listed but there is nothing recorded; Catalina López's testimony is on pp. 19–20; and Bartolomé de Badajoz's statement appears on p. 20. This last witness as well as his daughters testified frequently; he was a converso who had been reconciled to the church and even housed inquisitorial inspectors in his home. See vol. 4, p. 421.
102. For details, see Beinart, *Records* 2:25.
103. Juana was a former servant who had left their service because Marina had hit her; it seems that she had been paid in advance and then disappeared with the funds. Francisco also referred to her as a whore, a gossip and a drunk. See Beinart, *Records* 2:25–26. The next suspect, Mayor, was also a servant of theirs whom Marina had suspected of having an affair with her husband and subsequently had thrown her out of the house by her hair. Mayor, in turn, had called Marina a Jewish whore and threatened to have her burned, but this sincere enemy did not provide testimony either; Beinart, *Records* 2: 26. The third woman was described as simple, shameless and impoverished. Marina had given her various things from the house,

but Catalina demanded more and ultimately called Marina a Jewish heretic; Beinart, *Records*, p. 26. Marina had disliked the next suspect because she considered her to be lazy and had told this woman's employer to punish her; Beinart, *Records* 2:26–27. Marina had spoken ill of the following woman in the list as well; Beinart, *Records* 2:27. Marí Ruíz had been their neighbor in Almagro and when they closed up their home, she entered through the common entrance to the two houses and appropriated some of their belongings, an act which led to a fight between the two; as a result, she too had threatened the defendant; Beinart, *Records*, p. 27. Francisco recalled fights between the next candidate and his wife; Beinart, *Records* 2:27. Another woman had broadcast the fact that Marina was reconciled and had threatened her; Beinart, *Records* 2:27. Details of her fights with Catalina la Toledana appear in the next *tacha*, for she claimed to know that the defendant persisted in her heretical ways; Beinart, *Records* 2:27. Another neighbor and his wife had stopped speaking to one another and it was assumed that she also wanted to do Marina ill; Beinart, *Records* 2:27–28. The following suspect, Gracia de Espina, was indeed the fifth witness for the prosecution (see note 98), and is discussed further. The next woman on the list had been another neighbor who had received various things from Marina and then had threatened her when she discontinued this treatment; Beinart, *Records* 2:28. The next to last woman on the list had been a servant living nearby whom Marina suspected of pilfering; Beinart, *Records* 2:28. The last *tacha* concerned Juana la Cuchilla who had been their neighbor in Almagro and was embittered when Marina stopped giving her various items from the house; Beinart, *Records* 2:28.

104. Beinart, *Records* 2:28.
105. This was not standard practice; lists were left untouched in files, but when the name of an actual prosecution witness was included in the defense list, a special mark appeared in the margins of the folio to signify precisely that.
106. The suspects were Torres and his wife Marí Godias. See Beinart, *Records* 2:30.
107. Beinart, *Records* 2:30.
108. See Beinart, *Records* 2:30.
109. Beinart, *Records* 2:31.
110. See Beinart, *Records* 2:30–31.
111. Beinart, *Records* 2:31.
112. Beinart, *Records* 2:32–34.
113. Beinart, *Records* 2:34.
114. Beinart, *Records* 2:36–37.

CHAPTER 3

THE INQUISITORIAL PERSPECTIVES OF AN UNMARRIED MULATTA WOMAN IN MID-SEVENTEENTH-CENTURY MEXICO

Amos Megged

One of the most unusual and elaborate cases to be found in New Spain's inquisitorial records regarding caste women in the mid-seventeenth century is that of Isabel de Montoya. The confinement and trials of this unmarried mulatta, a midwife, extended over thirteen years, between 1650 and 1663, and were recorded in two large volumes in the records of the Holy Office. In this particular life history, one is clearly able to identify the principal themes of the "alternative single woman's household," of matriarchal-matrilocal patterns among caste women, as well as these women's distinct mechanisms of survival which consistently foreshadowed the "stable patriarchy" in seventeenth-century Mexico. The records also expose the central themes of honor and shame, moral and sexual transgression, seduction, abduction, and "liberation." Isabel's life history, from her own accounts to the interrogators in the inquisition chambers, and from the testimony of a great variety of acquaintances who knew her at different times in her life, consists of a fascinating accumulation of collective and private memories, in which, very often, time seems to stand still.

Nevertheless, her recollections are indeed fragmented. One could find in her testimony the gradual emergence of a personal narrative that could be properly referred to as "explicit memory." This is because it is in the very nature of traumatic memory of women of Isabel's social standing and caste who must all have fallen prey to similar circumstances, to be dissociated. Moreover, the story as a whole may be divided into distinct layers and themes or leitmotifs, that are superimposed on the given text in keeping with the predicaments and prejudices of the seventeenth century and following the structure and norms of the inquisitorial discourse.

Isabel de Montoya was born and baptized in 1614 in the parish church of Santa Veracruz in Mexico City (a few hundred meters from the Alameda Central, where the Plaza de Santa Veracruz today stands).[1] She was the legitimate daughter of Diego de Montoya y Guzmán, a Spanish immigrant (*gachupín*) shoemaker, and his mulatta wife, Luisa Hernández, a healer by profession. When Isabel de Montoya was interrogated by the Holy Office many years later about her ancestry, she responded by saying that on her mother's side, they were all *mestizos blancos*, and "all of them were true Catholics, and none of them had been sentenced by the Holy Office; she was the only one in the family to be sentenced to serve in the Amor de Dios hospital for two years."

Grandparents on her father's side included Juan de Montoya, a weaver who came from Spain and by 1662 had already been dead for many years; he had died in the same hospital where she completed her sentence. She did not know her grandmother nor her name, but she knew that she was born in Puebla, but was unaware of the place where she had died or when. Relatives on her mother's side, included: (1) her grandfather, Miguel Hernández, a miller and a castizo, who had died in the province of Chalco, where he lived all his life; (2) her grandmother Cathalina Martin, a mestiza, who was also dead for many years (by 1662); and (3)uncles, her father's brothers: Juan de Vanegas, who lived in Puebla. She did not know the rest. Her mother's relatives included: (1) her mother's brother, Juan López, a castizo, who had been exiled to the Philippines for having murdered his wife, and she does not know if he was dead or alive; and (2) Ana Martin who was dead already. "Neither her nor Juan Lopez had any children."[2]

Beside Isabel, the Montoya family had three more children: (1) Juana de Montoya, who had died in 1638; she was described as a castiza, (not a mulatta) and was married to a cart-driver, called Gallardo, with whom she had three children. Her sister's second son, Nicolas, became a tailor of woolen cloths, and died unmarried in Puebla, at the age of nineteen. Her third son, Juan, died at the age of three in Mexico City; (2) Nicolás, Isabel's other brother, who had also died by 1662, was put in prison in 1647 because of his close association with Isabel, and there married a mestiza, Isabel Renjito, who had died a few years after their marriage, childless; and (3) the youngest of the Montoya children, Josephe, had also died at the age of eight, in Puebla.[3]

In mid-seventeenth-century New Spain blacks and mulattoes outnumbered by far all those termed *españoles* (whites, castizos, and mestizos—i.e those of mixed Indian and Spanish parentage), the former remaining in the lowly status of servitude to the latter. Mulattas were usually the household slaves or free servants, maids, midwives, wet-nurses, cooks, washerwomen, bakers, and food and flower-sellers in the city markets. Certain popular arts and crafts, as well as professions in which they specialized, such as healing, offered these women limited pathways along which they might advance socially.[4]

At seven Isabel was confirmed as a Roman Catholic in Mexico City's cathedral, by a secular priest by the name of Lic. Benavides, who was the priest of that parish, who served as her godfather and a black woman by the name of Malchora de Fustamante, who was a slave of a public notary, was her godmother.[5]

By the age of ten Isabel, who could not read or write, had been trained under the close instruction of her mother and her aunt to work as a healer, using a great variety of medicinal plants to produce ointments, lotions, and potions of her own concoction. Isabel was born into a family of healers; the knowledge and practice of healing was strictly matriarchal, and passed on in this family from mother to daughters for three generations. The initiator of this family tradition was Isabel's grandmother, renowned in the neighborhood for her skills; she had passed on her knowledge to Luisa, Isabel's mother, as well as to her two aunts. One of these, Isabel Martín had, moreover, bridged a wide gap in the medical services hierarchy of that day by marrying a Spanish surgeon thought to be the best in the city; and it was she who served as Isabel's principal mentor in the craft. This fact might well highlight the "dialogue" that developed between "high" and "low" medical practices in Mexico, by the early seventeenth century. It resonated in the manner whereby forms and usage of herbs and medicines traditionally employed by the Indians of Mexico for magical curative purposes were increasingly appropriated and accommodated into the formal medical practice of the Spanish controlled colonial institutions.[6]

In 1624 a Spaniard came to the house of Isabel's parents and, with their consent, took her away to live as a servant in his mother's home. There it was announced that the Spaniard intended in due time to marry her; and Isabel was entrusted to two mulatta servant-women, Francisca Ruiz and her daughter, Juana de la Cruz, to be trained in the domestic arts while she completed the transition to womanhood. She remained in that house for four years. Francisca Ruiz was an active participant in local church activities, and served as a godmother for baptisms (*madrina de bautizmo*) to quite a few of the black and mulatto newborns in the parish. She instructed them in the Catholic religion as well as the practice of local folk religion, and kept watch over their moral education. A devout member of the parish, Francisca Ruiz was also in charge of knitting clothes with which to dress the image of the local patron, Our Lady of Carmen, and taught Isabel this craft. Isabel also accompanied her to all the parish processions during feast days proceeding to the metropolitan cathedral in the Plaza Mayor, the city's main square.[7]

The cathedral stood at the forefront of this huge square, on its northern side. To the south stood the Lord Mayor's office, the police, judge's residence, the public granary, and the metropolitan prison. Behind, one would come through the major storehouses of the city. The mansions of the most prosperous merchants and city officials occupied most of the western part of the square, together with five or six storehouses selling golden embroidery styled in Europe. To the east was the palace of the Viceroy, the Royal *Audiencia*, the university and Santo Domingo College, and the Holy Office, at the corner of which stood the Casa de Moneda. The nearby Plaza de Volador, founded in 1624, was a bustling public area southeast of the Plaza Mayor. It became the main arena for the "running of the bulls" (*corrida de toros*) and public games during festivities and holy days. It also became the capital's main marketplace for castes, and Indians alike. Indian fruit and vegetable merchants reached this site from the floating markets of Chalco and Xochimilco, arriving by canoe through the Royal Canal (*La Aceqay Real*), which began in the town of Tláhuac, to the south of the capital. From there hundreds of canoes, traditional vessels called *chalupas* and *trajuneras* carried the city's supply of fresh fruit, vegetables, and flowers. The most prestigious commerce (retail merchants; imports) remained in the hands of powerful Spanish and Creole tradesmen who established themselves at the Parían market located on the west side of the Plaza Mayor. The Plaza de Volador was also the most popular space in the city for Spaniards, Creoles, and Indians, as well as the different castes, to meet and interact informally. The nearby Alameda Central, the first public park in Mexico City in the early seventeenth century, was not the place for Isabel and her kind to wander about in. It was intended at that time only for the "upper classes." Official documents of this period show that the local police were ordered to ban "coarsely dressed people, barefoot, beggars, or nude or any other indecent people."

In the Plaza de Volador also, at the age of fourteen, Montoya presumably caught the eye of the treasurer of Mexico City's Minting House, who persuaded her to become his mistress. He installed her in a rented house of her own under the care of an African slave whom he purchased to look after her, where she cooked and knitted for a year in anticipation of his daily visits. On September 21 that year (1629), the capital of New Spain was struck by blasting winds and torrential rains. The mounting waters of Lake Texcoco broke the dikes defending the city and inundated the streets, which remained impassable for a few more months following the catastrophe, except for travel by canoe. Thousands of houses throughout the city were ruined, and hundreds of persons and animals were drowned, especially in the poorer neighborhoods. Isabel was then spirited from her house by Don Gabriel de Cabesco, a sergeant major in Mexico City's local militia. He too rented a house for her where he kept her as his concubine for the next six years, during which time she was also employed as his personal servant.

During these years Isabel remained in close touch with her two aunts on her mother's side, continuously learning from them about new forms of healing. She regularly frequented the marketplace at the Plaza de Volador where she established close working relations with Indian herb sellers, who taught her about the qualities of their herbs. Her foremost craft of healing with magical formulas was also passed on to her by a mulatta, Isabel de Vivanco, who lived next to the Alameda Central and who was knowledgeable in many matters of this kind. One day the mulatta asked for a table, "opened a cloth in which she had some dry Ava-Ava leaves, a piece of carbon, a piece of silver, a piece of mineral salt, and a piece of brimstone, all spread on a piece of taffeta."[8] Isabel returned to live for a while in her parents' house; since, as she testified to her inquisitorial interrogators, she had "lived a scandalous life" (*"como mala mujer"*) during these years.[9] She now maintained a new and exciting relationship with one of the city's treasurers, Juan Serrano, this time of her own free will, from whom she became pregnant.

At 21, Isabel was still under the *patria potestas* of her parents who, acknowledging her pregnancy, finally compelled her to marry him in church. It is significant to note here that in mid-seventeenth-century New Spain, the church as well as public attitudes followed the norms established back in 1563 by the Council of Trent's decree on marriage. It promoted free will and free choice and opposed parental compulsion of those about to be married, while the *patria potestas* became marginalized.[10] Isabel defied her parents, and then escaped from the house, and returned to living "immorally" on her own, thereafter giving birth to her only child, the illegitimate daughter, Ana María de Montoya, who later in life became a seamstress. Outraged by her audacity, Isabel's parents took the child away from her, and paid one of the city's councilors to forcibly deposit her at the House of Seclusion run by the church of Santa Monica in the city.[11] There, like all other immoral persons condemned by the bishop and the city authorities to such imprisonment and reprimand, she was expected to pay for her wrongful behavior and to reform, under the close guidance of the priest and nuns.

Isabel's early life seems to have been an unbroken sequence of lingering violation, compulsion, subjugation, "free spirit" and shame, from an extremely young age; it could be defined indeed as a "post-traumatic complex disorder."

Contemporary studies on post-traumatic disorder do show that women who claimed to have been abused as children were even as adults unable to give a coherent account of what had happened to them. They had only fragmentary memories that supported other people's stories, and their own intuitive feelings, that they had been abused; Isabel's own narrative clearly demonstrates this. The combination of a fragmented autobiographical memory, continued dissociation that includes victimization, helplessness, and betrayal was an inseparable part of the molding of her adolescent life in the form of a repeated return to the initial trauma, as most recent studies on post-trauma show. Isabel's early trauma, therefore, surely left permanent wounds on her later upbringing and choice of love, occupations, and union, as can be seen from the following.

While serving her term at the House of Seclusion she met the first available man around, Gaspar de la Peña, who had formerly served as a cabin boy for the Conde de Santiago; she agreed to marry him with no further ado, and their marriage was approved by the local priest (despite his knowledge of her motherhood). They remained formally married for more than twenty years, but lived together for only eight days, after their release. Then, following repeated beatings, Isabel reported her new husband to the city authorities, who threatened to throw him into jail. Gaspar de la Peña fled the city leaving Isabel with no children from him. It was only in 1655, back in Mexico City, that Isabel met him again, briefly. On that occasion he came from Cocula, a village near the city of Guadalajara, where he lived, and asked her if she wished to live with him again. That night he stabbed her with a knife, badly wounded her, and also tried forcing her to go with him to Cocula, but she resisted. He then offered 200 pesos to a mulatto slave to do away with her, "because she had had an affair with another man." When the local police uncovered the plot he again fled, and Isabel never saw him again. She only heard after a while that he continued to live in that small village, and that "he had become very rich."[12]

In 1635, at the age of twenty-one, Isabel left the capital city of the viceroyalty and took up residence in the nearby city of Puebla de los Angeles. She earned her living there as a part-time prostitute and a healer, making ointments and selling them, through an Indian artisan, at the local market. In one of the inquisitorial hearings of her case, Montoya had thus characterized her first five years in Puebla as "living totally promiscuously." The English missionary and traveler Thomas Gage, who visited Puebla during these very years also attested how it was "an accepted norm" among attractive black and mulatto young women to become the courtesans and concubines of rich and powerful merchants and public officials there. They were also depicted as "dressed in their particular seductive style, with abundant jewelry and silk pieces, which made the Spaniards depreciative of their own wives."[13]

Isabel's home in Puebla, as the inquisitorial proceedings attest, was regularly crowded between 1635 and 1640 with laymen, as well as priests from the nearby Franciscan monastery. They came to find cures for their bodily pains and frustrated love, and also to obtain magical remedies against bewitchments. Most of the clientele were women of all classes, who sought different means (love potions and magical substances, usually, hearts of wax and healing-minerals) to retrieve the men who had abandoned them (either these lovers or their husbands, who had engaged themselves to other women). In addition to its function as a popular healing sanctuary, the place soon became a shelter for deserted women of the lower caste and class, household maids, wet-nurses, cooks and midwives, who had escaped their former afflictions. Some of these women remained behind, living there for a while, serving as apprentices to Isabel. They assumed the role of mediators with the repressed world of the supernatural, and were sought by many for specific needs outside the conventional procedures of medicine and the Catholic liturgy. They were able to help each other mold a gender consciousness of self-defense, under a permanent situation of compulsion and repression. The collective practice of healing, the knowledge of which they passed on to each other while staying there, became for these women alternative grounds for social and ritual subversion against the male-dominated "caste system" of the colonial arena.

They were thus able to fulfill their desires to attract and reunite with men of higher status and prestige in the local market place, where the latter would stroll or take their sumptuous afternoon luncheon. They could also meet them at the public baths of Atoyaque or during festivities at the plaza, when blacks and mulattoes wearing their traditional clothes mounted theatrical representations and other amusements such as dances and music. Nevertheless, all such pursuits, amusements, and "public scandals" virtually ended upon the inauguration in 1640 of the new and repressive rule of the new bishop, and ex-Viceroy, Juan de Plafox y Mendoza in Puebla. Under his rigorous moral and ecclesiastical reforms in the city, all dances, music, and games enjoyed by blacks and mulattoes, women and men on Sundays and holy days were suspended indefinitely. Prostitution, as well as other lesser immoral transgressions of the strict observance of the norms of proper behavior and living, were severely punished.

As the records suggest, many of these women were able to mold powerful ways of ignoring and transcending both race and class barriers, as well as operating skillfully outside the bounds of family and marriage, in a multi-faceted cultural environment. In spite of being marginalized due to "race" and also as an outcome of their loss of sexual honor, their personal histories are, in fact, laden with important insights into their replacement of the conventional family model with forms of alternative kinship. In 1629, for example, Luisa Franco and Inés, both widowed mestizas, clothing sellers in their profession, were accused in the Puebla court of "dressing like Indians, and causing public scandals." The litigation records describe them as selling regularly the forbidden pulque liquor in their houses. "They made many of the Indians become drunk everyday, and instructed them to avoid work, nor go to hear mass on feast days. In addition, they lived unmarried with two Indians."[14] Forty-year-old Luisa Franco was the widow of Juan, an Indian stone-cutter, and then the pregnant concubine of Pedro Juarez, the Indian alcalde of the San Francisco *barrio* in Puebla. Inés, her friend, was described as unlawfully living with another Indian, a tailor. The two, who were eventually detained by the city authorities for innkeeping, for leading immoral, scandalous lives, and for concubinage, "violently resisted their arrest" and were sent off to the public prison.[15]

Living as concubines did not necessarily imply "living in sin" for unmarried women and single mothers of *hijos naturales*. However, the main concern over the unruly life of unmarried girls remained throughout the preservation of honor and the confinement of overt sexual promiscuity. Therefore, Guido Ruggiero's recent claim that "crucial was the disciplining power of a complex web of concepts that turned on honor and reputation and their association with female sexuality" was valid in northern Italy as much as in New Spain.[16] Informal marital arrangements, especially among the lower classes of the racially mixed, and the practice of abduction of young girls for the sake of elopement were far more common than in other European countries at that time, as Richard Boyer has shown in his recent study on bigamy in New Spain. However, he has also noted that the parish clergy censured illicit, informal unions of any duration and demanded that the couple should either separate or marry. The general public often reported such couples to the authorities, but also "tolerated a good deal of it."[17] As this chapter indicates, the concubines themselves were not always happy with this confining arrangement. Steve Stern has recently described how "even when a woman questioned a man's sincerity and intentions or when marriage clearly lay outside the prospective horizons of a relationship, a poor woman could not easily afford to rule out sexual liaison."[18] Therefore, kidnapping young girls and turning them into concubines was in effect a drama of virility. "It affirmed male-on-male rivalry between men who wished to possess the same woman, and this implied that possession of a woman was permanent unless one man robbed sexual property from another." The drama was also one of familial ownership: "the woman was subject to overlapping claims of family that rendered possession less than permanent or final."[19] The populace across New Spain tolerated these acts, as well as those of such women, only to the point where immoral living combined with supernatural transgressions became a real menace.

These two women do, indeed, portray a multifaceted case in which immorality, promiscuity, as well as the transcending of race affiliation, is clearly present. Under such circumstances in Puebla the usual penalty for these women was to be sent to the Magdalena Casa de Recogimiento (House of Seclusion), to improve their lives. Only one year earlier, as the local records show, Francisco de Trujillo, a merchant, was accused in court of having kidnapped Francisca, his mestiza concubine from the same Casa de Recogimiento and instead placed his own wife there.[20] Cases involving kidnapping, the sexual abuse of single servants and slaves, and "living in sin" as concubines are numerous in the Puebla records for 1629–1648. Most of them cite single, caste women, either widowed or unmarried, who usually lived together and shared strategies of survival.[21] In 1648, one of them, Juana Bautista, a free mulatta, a widow, sold the house of her late husband located in the *barrio* de Analuco, in the street behind the parish church of San Angel de la Guardia, and next to the Jewish baker's houses, for the price of thirty golden pesos. She then moved to share a new household with a few of her female inmates.[22]

In 1641 Isabel was therefore flogged by the bishop's orders and placed in Puebla's House of Seclusion. She had spent a year and a half there together with not a few other "indecent" women of her kind, ordered by the new bishop to be "reformed." There, Isabel had first befriended María de Rivera, a mulatta and a bread-seller, one of the regular visitors to the place. María had provided her with badly needed food and clothing and, in return, Isabel had taught her new friend a body of supernatural crafts: how to perform magic with herbs; to cast lots from Ava-ava leaves, from which an intoxicating liquor could be produced, as well as foretell the future by casting grains of corn into a glazed earthenware pot.[23] After her release in 1643, Isabel invited María to share her lodgings with her, and also her knowledge of supernatural arts. Likewise, Isabel once directed her to go to a mulatta who lived in Puebla, called Josepha de Miranda, who owned a wax heart and who had been known to have cured a friar with it. While staying at Isabel's place, Rivera apparently transferred a whole set of ritual gifts of knowledge and practice to Isabel. The latter actually witnessed Rivera performing a number of ritual practices intimately linked with the theme of ritual gifts. According to the testimony presented to the court by both, these included nocturnal offerings to the Lord of the Street. It was a ritualized image of an "upper class" man, to whom Rivera offered bread and cheeses, and used a vapor-maker of violet silk, golden lace and rosemary, with which she sprayed the street for the lord's dinner. In exchange, Isabel taught Rivera a method by which the man she chose as a prospective partner would become rich: one must go to the merchants' street (Calle de Mercaderes) in Mexico City to collect a small quantity of soil from each of the four sides of the street and spread it on the doorway of the relegated person. The following should then be recited with a wax heart placed in the palms of both hands:

> In the name of the Street, Lord, Godfather,
>   Where you wished someone to belong,
> Do not let him halt, nor provide him with lodging
> Until he comes to look for me. If it is true, then
>   give me a signal, That of one dog or that of a
>   crowing cock, or that of
>   a passing horse.[24]

Isabel also witnessed Rivera pour hot chocolate on the ground in front of two men who came to visit her. Rivera also possessed a vapor-maker filled with rosemary, in which she burnt copal resin and horse dung to purify her relegated partner's intimate parts before and during lovemaking. Once, ill in bed with an Indian herbal specialist beside her, she asked Montoya to buy from the Indian some *peyomate*, dry grass and roses, called "la doradilla," to be given to drink by the man who wanted her. The two women had exchanged earlier versions of such recitations intended also "for protection against vengeful men who wished to do away with their women or hurt them" during mass, when they were both in Puebla's House of Seclusion.

One particular aspect of single women's strategies of survival which might throw more light on the "survival mechanisms" among single women is the chain of ritual gifts among these women themselves and between them and men; which, we suggest, were also closely linked with the rule of concubinage, honor, and shame involving local realities. The testimony presented here sheds light on the types of ritual actions, and the social aspirations in their repertoire. Fertility rites, and "love-magic" in particular among such single women in Puebla, Mexico City, and elsewhere in the countryside of New Spain, aimed at attaining progeny, motherhood and ultimately matrimony on the one hand; and they challenged the stigmas attached to the unmarried, living outside proper family structures, the racially inferior, and barren on the other.[25] The tales of the supernatural practices they used, to challenge their impregnable status, are filled with rich details about networks of patients, entourage, and lovers, up and down the social and racial ladders, from inquisitors and priests, down to petty seamen. Their use of "love magic" to attract men of a superior race and class, were more suited to proper marriage rather than their restricted choices; their "sisterhoods" and mutual ritual practices, all have a social significance as yet unexplored.

Menstrual blood, as well as the caul of newborn babies, was inter alia both a benevolent and malevolent gift in those fertility rites, given to men either simultaneously, or, separately, as one might presume from the sources, although there is no evidence indicating the former. The recipients undoubtedly believed in the powers attributed to these gifts in order to accept them, but one of the two gifts was regarded by the recipients to be purely benevolent; the other, to be sour and dangerous. It could be compared to one of the female spirits in Tyrol mythology, *Langtuttin*, from whose breasts poured both milk and venom respectively.[26] In contemporary New Spain, fertility rites among blacks, mulattas and mestizas involved diverse uses of the old, familiar "love-magic" but also entailed a whole package of syncretistic practices added to it.

The sources for the various substances and practices disseminated by women belonging to the three groups of mulattoes, mestizos, and Indians were quite different. For Indian and mestizo women, it was mainly the rich, idiosyncratic repertoire of the still-maintained Nahua magical traditions, whereas for the mulattoes and blacks, it was basically the syncretistic combination of Iberian tradition, based on Arabic and Romany magical practices, together with inherited African cultural usage. Magical practices were transferred to the colonies from Spain and Portugal as an inseparable element of the slave trade. Such practices involved a wide variety of source materials extending from the knowledge and use of magical curative substances of love magic to counter-magical spells, as well as the invocation of Satan, and sorcery, representing the synthesis of European and African traditions.[27] Thus, while mulatto and black women, as ex-slaves brought from the Iberian Peninsula by their masters, were popularly considered the cultural carriers and proselytizers of mainly Spanish-Morisco magical traditions, Indian and mestizo women were predominantly conceived as mentors and initiators for the autochthonous, "natural" resources of the supernatural.[28] The practice of "love-magic" would combine resources originating from the three groups, and was used within the alternative kinship framework. The components included the use of wax hearts, vapors, *puyomate* (an indigenous plant widely applied for purposes both of attraction and repulsion in colonial times) bundles sown under the clothes containing stuffed hummingbirds; various lotions and potions, herbs, and ground soil. Menstrual blood mixed with drinks of cocoa or pulque was one of the most striking among their syncretistic repertoire and may have originated from pre-Columbian indigenous practices rather than from its counterpart in Europe, as the Franciscan chronicler, Fr. Bernandino de Sahagún informs us.[29]

Another of Isabel's new relationships originating in the House of Seclusion was with a Franciscan priest, who served his sentence there for having applied "many falsehoods and frauds," one of them on the inquisitor of Puebla's cousin. She became a close friend of this friar who had mastered many remedies which he taught her. But his specialty was to teach Isabel the very basics of applied astrology, that forbidden art. Likewise, every day, at midnight, they would both sneak together into the prison's patio and there they would stare into the pool "to know where the stars went."[30] According to Isabel, this priest, with his magical powers could also compel María de Rivera "to come to prison to have a carnal act with him." María herself later testified that Isabel also persuaded her that the priest was "a rich man and she should sleep with him" which she once did, in his cell.

Another of these women who lived with Isabel for a while after her release from prison was Juana de Sosa, a native of Puebla and a seamstress, who sold the intoxicating yellow *pulque*, an intoxicant based on the agave plant, in the local market place until 1648, when she was put under surveillance by the Holy Office.[31] The three women set themselves up as housemates and partners in the illicit pulque trade under the constant danger of being exposed by the local police or the Holy Office for their clandestine activity of selling hallucinogens such as the forbidden peyote plant, and yellow pulque. The use of Indian herbs was, at that time, often associated with magic and thus, in 1620 in the Edict of Faith, the Mexican Inquisition prohibited the use of peyote "and any others of the type that hold the virtue of causing fantasies and representations upon which divinations are found." Fearing that she would be arrested by the inquisition for trading in intoxicants, Juana fled in 1648 to the nearby town of Cholula. Isabel went occasionally to Cholula, where the two continued to meet. On one occasion, Isabel had the opportunity to demonstrate her skills as a midwife. Her friend's daughter, Isabel de los Angeles, a 25-year-old wool weaver, was carrying the child of a man from Tlascala, who had promised marriage and then abandoned her. Isabel de Montoya found the girl to be extremely weak, predicted a miscarriage, and then told her that "she would entrust her daughter to God's will." Some months later, Juana returned to Puebla. There, Isabel scolded Juana for not having cared for her daughter as she had promised her earlier on in Cholula. Isabel had also advised her that she should sow seeds in the earth, "to know whether the man who had left her daughter would come back to marry her." Isabel had also instructed an Indian practitioner to light some candles, and had given him some wine, to make him foretell whether the man who had abandoned Isabel de Los Angeles was about to return and whether she should marry him. By then, Isabel apparently, had already established close working relations in Puebla with local Indian practitioners who regularly assisted her in her own practice of healing and fortune-telling. Such cooperation clearly taught her traditional curatives, such as the use of peyote. Once, Juana later recalled,

Isabel asked her to bring a jar into which she poured water together with some powders and two peyote plants. Isabel then gave her the potion to drink and advised her to remember well what she would dream. Isabel had taken out the peyote plants from the water and placed them in the sun to dry, and kept them hidden in a rolled cloth. In her work as an intermediary with the supernatural, Isabel de Montoya relied heavily on Indian knowledge and practice which she also passed on to her adherents. While at Isabel's home, Juana regularly consulted an Indian herbal specialist who taught her how to refine her pulque.

Monica de la Cruz, a single mestiza, lived in Cholula when she and Isabel had first met in the marketplace of Cholula, on the feast day of Our Lady of the Mountain. Monica, who was still unmarried, was born in Puebla, and used to live there in the Bishop's Palace. She was fifty years old, had been baptized and confirmed by the church; as she attested, "on her father's side she was a descendant of Creoles and of Christianized Indians, on her mother's side." She made her living there as a cook in households of local Spaniards preparing *bonuelos* and *tamales* on feast days, and also as a balladeer, reciting popular prayers in the streets while selling various foods.[32]

Yet another of Isabel's adherents during these years was Margarita de Palacios; a native of Puebla, she was married to Gaspar de Morales, a lime-burner. She had first become acquainted with Isabel through María de Rivera. In about 1646, ill with malaria, she went to María for a cure and was given some winter vetch and told to dissolve it in water, pour some of it onto her chest over her heart and drink the rest, "by which she would be cured of that habitual lack of integrity [in her health]." Two days later she visited María at home and was invited in to meet Isabel, who offered her some dry, green herbs which from then on, she always kept with her. The following year and a half we find her sharing the same house with Juana de Sosa, whom she called sister-in-law because Juana had relations with Margarita's brother, Francisco de Palacios. Confessing to Fr. Mateo de la Cruz in the monastery of El Carmen, Margarita de Palacios told him about the herbs she had received from Isabel and he instructed her in turn to tear and cut them into small pieces. Then, praying, he absolved her and warned her never to see Isabel and her colleagues again, an admonition she evidently did not heed. In June 1654, Margarita was arrested on orders from the Holy Office in Puebla, held there for ten days and then taken to Mexico City, to be held in the monastery of El Carmen until she could stand trial on charges of "bewitching and using superstitious herbs and frauds." Isabel was also a close friend of Bernardina, also known as "Señora la Grande," a mestiza who lived in the Gualaquilla area of Puebla, and who later on was also sentenced to penitence by the Holy Office.

Isabel and her colleagues were all roughly the same age, about thirty years old, at the time. They were all devout Catholics, who partook regularly in the church rites and the holy feasts. They were able to recite the Credo, the Ave María, and the Salve Regina, as well as some of the Articles of Faith, and part of the Ten Commandments. Their knowledge of the Catholic faith was somewhat better than that usually found among New Spain's popular classes. Examining the list of items which Isabel had brought with her to the inquisition's prison in Mexico City on July 24, 1662, one finds fair evidence for her own piety to the cult of the saints, analogous to the rich collection of powders and herbs that she possessed. Her devotional objects, which would not have put to shame ladies of the Spanish colonial aristocracy, included, inter alia, a black rosary with an insignia of the Immaculate Conception; two small slips of cloth with an engraved image of Our Lady of Carmen; small ceramic plates engraved with the image of St. James; a rectangular plate, with an engraving of St. Anthony, holding a branch in his left hand; a copper plate with an engraved image of Our Lady of Solitude, together with a painted figure; an image of the adoration of St. Mary Magdalene holding the cross; six sheets of paper bearing the figures of male and female saints; Agnus Dei with a painted cloth; a roll of bread of St. Nicholas; a paper with the image of Christ; a bull of the Holy Cross; a calf of St. Anthony, and two small ivory images of St. Francis and St. Mary Magdalene coiled in paper.[33] Some of these objects were probably donated to her either by the friars who frequented her house, or by others whom she regarded as her closest patients.

Isabel's teachings to her housemates, apart from the practice of healing and counter-magic, included popular devotions to her favorite saints. For example, "to make the man come and stay, they should place in his shoes or in the folds of his shirt a certain grain which she gave them, accompanying it with a certain recitation":

> Marta Martilla, compadre la mala,
>   que lo ruega a la de la falle,
> que donde estuviera Juan, no lo de desparar,
>   ni llegar hasta que me venga a buscar.[34]

[Martha Martilla, the bad one's godfather, so that she would plead before that of the trickster kind, that where Juan would dwell, do not awaken him, nor go there until he comes to look for me.]

María de Rivera was instructed by Isabel to become a devotee to Saint Martha. She instructed her to go to a mulatto artist who worked at the marketplace, and to ask him to paint an image of the saint for her. Isabel had also handed her a popular chant in honor of that saint, which she had kept with her since early childhood, written on a piece of paper. Popular chants such as those to Saint Martha, were composed and recited at that time by street-balladeers and performed among the castes; once Montoya had inscribed for María de Rivera the prayer of Santa Marta on a piece of paper which she carried with her. It went thus:

> Santa Marta,
> en el Monte Tabor entraste,
> con la gran sierpe encontraste,
> con el eslopo del agua vendita
> la arostaste,
> con el cordon la amarraste,
> credo y cerdo que seamanse,
> el que conmigo estuviere tirado.[35]

[Santa Martha, into Mount Tabor you entered, and with the great serpent you have met, and with the water-sprinkler of holy water you have challenged him, with a cord you have tied him, so that credo and pig would fall in love, (if) he will fall for me.]

This present version appears to be a popular variation on the same theme as manifest in a yet more complete text, in an inquisitorial manuscript dating from 1617:

> En el Monte Olibete entraste, con laserpiente fiera encontraste braba la hallaste, con vuestros santos conjuros la conjurastis, con vuestro hisopo la rosiastiscon vuestra sinta la atastis. . .madre mía, Santa Marta, con aquellos conjuros que conjurastis a la serpiente, me conjuréis al Fulano y así me pongáis. . .[36]

The representation of the serpent, and the act of tying him up (as the devil), might well have been an amalgam of the traditional teachings on Christ raising Lazarus from the Dead. It first appeared in its visual form in the *Byzantine Barbarini Plaster*, in which the devil is seen lying in chains, an image related to Christian-African syncretistic beliefs about the devil. These were usually the by-product of the liturgy, blended with Indian and African myths. Such syncretistic beliefs, held also by Montoya and her companions, were also pictorially documented, sometimes reflecting a reversed version. In a rare and fascinating illustration, painted probably by one of the mulatta female internees imprisoned in the inquisitorial prison in Mexico City during the 1620s, and annexed to a manuscript of inquisitorial records of New Spain,[37] a black/mulatta culprit, possibly the artist herself, is seen holding a snake on her left hand, and facing the devil, who, himself holds a rope (see figure 3.1). Yet another rope is hanging up from the culprit's neck and tied to the banister above her head. This illustration, which possibly combines African and Christian beliefs about the devil, can be deciphered to convey a message according to which the devil either wishes to lure her with the rope, while the snake here plays the role of "seduction" per se, or, he uses the rope for the sake of possibly tying up/ subjecting the snake, who is the object of seduction.

Such popular traditions were basically the combination of Iberian tradition, based on Arabic and Romany (gypsy) magical practices, inherited African cultural usage, and learnt indigenous usage. Magical practices had been transferred to the colonies from Spain and Portugal as an inseparable part of the slave trade. They involved a wide variety of source materials extending from the knowledge and use of magical-curative substances of love magic to counter-magical spells, the invocation of Satan, and sorcery, representing the synthesis of European and African traditions.

From what we know, Isabel and her colleagues were actively involved in the annual procession of the confraternity of the Holy Sacrament in Puebla, enacting the burial of Jesus, wearing black tunics, ropes around their necks and a crown of thorns on their heads. They frequented the city's churches, praying for their beloved saints—Our Lady of the Rosary, Our Lady of Cármen, and went to confess to the priests in the El Carmen convent, to the San Antonio monastery and to the Franciscan convent. Their interaction with the priesthood in the city convents and at Isabel's place undoubtedly enriched their knowledge of the liturgy. Nevertheless, it also provided them with additional channels to the supernatural through the deliberate assumption of noncanonical roles.

The three years between 1647 and 1650 were especially significant in Isabel's private recollections, as much as in the collective histories of Puebla's inhabitants. Throughout the summer of 1647 Puebla witnessed a campaign mounted against Bishop Palafox, initiated by the Holy Office and the Jesuits. On June 7 of that year, upon the sounding of the cathedral's bells, a great crowd of Bishop Palafox's adherents gathered in the Plaza Mayor and the bishop gave a stern sermon admonishing his enemies. On June 14, the bishop abandoned the city and fled to the mountains of Tepeaca, leaving the city behind to the "triumph of moral decay" and to the triumphant processions of both Dominicans and Jesuits who marched through the center of the city. For the feast day of their patron saint, St. Ignacio Loyola, the Jesuits organized a procession headed by a column of students, followed by black slaves, and other persons commissioned by the Company, all of them wearing masks and escorted by soldiers and officials. The procession carried a grotesque representation of Palafox and a triumphal chariot with the image of St. Ignacio. On September 24 of that year,

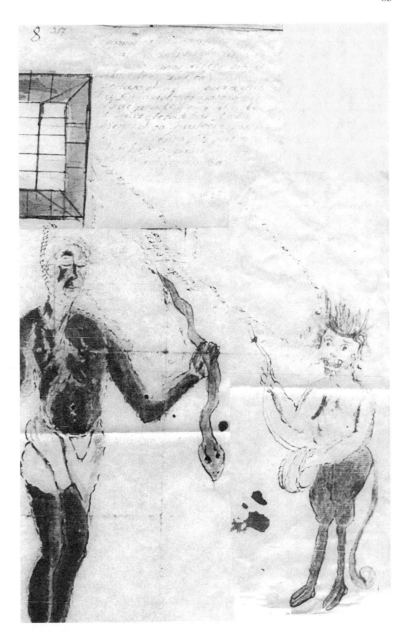

Figure 3.1 Facing the Devil.

Source: (Courtesy of Archivio General de la Nación)

ringing the cathedral bells, the pro-Palafox faction again gathered a great number of people in the city center throwing stones and shouting *Víva Palafox, virrey, visitador general!* ("Hale Palafox, viceroy and general visitor.)" Other groups also swept through the city streets causing damage to the houses of those opposing the bishop. On November 10, Palafox finally returned to his episcopal seat, after an absence of four months, and after seeing to it that the Viceroy, Conde de Salvatierra, his greatest enemy was disposed. On the 25th of that month, the return of Palafox was celebrated with great presentations of dancing, music, and thanksgiving processions.[38]

Holy Week of 1648 was followed by many days of blustering rains: the streets were flooded by water, mud, and garbage. The worst situation occurred near the Saint Catherine's baths and the San Pedro hospital, next to the Río San Francisco. At the end of August that year a terrible epidemic struck Puebla, causing numerous deaths. The local hospitals and hospices were filled with the sick and dying. Under Bishop Palafox's instructions, Isabel and the rest of the populace who had escaped the catastrophe proceeded to the now-renovated cathedral, carrying the image of the city's patron saint, St. Joseph, and holding special prayers to counteract the plague.

In 1648 also, Isabel traveled to Cholula especially for the feast day of Our Lady of the Mountain, hoping for easy profits by selling her remedy of the intoxicant yellow peyote to the crowds gathering at the marketplace. Isabel and Juana had met there, at Juana's stand, where she sold Isabel some silver lace which she exhibited on an open cart to the groups of bystanders. Two years later, in the same town of Cholula, in the inquisitorial procedure that took place there, a total of 101 cases were brought before the district commissioner: 32.6 percent of whom were male culprits and 67.3 percent females.[39] In the inquisitorial inventory of the cases prosecuted in 1650, it is mentioned that Margarita de Palacios was being accused of living in concubinage (*amancebada*) with María de Rivera, a mulatta, "who prepared for her a heart of wax which she carried hung with two nails and another bound inside an amulet, for the sake of retrieving a man with which she was living in concubinage."[40]

In April of 1650, during Holy Week, Isabel was among the massive crowd which gathered in the main square to witness the celebrations of the grand completion of the prolonged renovation of the city cathedral. At noon, after all the streets were thoroughly swept and the buildings decorated, the alcaldes and *regidores* (city officials) enacted the game of the spears (*juego de cañas*), and thirty-two actors dressed in silk mounted on horses participated in the ritual battle between Christians and Moors. That night, a special procession headed by the bishop, rector, and sacristans proceeded through the main streets of the city to the cathedral where a special mass was held. The *cabildo* (municipal hall) building and the archways were illuminated by numerous torches, and the parishioners gathered at the atrium of the cathedral awaiting the call to enter and receive the Holy Sacrament.[41]

For the next four years Isabel moved to reside for short periods in the nearby towns of Cholula, San Salvador, and Huejotzingo, in order to avoid the inquisition's close surveillance, especially over her trade in the illegal yellow peyote. In these towns she was probably a boarder in the households of her close unmarried female acquaintances; she made her living as a healer and a midwife but, occasionally, she also served as a cook for local dignitaries and the Franciscan friars. In these towns she had established her name in the healing profession, as well as extending her body of women adherents even as far away as the distant port town of Vera Cruz. Juana de Sosa, Margarita de Palacios, and María de Rivera all appear in the 1650 inquisition's records from Puebla, as having submitted voluntary confessions describing their "immoral acts," their magical practices, as well as their intimate relationship with men.[42]

Possibly following her friends' confessions to the Holy Office, and the close inspection that followed, on June 25, 1652, Isabel was taken into the penitentiary of the Holy Office in Huejotzingo, together with a few of her belongings: two shirts and a mattress, and her powders and herbs. She was placed under the custody of the parish priest of the San Salvador barrio, Don Joseph de Goitias. One week later she was transferred to Mexico City, to the Holy Office's prison. The original allegation, read before her by Huejotzingo's inquisitors, was that she had continuously abused her local profession as a midwife, having treated her patients with illicit means.[43] In the Mexico City courtroom the prosecutor, Tomás López de Erenchun, added to the allegations, describing Isabel "a famous healer, who used herbs, roots, vapor-producing substances, and powders, all for the sake of evil ends, reciting superstitious words and prayers, and forming an explicit pact with whom she consulted and communicated those matters. . . ."[44]

On February 16, 1653 after seven months of imprisonment and torture, Isabel was finally sentenced to an auto-da-fé, a hundred lashes, exile from her city, Puebla, and a three-year penitence in Mexico City's hospital, Amor de Dios. This hospital was first founded by Bishop Zumarraga in 1539, exclusively for patients suffering from syphilis, since they were excluded from Cortes's general hospital or Hospital General. On February 17, Isabel was taken from the Santo Domingo monastery, stripped from the waist upward, mounted on a pack-saddle, wearing a *coraza* with the insignia of a witch, holding a green wax candle in her hands, through the city streets, to the main square, where the town crier pronounced her sentence. She was then tied and publicly flogged.[45]

In 1656, after her release in Mexico City, Isabel lived in a small adobe house in the area where she was born, in the Santa Veracruz *barrio*, in an alley behind the San Juan de Dios convent, several hundred meters from the palace of the Holy Office. Juan Serrano, Isabel's first and by then deceased lover, had bequeathed the house to Isabel's daughter, 24-year-old Ana María de Montoya. At first Isabel shared her lodgings there with two other mulattas; later, some of the rooms were rented out to five different tenants, each paying between four and six reales a month.[46]

Among Isabel's acquaintances during this period was young Juana, the 28-year-old wife of Juan Alvárez, a water-carrier, who lived in San Bernardo Street. Juana had been left confused, perplexed, and bedridden by a sexual encounter with her lover. On the recommendation of a Chichimeca Indian woman of her acquaintance who was a servant in Isabel's house, as well as of a neighbor who had once been cured of an illness by Isabel, Juana sent her own servant-girl to fetch the famous healer to her bedside. Isabel had come to her, and had restored her health with a soup prepared with the flesh of black-plumed chickens. She had also provided Juana with a powder to sprinkle on her lover's clothes, claiming that it should cause him to want her; and she had received in payment for these services one turkey, some pearls, and four pesos. After a while, when her lover failed to return, Juana felt cheated and went to confess the whole affair to her parish priest.

Another client was a Creole lady named Doña Isabel Velázquez de la Cueva, aged thirty-nine, who lived on Tacuba Street, in the "Las Briviescas" houses, next to the house of the *alguacil Mayor* of the inquisition. Two weeks after Holy Week, 1661, Isabel Velásquez was seized by fits while visiting a friend. The friend recommended that she visit a mid-wife nicknamed La Centella (The Spark of Lightening), who had delivered her daughter "extremely professionally" and was also an expert in "love-magic." Anxious to relieve her suffering Velásquez went to an alley at the corner of the Santa Clara convent, where she met a black man who informed her that La Centella had moved three days earlier to the backyard of the San Juan de Dios church nearby. That night she mounted a mule and ventured out to seek the midwife. In an alleyway an Indian woman indicated to her where Isabel lived. Having entered the house she saw a number of women who had come to be cured. She asked her if she knew how to cure or deliver a baby, and Isabel replied positively, adding that, "many gentlemen and priests also came to visit her." Velázquez got undressed, and was helped to lie down. Then Isabel anointed her with a green unguent, at the same time reciting: "in the name of the Holy Trinity, the Father, the Son, and the Holy Ghost." The following morning Velázquez returned to Isabel's house, where she breakfasted with her.

Isabel urged her to confess her sins, and "trust God, who cures all." Twelve days later, on Ascension Day, Velázquez was called to return, and was given some rosemary leaves rolled in paper, and some *chocozote* to produce incense. Isabel then sent her a small jar with water and ground herbs, and she drank it in the company of an Indian woman who served at her place. Velázquez then went to confess to her priest, but he denied her penitence, stipulating that she should bring him everything that Isabel had administered to her. She did so, whereupon he absolved her and warned her against venturing into Isabel's lodgings again.[47]

Nevertheless, the following year, on the octave of St. Anthony's Day (January 17, 1662), Velázquez was fetched by one of Isabel's assistants. The assistant gave her some love magic powders to place in her intimate parts. Two days after St. Elizabeth's Day (July 8) that year, Isabel had asked her about the men she wished to possess, and when Velázquez responded that she preferred someone who was neither a Creole nor an official Isabel promised to introduce her to two men who worked on a canoe in the Royal Canal, and called her "their mother."

The iconography of Isabel's devotional objects and her ritual means and methods represented, indeed, a spectacular combination of lotions, potions, herbs, vapor-producing substances, minerals, and hallucinogens, all of them "borrowed" mainly from local cosmology, and merged with chants, prayers, and ritual actions of the Catholic liturgy, as well as popular devotions to the cult of the saints. The dates on which she performed ritual healing also coincided with the church's calendar of feast days. One key representation in this particular life-history is, therefore, the willful assumption by a pious and spiritually powerful woman of the church, of non canonical roles which the male hierarchy is at pains to deny her, that is, the control and claim of effectiveness of both healing and intercession with the divine.

In 1662, Don Miguel de Guevara, the ex-alcalde of Suchiapa and a respected citizen of Mexico City, was sweating feverishly in his house on Doncellas street in the city center, when Isabel was called to minister to him. By 1662, Isabel was then described as "quite an old woman who appeared to be either a mestiza or a mulatta." Isabel arrived at Don Miguel's house accompanied by a Creole woman dressed in a short green cloak. Doña Juana Alvárez de Vosmediano, Don Miguel's wife, described how immediately upon entering the house Isabel instructed them to remove the image of Holy Christ, the miracle-maker, from above the client's bed, and that "until his death it was not to be placed back." Her diagnosis was that he had been bewitched by his wife, his mother-in-law, and his sister, during his term of office in Suichiapa. The spell, she said, was carried out by their taking a small piece of bread chewed by Don Miguel, placing it in the mouth of a toad, and nailing the toad to the hinge of a door. In the presence of some other women Isabel poured out some holy water which she had acquired from a priest at the Franciscan monastery, and placed a *lignum cruces*—a relic of the cross of Christ—by his bed; she prescribed him some potions made of peyote to counter the spell. This caused him "to behave madly" for the following three days. Throughout his last fits Isabel remained in the household kitchen, together with all the other servants. During that time, Don Miguel's aunt overheard Isabel tell Don Miguel how, the other night, while "asleep with the other women, she had envisioned a handsome man surrounded by green light who appeared to be St. Michael, Don Miguel's patron, and who told her that he had come to cure him." The aunt was heard later to have said that "Don Miguel must have been with witches." Don Miguel himself, before returning his soul to the creator, divulged to his wife that he had seen the devil himself.[48]

Isabel was not always ready to go to the bedside of any sick person. When María de Jesús, the mulatta wife of Juan de la Mota in Doncelles Street, found that her mother Augustina was suffering from arthritis, in April 1662, she had her treated in vain by several licensed doctors. Then neighbors recommended Isabel. But when she went to find "an extremely black old woman, who cured the sick and dying," she was told that she would attend to her "only if driven by coach or by a sedan chair." She then gave her some powders rolled up in paper, which María threw away. She went to confess the affair to her priest, who in turn directed her to go and testify about the matter to the inquisition.

Catalina de Arcila was a single woman of thirty who lived in the houses of the *cofradía* of the Holy Sacrament in Isabel's native parish of Santa Veracruz where, as a *madrina de bautizmo* (baptismal godmother), taught girls of this parish reading, writing, praying, and domestic skills. It was her fate not to be the beneficiary of Isabel's spiritual power and her gift for healing, but to fall foul of her. One day, while she was alone in her home, a priest arrived and asked her: "Girl, when will your hand be cured?" she responded that "only God was able to cure." The priest's inquiry sparked some festering memories for Catalina. Back in 1653, when Isabel was publicly flogged through the streets of Mexico City, Catalina was one of the bystanders. In 1658, after Isabel's release, she met her at the raw silk stalls in the marketplace near the Santa Clara convent. Isabel approached her and told her that "she should not be working for the church, and should come instead and live with her," and "after only fifteen days even her own mother would not be able to recognize her." Catalina still remembered that when Isabel could not persuade her to follow her to her house, she caused her right hand to become permanently swollen.

Then, four years later, a few days before Nativity of 1662, an old Indian passed along the street and publicly pronounced a variety of remedies. When Catalina showed him her swollen hand the Indian indicated to her that there was no cure for it because it was "a spell, and only the person who had caused it could cure it." He added that a woman had done the deed with her thumb when she extended her hand to her. After having confessed this incident to the priest, the latter at once pressed her to go and divulge it before the wise priests at the Dominican convent "because it was contrary to our faith."[49]

One might well ask at this point: why, when Isabel was living so close to the Holy Office, did so many years elapse before she was finally arrested again, in 1663? The answer to that is to be found in the list of some of her clientele, among whom were prominent members of the local elite, and with whom she maintained intimate relationships. Highly placed city women and learned friars, as well as one of the inquisitors themselves, Don Francisco de Estrada, helped considerably in concealing Isabel's activities and provided her with an alibi when there was danger of her being exposed to the authorities.

In 1663, following her arrest, among other activities denounced by the Holy Office were the selling and use of unguents mixed with wine and wafers in the form of small loaves of bread and saturated soil, which Isabel gathered from the holy relics of San Diego and St. Michael for the purpose of healing her patients. Thus, as the inquisitors described it, "she committed grave offenses just like real witches, mixing evil with the pure and benevolent." In addition, she was accused of having applied in her magical healing "false visions and spurious divine revelations, by which she pretended that the saints communicated with her." Handcuffed in the torture chamber of the inquisition's prison in Mexico City, in April, 1664, Isabel described how night after night she dreamed that she saw St. Michael. Questioned by the inquisitors about his appearance, she described the saint as dressed in an orange-colored jacket with majestic green sleeves and, over this, an open, green taffeta cloak with gold buttons. Under it he wore a white tunic and on his head, a woolen cap. Each night, appearing before her, the saint urged her to undertake the healing of the sick and needy. Asked how she could recognize that the apparition that she saw so often was indeed St. Michael, and not the devil, and how she could identify that it was a dream or a revelation and "that it was St. Michael and no other angel," Isabel replied that as his longtime devotee, she knew him well, and that "the fact that he carried a spade signified that he was not the Devil."[50]

Isabel's own deposition about her supernatural powers seriously disturbed her interrogators on a number of points. In particular was her sophisticated balancing of her testimony; on the one hand she openly acknowledged that all evil was caused by the devil but, on the other she fiercely insisted that she was able to overcome the evil, by "invoking the saints, whom she knew could easily undo the works of the devils." On one occasion she even went as far as saying that "she was more knowledgeable than the devils themselves." Describing her magical procedures to the interrogators, she also emphasized that prior to curing a patient bewitched by the devils, she instructed him or her to recite two masses for the saints. She knew that masses had the property of curing spells caused by the Devil and that "each day thousands of masses are said all over the world to do away with spells." Isabel's own testimony further informed the interrogators about her habitual arrogation of functions reserved for the priesthood and confessed that, in the medical potions that she had prepared for her patients, she mixed "saintly substances" (*cosas de santos*), "for additional help." The potions were made of oil and "very holy" ground herbs, which she said "God grants to only a few virtuous persons in order to cast spells in this form, and not in any other, and likewise God had bestowed these powers upon her." According to her, numerous ill persons came to her after having fruitlessly sought a cure by others, and she had cured them all "in the name of God and the Holy Trinity."[51]

Incessantly challenging her interrogators, Isabel further insisted that some of her magical know-how proceeded directly from men of the church. She illustrated how on one occasion she had been taught by Fr. Joseph de Paona of the Franciscan monastery in Puebla that the Bull of the Crusade gave protection against witches if placed under one's pillow. Fr. Joseph, Fr. Andres, her confessor, and some other Franciscan friars in Puebla used to dine with her and she would wash their clothes. They had also occasionally shared some of their astrological knowledge and magical formulas with her. The penumbra embracing licit and illicit knowledge, the magic operating within the church and that appropriated by experts outside it, was obviously wide and ever expanding at the time.

The Mexican Inquisition subjected Isabel de Montoya to a trial lasting nearly two years, between 1662 and 1664, at the then considerable cost of two hundred and thirteen pesos for her meals and lodging. At length, on Sunday morning, May 4, 1664, in the chapel of the Santo Domingo convent in Mexico City, after 677 days of solitude and suffering since her inquisitorial process first began, Isabel was charged with both heresy and sorcery. "Heresy" was attributed by the judges to the use of false revelations, as well as the misuse of sacramental objects and formulas in her healing procedures. Thereupon, in the presence of the Holy Office's dignitaries, the heads of the three mendicant orders, and many other honorary citizens of the city, Isabel de Montoya's confession took place. At ten o'clock in the morning the next day, as the formal procedures command, led through the Alameda, Isabel's sentence was publicly proclaimed by the town crier; she was lashed, and then returned to the prison.[52]

On May 15, 1664, at the age of fifty, Isabel entered the Hospital Real del Amor de Dios hospital, on the San Francisco street in Mexico City, where she had been sentenced to serve the poor for three years. In the course of this period she was expected to recite the rosary cycle every Friday, standing before the altar. In the sentence it was stipulated that she "should be prohibited from curing, or teaching others to cure, or transferring to others the virtues and properties of herbs, or what their names were." The professional staff of the Amor de Dios hospital included by then a chaplain and a sacristan mayor, in charge of religious instruction for the patients; the medical services were placed under a medical practitioner, two surgeons, two head nurses, and various other assistants.

In one of Isabel's several letters delivered to the inquisitors from the hospital during the last days of her life, she told how she had bled heavily from the lungs more than eight times without being treated. She asked to be permitted to leave the hospital and look for someone who could take care of her and heal her pains. But at noon on June 18, 1664, a young man from the hospital entered the reception hall of the inquisition palace and notified the inquisitor, Don Pedro de Medina Rico, that Isabel de Montoya had died that day while working, after prolonged suffering from pneumonia.[53]

On June 19 all of Isabel's belongings found at her lodgings were confiscated by the inquisitors. Juan Domingo and Catalina María, Indian practitioners who sold herbs and other medicines at the Plaza Mayor, were called in by the inquisitors to identify the qualities, substances, as well as the efficacy of the herbs and lotions and other items left in Isabel's room in the small adobe house where she had lived before her arrest. The items examined made up an entire corpus of contemporary popular medicine. They said that one of the herbs was for curing Pulque, "and not to cause evil." They indicated that other herbs called *Guaiesla* were applied to heal *hinchazones* (swellings). The body of a viper was credited with curing contraction of the tendons, while a hare's ear was regarded as a remedy for hearing problems. Deer's excrement was said to be effective against *mal de aire*, while the trunk of a rubber-tree was said to heal *Mal de Madre* (vaginal pains). A piece of *Coquintl*, they said, was applied by Indian women against headaches, while a toad's grass was effective against urinary problems. A *Paloncapatl* was to cure ulcer, while herbs identified as *Talayotl* were given for healing the gout. There were other unidentifiable variants of powders and other substances that they identified as remedies for babies' indigestion.

The total value of her belongings was a mere 12 pesos. An additional sum of 220 pesos was paid by Joseph Hurtado, a local *vecino* for the small adobe house near the San Juan de Dios church, and also put up for sale.

Three wooden boxes, together with her bed and mattress, healing powders, and roots were all brought into the merchants' courtyard in the Plaza Mayor in Mexico City and auctioned by Diego Martínez, the secretary of the Holy Office, to the public.

As the inquisitorial papers cite from a person who stood by her at the hospital on her deathbed, on June 18 Isabel uttered a final farewell to her sacred guardian, St. Michael:

> The most sacred of my soul. A poor woman like me does not owe these pains even to the Holy Virgin, nor to the Virgin of Carmen, nor to the Mother of God. My beloved angels, you should keep on flying above and refrain from seeing me in such pain. Nor am I obliged to Jesus. . .nor to St. Gregory, Jesus Mary, or St. Joseph. . . .And for the love of God, that I die without sin, my lords you should not see me come out of this pitfall, in case I am obliged to you. . .[54]

Conclusion

Isabel de Montoya was only one among 190 women of mixed race and impure blood found in the records to have been persecuted for witchcraft by the Holy Inquisition in New Spain, by the colonial church and local police in Mexico City and Puebla, between 1572 and 1770. However, her story is undoubtedly unique in both detail and variety; it is clearly divided between two competing voices, that of the church and that of Isabel. One can also clearly identify here the grand themes of women's popular cultural heritage, as well as subjugation in colonial Mexico. The development of this "gender canon" in the matched and interweaving testimony emerges diachronically. In Isabel's personal narrative it begins with "race" and "class" affiliation, and also with fate, as prescribed by "class" and matriarchal impact. The narrative continues with the central themes of honor and shame regarding moral and sexual transgression; seduction, abduction and "liberation"; the fall into carnal sin and "diabolical freedom"; the practice of love-magic against men; seclusion and damnation. And it draws to an end with the act of confession in the torture chambers, the performance of enforced penitence, and inevitable death.

Notes

1. In 1578 the church was elevated to the status of a parish church. Hernando Cortés first founded the Arch-confraternity de la Cruz, an organization composed of noblemen whose aim was to comfort, in their last hour, and bury criminals condemned to execution. A papal bull of January 1573 conceded

to this privileged brotherhood the name of Santisimo Cristo de San Marcelo, and a hundred days' indulgence to the faithful who would visit the sacrosanct image to which the arch-confraternity was dedicated. The image, which is highly venerated, was brought to Mexico City by the conquistadores. It was always covered with seven veils and was known as El Señor de las Siete Velas.

2. *"Proceso y causa criminal de Isabel de Montoya, mulata ó castiza llamada La Centella, Mexico City, 1652–1661,"* Philadelphia, University of Pennsylvania, Van Pelt Library, Special Collections, MS Lea 160 (Sp.), 2 vols., 302 folios, vol. 1, fol. 252v.

3. *"Proceso criminal. . .,"* MS Lea 160 (Sp.), 2 vols., 302 folios, vol. 1, fol. 252v.

4. For social stratification in seventeenth-century New Spain see also, Rodney D. Anderson, "Race and Social Stratification: A Comparison of Working-Class Spaniards, Indians, and Castes in Guadalajara, Mexico, 1821," *Hispanic American Historical Review* (hereafter *HAHR*), 68 (1988): 209–244. Also, Patricia Seed, "Social Dimensions of Race: Mexico City, 1753," *HAHR*, 62 (1982): 569–606.

5. *"Proceso criminal. . .,"* MS Lea 160 (Sp.), 2 vols., 302 folios, vol. 1, fol. 91v.

6. On the "dialogue" between "high" and "low" medical practices in Spain and across the Atlantic see, for example, Luis Garcia-Ballester, "Academicism versus Empiricism in Practical Medicine in Sixteenth-Century Spain, with regard to Morisco Practitioners," in *The Medical Renaissance of the Sixteenth Century, ed.* Andrew Wear, R. K. French, and I. M. Lonie eds. (Cambridge: Cambridge University Press, 1985), pp. 246–70. On the amalgamation between Old World and New World popular medical practices in sixteenth-century Spain, see Juan Fragoso's famous treatise, *Discurso de las cosas aromáticas. . .de las Indias. . .para uso de medicinas* (Madrid, Casa de Francisco Sánchez, 1570); also, Guenter B. Risse, "Medicine in the New World," in *Medicine in the New World*, ed. Ronald L. Numbers (Knoxville: University of Tennessee Press, 1987), pp. 32–54; Luis Garcia Ballester, *Los moriscos y la medicina, Un capitulo de la medicina y la ciencia marginadas en la España del siglo XVI* (Barcelona: Labor, 1984), pp. 114–18; Madrid, Biblioteca Nacional, MS 18.586–587, IV, No. vi; Luis Sánches Granjel, "Medicina y brujeria," *Cuaderno de Historia de la medicina Española*, 11 (1972): 407–20; Manuel Herrero, "Tipologia social del siglo XVII-ensalmadores y saludadores," *Hispania*, 15 (1955–56): 173–90; Inés Yañez Polo and Juan Ramón Zaragosa Rubira, "Spanish Folk Medicine of the XVIIth Century," in *Acta Congressus Internationalis XXIV: Historiae Artis Medicinae* 2 vols. (Budapest: Semmelweis Museum, 1976), 2:1287–93; Manuel Parrilla Hermida, "Apuntes historicos sobre el protomedicato," *Anales de la Real Academia Nacional de Medicina-Madrid*, 64 (1977): 475–515; Eduardo Malvido, "Efectos de las epidemias y hambrunas en la poblacion colonial de Mexico," *Salud Pública de México, Epoca V*, 17 (November–December 1975): 793–802; John Tate Lanning, *The Royal Protomedicato: The Regulations of the Medical Professions in the Spanish Empire*, ed. John J. Tepaske (Durham: Duke University Press, 1985); Nicolas León, "Apuntes para la historia de la enseñanza y ejercicio de la medicina en Mexico desde la conquista hispana

hasta el año de 1833," *Gaceta de Medicina Mexicana*,3ª, 11 (1918): 210–286, and 14(1921): 3–48; *Hospitales de la Nueva España*, 2 vols. (México: Edición Jus, 1956–60), 1:36–48; Naomi Quezada, "La herbolaria en el México colonial" in, *Estado Actual del Conocimiento en Plantas Medicinales Mexicanas*, ed. Xavier Lozaya (Mexico: Institúto Mexicano para el Estudio de las Plantas Medicinales, 1978), pp. 51–68; Saul Jarcho, "Medicine in Sixteenth-Century New Spain," in *Essays on the History of Medicine: Selected from the Bulletin of the New York Academy of Medicine*, ed. Saul Jarcho (New York: Science History Publications, c1976), No. 49, 431–39; Juan Comas, "Influencia indígena en la medicina hipocrática en la Nueva España del Siglo XVI," *América Indígena*, 14 (1954): 327–61; Agustin Farfan, *Tractado Breve de medicina* (Obra impressa en México, por Pedro Ocharte, en 1592; rpt. Madrid: Edición Cultura Hispánica, 1944).

7. "*Proceso criminal. . .*," MS Lea 160 (Sp.), 2 vols., 302 folios, vol. 1, fol. 253v.
8. "*Proceso criminal. . .*," MS Lea 160 (Sp.), 2 vols., 302 folios, vol. 1, fol. 93v.
9. "*Proceso criminal. . .*," MS Lea 160 (Sp.), 2 vols., 302 folios, vol. 1, fol. 253v.
10. On the meaning of the *patria potestas* in New Spain and on the development and change in New Spain's attitudes toward marriage see also, Patricia Seed, *To Love, Honor, and Obey in colonial Mexico: Conflicts over Marriage Choice, 1574–1821* (Stanford: Stanford University Press, 1988), chapter 1: "The Mexican Background," pp. 17–31; chapter 2: "Will," 32–46; chapter 6: "Changing Attitudes Towards Honor," 95–108; chapter 7: "Changing Attitudes Towards Love and Will," 109–122; Chapter 8: "Interest and Patriarchy," 123–35; also, Silvia Marina Arrom, *The Women of Mexico City, 1790–1857* (Stanford: Stanford University Press, 1985), chapter 2: "Legal Status," pp. 53–81; Chapter 3: "Demographic Patterns," 111–53. Also Deborah Ellen Kanter, "Hijos del Pueblo: Family, Community, and Gender in Rural Mexico, the Toluca region, 1730–1830," (Austin: University of Texas Press, 2004), chapter 4: Marriage and Family, "Women, Men , and Married Life"; chapter 5: "Household, Family and the Meaning of Kinship."
11. "*Proceso criminal. . .*," MS Lea 160 (Sp.), 2 vols., 302 folios, vol. 1 fol. 92r. The house was first founded as a hospice for noble women of Puebla, between 1606 and 1609. Its founders were Francisco Reynoso and Julian López. Such women were those who were unable to support themselves economically or were under other poor circumstances, such as having been abandoned by their husbands who went to Spain, or for other reasons. In 1677, the house was turned into a place of forced seclusion for "lost" women, mostly prostitutes, under the advocacy of Santa María Magdalena Penitent. Being nearly empty the whole year, or, "caused too many scandals by the women put there by the justice authorities of the city," as the bishop of Santa Cruz put it, the house was finally shut down in 1681. It was replaced by a college for young women, girls, and widows, for poor women, virtuous and notable. Its penitents were now transferred to another house, on the same street, under the protection of Santa María Egipciaca,

that was opened on June 11, 1680, by the same name of Santa María Magdalena, until when it held 14 girls, its name was then changed into Santa Mónica. Rosa María Garza Marcué y Cecilia Vázquez Ahumada, "Los recogimientos de mugeres en Puebla, Caso Santa Mónica," *Segundo Coloquio sobre Puebla* (Puebla: Colección Ventura, El Gobierno del Estado de Puebla, 1992), pp. 427–41.

12. *"Proceso criminal. . .,"* MS Lea 160 (Sp.), 2 vols., 302 folios, vol. 1, fol. 251v.

13. *Thomas Gage's Travels in the New World*, ed. and introd. J. Edward. S. Thompson (Norman: University of Oklahoma Press, 1969), pp. 116–17.

14. According to the 1811 population census in Mexico City, only 44% of mature women (above the age of 25) were listed as married, and 16% had never married; 52,500 women of the total population visited were either unmarried or single (widowed, or deserted). Arrom comments that, "Despite the emphasis on marriage in didactic literature, there were socially viable alternatives to matrimony in the Mexican capital." Arrom, *The Women of Mexico City*, p. 116.

15. *"Causa criminal promovida por Pedro Juarez, alcalde de los Indios del barrio de San Francisco, contra Luisa e Inés, Mestizas viudas, que visten en ropas de Indios, por causar escandólo y vender publicamente pulque de tepache en sus casas y estar amancebadas,"* Puebla, Institúto Nacional de Antropólogia e Historia (INAH), El Archivo Histórico Judicial MS, exp. 1538 (1629).

16. Guido Ruggiero, *Binding Passions, Tales of Magic, Marriage, and Power at the End of the Renaissance* (Oxford: Oxford University Press, 1993), p. 59.

17. Richard Boyer, *Lives of the Bigamists: Marriage, Family, and Community in Colonial Mexico* (Albuquerque: University of New Mexico Press, 1995), pp. 31, 65, 96–97.

18. Steve J. Stern, *The Secret History of Gender, Women, Men, and Power in Late Colonial Mexico* (Chapel Hill: University of North Carolina Press, 1995), pp. 270–71.

19. Stern, *The Secret History*, p. 234.

20. "Proceso criminal contra Francisco de Trujillo, mercader, vecino de la ciudad, por haver secuestrado a Francisca, Mestiza del servicio de la rectoria, del recogimiento de la Magdalena y por haver metido a Catalina de Peralta, su muger en dicho recogimiento," Puebla, INAH, Archivo Histórico judicial de Puebla, exp. 2017 (1628).

21. Current research on the subject of concubinage in early and mid-colonial New Spain is abundant; not a few of those venturing into this theme deal also with the degree of autonomy granted to single women. It is worth mentioning here one particular essay, Thomás Calvo, "The Warmth of the Hearth: Seventeenth-Century Guadalajara Families," in *Sexuality and Marriage in Colonial Latin America, ed.* Asunción Lavrin (Lincoln: University of Nebraska Press, 1989), pp. 287–312. Concerning the wide phenomenon of single women households in mid seventeenth-century Guadalajara, Calvo observes that: "We should not mistake this situation for one of female independence. . .since the female heads of households were often condemned

to such a status once they stopped being concubines due to an old age."
Calvo, "The Warmth of the Hearth," p. 292. See also, Boyer *Lives of the
Bigamists*, pp. 15–33.

22. Puebla, INAH, Archivo Histórico Judicial de Puebla, exp. 2017, no. 13
    (1648).

23. "*Proceso criminal. . .*," MS Lea 160 (Sp.), 2 vols., 302 folios, vol. 2, fol. 94r.

24. Author's translation, "*Proceso criminal. . .*," MS Lea 160 (Sp.), 2 vols., 302
    folios, vol. 2, fol. 27r. Similar but variant versions of this incantation are to
    be found in the recently published compilation entitled, *Oraciones, ensalmos
    y conjuros mágicos del Archivo Inquisitorial de la Nueva España*. Estudio prelim-
    inar, Araceli Campos Moreno (Mexico City: El Colegio de México, 2001),
    under, "*Conjuro del Anima sola*," pp. 118–19.

25. The use of love magic in general and menstrual blood in particular, by
    women across Europe is extensively documented as early as the eighth cen-
    tury. Rabanus Maurus (780–856) illustrates the uses for this blood when he
    inquires, "What sort of penance should a woman perform who has mixed
    her menstrual blood in food or drink and given it to her husband to
    consume. . .in order to overcome some weakness?" Similarly, the canonist
    Burchard of Worms (ca. 965–1025) remarks, "Some women. . .collect their
    menstrual blood and mix it in food or drink and give it to their husbands to
    eat or drink so that they would desire them more. If you have done so, do
    penance for five years on proper feast days." Irven M. Resnick, "On Roots
    of the Myth of Jewish Male Menses in Jacques de Vitry's *History of
    Jerusalem*," unpublished paper. I am grateful to the author for allowing me
    to cite this study. During the second decade of the fourteenth century, in
    Béatrice de Planissoles' trial in Pamiers, conducted by Jacques Fournier, this
    accusation becomes a central issue discussed by the judges. Jean Duvernoy, ed.
    and trans., *Le Registre d'Inquisition de Jacques Fournier 1318–1325*, 3 vols.
    (Paris: Mouton, 1978), 1:260–90; also, Michael Goodich, ed. and trans.,
    Other Middle Ages, Witnesses at the Margins of Medieval Society (Philadelphia:
    University of Pennsylvania Press), 201–215; in Italy, during the late sixteenth
    and early seventeenth century, the Venetian Inquisition was also much con-
    cerned about these practices. See, for example, Ruth Martin, *Witchcraft and
    the Inquisition in Venice, 1550–1650* (Oxford: Oxford University Press,
    1989); Guido Ruggiero, *Binding Passions*. On sixteenth-century Spain:
    Maria Helena Sánchez Ortega, "Women as a Source of 'Evil' in Counter-
    Reformation Spain," in *Cultural Encounters*, ed. Ann Cruz and Mary
    Elizabeth Parry (Berkeley: University of California Press, 1992), pp. 196–215.
    Published research on the theme of love magic in the New World is com-
    prehensive, and could not, of course, be fully listed here. Nevertheless, like
    their European counterparts, such studies did not challenge this practice
    from our own point of departure associated with gift-giving ritual action.
    See, Amos Megged, "The Social Significance of Benevolent and Malevolent
    Gifts among Single, Caste Women in Mid Seventeenth-Century New Spain,"
    Journal of Family History, 24 (1999): 420–41. The most significant contributions,
    to my mind, are: Solange Alberro, "Herejes, Brujas y Beatas: Mugeres ante

el Tribunal del Santo Oficio de la Inquisición en la Nueva España," in *Presencia y transparencia: La muger en la historia de México* (Mexico City: Colegio de México, 1987), pp. 79–94; Alberro, *Inquisición y sociedad en México 1571–1700* (Mexico City: Fondo de Cultura Económica, 1988), especially pp. 180–92, 456–72; Gonzalo Aguirre Beltán, *Medicina y magia: El proceso de aculturación y el curanderismo en México* (Mexico City: Instituto Nacional Indígenista, 1955); Jean Franco, *Plotting Women, Gender and Representation in Mexico* (New York: Columbia University Press, 1989), pp. 55–79; Ruth Behar, "Sex and Sin, Witchcraft and the Devil in Late-Colonial Mexico," *American Ethnologist* 14 (February 1987), no. 1:34–54.

26. Arne Runeberg, *Witches, Demons and Fertility Magic, Analysis of their Significance and Mutual Relations in West-European Folk Religion* (Norwood, PA: Norwood Editions, 1974), pp. 126–27.

27. On the role of magical practices among black slaves in Portugal see, A.C. de C.M. Saunders, *A Social History of Black Slaves and Freedmen in Portugal 1441–1555* (Cambridge: Cambridge University Press, 1982), pp. 162–64.

28. Solange Alberro, *Inquisición y sociedad en México 1571–1700* (México: Fondo de Cultura Económica, 1988), pp. 342–51.

29. Fr. Bernadino de Sahagún, *Historia general de las cosas de la Nueva España (Códice Florentino)*. Introduction and notes by Alfredo López Austin and Josefina García Quintana (reprint of the 1577 manuscript form, Madrid: Alianza Editorial, 1988), vol. 2:150–51.

30. "*Proceso criminal. . .*," MS Lea 160 (Sp.), 2 vols., 302 folios, vol. 2, fol. 25r.

31. "*Proceso criminal. . .*," MS Lea 160 (Sp.), 2 vols., 302 folios, vol. 2, fol. 61r-61v.

32. "*Proceso criminal. . .*," MS Lea 160 (Sp.), 2 vols., 302 folios, vol. 2, fol. 70v.

33. "*Proceso criminal. . .*," MS Lea 160 (Sp.), 2 vols., 302 folios, vol. 2, fols. 23r; fols. 110v, 252v, 312v; Mexico City: Archivo General de la Nación (AGN), Ramo Inquisición, vol. 447, exp. 8, fols. 308r–326v: "Inventario y sequestro de vienes de Isabel de Montoya, 5–25 Julio 1662."

34. Author's translation, "*Proceso criminal. . .*," MS Lea 160 (Sp.), 2 vols., 302 folios, vol. 2, fol. 14r.

35. Author's translation, "*Proceso criminal. . .*," MS Lea 160 (Sp.), 2 vols., 302 folios, vol. 2, fol. 23r.

36. AGN, Ramo Inquisición, vol. 366, exp. 14, fol. 223v, in *Oraciones, ensalmos y conjuros mágicos del Archivo Inquisitorial de la Nueva España*, 123–24.

37. "Proceso criminal contra Leonor de Isla, mulata, vecina de la ciudad de Nueva Vera Cruz y natural de Cádiz, 1622." AGN, Ramo Inquisición, vol. 341, exp. 1, fol. 8r.

38. Jonathan Israel, *Race, Class and Politics in Colonial Mexico, 1610–1670* (London: Oxford University Press, 1975), pp. 238–41.

39. "Proceso criminal. . .," vol. 2, fol. 62v; "Testificaciones y deposiciones voluntarias remitidas a este tribunal de diferentes partes del distrito de esta Inquisición- en virtud de los edictos generales de la fe, que se publicaron dicho año 1650." AGN, Ramo Inquisición, vol. 435, 1a parte, fol. 293r, 2.3.1650.

40. AGN, Ramo Inquisición, vol.447, 1st part, 1650.

41. Israel, *Race, Class and Politics*, 237.

42. "*Proceso criminal. . .,*" MS Lea 160 (Sp.), 2 vols., 302 folios, vol. 2, fol. 47r.

43. "*Proceso criminal. . .,*" MS Lea 160 (Sp.), 2 vols., 302 folios, vol. 2, fol. 87v.

44. "*Proceso criminal. . .,*" MS Lea 160 (Sp.), 2 vols., 302 folios, vol. 2, fol. 115r.

45. "*Proceso criminal. . .,*" MS Lea 160 (Sp.), 2 vols., 302 folios, vol. 2, fols. 194r-96v.

46. AGN, Inq. vol. 447, exp. 8, fols. 308–326: "Inventario y sequestro de vienes de Isabel de Montoya, 5–25 Julio 1662."

47. "*Proceso criminal. . .,*" MS Lea 160 (Sp.), 2 vols., 302 folios, vol. 1, fol. 210r.

48. "*Proceso criminal. . .,*" MS Lea 160 (Sp.), 2 vols., 302 folios, vol. 1, fol. 218v.

49. "*Proceso criminal. . .,*" MS Lea 160 (Sp.), 2 vols., 302 folios, vol. 1, fol. 240v.

50. "*Proceso criminal. . .,*" MS Lea 160 (Sp.), 2 vols., 302 folios, vol. 1, fol. 303r.

51. "*Proceso criminal. . .,*" MS Lea 160 (Sp.), 2 vols., 302 folios, vol. 1, fols. 304r–312v.

52. "*Proceso criminal. . .,*" MS Lea 160 (Sp.), 2 vols., 302 folios, vol. 1, fol. 344r–344v.

53. "*Proceso criminal. . .,*" MS Lea 160 (Sp.), 2 vols., 302 folios, vol. 1, fol. 349r: Isabel de Montoya's Notice of Death (June 18, 1664): "At noon entered the reception hall of the Inquisition a man from the hospital and notified the Inquisitor Don Pedro de Medina Rico that Isabel de Montoya had died at the hospital that same day."

54. Author's translation, "*Proceso criminal. . .,*" MS Lea 160 (Sp.), 2 vols., 302 folios, vol. 1, fol. 349r.

CHAPTER 4

THE MULTIPLE MISERIES OF DULCIA OF
ST. CHARTIER (1266) AND CRISTINA OF
WELLINGTON (1294)

Michael Goodich

Canonization records provide unusually rich raw material for those interested in exploring the lives of the subaltern classes. Beginning in the twelfth century, each dossier included the testimony of hundreds of persons who claimed either to have witnessed or experienced a miracle attributed to a putative saint.[1] These reports were recorded by scribes and notaries employed by either the curia or local ecclesiastical authorities applying the principles of Roman and canon law to the deposition of witnesses. While the aim was to compile a dossier of reliable examples of credible miracles, the deponents often provide us with a glimpse into such secondary themes as family structure, ties of dependence, contemporary medical knowledge, and notions of space and time. The seasoned inquisitor Bernard Gui in his handbook for those investigating heresy warned of the dangers of allowing witnesses to stray from the central subject at hand, and cautioned fellow inquisitors to maintain firm control of the inquiry.[2] But just as historians of heresy have nevertheless been able to exploit such trials as a means of studying the mores and beliefs of otherwise inaccessible medieval folk, the canonization records may prove equally fruitful.[3]

Two extensive dossiers are particularly useful in the attempt to go beyond the official diplomatic documents of court and curia, the cases of Philip of Bourges and Thomas of Hereford. The process of Bishop Philip of Bourges (d. 1261), nephew of William of Bourges (d. 1218), who had been canonized by Honorius III in 1218, was heard in 1264–26 at

Beaugency, Bourges, and Orléans.[4] His unpublished dossier is particularly rich, containing the following items: (1) copies of the protocol of the original process held under Popes Urban IV and Martin IV, including a narrative account of the canonization process;[5] (2) a rubricated *relatio* including summaries of each miracle along with remarks made by each relevant witness, prepared for perusal by the curia by Cardinals Guglielmo of Sta. Sabina, Pietro of St. Praxed and Jacopo of St. Giorgio, possibly in 1331, when the case was reexamined;[6] and (3) a brief summary of seventeen miracles with notes concerning the points of agreement and disagreement among the witnesses.[7] The summarized miracles reported in the *relatio* are followed by a list of witnesses, stating whether they were present at the miracle, heard and saw it performed, whether they had seen the recipient of the miracle both before and afterward, and how their testimony might differ from others. In addition, a *Vita et miracula* was composed (perhaps by a participant in Philip's inquiries) which is taken verbatim from the summary, but doesn't include all the miracles attributed to Philip.[8]

Philip's case had gone through a number of stages spanning a period of over seventy years. On October 3, 1329 during the pontificate of John XXII it had been proposed in the College of Cardinals that Philip's case should be reconsidered.[9] After a short delay, on November 5 three cardinals met in the chambers of Bernard, bishop of Tusculum (Frascati), along with several notaries and scribes in order to reexamine the case. On this occasion the full contents of Philip's file was noted. This included copies of the earlier inquiries held under Urban IV, Martin IV, and Clement IV (made at the Dominican house of Orvieto), papal letters, and letters from Odo of Châteauroux, former cardinal-bishop of Tusculum, who had been involved in the original process. It is reported in the summary written at this time that the dossier had been examined earlier at Viterbo in October 1270 by Odo and several others, including his personal chaplain.

During Philip's canonization process forty-five miracles were recounted by a hundred and forty witnesses, of whom forty-five were laywomen, forty-six were laymen, and forty-nine were clergy.[10] This preference for miracles reported by the clergy and the apparent suspicion of miracles reported solely by the laity is reflected in the contemporary biography drawn from the protocol and suggests that Philip's cult appealed to a local and ecclesiastical audience. His miraculous discovery of the relics of St. Severa, reported by only one cleric, is given pride of place. Many of his miracles demanded confirmation by a clerical witness, in addition to the laity. On the other hand, papal bulls of canonization markedly prefer miracles performed among the laity as evidence of a wide constituency and as a means of spreading and maintaining the cult. This presumably reflects the audience for whom the saints' cults were intended and may explain

Philip's failure to achieve medieval canonization, despite efforts to revive the case in 1329 and later.[11]

Philip's miracles are less varied and rich than other contemporary cases such as those of Margaret of Hungary and Richard of Chichester, since nearly all concerned the thaumaturgical cure of the blind, paralyzed, lame, mute, and others, and do not include rescues at sea, miraculous military escapes, the transformation of water into wine, or other such miracles. Nevertheless, by breaking down each one into at least thirty schematic elements reflecting the traditional "who, what, when, where, why, and how" of any miracle narrative, it is possible to draw out the social environment of Philip's cultic community.[12] A map of the geographical boundaries of the cult and its adherents, where they were born and lived, how far they were willing to travel in pursuit of a cure, and whether the cures occurred in close proximity to the tomb or elsewhere may be drawn up.[13] Professional background, age, kind of affliction, symptoms, access to medical care, marital status, and personal acquaintance with the saint are among the details provided. Since several family members frequently testified, we are able to learn about the dynamics of family structure and ties of affection.

The commissioners in Philip of Bourges' process referred to themselves as "inquisitors," a practice which seems to have begun under Pope Honorius III (1216–27), whose pontificate also witnessed the establishment of the inquisition into heresy. This reflects the fact that an inquisition was the form of trial procedure employed in the investigation of both heresy and sainthood, although it could be used to investigate usury, marriage cases, episcopal appointments, clerical disorder, simony, unorthodox sexual behavior, and other acts which might brand the offenders with the charge of infamy in ecclesiastical contexts.[14] The same personnel were also often employed in both kinds of cases, beginning with Conrad of Marburg, who has been regarded as the first papal inquisitor, appointed in the late 1220s to investigate heresy in Germany, persecuting the Luciferians, Waldensians, Cathars, and Stedingers. In 1232 he was likewise entrusted with looking into the case of his pupil Elizabeth of Thuringia (d. 1231). The papal investigation of putative saints was conducted according to the guidelines of the canons *De testibus et attestationibus*, *De inquisitionibus*, and other relevant canons. These were probably inserted into canon law around 1206 under Innocent III.[15] According to this procedure, should there be any rumor of legal transgressions in his diocese, an ecclesiastical judge was allowed to initiate an inquiry on his own. In 1234 these canons were formally included in Gregory's IX's decretal collection, which was edited by the Dominican papal penitentiary Raymund of Penyafort (d. 1275).[16] This development parallels the organized papal investigation of heresy, and therefore the conduct of heresy trials was probably influenced by such cases. The first extant "charge to the jury" in a canonization trial is found in Elizabeth of Thuringia's case, in which Raymund was also involved along with the inquisitor Conrad of Marburg.[17]

Dulcia of St. Chartier

The illustration selected from Philip's protocol provides the social historian with a record of the role of faith in the supernatural among the subaltern classes. One of the miracles contained in Philip's original hearing concerned the cure of insanity of Dulcia of the parish of St. Chartier.[18] It had been heard between Thursday, July 1 and Saturday, July 3, 1266 in the presence of Robert de Marzy, bishop of Nevers, the Dominican prior of Bourges, and the notary Gaufrid of Bourges. Another member of the investigating commission, Pierre de Minci, bishop of Chartres, had excused himself from the hearings, and was therefore not present. A total of about twenty-one witnesses were either present at the time of Dulcia's deposition or were at the hearing during this three-day period, so that her case was probably known to a circle larger than the six persons who testified about her cure, that is, witnesses #97–102.[19] Those present at the hearing had come to testify concerning five miracles, including Dulcia's.[20] Three of these were cases in which possession or emotional disorder played a central role, while two involved paralysis. In one case, the parish priest, brother of the victim, reported that his brother had begun to spit at those who approached him, uttered strange words, was unable to eat, and was therefore bound hand and foot for eight days until he was cured.[21] In another case, the victim had lost his mind after having drunk some wine.[22] The witnesses in these cases probably had an opportunity to become acquainted, since they came from different parishes, and to compare their own experiences. Such a meeting of witnesses, their families, friends, and neighbors helped to create a community of the faithful, which would surely reinforce their allegiance to the cult of Philip of Bourges. Possession and exorcism were among the premier miracles performed by contemporary saints, since they so well highlighted the battle between God and the devil that was at the core of the Christian message.[23] This is well illustrated by Laura Smoller's chapter (6) in this volume.[24]

Although the twenty-year old Dulcia herself might be regarded as the main witness, she had clearly been indisposed during many of the events described, and the local chaplain Pierre of St. Chartier provided fuller evidence, along with the other witnesses. The local curate or another ecclesiastic often appeared in such cases as both a kind of character witness and the person regarded by church authorities as a more reliable reporter than the laity. Pierre had been present at many of the events, and had also heard Dulcia's confession immediately after her cure. She reported that beginning in 1256 or 1257 her husband and his "whore"[25] or strumpet had made her lose her memory, and had driven her so crazy that she could recognize no one, including her own mother, and was therefore not responsible for her actions. This condition had lasted until 1261, when Philip of Bourges died. Other witnesses testified that she would roam about the fields and vineyards day and night tearing her clothes with the aid of a stick she carried everywhere. Dulcia remembered that during this period she had envisioned herself taken to Philip's tomb at the cathedral of St. Etienne in Bourges for a cure. After the vision, she had demanded that she be led there during Quadragesima 1261, that is, late April. Accompanied by her mother, Dulcia had made an offering and was cured, although neither she nor anyone else could recall the words of her invocation. Others reported that she had remained at the tomb with her mother for three days and was cured on a Saturday evening.

The chaplain Pierre and the four other witnesses agreed that she had been poisoned by her husband and his harlot with some drug given to them by an old witch (*vetula*) or "crone" (the "old hag" was a stereotypical figure in accusations of witchcraft). Both her husband and his paramour had confessed, and, as a result, he had been hung by order of a secular judge, she had been burned, and the witch had fled. The witnesses differed concerning the nature of the poison administered to Dulcia. Ralph Iosius said it had been a cat's or toad's brain fed to her in bread; one of her brothers, Bonitus Amelorum (or Amelon), said she had been fed a snake. As the scholastic William of Auvergne (d. 1259) noted, these creatures were especially likely to serve as agents of the devil.[26] Her other brother Jean, along with another lay witness, Diccus, provided no evidence concerning the kind of poison. All however, agreed about the circumstances surrounding her illness, having witnessed the execution of her husband and his paramour. Claudia Opitz has suggested that, "whereas law codes and public opinion at the time prescribed the death penalty for adulteresses, men who committed the same act went unpunished," while women would have to endure a great deal before leaving an unfaithful husband.[27] If this were true, then Dulcia's spouse would have been hanged for attempted murder and the use of magic, rather than adultery.

The subsequent versions of this story indicate some severe expurgation by those in the curia or local commission who had handled the dossier. The rubricated summary or *relatio* intended for perusal by the cardinals before considering the case makes no reference whatsoever to the poison and its contents, Dulcia's husband's unfaithfulness, the conspiracy, his lover, their execution, and the flight of the "witch."[28] In this bowdlerized version, Dulcia was merely cured of insanity through a pilgrimage to Philip's shrine.

This abbreviated and censored version appeared in the biography which was a product of the *relatio*, and is thus absent from the saint's legend.[29] Furthermore, in the list of those miracles deemed worthy of further investigation found in a Bibliothèque Nationale manuscript, prepared by some unidentified official, this case is entirely absent, although such a miraculous instance of Christian victory over witchcraft and sexual deviance would appear to be a highly suitable example to be included in the putative saint's dossier of achievements.[30] The condemned practitioner of witchcraft was among the increasing number of "sources of social contamination" that were excluded from Christian society, which encompassed heretics, sexual nonconformists, and lepers, among others.[31] William of Auvergne had spoken of *vetulae* as evil spirits or demons of the night masquerading as old women. Women, he suggested, are more vulnerable than men to the devil's wiles and may be subject to delusions, partly due to their melancholic natures. On the other hand, if the physician's art may be ineffective in such cases, the prayers of holy persons may be of assistance.[32] Stephen of Bourbon (d. 1261) further argued that witchcraft could be employed to impede matrimony, just as the serpent had served as an agent of the devil in order to tempt womankind and the corruption of the first sin is intimately related to human sexuality.[33] In 1258, Pope Alexander IV empowered inquisitors to deal with witchcraft only if it "savored of heresy," otherwise regular courts continued to deal with the matter.[34] Europe was not yet in the grip of the great witch persecution that was to begin in the fifteenth century when the subversive witch was blamed for all manner of ills. Dulcia's case does not suggest that any of the guilty parties was stained with heresy, only that they had engaged in a poisoning or attempted homicide. The identity of an "old hag" as the practitioner of witchcraft conforms to the traditional view that witches were recruited from among the poor, ugly, aged, foreign, marginal, and excluded sectors of the population. A variety of hypotheses have been offered to explain this stereotypical view.[35]

Dulcia's woes had not occurred in a region free of public controversy and conflict. During Philip of Bourges' term as bishop in 1251 the Pastoureaux had invaded the city of Bourges and its diocese. They were termed by Matthew Paris as "thieves, vagabonds, fugitives, excommunicates, persons who are customarily called in France *ribaldi*." These *ribaldi* were regarded as debauched troublemakers, who spent their time gambling, swearing, drinking, and whoring. Upright citizens might be expected to incur a fine should they receive them into their homes. Within the military context, they may be termed camp followers or army drudges, the lowliest foot soldiers who performed the most disreputable tasks, such as setting fire to churches, and were often the first into battle shouting scurrilous insults at the enemy in order to provoke him to anger.[36] Another observer termed the *Pastoureaux* "thieves, outlaws, apostates, pagans, heretics and prostitutes," although they were more likely shepherds, cowherds, servants, farm laborers, and other socially disadvantaged persons. They had been aroused by recent calls for a crusade in the east to liberate the captive King Louis IX and the Holy Land, and a papal call for a crusade against the recently deposed Hohenstaufen dynasty in the Empire. Bearing banners emblazoned with images of the cross, the lamb, and the Virgin, they may have originated before Easter 1251 in Flanders or Brabant, and spread into France. They reached Paris, Orléans, Tours, and Bourges. Under the alleged leadership of the "Master of Hungary," the Pastoureaux may have changed their aims, and displayed sacrilegious, violent, anticlerical and anti-Semitic behavior.[37]

Despite Philip of Bourges' efforts to bar their entry, synagogues were attacked, Jewish books were burned, and homes pillaged.[38] Either inside or near the city the legendary "Master" was killed. Their leaders were captured and hung, and their followers dispersed. After these events, civil disorder nevertheless continued at Bourges. In 1252 a fire broke out, followed by a riot against the archbishop and papal legate Aubert, in the course of which stones were thrown at the archiepiscopal palace, for reasons unknown. The king intervened, arrests were made, and a heavy fine imposed.[39] Thus, contrary to the view of the medieval countryside as a pastoral Eden, Dulcia, her family, and fellow villagers were touched by the social and ideological conflicts of the day, and may themselves have been active participants. Her husband's lover and the "old hag" may have been part of the remnant left by the Pastoureaux in their passage through the area. The testimony at a canonization trial can provide more down-to-earth evidence of the immediate implications of public events on a local community than can traditional diplomatic sources.

The cases of Dulcia and others in Philip of Bourges' process were not immediately adjudicated. Rather, the material relating to this abortive dossier was read and collated by Odo of Châteauroux (ca. 1200–73), cardinal-bishop of Tusculum, who also delivered two unpublished sermons on Philip's virtues.[40] It may well be Odo who undertook to censor the undesirable testimony in Dulcia's case, with the assistance of the large papal bureaucracy of procurators, scribes, notaries, correctors, and other officials.[41] Odo was one of most prolific preachers of his time, having left at least a thousand sermons found in a large number of manuscripts throughout Europe, and one of the most active proponents of papal policy. He had served as chancellor of the University of Paris (1238–44) and consecrated Louis IX's Sainte-Chapelle at Paris (1248). His experience as a persecutor of the unorthodox was extensive, which would have qualified him to judge the reliability of testimony concerning the use of magic reported in Dulcia's case. As chancellor he had been involved in the decision to burn the Talmud and may have written a refutation of its errors. He was then appointed to serve as the head of the Anagni commission that examined the orthodoxy of Gerard of Borgo of San Donnino's Joachitic *Introductorius* (1255), which had suggested that the papal church would soon be replaced by a new religious dispensation. Furthermore, he served with Louis IX in the Holy Land (1248–54) and was papal legate to France.[42] Many of his sermons were highly topical, such as the sermon delivered on March 18, 1229 to the people of Paris on the occasion of the killing of several scholars of the new university.[43] The sermons he delivered at Paris in late 1230 and early 1231 attacked wealthy clergy, simoniacs, Jews, heretics, excommunicates, irregular monks and "gentiles," that is, other non-Christians, placing him in the forefront of those who formulated the increasingly repressive policies of the church.[44]

As dean of the Sacred College after 1254, Odo was involved in at least four canonization processes, and delivered sermons devoted to such new saints as Philip of Bourges, Richard of Chichester, and Hedwig of Silesia. The same manuscript containing Odo's two sermons on Philip, which includes a hundred and twenty-nine sermons on saints (*sermones des sanctis*), also includes a sermon or panegyric devoted to the recently canonized (1262) Bishop Richard of Chichester, setting forth a systematic formulation of the Christian theology of miracle which was being developed among contemporary scholastics such as Thomas Aquinas, Albertus Magnus, and Engelbert of Admont. As a fellow countryman, canon, and former chancellor of Bourges (1230–37), Odo was well acquainted with Philip of Bourges and was well qualified to deal with his case. But his sermons on Philip make no mention of miracles, stressing only his acts of charity. This may be because they had not yet been approved by the curia and Odo could thus not be sure of citing fully authorized miracles, unlike the sermon on Richard, that summarizes those miracles which appeared in his canonization bull. The absence of any reference to Philip's miracles in these sermons reveals the tension between popular and learned views of sanctity: the people needed "signs and miracles"; while the learned demanded a virtuous life. Scholastic theologians had begun to apply the principles of natural law to the study of the supernatural, even questioning whether the death of Christ had been natural or supernatural.[45] In his sermons, Odo of Châteauroux likewise prefers to survey Philip's career and lineage, his ties to the Cistercian order, his chastity, service to the poor and other virtues rather than his miracles. This reflects a long hagiographical tradition. John of Salerno in his life of Odo of Cluny had said: "Those who like to heap praise on exorcists, on those who raise the dead and on others famous for their miracles may do so. I would rather praise Odo [of Cluny] for patience as his prime virtue."[46]

A case in Philip's dossier parallel to Dulcia's, involving the cure from insanity, apparent post-natal depression, and paralysis in 1263 of the thirty-year-old Jeanne Laboysans from the village of Crosses, about six miles from Bourges, was reported by twelve witnesses, including the victim herself, her husband, mother, the local curate, and a Benedictine prior. Jeanne's pilgrimages to such faraway shrines as Notre-Dame de Rocamadour, St.-Gilles-du-Gard, near Nîmes, and St. Vrain near Orléans before achieving a cure for her various afflictions at St. Étienne de Bourges are also reported. A series of visions of the saint punctuate Jeanne's serial cures.[47] But Jeanne's, Dulcia's, and other cases reveal a local cult that failed to breach its narrow geographical boundaries, unlike those of more celebrated saints such as Francis of Assisi, Dominic, Louis IX, and others. Philip's cult contains no miracles outside the confines of the diocese of Bourges and its environs. No leading ecclesiastics or nobility testified to his thaumaturgic powers. As noted, the miracles are rather typical of semirural cults: children saved from drowning, exorcisms, faith-cures. The local clergy play a central role as witnesses.

Although the investigators were presumably interested in maximizing points of agreement among witnesses, in the cases of Jeanne Laboysans of Crosses and Dulcia of St. Chartier this was not always possible. The separate curial list summarizing the points of discord among deponents (whose collator is not identified) reflects greater skepticism about the supernatural among experts than among the lay and ecclesiastical witnesses to particular miracles. In this list, because of inconsistencies in the testimony only seventeen of Philip's alleged forty-five miracles were singled out for possible further scrutiny. More difficulties would no doubt have been discovered had both Jeanne's and Dulcia's cases not been discontinued. Already in the earlier canonization cases of Elizabeth of Thuringia and Stanislaus of Cracow note had been taken of miracle reports in which the witnesses were not in full agreement, or which lacked corroborating evidence, especially in the case of miracles accompanied by a vision to which the only witness was the visionary.[48] In the dossier of King Louis IX, rigorous examination by Cardinal Pietro Colonna of the case of a woman cured at his shrine in St. Denis involved citation from scripture, canon and Roman law, and Seneca, along with the application of reasoned argument. In the dossier of Pope Celestine V, the summary of his miracles examined by the curia indicates that some cardinals were highly critical of miracle stories, following the theologians' longstanding preference for stressing a virtuous life over miracles in the adjudication of sainthood. For example, the future Pope John XXII rejected many of his predecessor

Celestine V's proposed miracles, due to political rather than theological considerations.[49] Even Celestine's biographer Gaetano Stefaneschi voiced sharp doubts, and only those fully accepted by the most skeptical Cardinal Richard Petronius of Siena, finally appeared in the bull of canonization.

Dulcia's case tends to support the view that a gap divided learned and popular religious culture. The extensive report of her experience reported at the first canonization hearing was later transformed and expurgated in the course of subsequent summaries prepared by the curia in an attempt to expunge questionable testimony from the trial record. The witnesses in this case, including the local cleric, believed in the simultaneous power of both God and the devil, acting through their agents Philip and the witch. Satan's influence was only counteracted through the acts of pilgrimage and incubation at Philip's shrine. Subsequent versions appear to credit Dulcia's recovery to her ceasing to ingest a poisonous potion (after her husband, his paramour, and the witch had exited from the scene) rather than supernatural intervention.[50]

Cristina of Wellington

A second rich source for the social history of the subaltern classes is the canonization inquest of Bishop Thomas of Hereford, which was conducted during a four-month period in 1307 at St. Paul's, London and the chapel of St. Catherine, Hereford.[51] Over three hundred miracles reportedly occurred between 1287, when Thomas's relics were translated, and 1299. These miracles acquired a wide currency. As one witness testified, he himself had heard of a thousand.[52] A summary record was made by the clerics of Hereford of those who appeared at the bishop's tomb, mostly in fulfillment of a vow to undertake a pilgrimage. In addition, thirty-eight miracles were examined in depth, of which twenty-six were given special attention by the curia before Thomas's canonization by John XXII in 1320. This extensive dossier provides more raw data for the social historian than Philip's case, reflecting the increasing bureaucratization of the curia during the Avignon period, the refinement of the theology of the miracle and the wider geographical distribution of Thomas' cult.[53] The simple list of questions reported in Elizabeth of Thuringia's and Philip of Bourges' cases was replaced by a long list that stressed the need to provide more corroborating evidence of the symptoms of the victim's afflictions and to report any attempt to use natural means to bring about a cure before resorting to the supernatural. Furthermore, deponents were asked about the possible use of "incantations, trickery or other forms of deceit." This suggests sharpened concern about expressions of skepticism regarding the institution of sainthood, a possible confusion among believers between magic and miracle, and the challenges posed by late thirteenth-century false saints. It was indeed often difficult to distinguish heresy from orthodoxy, as in the cases of Ermanno Pungilupo, Guglielma of Milan, and Gerardo Segarelli.[54] In addition, the inquisitors undertook to inquire about the social status of each witness, whether noble or not, rich or poor, and his or her knowledge of Latin.[55]

One case merits comparison with the case of Dulcia of St. Chartier. It concerns the miraculous rescue from hanging for the theft of a pig of a certain Cristina Cray or Cragh from the parish of Wellington on the Lugg River, about four miles north of Hereford and about a mile from the village of Marden. Marden is at present connected to Wellington by the Leystone Bridge across the Lugg, probably preceded by the "Wisterton Bridge." A large parish and site of the church of St. Mary the Virgin, Marden was the home of many deponents at Thomas' trial, including the witnesses in the case of Joanna, who was saved from drowning by the merits of Thomas of Hereford.[56] Wellington was the site of a recently constructed parish church built of local sandstone and ashlar, much of which is still standing.[57] It was also the home of several other persons who had benefited from Thomas' charisma. In 1288 the daughter of Richard Pinke of Wellington was miraculously saved from strangling after her cradle was tipped over while under the care of another child. Another *miraculé*, William Gayut of Wellington had suffered with a paralyzed hand for three years; while a certain Richard (perhaps the same as the aforementioned Richard Pinke) of Wellington was among those who testified in Thomas' support during the special hearing held to investigate his excommunication by Archbishop John Peckham of Canterbury, which had to be cleared up before Thomas' could be canonized.[58]

Cristina of Wellington's case was reported by six male witnesses on November 10 and 11, 1307 at St. Catherine's chapel in Hereford cathedral.[59] Four of the witnesses had also reported other miracles, and may thus be considered strong partisans of Thomas's cult. One spoke in French, the others in English, although two reported knowing Latin. Although many women testified at this process, in this case only men testified. All were described as free men, one living on royal land, another on the lands of the priory of St. Guthlac, the patron saint of Hereford. Their firsthand knowledge of the miracle is uneven, and their testimony does not always agree. Perhaps for this reason this miracle was not included among those confirmed by John XXII in his bull of canonization.

A reconstruction of the events is therefore difficult; nevertheless, I will attempt to recreate the circumstances of Cristina's miracle. Cristina had allegedly stolen a pig, which she added to her own herd, and then sold it. After being apprehended and incarcerated at the royal fortress (*castrum*) in

Hereford, she was sentenced to hang, along with between five and ten other criminals, probably at noon on the Saturday after Pentecost, 1294. Such mass hangings seem to have been a common phenomenon, perhaps due to the severity of the laws, the disturbed and lawless nature of the border region where Hereford was situated, and infrequent visits by royal judges.[60] In order to counteract such lawlessness, Edward I had undertaken to impose stiffer penalties, and execution for theft was not unusual.[61]

Cristina was led to the gibbet about a quarter of a mile from the church of St. Martin.[62] Since neither friends nor family had prepared a burial spot for her (as was customary), unlike the other criminals, Cristina was left hanging until vespers. Although a network of family and friends commonly bound rural folk together in mutual ties of community solidarity, encompassing persons from a variety of social classes, declining standards of living and widowhood, for example, might severely weaken such bonds. As a member of the confraternity of the hospital of St. John of Jerusalem, Cristina was then to be taken by family and friends to the cemetery for burial. This order was well patronized by the crown, with large holdings in Wales and the Welsh borders. A hospice of the knights of St. John was situated close to Cristina's parish; the order also owned seven houses in Hereford itself, along with thirty acres and a meadow, on which a large hospice was built, adjacent to the north gate of the city.[63]

Apparently dead, with the rope still tied around her neck Cristina was bound to a bier and carried to the church of St. Martin, just outside the city. There, a woman of the parish cried out that one foot was still stirring. It was later reported that before her execution Cristina's son and daughter had measured her with a wick at the prison gate in order to provide an offering to Thomas of Hereford. This was a peculiarly English practice, as had been noted in other cases at Thomas's canonization inquiry. Cristina had also made her confession near the church of St. Martin to an unidentified Franciscan friar and the royal justices and others present at the hanging reported that she had invoked Thomas's aid. The Franciscans were active at Hereford, and appear in other cases. St. Martin's was situated in the southern suburbs of the city, just across the Wye River. Since there were still signs of life, a local woman prepared some warm beer for Cristina to drink. This use of beer is, again, a peculiarly English phenomenon and appears in other contemporary miracles; although in the resuscitation of another hanging victim at Swansea (also in Thomas' protocol), chicken soup was used to help revive the victim. Cristina immediately spat up blood and her body was found to be warm, both clear signs of life. Therefore a local surgeon, the son of an apothecary, applied pressure to her neck so the coagulated blood would begin to flow. When she was revived, Cristina reported that during the hanging she had had a vision of Thomas of Hereford dressed in his white episcopal robes supporting her feet and placing his hand between her neck and the rope, telling her that she would not die. At the time, it had been found that not even a man's finger could be inserted between her neck and the rope. As in Philip of Bourges' cult, visions play an important role among Thomas of Hereford's adherents. For example, a mute man of Doncaster whose tongue had been torn out by thieves in 1289, after having made pilgrimages to many holy places, finally had a vision in his sleep of Thomas preparing to celebrate mass; the saint put three fingers in the man's mouth and he spat blood. The next day, at Dunelm where he was staying, bystanders saw the blood and he was cured.[64] In 1309, a clerical member of the count of Pembroke's household was cured of severe swelling of his body, in the course of a dream.[65]

Following the resuscitation, Cristina took advantage of the right of refuge and remained safely in the church for three weeks for fear of again being taken by the royal officials to be hung. Such an event often became the occasion for the gathering at the church of parishioners from the surrounding region who could take part in the general commotion surrounding the miraculous event. As Cristina held a cross in her hand, churchgoers praised and glorified God and Thomas Cantilupe. In the end, due to her miraculous revival she was sentenced to leave Hereford for Ireland, cross in hand. At this time, the counties of Ulster, Leinster, Munster, and Meath had been heavily colonized by settlers from Wales and the marcher lordships. The local population had generally been reduced to servile status, but the crown and its allies in Ireland continued to require fresh settlers on the feudal estates, in addition to soldiers given land grants in return for service during the conquest, and those brought in by recruiting agents.[66] Cristina's miraculous revival, pardon, and exile to Ireland therefore also benefited the crown.

One of the witnesses claimed to have later seen her visiting the tomb of Thomas of Hereford, but otherwise no one knew what had become of her and neither Cristina nor any members of her family testified at the canonization hearing. Her pilgrimage cannot be confirmed from the surviving daily record of visitors to Thomas's shrine in which so many of the other miracles are noted. The 1294 record of pilgrims who claimed to have been aided by Thomas encompasses nineteen cases, including: a man who had suffered cruel imprisonment; a group of merchants nearly shipwrecked between Ireland and Flanders; the distinguished cleric and royal notary Master John de Lacy, who had suffered dysentery aboard ship; a man of Bristol who had nearly drowned at sea; the owner of a falcon whose life had been spared; the usual assortment of injured and dying children; along with paralytics, lame persons, pregnant women and others who customarily claim thaumaturgical cures.[67] Cristina does not appear among them.

This brief miracle story contains much of interest to the social historian. Does the theft of a pig and the serious penalty Cristina suffered indicate some kind of heightened economic distress at the time? As large tracts of woodland were converted to agriculture, the proportion of pigs among the local cattle population was dropping in Herefordshire, an area in which herding played an important role in the local economy. Although she reputedly had several pigs, the theft of a pig (as opposed to a cow, for example) suggests that Cristina would have been among the poorest members of a relatively impoverished peasantry, and may have used the adjacent Wellington wood for grazing. The continuing importance of pigs to the local peasantry is indicated in Thomas' dossier. One of the miracles reported in the protocol concerns the revival of twenty-one pigs at the priory of Wotton (which belonged to the abbey of Conches in Normandy) in the diocese of Worcester after they had been found dead one morning. A pig had been promised as an ex-voto offering to Thomas.[68] In another case, a cow had been promised as an offering in order to revive a man's wife.[69] There is considerable evidence that the economic position of the English peasantry was worsening in the sixty years before the plague. Debts, land sales, and burglaries directed against the rich were on the rise. Poor persons lacking resources (i.e., possessing fewer than five acres of land) were forced to live on a combination of charity, subsistence wages, and the little they might earn off their landholdings (if such existed). Despite Edward I's policies, as Judith Bennett has noted, "field crimes associated with poverty and economic hardship increased dramatically. . ."[70] There is even evidence of a sharp increase in women's criminality during this period, although only a small percentage of the total accused were women.[71]

Late thirteenth-century England was extremely litigious and lawless, and a considerable number of accusations appear in court records, although only a minority reached adjudication. The majority of cases involved theft, and it often appears that homicide was treated with far greater leniency than property crimes. Rape, for example, was only made a capital crime in 1285. Most thieves belonged to the underclass—vagabonds, poor, landless peasants, and strangers. While most accused thieves probably escaped, hanging was not uncommon for this offense, and the lower the social class, the greater the likelihood of punishment. In Cristina's case, several questions arise. Grand larceny, for which hanging might apply, entailed the theft of goods worth at least 12d. Pigs were not so highly valued. As Barbara Hanawalt notes, "Almost all the recorded pig and poultry thefts involved more than one animal because those animals were not so valuable and the thieves would probably not even be indicted unless they stole enough to be equal to a shilling value."[72] In Hanawalt's sample, no women were hanged for theft, even grand larceny, and pigs were rarely stolen.

Since the canonization record reports only the theft and resale of merely one pig, for which Cristina was allegedly hanged, there is clearly some missing information. Perhaps she was also a fence or receiver of stolen goods. That would imply that she had not stolen out of hunger, but rather was a professional involved in criminal activities. Leominster and Hereford were important regional centers for the sale of stolen goods and the criminal court records are filled with accusations of theft, although probably only a minority were prosecuted.[73] Perhaps she was a member of a criminal gang, involved in other kinds of illegal activity, a feature common to such lawless border areas.

Is the reported execution of so many criminals at the time of Cristina's hanging caused by infrequent visits by royal justices or some other administrative procedure? The long and unjust imprisonment of victims prior to a court hearing was often itself a cause for supernatural intervention. Shortly before Cristina's case an allegedly innocent man named William Talgar had broken his left arm while in prison due to the cruel treatment he received. He was subsequently released and his arm restored to health due to the assistance he believed he had received from the saint. Sometime afterward, because he had not fulfilled his vow, William began to suffer such pain that he was visited by demons and in his sleep imagined that his arm was again broken in the same place. In the course of a vision of Thomas and the Virgin he was told that he would be cured if he fulfilled his vow. His visit to Hereford cathedral was reported by the local clerics.[74] Such supernatural intervention is a perennial feature of miracles during wartime, when victims were held for long periods of time in cruel conditions or were asked to pay an exorbitant ransom they were unable to mobilize.[75]

Or is Cristina's planned execution related to Edward I's repressive policy toward the Welsh, the consequent civil disorder, and the recalcitrance of the local population? The 1280s and 1290s were a period of border skirmishes, frontier warfare, disregard of the law and general mayhem in Wales and the borders. Does the similarity between her name Cray or Cragh and that of a man executed for treason as a Welsh rebel in 1289, but saved due to Thomas of Hereford's miraculous intervention, suggest a family tie and a Welsh background?[76] Cristina's reported vision, after all, is almost identical to the like-named Welshman William Cragh's. Thomas of Hereford's shrine had in fact become a popular pilgrimage site for those taking part in the wars against the Welsh. His record of miracles reports that in September and October 1287 many came to Hereford to take part in the battle against the Welsh rebel leader Meredith, including Bishop John of Ely and William, Count of Cornwall; among them were those seeking a cure.[77] Such pilgrims naturally spread word of Thomas' cult beyond the narrow confines of Herefordshire.

Miraculous rescue from hanging accompanied by a vision makes its appearance in other canonization records. A case similar to Cristina's had been reported at one of the earliest papal hearings and concerned a thief named Johannes of Wolfhagen, near Kassel, whose miraculous rescue from hanging on December 21, 1234 was attributed to the intervention of Elizabeth of Thuringia.[78] The event had been witnessed by over three hundred spectators who had come from three parishes in order to take part in the hanging. In this protocol, which is far more cursory than Thomas', six persons testified, including the victim himself. Johannes testified that, in keeping with a common hagiographical *topos*, he had heard a voice in the course of the hanging telling him, "Firmly believe, and never remove this rope from your neck, which you should bring to Elizabeth's tomb at Marburg." The rope then broke, and he fell down from a great height, nevertheless remaining uninjured. Sixteen *denarii* were offered to Elizabeth, the parish priest gave a cloak and trousers as an offering, while the judge who had presided, freed the victim. In another case in the same dossier, a man of Grünbecke near Altena in Westphalia who had been incarcerated for nearly three months, had been hung and taken for dead.[79] His friends dug a grave and beseeched Elizabeth's aid. During his incarceration, he had asked for the assistance of both Elizabeth and Conrad of Marburg, the former inquisitor, confidant of the saint, and one of the commissioners in her case, who had recently been killed. Both had appeared to him in a vision consoling him. His paternal uncle invoked the Virgin Mary, Elizabeth, and master Conrad. This tale, however, was contested by the local priest, swearing under oath.

The theme of the vision that precedes the performance of a miracle appears equally in the tales of Dulcia of St. Chartier, Jeanne Laboysans, and Cristina of Wellington. Although the vision reflects clerical expectations, this does not necessarily deny the possibility that victims would have been subject to such an auto-suggestive experience, especially given the ever-present use of dream in contemporary culture. In his classic *Varieties of Religious Experience* William James posited that the predisposition of the recipient and his or her audience to experience spiritual phenomena is the single most important causal factor in the occurrence of such events. Despite the caution voiced by Innocent III and others that some visions may be sent by Satan in order to befuddle believers, the widespread appearance of visions in hagiographical narrative sources suggests that both learned and popular culture shared a common faith in their providential nature.[80] Even the inquisitor Bernard Gui had been subject to vision. His nephew reported that when he was resting in the infirmary while serving as Dominican prior of Carcasonne he had dreamt of Friar Martin Donadieu (whose biography Gui subsequently wrote) in glory among the angels.[81]

The vision may appear in a variety of contexts, for example, as a means of calling the recipient to act in pursuit of a long contemplated goal: for example, prior to the liberation of a prisoner from captivity; as a means of identifying the site of long-buried relics or the place to establish a church or monastery; or as the medium during which victims are cured through a saint's touch, often in the course of incubation at the saint's tomb.[82] Such popes as Innocent III, Gregory IX, Clement IV, and Clement VI were themselves allegedly subject to dreams that prodded them into action, by confirming policies which they had long contemplated. In the lives of Jeanne, Cristina, and Dulcia, such a vision serves both a private and public role: as a reflection of the victim's desire to undertake a pilgrimage to the shrine of a popular and politically important miracle worker in pursuit of a cure; as confirmatory evidence of the saint's supernatural powers and claims to sainthood; and as a socially acceptable means of resolving their predicaments. But despite the willingness of both the learned and subaltern classes to be influenced by visions and dreams, they were nevertheless often rejected by investigators at canonization hearings. Only the recipient could testify that a vision had appeared, and it was therefore not verifiable.[83] A vision had to appear three times before it might be considered as reliable and God-given, rather than demoniacal.

Conclusion

Neither Cristina's nor Dulcia's experiences survived in the continuing traditions of the cults of Thomas of Hereford and Philip of Bourges. Cristina's case was not included in the twenty-six miracles closely examined by an anonymous curialist in 1318 for possible inclusion in the bull of canonization.[84] Due to many inconsistencies in such cases, no rescue from hanging appears in any of the medieval canonization bulls, although they appear in the hagiographical traditions of several saints. Dulcia's case was also censored early in the history of Philip of Bourges' dossier. Her cure could readily be attributed to the fact that after her husband was apprehended she was no longer being fed poisonous food. Divine intervention was not needed. A further reason for the absence of these cases for later consideration may be the greater suspicion with which the testimony of women was regarded by such figures as John Gerson.[85] Although the clergy and nobility were active, and even decisive participants in the creation of new cults; nevertheless, the common folk were regarded as more credulous and the learned imposed a more rigid standard in discernment of the miraculous.

Nevertheless, we owe a debt of gratitude to those officials who investigated the miracles of Philip of Bourges, Thomas of Hereford and others and to the notaries, procurators (who drew up the lists of witnesses and questions to be posed), scribes and translators who recorded the deponents' testimony.[86] Despite the presumed commitment of the court's personnel to the virtues of the putative saint, their probing questions allow us to recreate the otherwise lost private worlds of a host of otherwise silent denizens who populate our historical imagination. These public notaries, often officials of the papal chancery and members of the notarial college of the Roman curia, were appointed by the emperor or pope. But they were authorized to record and draw up public instruments anywhere, including France, England or Spain, and were well trained in canon and Roman law.[87] Their records give a voice to, among others, a woman from Bourges whose husband and his lover attempted to poison her, an emotionally distressed pregnant woman from the village of Crosses and a convicted felon, Cristina of Wellington, among a host of others drawn into the web of a nascent cult. Although the clergy may have intervened in the deposition of their testimony and of other rural and urban folk at canonization processes, it may be possible to come closer to the lives of such historically neglected persons, especially when the witnesses stray from the inquisitor Bernard Gui's caveat to avoid nonessentials in inquisitorial trials.[88] Just as historians of heresy have exploited trials as a rich source for the more mundane, less ideologically charged environment of their deponents, miracle tales may likewise be mined to permit a microhistorical reconstruction of the concrete milieux in which the miraculous has been experienced by those left out of the traditional historical narrative.[89]

These cases reveal the severe punishments meted out to those among the rural and urban subaltern classes who broke the law, whether adulterers or thieves, and the consequent appeal to the supernatural. If women are underrepresented in traditional histories, they play a central role in the genesis of many religious cults. Miracle collections provide us with concrete examples of the spiritual world, family and material lives that lay at the basis of our understanding of medieval culture. Much medieval piety found its expression within the smaller confines of a community, which was brought together through a common experience of what was perceived as providential intervention in the lives of the faithful.

Notes

I would like to thank Gábor Klaniczay, Amos Megged, Laura Smoller, and Daniel Smail, for their useful comments and suggestions.

1. See e.g. André Vauchez, "Les origines et le développement du process de canonisation (XIIe-XIIIe siècles)," in *Vita Religiosa im Mittelalter. Festschrift für Kaspar Elm zum 70. Geburtstag*, ed. Franz J. Felten and Nikolas Jaspert (Berlin: Duncker & Humblot, 1999), pp. 845–56.

2. Bernard Gui, *Manuel de l'Inquisiteur*, ed. Guillaume Mollat and Georges Drioux, 2 vols. (Paris: Les Belles Lettres, 1926–27), 1:32; Caterina Bruschi, " 'Magna diligentia est habenda per inquisitorem': Precautions before Reading Doat 21–26," in *Texts and the Repression of Medieval Heresy*, ed. Caterina Bruschi and Peter Biller (Woodbridge: York Medieval Press, 2003), pp. 81–110. The phrase employed by John Gerson, "Tu quis, quid, quare, cui, qualiter, unde require," is cited in Gábor Klaniczay, "The Process of Trance, Heavenly and Diabolic Apparitions in Johannes Nider's *Formicarius*," Discussion Paper Series 65 (Budapest: Collegium Budapest, 2003), p. 52.

3. See e.g., Sharon Farmer, *Surviving Poverty in Medieval Paris. Gender, Ideology and Daily Lives of the Poor* (Ithaca: Cornell University Press, 2002); Robert Bartlett, *The Hanged Man. A Story of Miracle, Memory and Colonialism in the Middle Ages* (Princeton: Princeton University Press, 2004); Ronald Finucane, *The Rescue of the Innocents. Endangered Children in Medieval Miracles* (New York: St. Martin's, 1997); Laura Smoller, "Miracle, Memory, and Meaning in the Canonization of Vincent Ferrer, 1453–54," *Speculum*, 73 (1998): 429–54; Laura Smoller, "Defining the Boundaries of the Natural in the Fifteenth Century: The Inquest into the Miracles of St. Vincent Ferrer (d. 1419)," *Viator*, 28 (1997): 333–59; Christian Krötzl, *Pilger, Mirakel und Alltag. Formen des Verhaltens in skandinavischen Mittelalter (12.15. Jahrhundert)* (Helsinki: SHS, 1994).

4. On Philip, see e.g. *Bibliotheca sanctorum*, 12 vols. (Rome: Istituto Giovanni XXII, 1969–80) 3:87–88; A. Baudrillart, ed., *Dictionnaire d'histoire et de géographie écésiastiques*, 27 vols. to date (Paris: Letouzey et Ane, 1912–1999) 8:92–98.

5. *Processus supra vita et miraculis domini Philippi archiepiscopi Biturcensis*, in Vatican City, Bibliotheca Apostolica Vaticana MS Vat. lat. 4019 and Paris, Bibliothèque Nationale de France MS lat. 5373A, fols. 1v–61v.

6. Vatican City, Bibliotheca Apostolica Vaticana MS Vat. lat. 4021.

7. Paris, BNf MS lat. 5373A, fols. 1r–3v.

8. *Vita sancti Philippi archiepiscopi Biturcensis*, in Edmond Martène and Ursin Durand, eds., *Thesaurus novus anecdotorum*, 5 vols. (Paris: Sumptibus F. Delaulne, 1717–26), 3: cols. 1927–46.

9. Vatican City, Bibliotheca Apostolica Vaticana MS lat. 4019, fols. 1r–14v.

10. Such a large proportion of women is not uncommon. In the case of Margaret of Hungary, the gender breakdown of recipients of miracles is 50/50. See Gábor Klaniczay, "Speaking of Miracles. Oral Testimony and Written Record in Medieval Canonisation Trials," which I have kindly seen in typescript.

11. This was the occasion for the production of the Vatican manuscript, which is a copy of the original, including an account of its treatment by Rome.

12. See n. 18 for the list of questions in Elizabeth's case. For Philip's questions, see Vat. lat. 4019, fol. 9r–v: "Testos legitimos quos super vita coversationem et miraculis recolende memorie Philippi bituricensis archiepiscopi recipere prius ab eis prestito iuramento diligenter examinare curetis et de

omnibus que dixerint interrogetis eosdem quomodo sciunt quo tempore quo mense quo die quibus presentibus quo loco ad cuius invocationem et quibus verbis interpositis et [de] nominibus illorum circa quos miracula facta dicuntur et si ante cognoscebant et quot diebus ante viderunt eos infirmos et quanto tempore fuerunt infirmi et quanto tempore visi sunt sani et de quo loco siunt oriundi et interrogetis de omnibus circumstanciis et circa singula capitula. . ."

["You should take care to diligently examine under oath upright witnesses concerning the life, conversation and miracles of Philip of blessed memory, archbishop of Bourges. Regarding everything they say you should ask how they knew, what time, month and day [the events had occurred], who was present, where they had occurred, at whose invocation, what words were used, the names of those for whom the miracles had been performed, if they knew them beforehand, for how many days before they had seen them ill, how long they had been ill, how long they had seen them healthy, where they came from; you should ask about the circumstances and about each of the chapters [of the inquiry] separately. . ."]

The questions posed by Innocent V in the 1276 case of Margaret of Hungary are identical. See Vilmos Fraknoì, ed., *Inquisitio super vita, conversatione et miraculis beatae Margarethae virginis*, in *Monumenta romana episcopatus Vesprimiensis*, 12 vols. (Budapest: Ráth, 1874–1917) 1:161–62.

13. Christian Krötzl, "Miracles au tombeau—miracles à distance: approches typologiques," in Denise Aigle, ed., *Miracle et Karáma* (Turnhout: Brepols, 2000), pp. 557–76 notes the greater frequency of miracles far from the shrine in the thirteenth and fourteenth centuries. This parallels the substantial rise of miracles which occur in the presence of movable altarpieces, particularly in Italy.

14. James Brundage, "Playing by the Rules: Sexual Behavior and Legal Norms in Medieval Europe," in *Desire and Discipline. Sex and Sexuality in the Post-Modern West*, ed. Jacqueline Murray and Konrad Eisenbichler (Toronto: University of Toronto Press, 1996), pp. 23–41.

15. Winfrid Trusen, "Der Inquisitionsprozess: Seine historischen Grundlagen und frühen Formen," *Zeitschrift der Savigny Stiftung für Rechtsgeschichte. Kanonistische Abteilung*, 74 (1988): 168–230. On its spread use see Adhémar Esmein, *A History of Continental Criminal Procedure with Special Reference to France*, trans. John Simpson (South Hackensack, NJ: Rothman Reprints, 1968). Innocent's first explicit reference to the inquisitorial method of investigation dates from a September 22, 1198 letter regarding clerical discipline in the Milanese church.

16. Raoul Naz, "Inquisition," *Dictionaire de droit canonique*, ed. Raoul Naz, 7 vols. (Paris: Letouzey et Ane, 1935–65) 5:1418–26. The inquisitorial procedure was imported from Roman law. Elements already appeared in a canon dated September 22, 1198. See *Deretales Gregorii IX*, in Emil Friedberg and Emil Richter, *Corpus iuris canonici*, 2 vols. (Leipzig: B. Tauchnitz, 1879–81), II. Tit. xxiv. C. 21. See also Decr. III. Tit. xii.c. 1; Decr. V. tit. 34. c. 10; Decr. V. tit. 1. c. 17; Decr. V. tit. 3. c. 31, c. 32; V.1.17; V.1.24; Brundage, "Playing by the Rules."

17. Lucien Auvray, ed., *Registres de Grégoire IX*, 4 vols. (Paris: A. Fontemoing, 1896–1955) 1:548: ". . .quomodo sciunt, quo tempore, quo mense, quo die, quibus presentibus, quo loco, ad cujus invocationem, et quibus verbis interpositis, et de nominibus illorum circa quos miracula facta dicuntur, et si ante cognoscabant, et quot diebus ante viderunt eos infirmos et quanto tempore fuerunt infirmi, et de qua civitate sunt oriundi et interrogantur de omnibus circumstantiis diligenter."
[". . .how they knew, when it occurred, the month and day, who was present, where it had occurred, at whose invocation, the words that were used, the names of those for whom the miracle had been performed, if they knew them beforehand, how long they had seen them ill and how long they had been ill, what city they came from, and other circumstances."] (Bull of Gregory IX, *Ut ceci viam*, October 13, 1232).

18. In 1251 this village was granted a charter of rights by the seigneur of Levroux. See Louis Raynal, *Histoire de Berry*, 4 vols. (Bourges: Librairie de Vermeil, 1845) 2:211. The parish was among the fifty-three parishes subject to the archpriest of Le Châtre. See Louis Raynal, *Histoire de Berry*, 4 vols. (Bourges: Librairie de Vermeil, 1845), I:xxxi; Maurice Prou, Ch.- Edmond Perrin, and Jacques de Font Réaulx, *Pouillés de la province de Bourges*, 2 vols. (Paris: Impr. Nationale, 1961–62) 2:646.

19. Vat. lat. 4019, fols. 75r–76v; Paris, BnF MS lat. 5373A, fols. 28v–30r.

20. Vat. lat. 4019, fol. 8r. These witnesses testified concerning miracle numbers 16, 19, 17, 18 and 43. See Martène and Durand, *Thesaurus novus anecdotorum*, 3: 1941, 1944.

21. Vat. lat. 4019, fol. 79v.

22. Vat. lat. 4019, fol. 76v.

23. The first canon of the Fourth Lateran Council of 1215 had reiterated the continuing presence of the devil. For special prayers for the exorcism and interdiction of the devil, see Adolph Franz, *Die kirchlichen Benediktionen im Mittelalter*, 2 vols. (Freiburg-im-Breisgau: Herder, 1909) 2:586–96, 603–615.

24. Laura A. Smoller, "A Case of Demonic Possession in Fifteenth-Century Brittany: Perrin Hervé and the Cult of Vincent Ferrer," in this volume.

25. The term used is *garcia*. See Vat. lat. 4019, fol. 75v.

26. William of Auvergne, *De universo*, III, in *Opera omnia*, 2 vols. (Lyons: F. Hotet, 1674), 1:1021.

27. Claudia Opitz, "Life in the Middle Ages," in *A History of Women in the West*, 2 vols., ed. Christiane Klapisch-Zuber (Cambridge: Harvard University Press, 1992) 2:277.

28. Vat. lat. 4021, fol. 15r.

29. *Vita* in Martène and Durand, *Thesaurus novus anecdotorum*, 3:1943C.

30. Paris, BnF lat. 5373A, fols. 1r–3v.

31. Robert I. Moore, *The Formation of a Persecuting Society: Power and Deviance in Western Europe 950–1250* (Oxford: Basil Blackwell, 1987), p. 99. The discussion by Ruth Mazo Karras and her interlocutors in "Prostitution and the Question of Sexual Identity," *Journal of Women's History*, 11 (1999): 159–77 is a provocative contribution to the theme.

32. William of Auvergne, *De universo*, p. 1042, 1066.

33. Joseph Hansen, *Zauberwahn. Inquisition und Hexenprozess im Mittelalter* (Munich: R. Oldenburg, 1900), for many contemporary sources; Julio Caro Baroja, "Witchcraft and Catholic Theology," in *New Perspectives in Witchcraft, Magic and Demonology*, ed. Brian Levack, 5 vols. (New York: Routledge, 2001) 1:1–43. See also Alan Kors and Edward Peters, ed., *Witchcraft in Europe 400–1700. A Documentary History*, rev. ed. (Philadelphia: University of Pennsylvania Press, 2001), who note how the scholastics organized folklore into a diabolical system.

34. Edward Peters, *The Magician, the Witch and the Law* (Philadelphia: University of Pennsylvania Press, 1978), p. 99.

35. For a useful survey of the literature see Elspeth Whitney, "The Witch 'She'/The Historian 'He': Gender in the Historiography of the European Witch Hunts," *Journal of Women's History*, 7 (1995): 77–101.

36. Charles de Fresne Ducange, *Glossarium mediae et infimae latinitatis*, 10 vols. (Graz: Akademische-U. Verlagsanstalt, 1954) 7:183–84 contains a considerable number of contemporary citations.

37. Gary Dickson, "The Advent of the *Pastores* (1251)," *Revue belge de philologie et d'histoire*, 66 (1988): 249–67; Malcolm Barber, "The Crusade of the Shepherds in 1251," *Proceedings the Western Society for French History*, 11 (1984): 1–23; on Bourges, see Gaspard Thaumas de la Thaumassière, *Histoire de Berry*, new ed., 4 vols. (Bourges: A. Jollet Fils, 1865) 2:74–75.

38. Raynal, *Histoire de Berry*, 2:235–36.

39. Guy Devailly, *Le Berry du xe au milieu de xiiie. Étude politique, religieuse, social, et économique* (Paris: Mouton, 1973), p. 466.

40. Rome, Biblioteca Angelica MS 157 (B.6.10), fols. 93v-95v for his sermons. I would like to thank both the Biblioteca Angelica and the Institut de Recherche et d' Histoire des Textes for their assistance. This stress on virtues rather than miracles by preachers is clear in the over sixty sermons concerning Clare of Assisi examined in Marina Soriani Innocenti, "I sermoni latini in onore di Santa Chiara," in *Chiara di Assisi. Atti del XX Convegno internazionale, Assisi, 15–17 Ottobre 1992*, in *Società internazionale di studi francescani*, Nuova serie, 3 (Spoleto: Centro italiano di studi sull'alto medioevo, 1993): 357–80. The downplaying of miracles as opposed to saintly virtues characterized the Franciscan order. See Gábor Klaniczay, "Proving Sanctity in the Canonization Processes (Saint Elizabeth and Saint Margaret of Hungary), 3. The typescript was kindly given to me by the author.

41. Gerd Friedrich Nüske, "Untersuchungen über das Personal der päpstlichen Kanzlei, 1254–1304," *Archiv für Diplomatik*, 20 (1974): 39–240; 21 (1975): 249–431 for a thorough census of the staff of the papal curia during this period.

42. Maria Magdalena Lebreton, "Eudes de Châteauroux," *Dictionniare de spiritualité*, ed. Marcel Villers et al., 12 vols. (Paris: G. Beauchesne et ses fils, 1932–95) 4.2: 1675–78.

43. André Callebaut, "Le sermon historique d'Eudes de Châteauroux à Paris le 18 mars 1229 autour de l'origine de la grève universitaire de de l'enseignement des mendiants," *Archivum fratrum historicum*, 28 (1935): 61–114; for his attack on the Jews, see David Behrman, "Volumina vilissima, a sermon of Eudes of Châteauroux on the Jews and their Talmud," in *Le brûlement de Talmud à Paris 1242–1244*, ed. Gilbert Dahan (Paris: Les Éditions du Cerf, 1999), pp. 191–209.

44. Marie-Madeleine Davy, *Les sermons universitaires parisiens de 1230–1231* (Paris: J. Vrin, 1931), pp. 179–213.

45. Alain Boureau, "Miracle, volonté et imagination: la mutation scholastique (1270–1320)," in *Miracles, prodiges et merveilles au moyen âge. XXVe Congrès de la J.H.M.E.S* (Paris: Publications de la Sorbonne, 1995), pp. 159–72.

46. John of Salerno, *Vita Odonis*, in PL 133:49.

47. Vat. lat. 4019, fols. 56v–63v; Paris, BnF MS lat. 5373A, fols. 16r–19r; *Vita* in Martène and Durand, *Thesaurus novus anecdotorum* 3:1927–46, here 1942–43, "xii: De alienatis a sensu, intellectu, memoria et loquela liberates."

48. Zbigniew Perzanowski and Janina Pleziowa, eds., *Miracula S. Stanislai*, in *Analecta Cracoviensia*, 2 (1979): 78, 80, 92, 98 for such cases.

49. Fernand van Ortroy, ed., "Procès-verbal du dernier consistoire secret préparatoire à la canonisation du Célestin V," *Analecta bollandiana*, 16 (1897): 475–87.

50. An example of a possessed girl in the process of Margaret of Hungary, whose case was reexamined, is reported in Klaniczay, "Proving Sanctity," p. 28.

51. *Processus canonizationis Thomae de Cantilupo*, in *Acta sanctorum*, ed. Socii Bollandiani, new ed., 68 vols. (Paris: V. Palmé, 1863–1940), 2 October 1:582–696 (Hereafter *AASS*). The commissioners were William Durand, bishop of Mende, the papal nuncio in England William de Festa, and Ralph Baldock bishop of London, assisted by the canon and archdeacon of Hereford, Henry de Schorne. This cult is also dealt with in this volume by Ronald Finucane, "The Toddler in a Ditch: A Case of Parental Neglect?".

52. Vat. lat. 4015, fol. 79v: "Ipse tamen testis non vidit aliquod miraculum de praedictis audivit de mille miraculis ut credit quod Deus dicitur operator fuisse per dicto domino Thomas." "This witness had not seen any of the preceding miracles, but had heard about a thousand, so he believed that God had acted through lord Thomas."

53. See Christian Krötzl, "Prokuratoren, Notare und Dolmetscher. Zur Gestaltung und Ablauf der Zeugeneinvernahmen bei spätmittelalterlichen Kanonisationsprozessen," *Hagiographica*, 5 (1998): 119–40; Christian Krötzl, "*Vulgariter sibi exposition. Zu Übersetzung uns Sprachberherrschung im Spätmittelalter am Beispiel von Kanonisationsprozessen," *Das Mittelalter*, 2 (1997): 111–18 on Thomas's trial. See also the articles in Meryl Jancey, ed., *St. Thomas, Bishop of Hereford. Essays in His Honour* (Hereford: The Friends of

Hereford Cathedral, 1982). Such scholastics as Thomas Aquinas, Engelbert of Admont and Albertus Magnus wrote about the nature of miracles.

54. *Processus Thomae*, in *AASS*, October 2, 1: 585–86; Gabriele Zanella, "Armanno Pungilupo, eretico quotidiano," in Gabriele Zanela, *Hereticalia. Temi e discussioni* (Spoleto: Centro italiano di studi sull'alto medioevo, 1995), pp. 3–14; Daniele Solvi, "Santi degli eretici e santi degli inquisitori intorno all'anno 1300," in *Il pubblico dei santi. Forme e livelli di ricezione dei messagi agiografici*, ed. Paolo Golinelli (Rome: Viella, 2000), pp. 267–86. For the attempt to distinguish between saints and witches, see Peter Dinzelbacher, *Heilige oder Hexen? Schicksale auffälliger Frauen in Mittelalter und Frühneuzeit* (Zurich: Artemis & Winkler, 1995); Gábor Klaniczay, "Miraculum and Maleficium: Reflections Concerning Late Medieval Female Sainthood," in *Problems in the Historical Anthropology of Early Modern Europe*, ed. Ronnie Po-Chia Hsia and Robert E. Scribner, in *Wolfenbüttlicher Forschungen*, 78 (1997): 49–71. On Armanno see Carol Lansing, *Power & Purity. Cathar Heresy in Medieval Italy* (Oxford: Oxford University Press, 1998), pp. 92–95. On Guglielma, Marina Benedetti, ed., *Milano 1300: I processi inquisitoriali contro le devote e i devoti di santa Guglielma* (Milan: Scheiwiller, 1999).

55. Vat. lat. 4015, fol. 3v: "conditio dictorum testium, scilicet an sint literati vel illiterati, nobiles vel plebei, divites vel egeni" (*Processus Thomae*, in *AASS*, October 2, 1:589).

56. Finucane, *Rescue*, 169–206 for a translation of the testimony in this case, found Vat. lat. 4015, fols. 123r–40r.

57. *Herefordshire, vol. II. East.* (London: Royal Commission on Historical Monuments, 1932), pp. 136, 200–202.

58. Vatican City, Bibliotheca Apostolica Vaticana MS lat. 4015, fols. 247v, 252v; Vatican City, Bibliotheca Apostolica Vaticana MS lat. 4016, fol. 35r.

59. Vat. lat. 4015, fols. 230v–34v; *Processus Thomae*, in *AASS*, October 2, 1: 637. For other testimony see fols. 183r–83v, 205v–206r, 227v–30r.

60. I have been unable to find a reference to such cases in the suitable rolls of the King's Bench for Easter, 1294, taken from a variety of courts, including Hereford. See London Public Records Office MS KB 27/140 (22 Edward I).

61. Michael Prestwich, *Edward I* (London: Methuen, 1988), p. 183. See e.g., a 1293 hanging for theft in George O. Sayles, ed., *Select Cases in the Court of the King's Bench*, 3 vols. (London: B. Quaritch, 1938) 2:197.

62. In addition to the church of St. Martin situated outside the town on the other side of the Wye, there was a chapel of St. Martin in the castle bailey in the King's chamber. It is unlikely that Cristina would have been taken to this chapel after her execution. See Roy Shoesmith, *Hereford City Excavations*, 3 vols. (London: Council of British Archaeology, 1980–86) 1:5.

63. William Rees, *The Hospital of St. John of Jerusalem in Wales or on the Welsh Borders* (Cardiff: Western Mail and Echo, 1967), p. 44; John Le Neve, *Fasti Ecclesiae Anglicanae, 1300–1541*, 10 vols., ed. Joyce M. Horn (London: Institute of Historical Research, 1962) 2:50. For further material on the geography of medieval Hereford and the village of Wellington, see Shoesmith, *Hereford City Excavations*; see also the Ordinance Survey maps of

the area. The important topographic features of the village of Wellington are Wellington marsh, wood and brook.

64. Oxford, Exeter College MS 158, fol. 39v.
65. Oxford, Exeter College MS 158, fols. 44v–45r.
66. Kevin Down, "Colonial Society and Economy in the High Middle Ages," in *A New History of Ireland. II. Medieval Ireland, 1169–1534*, ed. Art Cosgrove (Oxford: Clarendon Press, 1987), pp. 439–91.
67. *Processus Thomae*, in *AASS*, October 2, 1: 681–82.
68. *Processus Thomae*, in *AASS*, October 2, 1: 668.
69. Oxford, Exeter College MS 158, fol. 7r.
70. Judith M. Bennett, *Women in the Medieval English Countryside. Gender and Household before the Plague* (New York: Oxford University Press, 1987), p. 190. While this book is based on the Northamptonshire village of Brigstock, much further contemporary evidence is drawn from other regions.
71. Bennett, *Women in the Medieval English Countryside*, p.189 notes a rise from 26%–35% of women among the criminal population from 1301–1343. Anne Reiber DeWindt and Edwin Brezette DeWindt, eds., *Rural Justice and the Medieval Countryside. The Huntingdonshire Eyre of 1286, the Ramsay Abbey Banlieu Court of 1287, and the Assizes of 1287–88*, 2 vols. (Toronto: Pontifical Institute of Mediaeval Studies, 1981) 2:60 note that only 3% of their accused were women, although they constituted 22.5% of the victims.
72. Barbara A. Hanawalt, *Crime and Conflict in Medieval Communities 1300–1348* (Cambridge: Harvard University Press, 1979), p. 72.
73. Hanawalt, *Crime and Conflict*, p. 94.
74. William Talgar visited Thomas's shrine on June 6, 1293 and reported his experience. Exeter College MS 158, fols. 27r–28v:

Item anno eodem [1293] viii idus iunii vir quidam Willelmus Talgar nomine cum per dominum suum terrenum innocentus fuisset missus carcerem et tanto pondere ferri constrictus ut eius sinistrum brachium frangeretur. Cum ipse tam squalore carceris quae fractura praedicta nimium torqueretur. Pro sua liberacione et sanitate servi dei auxilium invocavit votum emittens quod eius tumulum in persona propria visitaret quaecito ipsum contingeret a carcere liberari. Et ecce brachio eius statim sanato et ipso in brevi postmodum de carcere liberari. Et ecce brachio eius statim sanato et ipso postmodum de carceralibus vinculis liberato. Ille sui benefactoris et voti frus immemor et ingratus processus temporis gravissime egrotabat in tantum ut frenesim incurrerat et fieret velud arrepticius a demonibus cruciatus ut sibi videbatur in sompnis et in tantum torquebatur insanus ut brachium eius frangeretur in loco ubi primitus fuit fractum. Et cum quadam vice aliquantulum dormitaret vidit in sompnis gloriosissimam matrem dei dicentem servo dei Thome pontifici qui ut sibi videbatur tunc astabat ibidem. Amice adiuva miserum istum. Qui statim respondit virginum gloriose. Illusit mi homo iste promisit enim quod me ante hec tempora visitasse et non venit ut redderet votum suum. Et mater misericordie iterum dixit ei.

Ipse venietur ad te. Adiuva illum rogo. At ille respndit veniat tunc die pen-
tecostis et sanabitur in nomine domini. Quibus dictis praedictis referens
astantibus visionem postmodum ductus est ad tumulum viri dei die praedicta scilicet qui fuit viii ides junii. Et ibidem tam a brachii fractione qui a
frenetica passione ipsa die fuit divinitus libertus per intercessionem virginis
gloriose et merita servi dei praedicti.

[In the same year [1293] on the 8 Ides of June [June 6, there came] an innocent man named William Talgar had been sent by his earthly lord to prison
and was bound with a heavy iron weight so that his left arm was broken. He
was tortured excessively by the squalor of the prison in which he was
injured. In order to be freed and made healthy, he made a vow to the servant of God [i.e. Thomas of Hereford] to visit his tomb in person as soon as
he was freed from the chains of prison. His arm was immediately cured and
shortly thereafter he was let out of prison. Since he had forgotten his bene-
factor and the vow he had made, the ingrate fell gravely ill in the course of
time, went mad, and suffered as if possessed by the demons. In a dream he
suffered terribly and it seemed that his arm had been broken in the same
place as before. On another occasion in his sleep he saw the glorious
Mother of God speaking to the servant of God Thomas the bishop whom
he saw standing there, "My friend, help this wretched man." He immediately responded to the glorious Virgin, "It seems to me that this man
promised before to visit me but did not come in order to fulfill his vow."
The mother of mercy again said to him, "He will come to you. I ask you to
help him." He replied that he should come on the day of Pentecost and will
be cured in the name of the Lord. After these things were said in the vision,
he was taken to the tomb of the man of God on the day that was mentioned, which was the 8 Ides of June. On that day he was divinely freed of
the broken arm from which he had suffered in his madness, by the intercession of the glorious Virgin and the merits of the aforesaid servant [i.e.
Thomas] of God.].

75. Michael Goodich, "Die wundersame Gefangenenbefreiung im mittelalter-
     lichen Kanonisationsdocumente," in *Hagiographie im Kontext*, ed. Klaus
     Herbers and Dieter Bauer (Stuttgart: Steiner Verlag, 1999), pp. 69–84.
76. On this case, see Michael Goodich, "Foreigner, Foe and Neighbor: the
     Religious Cult as a Forum for Political Reconciliation," in *Meeting the Foreign
     in the Middle Ages*, ed. Albrecht Classen (New York: Routledge, 2002),
     pp. 11–26; Michael Richter, "Walser und Wündermänner um 1300," in
     Spannungen und Widersprüche; Gedenkschrift für František Graus, ed. Susanna
     Burghartz (Sigmaringen: J. Thorbecke Verlag, 1992), pp. 23–36; idem,
     "William ap Rees, William de Braose and the Lordship of Gower, 1289 and
     1307," *Studia celtica*, 32 (1998): 189–200; Bartlett, *The Hanged Man*.
77. Exeter College MS 158, fol. 6r. See also Vat. lat. 4015, fols. 250r–51v for a
     man of London whose demonic visions were driven away by the saint;
     Exeter College MS 158, fols. 257r–57v for a man cured by the saint during
     a nocturnal vision. *Processus Thomae*, in *AASS*, October 2, I: 670 for a

demoniac of Cornwall who had mocked Thomas by saying, "I believe he is as much of a saint as Simon of Montfort, who people regard as a saint, but who was buried at Evesham." He became ill, was rebuked in a vision by the saint, and then cured.

78. Albert Huyskens, *Quellenstudien zur Geschichte der hl. Elisabeth* (Marburg: N. G. Elwert, 1908), pp. 255–57 for the following cases. See also Baudouin de Gaiffier, "Un theme hagiographique. Le pendu miraculeusement sauvé," in *Études critiques d'hagiographie et d'iconologie* (Brussels; Société des Bollandistes, 1967), pp. 194–226 and Baudouin de Gaiffer, "Liberatus a suspendio," in *Études critiques d'hagiographie et d'iconologie*, pp. 227–32.

79. Huyskens, *Quellenstudien zur Geschichte der hl.*

80. The literature is considerable. See e.g., Peter Dinzelbacher, *Vision and Visionsliteratur im Mittelalter*, in *Mongraphien zur Geschichte des Mittelalters*, 23 (Stuttgart: Anton Hiersemann, 1981). A brief, but still useful study is Peter Burke, "The Cultural History of Dreams," in *Varieties of Cultural History* (Cambridge: Polity Press, 1997), pp. 23–42, first published in 1973.

81. Martin asked that the following inscription be inscribed on his tomb: "Vita fuit munda Martini, lingua facunda." See Thomas Kaeppeli, ed., "Vie de frère Martin Donadieu de Carcasonne, O.P. (1299) écrite par Bernard et Pierre Gui," *Archivum fratrum praedicatorum*, 26 (1956): 288.

82. See e.g., Vat. lat 4015, fol. 257r–v for a nocturnal vision in which a man is cured by the saint.

83. Wojciech Ketrzyński, ed., *Miracula sancti Stanislai*, in *Monumenta poloniae historica*, 6. vols., ed. A. Bielowski (Lwow: W. Komisie Ksiegarni Gubrynowicza I Schmidta, 1864–93) 4:285–318, especially miracle numbers 23, 27, in which the anonymous curialist notes that since only one witness testified about a vision, it had to be rejected.

84. See André Vauchez, *Sainthood in the Later Middle Ages*, trans. Jean Birrell (Cambridge: Cambridge University Press, 1997), pp. 540–54 for text; for discussion see pp. 488–98. See also Ronald Finucane, "Authorizing the Supernatural: A Curialist's Analysis of Some English Miracles around 1318," Paper presented at International Medieval Congress, University of Leeds, July 14–17, 2003.

85. Dyan Elliot, "Seeing Double: John Gerson, the Discernment of Spirits, and Joan of Arc," *American Historical Review*, 107 (2002): 30.

86. Christan Krötzl, "Prokuratoren," pp. 119–40 about the officials at Thomas of Hereford's process.

87. Christopher R. Cheney, *Notaries Public in England in the Thirteenth and Fourteenth Centuries* (Oxford, 1972); Dietrich Lohrmann, "Berard von Neapel, ein päpstlicher Notär und Vertrauter Karls von Anjou," in *Adel und Kirche: Festschrift Gerd Tellenbach* (Freiburg: Herder, 1968), pp. 477–98 on a notary involved in drawing up canonization bulls.

88. Bernard Gui, *Manuel de l'Inquisiteur*, 1:32.

89. Carlo Ginzburg, "Morelli, Freud and Sherlock Holmes: Clues and Scientific Method," *History Workshop*, 9 (1980): 15–16.

CHAPTER 5

THE TODDLER IN THE DITCH:
A CASE OF PARENTAL NEGLECT?

Ronald C. Finucane

On the morning of September 7, 1303, inhabitants of the royal stronghold of Conway (Conwy)—representing castle, church, and community—were wrenched from humdrum routines by the discovery of the frost-covered body of a little boy. Roger, age two years and two months, son of Gervase and Dionysia, was lying at the bottom of a ditch at Edward I's relatively new Welsh castle. Thanks to appeals to the dead Thomas Cantilupe, a Hereford bishop who would be canonized in 1320, Roger "returned from the dead." Because of Roger's mishap and miracle, reactions and interactions of Conway's various ranks, from servants to mayor, over a single night and day, are briefly but brilliantly illuminated.

Unusually, we have a letter about the event—sealed by numerous members of the local secular and ecclesiastical elite—composed that very morning.[1] It was written in St. Mary's church, where the revived child was carried by his thankful mother trailing a joyous crowd. A few weeks afterwards, several people involved in the miracle (including Roger and his parents) went on pilgrimage to Thomas's shrine in Hereford cathedral, telling their tale to the canons and leaving the letter as evidence of the wondrous event. Four years later a small group of Conway people arrived at Hereford, summoned to testify about this miracle at the local fact-gathering (*in partibus*) phase of Cantilupe's canonization process, overseen by three papal nominees. Transcripts of their depositions form the documentary basis of this essay.[2] In addition, the letter of 1303 was introduced and copied into the record; among the eight Conway people who testified in October 1307, two had appended their seals to that letter. The witnesses' statements and different interpretations, though structured by a list of interrogatories, reveal how each witness had created unique memories of that September morning, and what led up to it the evening before, when the toddler "died."

The Body

Conway castle and town were divided by a man-made ditch spanned during the day by a drawbridge. Excavations indicate that the ditch was about twenty-four meters wide and at least nine meters deep.[3] About sunrise on that morning four years earlier, gatekeeper John Griffin testified, as he was about to lower the bridge, that John de Havering's son Nicholas, whose room was in a castle tower, told him that just before going to bed the previous evening he'd heard a child cry out in the ditch.

Fearing that it might be his own child, John found Roger lying under the bridge on the "town side" of the ditch. One leg was bent, the other straight; only the whites of his eyes were visible; there was frozen spittle on Roger's closed mouth; the unclothed body, cold and stiff, was covered in white frost. John could detect no signs of life, though there was nothing broken in Rogers' limbs, bones or skin; there was no bleeding, just some redness on the left jaw, on which the boy lay. Griffin told the pope's committee that Roger was dead for as long as it took to walk three English leagues, a common mode of measuring time.[4]

Meanwhile, William de Cicon, constable of the castle (and Conway's mayor), and others, including his seneschal John de Boys and the vicar of St. Mary's church Simon of Watford—all castle residents—were watching from the bridge.[5] When Griffin picked up the child to take him from the ditch, Cicon instructed him to put Roger down, to await the coroners. John returned the boy to the spot where he had lain, and in the same state. Then, at Cicon's mandate, John went to summon the coroners.[6]

The coroners (Stephen de Gamowe/Gannowe, and William of Nottingham, burghers of the town) arrived, with William—their clerk who also was the town's common scribe—and a jury of twelve. They and Griffin examined Roger and adjudged him dead. About this time vicar Simon, having seen enough, left the scene. The coroners asked for pledges or sureties from Griffin as first finder.[7] Before he could provide the requested sureties, and while he, the coroners and jurors were still in the ditch, he testified, Roger came to life. In concluding their reportage of Griffin's testimony on October 26, 1307, the notaries saved time and parchment by stating that his responses to the last six interrogatories were "in effect the same" as the replies given by the very first witness to testify (on the 23rd), vicar Simon.[8] Those interrogatories and replies were: (1) Was the miracle then and is still ascribed in Conway and nearby places to Thomas's merits? Yes. (2) Did he believe that, following human reason, Roger would have revived without a miracle? No. (3) Did he and other townspeople learning of the miracle become more devout, glorifying God and St. Thomas? Yes. (4) Did he know of, or believe or hear it said, that anything whatsoever about the miracle involved fraud, artifice, or machination; or any sortilege, superstition (*superstitio*), incantation or invocation of a demon (*demonum invocatio*); or whether anything natural or artificial had been involved in the miracle? No. (5) Did he have notification, with others, about proving the miracle? Yes. (6) (The usual final question put to witnesses in contemporary trials:) Did he testify at anyone's request or order, through fear, hatred or love, or for money given or promised; had he been coached, or had he agreed with other witnesses about their depositions? No.

Another person down in the ditch was John Syward of Conway, perhaps a lower-level official, for that morning in response to the constable's summons, while walking over the drawbridge he saw Roger on the rocks below.[9] Cicon ordered him too to notify the coroners.[10] Syward returned to the ditch with coroners, scribe, and jury; by then, many others had gathered round the body. To Griffin's description, Syward added that Roger was stone-cold (*frigidus ut lapis*), his limbs stiff as a dry stick (*ut lingnum aridum*). Among the jurors was Simon of Flint.[11] He claims to have been drafted (*assumptus*) for jury duty at the clamor of Roger's mother (*ad clamorem matris*). In the ditch before prime, he found the body bespattered with dirt and dross. He tried to straighten the bent leg but gave up, fearing to break the sinews. The jury then moved away to complete their report (back up to the bridge, says Simon of Flint; still in the ditch, Syward reports).

Gervase testified that he learned of his son's death from the constable, who met the cook as he was returning to the castle. Cicon refused his request to remove his son's body, since the coroners had not yet arrived. At the ditch, Gervase saw the dead boy lying on his side, unclothed. Conway's bailiffs asked him for sureties or pledges because of the death, but Gervase couldn't recall whether he provided them. After the coroners' arrival, he left his son's body since he'd heard that his wife, hearing of Roger's death, was nearly out of her senses (*quasi extra sensum suum*); he went to control (*regendam*) and console her. Dionysia was being restrained by neighbors lest she throw herself into the ditch with her son. Gervase says very little else about his encounter with his son's body. Dionysia testified that she'd been thrown into this frenzy when (at daylight) gatekeeper Griffin came to the house asking where Roger was; Dionysia didn't know.[12] When John told her that he lay dead in the castle ditch she collapsed to the ground in grief, nearly out of her mind (*esset quasi extra mentem suam*); her neighbors took, restrained, and bound her (*capta ligata et retenta*).

Richard of Newcastle, priest of Conway church, also witnessed the scene at Roger's body.[13] He testified that, on that morning, before prime and after sunrise, leaving the church after Matins and heading for the castle, he saw Roger in the ditch. He named the royal coroners Stephen de Gamowe and Robert Rossel of Flint, the only time this latter individual appears. Several others were present, including John Syward, in the ditch; on the bridge were vicar Simon, John de Havering, and William Cicon, "knights," Thomas of Cambridge, "clerk and royal counselor"; and Hugh of Leominster, "clerk and chamberlain of the Prince of Wales at Chester."[14] Many of these eminent folk had gathered at Conway for John of St. John's memorial service.[15] Though Richard went into the ditch he didn't examine Roger, accepting the general opinion that the boy was dead—everyone who touched him said so. John de Boys, seneschal whose household had once included Roger's mother Dionysia, testified that just after sunrise he'd heard (along with Cicon and the vicar) Griffin relate Nicholas de Havering's report about an infant who "lay dead in the ditch."[16] Boys went down with Griffin and others. The jury and coroners of the Prince of Wales "now king of England" arrived, whom Boys assisted. Finding that Roger was dead, Boys, the coroners and jury left the body in place, withdrew a bit, and began writing up their report.

The Parents' Explanation of the Accident

Gervase testified that he went to vigils for Gerard de Pyneye, the constable's servant, and Cecilia, maid to the constable's wife, around sunset, leaving his wife and Wenthliana (a castle servant) in the house, along with the three children: Agnes and Ysolda, then about three and five; the boy was bound (*ligatum*) into his cradle, as infants usually were.[17] About a (walk of an English) league later, the two women came into church. Dionysia, he claimed, left her daughters sleeping in one bed, Roger asleep in his cradle. Closing the door as they set out for church, the women didn't secure it with a bar (or bolt), or any other fastener because there was none on the outside of the door, and because the church was a stone's throw from the house. Although there was a bolt or bar (*barra*) on the inside of the door, the girls did not bolt it. The two women maintained a vigil in the church the whole night.

After Gervase had been in church for (a walk of) four English leagues, he returned to the house and found the door open, his daughters asleep, but not Roger; his bindings and clothing were in his cradle. Gervase searched in the neighborhood, particularly where master Thomas the *medicus* lived, and William Godeswey. They had been asleep a good hour, and knew nothing of Roger. Then, assuming that some other neighbors had taken Roger in, he returned to church, where he told his wife that Roger was not in the house; she replied that she would not leave the church all night.[18] Gervase remained in church until about midnight, when, being disturbed (*turbatus*) by Roger's disappearance, he took a light and went back home; as before, he wasn't there. Having looked in the neighborhood again, he returned to church; since it was so late, he hadn't awakened any neighbors. After sunrise, as Gervase was returning to the castle, constable Cicon hastened up and asked where he'd been that night. To the reply that he'd been at vigils, the constable retorted that he'd maintained a bad vigil as far as caring for his son, who was dead in the ditch.[19]

Gervase believed that Roger unwrapped himself in his cradle, but he didn't know if he'd done this at other times, since he didn't live continuously with his wife, but in the castle. Finding no one in the house but his sleeping sisters, Gervase postulated that Roger opened the unsecured door and took his usual path toward the castle. He fell into the ditch on a dark night; Gervase remembered this, because he'd used a candle when searching the streets for his son. The commissioners then asked a question suggested by another witness (Syward; see below): was he or his wife drunk that evening? No, replied Gervase. There was another question not put to other witnesses in quite this form: in the town of Conway, are there (*sunt*) any sorceresses (*mulieres sortilege*) by whose machinations he believed his son could have been carried into the ditch and/or (*vel*) killed? No. How did it happen that his son was not smashed up (*totus confractus*) after falling from a high place? Gervase, who estimated the drop to be about thirty-three feet, said he didn't know. The notaries wrote that he responded to the last six interrogatories, in effect, as the first witness had done. (Among those six, there is a question about demonic invocation and superstition, but no mention of *mulieres sortilege*.)

Dionysia, the only woman testifying to the miracle, stated that her son, bound in his cradle as infants were (*infantile more ligato*), was lying near her daughters Ysolda six, and Agnes five.[20] Leaving the house with Wenthliana that evening, echoing her husband's testimony, Dionysia deposed that she drew the door closed but didn't secure it, because there was no way to do this from outside. Nor was the door secured inside, because her children were sleeping (and therefore couldn't bar the door). The two women went directly to vigils for Gerard and Cecilia, whom Dionysia had cared for during her fatal illness. After they had been there for about a walk of two English miles, her husband left to go home, carrying a burning candle (*candela*). Around one English mile's duration later, he returned and told her that he couldn't find Roger in the house or in the neighborhood.

He believed a neighbor had taken him in. Dionysia, who remarked that she would not leave the church (*inde non recesserat se*), believing the same, didn't worry about going to look for him (*non curavit ire ad querendum eum*). She remained in the church with Wenthliana and others, among whom, she believed, was her husband, for over an eight-mile walk. At first she didn't dare leave the church because of the darkness. Then, by moonlight, she, Gervase and Wenthliana walked home before dawn and before Matins were said. Roger wasn't there; the girls were sleeping, and in the cradle were the bands with which Roger had been tied (*involutus*). Because this made her so sad, and because of her earlier vigils, about a mile's walk before sunrise she fell into a deep sleep that lasted until daylight.[21]

Dionysia assumed that her son got out of his cradle, which was low (about a foot high), sitting on the ground; he opened the door, and, not seeing her or his father, who were in church, he went toward the castle and fell into the ditch, by as much after sunset as a three-mile walk.

The Community's Explanations

First finder Griffin set out his (and a commonly held) reconstruction of the events leading up to the child's accident which generally resembled the parents' version. He added that, some time ago, he saw a certain John de Brok, a castle servant, blown off the bridge by the wind into the ditch, where he died instantly. The bridge about which Griffin and the other witnesses testified was a wooden drawbridge, parts of which were still extant in the seventeenth century. When Edward I's master mason James of St. George built the walled town and castle of Conway (mainly through the period 1283–87) entry to the castle from the "town" side was by way of a long artificial masonry ramp that ended abruptly above a man-made ditch.[22] During the day this ditch was spanned by the bridge, the end of which rested on the top end of the inclined ramp. Raising the drawbridge left a nearly vertical drop, as witnesses testified, of almost thirty feet. Little Roger didn't fall from the bridge, but from the top of the ramp. Griffin stated that Dionysia's house was a stone's throw from the castle; another witness claimed that it was, likewise, a stone's throw from St. Mary's church where the vigils took place; presumably, then, the house was somewhere between church and castle. Since the church, still in use today, is about 200 feet from the castle, Roger may have toddled perhaps 100 feet before tumbling into thin air.

When vower Syward testified about the accident, he raised a striking possibility: he had heard that it was related by the boy's mother (*se audivisse referri a matre dicti R.*), and it was commonly believed in Conway, that the night before Roger was found dead, she was drunk (*ebria erat*).

According to this scenario, she undressed Roger and put him to bed. After the boy's father left the house and went to the castle, and while his mother was not paying attention, Roger followed after his father. Since every night the bridge was raised for castle security, and it was especially dark, everyone assumed that Roger fell in when trying to cross the bridge. It was also commonly believed that his mother went through town looking for him that night, and didn't find him. None of this accorded with the parents' testimony.

Next morning, Syward testified that Nicholas de Havering told him and others that before he went to bed in the castle he had heard, just once, a weak, childish (*parvilem*) voice, and he and others conjectured that it had been Roger's voice as he fell. Syward saw the child lying in the ditch for about a walk of five English leagues. After commenting, as had Griffin, that the other path into the ditch was dangerous and not near Roger's body, Syward noted that anyone falling from the "stone" rising above the ditch on the town side would have landed in the middle, which, he claimed, is where Roger was found; other witnesses put him more toward the "town" side.

The juror Simon of Flint, whose testimony resembled other witnesses' as to the circumstances of the accident, added an interesting point: that evening, he claimed, some women saw Roger toddling about after leaving his house, but it was said that they didn't concern themselves about it. The other Simon, vicar of St. Mary's, believed that Dionysia had remained in church all night; in the morning, returning home and realizing that Roger was gone, it was said that she looked for him throughout the town, but couldn't find him, another variance from her own statements.[23] Vicar Simon then retold the story that was generally accepted regarding Roger's ending up under the bridge. The vicar had himself measured the distance from bridge to ditch bottom with a cord, and found it to be twenty-eight feet. Simon also noted that there was no water, mud, or earth in the ditch, excavated into the rock during the castle's construction. Priest Richard related the commonly accepted circumstances behind the accident, adding that Roger was in his mother's house without any watching (*sine aliqua custodia*).

The Miracle in the Community

John Syward, as he and the community believed, was the miracle's catalyst. He claimed frequent pilgrimage to Cantilupe's tomb (where he'd heard of many of the saint's miracles) prior to the accident. After the coroners and jury withdrew to write their report, disregarding the coroners' prohibition against interfering with the corpse, with some effort Syward straightened out Roger's leg, succeeding where Simon the juror had failed. He then made the sign of the cross on Roger's forehead with a silver penny. He bent the coin and tied it round Roger's neck.[24] Syward prayed openly to God to resuscitate the child through Thomas's merits, vowing that if this happened Roger's mother would take her son to Thomas's tomb in Hereford cathedral, along with the penny. Then, just before going off to do other things, Syward testified, he forced open Roger's mouth and saw his tongue move. Seeing this he said (to bystanders) that he hoped through God and St. Thomas the child was alive. Opening the mouth further, he saw more movement. He told the coroners and jury that he had hopes for Roger's life. Clasping the boy to his chest, he carried him into Richard the Mercer's house, near the ditch. While holding Roger near the fire to warm him, he deposed, the child emitted some weak cries and opened and moved his eyes for a little while. Syward then gave him to his mother Dionysia. From later testimony it appears that after the child was taken to the mercer's nearby house and warmed, he was carried to Dionysia's house. Since Roger was so cold, Syward continued, having lain on the rocks unclothed through a frosty night, Dionysia put him next to her skin under her clothing. She immediately carried Roger, still under her clothing, to the church, followed by a joyful crowd, including Syward, coroners, jury, and many others.

In church where they were celebrating St. John's memorial service, Syward, while in front of the Cross, some time between Communion and the end of Mass noticed that Roger seemed to be more lively under Dionysia's garments. At this, he began loudly to sing *Te Deum Laudamus*, the others (among his group) following (the singing) because of the miracle. At the conclusion of Mass, Anian, bishop of Bangor (1268–1305/6), Abbot David of Maenan, John de Havering, William de Sutton, William de Cicon, Thomas de Cambridge, Thomas de Esthall, and Robert de Chishulle (not mentioned in the letter) who had earlier—in Syward's presence—seen Roger lying dead and then, evidently, walked on to church, had a letter patent attesting to the miracle written in the church, sealing it as Syward looked on.[25] This letter, Syward continued, was exhibited to the lords commissioners by Hereford's proctor as proof (*ad probationem*) of the miracle. Syward couldn't explain why Roger didn't break any limbs, which one would naturally expect. Everyone was amazed (*mirabantur*), but they believed (*credebant*) that a little dirt, about a bushel (a measure usually containing two measures of horse fodder, Syward explains) thrown out of one of the castle towers into the ditch where Roger was found, was soft enough to prevent fractures. Juror Simon of Flint found Roger lying on some broken rock, but, he claimed, between him and the rock was about a finger's thickness of hard dirt (*terra dura*) that had fallen from the bridge.

The vicar of St. Mary's, Simon, and Richard the priest were the only ecclesiastics to testify in 1307. In recognition of their rank, Simon was the very first witness to be called, and then Richard. Since the vicar left the scene before Syward's vow, he knew of the miracle only through hearsay. He was the only witness, however, to state that the coroners had prohibited anyone from entering the ditch, which, as we've seen, Syward blatantly ignored. According to Simon, the ditch, excavated into rock, contained neither water, nor mud, nor earth.[26] He'd heard that after Syward's vow the boy's right arm moved a bit, as well as his tongue. Simon was in church when Roger was brought in, and was a party to the sealed letter. The day of the revival, about nones, Simon spoke with Roger: the child didn't seem to be in pain, and could walk about his mother's house, though not as well as before the accident. The bruise on his face vanished completely some days later, and Roger was walking normally after three days. Priest Richard's version of the miracle was, also, based on hearsay; after observing the dead child, the next time he saw Roger was in church, where Richard joined in the *Te Deum*. He too is mentioned in the letter. Both vicar and priest noted that the child would have died from exposure alone, regardless of the fall itself. Presumably they had discussed their version of the story beforehand.

One of the witnesses to Syward's manipulations of Roger was the castle seneschal, John de Boys, whose testimony raised a serious issue.[27] The fourth to be called to give evidence after the vicar, priest, and Syward had testified, he related that when Griffin wanted to bring Roger out of the ditch, Boys told him to wait for the coroners. The child was put back onto the rocks, sharp as the toe of a man's shoe.[28] There was no chaff, earth, or dust there, just rock and frost. Boys claimed that in the crowd surrounding the boy down in the ditch there was a certain Lombard (*quidam Lumbardus*) whose name he didn't know. Boys heard the Lombard say that he would bend a *denarius* over Roger's body in honor of the Holy Cross (in St. Mary's church) by which God very often worked miracles in Conway, for the boy's resuscitation. Boys saw the Lombard make the sign of the cross with the coin on the child's forehead and with both hands bend the *denarius* in honor of the Holy Cross. Boys couldn't recall whether he hung the coin round Roger's neck. After that, because Roger showed no signs of life, John Syward—in Boys's hearing—said that he would bend another *denarius* over Roger's body for his resuscitation, in honor of St. Thomas of Hereford, for whom God also worked miracles. As the seneschal watched, Syward took a coin from his purse and made the sign of the cross on the boy's forehead. He bent the coin, but Boys couldn't recall whether he placed it round Roger's neck. The seneschal, assisting the coroners, noted that just as the *scriptor* William put pen to parchment to begin writing up the inquest on this death, Syward shouted that he had opened Roger's mouth and saw his tongue move a little (though Boys didn't witness this). Going to Syward who held the child in his arms, Boys had him put Roger back on the ground; this done, Boys saw the child's shoulder move. He told Syward to quickly take the child to his mother so that she could warm him; and John Syward did so.

Then Boys immediately went to the church where Anian was officiating at St. John's memorial service, and told John de Havering (who had observed the activity round the inert body) and many others in the church (about Roger's revival); there was great joy, with many in tears. Havering told Boys to wrap the child in moist linen by a fire, which Boys did. Boys must have left the church to carry out Havering's suggestion. After about an hour, around prime, Boys gave Roger to Dionysia,[29] who, followed by Boys and others who were weeping and crying out, took him to church (Mass not yet finished); there, before the Cross, the bells were rung and a *Te Deum* sung because of the miracle. Later that week John de Boys saw Roger walking, and as well as before.

When the papal judges asked him whether the miracle was ascribed to the Holy Cross, to which Roger had been first signed and vowed, Boys replied no, because after this, no signs of life appeared in the child; not until Syward signed and vowed Roger to St. Thomas were there indications of resuscitation. The rest of Boys's testimony is unexceptional, apart from his roughly dating the fatal accident of castle servant John de Brok, swept off the bridge by the wind—it happened some sixteen years earlier (i.e., 1291, when the castle and town walls were in final stages of construction). In addition, Boys claimed that it was miraculous that Roger wasn't killed, falling such a distance, however much he may have been clothed, and though the wind may have supported him.

After dismissing Boys, who as noted was the fourth to testify, in considering his statements the papal commissioners realized that some discrepancies in testimony needed to be examined. Thus, "on account of the [testimony of the] preceding witnesses," ex officio they recalled the first three witnesses, the vicar, the priest, and Syward. They were examined on three points (*punctis*): (1) whether, while he was dead, Roger had been signed, measured, or vowed to the Holy Cross or to any other saint apart from Thomas; (2) whether, in the place where Roger lay dead in the ditch, there was any dirt, dross, or wood present, and (3) whether the ground there was smooth or jagged.

The first to be recalled, John Syward, now (on cross-examination, as it were) came clean: after he'd bent the coin and hung it round Roger's neck, for *maiorem gratiam* (greater grace, favor, or mercy) he measured him with a string to the Holy Cross through which God did many miracles in

Conway church.[30] He didn't think anyone else measured him to the Cross or Thomas or any other saint. He didn't mention a "Lombard" at all. Because the tongue moved after he'd vowed Roger to Thomas, he attributed the miracle to him and not the Cross. The measuring, then, occurring after signs of life appeared, was for insurance or "greater mercy." More than a hundred people were there when he measured the boy, but he didn't know whether everyone saw the measurement; many could have seen it. As for the ditch, he said it was as he'd deposed earlier: between the rock and Roger there was soft dust/ashes (*pulverem mollem*) thrown from a castle tower. To the third point he replied that the surface under Roger was flat, though there were sharp rocks about three feet (from the body).

When reexamined, vicar Simon now stated that he'd heard it said by some of his parishioners, whose names he can't recall, that after Syward signed Roger with the coin to the honor of God and St. Thomas, the boy was measured to the Holy Cross by which God worked miracles. He didn't know by whom, or whether before or after the resuscitation; but after the publication of the miracle, he hadn't heard it ascribed to the Holy Cross, but to St. Thomas. As to the second point, he said that it seemed to him, and he didn't vary from his deposition of yesterday (though clearly he did), that there was some hard sandy soil, he didn't know how thick, on the ground where the body lay; he believed that the dirt had come from the shoes of people crossing the bridge. On the third point, he hadn't gone into the ditch, but looking from the bridge it seemed that Roger lay on a surface not entirely flat, nor entirely rocky.

Finally, recalling the priest Richard of Newcastle, the papal commission now learned that Richard had heard from trustworthy persons of Conway, especially John Syward and Roger's parents, that he had been measured— he didn't know by whom—to the Holy Cross by which God worked miracles in the church. If Syward himself had measured Roger, presumably the priest would have known this, if Syward was his source of information. Before the measuring, however, he'd been signed with a *denarius*, after which the tongue was seen to move, and the miracle was ascribed to Thomas "and not to the Holy Cross." On the second point he believed that between the rock and the body there was some hard dirt (*terra dura*) that had fallen from the bridge in about the amount one could hold in an ordinary hood; he saw this but hadn't touched the dirt. The surface of the ditch bottom was level, though there were broken rocks about two feet from the boy.

When directly questioned on these points, all three of these witnesses backtracked and revealed what they had suppressed in earlier testimony, namely, that there was possibly a rival supernatural power at work in Roger's resuscitation, about which there was significant confusion in the testimony. Another "new" possibility was that the boy's fall may have been cushioned by material that had collected in the ditch. Subsequently all witnesses were asked about these points, added to the list of interrogatories that scripted the proceedings.

The sixth witness, gatekeeper Griffin, testified that Syward and "a certain Lombard" with about a hundred other people loudly invoked Thomas of Hereford to resuscitate Roger. It's unclear to whom the plural verb refers; Griffin probably meant that both Syward and the Lombard made vows though, as we have seen, the Lombard did not call on St. Thomas. He's the only other witness to mention the Lombard. After Syward signed with the coin and saw the tongue move, Griffin stated, he (Syward) then measured Roger to the Holy Cross. As to whether the miracle was ascribed to the Holy Cross to which Roger had been measured and then carried, Griffin replied no, but to St. Thomas. First the boy had been signed with the *denarius* while Thomas's name was invoked; then he'd been measured to the Holy Cross prior to the movement of the tongue. Here Griffin contradicts himself on the sequence of events. Griffin's testimony generally confirms Syward's on the measuring, as on the matter of the ditch itself. The place where Roger lay wasn't totally flat: the boy's head was somewhat higher than his feet, and between his body and the stone bottom of the ditch there was some rough earth that had fallen from the bridge, about two fingers thick. Griffin also stated that he put a little clean dirt and some soiled straw that he'd found nearby, under Roger when he put him back down. This suggests that the ditch was littered with all sorts of debris, which one would expect since the castle's construction had been completed more than eleven years earlier.[31] The gatekeeper testified that, learning of Roger's recovery and reexamining the boy, the coroners and jury joyfully dispersed, lauding the miracle. They took Roger to his mother in Richard the Mercer's house (*reddiderunt matri sue in domo Ricardi*), near the ditch. There is confusion here. Why not take the child to his mother's home? She herself testified (below) that she was in her own house when Roger was brought in. Griffin continued: Dionysia warmed Roger with her bare skin and the fire, carried him before terce to church and put him "before the cross" (*ante crucem*); bells were rung and there was singing (Griffin didn't know what was being sung). Four or five days later he saw Roger walking, but he didn't seem fully recovered for another fifteen days.

Griffin could not explain why Roger's body wasn't smashed up (*confractus*) after such a fall. He admitted that there was a path that many children used during the day when they went to beg alms from castle residents. By night, however, it was dangerous; Roger would have needed great care in going into the ditch before he would end up where he was found; anyway, the path wasn't near the place where Roger lay. (Priest Richard claimed that it was eighty feet from the body.)

Simon of Flint, deliberating with his fellow-jurors on the bridge, saw Syward sign with a coin, bend it, and put it round the child's neck while loudly praying to Cantilupe. After the tongue moved and the coroners withdrew, Simon went off on business to distant places. Returning three days later, he found Roger alive and as well as before the accident. Simon complicates his own testimony, however, in responding to the now-standard question, whether Roger was measured, signed, or vowed by anyone to the Holy Cross or any saint other than Thomas: he'd heard that Roger's mother had measured him to the Holy Cross after signs of life had appeared.[32] Still, he attributed the miracle to Thomas since life first reappeared after the signing. Nevertheless, we now have a "Lombard," Syward, unknown person(s), and Dionysia as the measurer.

Gervase, having viewed his son's body, didn't see Roger again, he testified, until he was carried into the church. That suggests that he'd left Dionysia, having "consoled" her, and gone to church. He'd heard that in his absence Roger was signed to Cantilupe, measured to the Holy Cross, and then brought, alive, to the church and put before the Cross while Anian celebrated Mass. In naming others in the church, Gervase added one more clerk of the Prince of Wales, William de Blibury.[33] On the advice of John de Havering, Gervase added, the miracle was confirmed in a letter with pendant seals. His wife testified that after she had been in her house (not Richard the Mercer's) until about the third hour, Roger was carried in; he seemed dead, because she felt no breath even though she put her tongue in his mouth; it was so cold that she couldn't keep her tongue there. Cutting the upper part of her clothing down to the belt, she put him to her bosom to warm him (*ad calefaciendum*). After holding him thus for a while, she carried him next to her bosom into the church and sat with him in front of the Cross, among many bystanders—more than 200, she believes. After Bishop Anian finished Mass, he came and made the sign of the cross with his thumb on Roger's forehead. The child looked at him in terror and Dionysia felt him move one elbow and his heart beat very quickly. She shouted out, fearing that on account of the (rapid) heartbeat he would die again (*iterum deberet mori*). But, seeing that he remained alive, she praised God and sweet St. Thomas of Hereford, thanking them, as did the bystanders. She'd heard that John Syward measured Roger to St. Thomas, and after the measuring or bending of a coin over him, signs of life appeared. She hadn't heard that he'd been measured or vowed to the Holy Cross or any other saint. She doesn't mention that she herself measured Roger, as juror Simon claimed.

When Roger was brought home, Dionysia stated, his only injury was a small lesion on the right side of the jaw, and a little bruising on the outer part of the hip. During the week Roger developed a painful swelling in his right eye which obstructed vision, and a seepage from his right jaw, on which he was said to have been lying when found. Other witnesses specified the left side, a common species of memory slip in trial testimony. The day he revived Roger could stand, and that evening Dionysia suckled him; he was walking within three days, though it took three weeks for him to recover his pristine health.

Dionysia claimed that, even before the miracle, she and her husband were especially devoted to Cantilupe: while she was pregnant with Roger she went barefoot—her husband was shod—to Thomas's tomb some eighty-five miles from Conway to pray that he would help her and her infant. Other than that, she and Gervase were not exceptional in matters of faith, when compared with their neighbors; though poor, they led a good life. Again, as in her husband's testimony, she was asked in particular whether there were any sorcerers or witches (*sorciarie* [sic] or *malefice*) in Conway parish, by whose *maleficiis* she believed Roger to have been borne into the ditch and/or (*vel*) killed; no. They didn't ask if she had been drunk that night, nor do the commissioners seem to have asked this question of any witnesses apart from Gervase.

Because of the miracle, within three weeks she and her husband took Roger to Thomas's tomb, out of devotion and to publicize the miracle. They were accompanied by William de Cicon, John de Havering, Thomas of Cambridge, Hugh of Leominster, and several others. After a week's stay in Hereford the party began the return trip; before they had gone forty miles Roger's eye and jaw were perfectly healed (*perfecte curatus*).

Evidently requiring verification on some points, on the same day (October 28, 1307) the papal commissaries recalled Gervase, whose words were the last to be recorded in this miracle-testimony. The same question was put to him: before the miracle, did he or Dionysia have any doubts as to the faith, or excellence of life beyond their neighbors, or greater devotion to Thomas than to other saints? Gervase replied that he had no hesitations as to the faith, that he led a good life but no more excellent than others' lives, and that he and his wife were more devoted to Thomas than to other saints. Prior to the miracle the two of them had gone thrice on pilgrimage to Thomas's tomb some ninety-three leagues from Conway. Finally, Gervase noted that when, within a month of the miracle, they took Roger to Hereford, they were accompanied by the same four men named by Dionysia, whom Gervase says are of the council (*de consilio*) of the prince, now king of England, and many others.[34]

The Miracle in the Letter

Because it was composed, witnessed, and sealed on the day of the event, then deposited at Hereford cathedral a few weeks later, the letter may represent Roger's story before it could be embellished or distorted through reinterpretation and elaboration by the Conway community. On the other hand, it contained its own species of departure from the oral testimony of 1307.

On October 22, 1307, the proctor of Hereford cathedral (presenting the case for Cantilupe) interrupted the commissioners' hearing of a miracle about a mute boy to introduce the Conway witnesses who, he stated, had come a long way and could tarry no longer in the city; at the same time he placed the letter in evidence. Many of its red wax seals were no longer decipherable. However, several individuals, present in the church that September morning, were named in its text. These included Bishop Anian and David whose seal identified him as abbot of Aberconway.[35] Listed separately as witnesses to the miracle, also attending St. John's service that morning, were three knights and three clerics, members of the council and household of Edward Prince of Wales;[36] and Simon of Watford, vicar of Conway church, along with three Conway priests.[37] As we have seen, the vicar and one of his priests also testified at Hereford (on October 23) four years later.

The sealed letter, copied into the canonization record, is straightforward: "On 6 September 1303 during the first hour of the night, at Conway castle in Wales Roger, an infant two years and three months old, son of castle servant Gervase and his wife Dionysia, fell from the castle bridge into a ditch twenty-eight feet below, and lay there on the hard rock, unclothed, until around the middle of prime next morning." The letter here is at odds with those witnesses who testified that the ditch bottom was not bare rock. "The coroners found that the boy was dead. Afterwards, a Conway resident, John Syward, took a *denarius* from his wallet; with this he made the sign of the cross on the infant's forehead and chest, vowing to God and Thomas Cantilupe that, if the boy revived, he [Roger] would visit Thomas's tomb." Syward makes no mention of signing Roger on his chest, nor is there any reference to measurement in the letter. "As if in the blink of an eye (*quasi in ictu oculi*) the boy revived and was immediately (*statim*) restored to his mother, who gave him her breast, which he sucked." Roger did not recover immediately, as is evident from the testimony of several witnesses, nor was he immediately restored to his mother, nor did she suckle him until that evening. "After very little time (*pusillum*), the boy was joyous and happy, without any wounds on his body." As Dionysia and others remarked, recovery took time, and the wounds did not heal for some three weeks. "The people and clergy took up the boy and went into [St. Mary's] church singing *Te Deum Laudamus*, in the presence of bishop Anian and Abbot David, who were there at that time celebrating John of St. John's memorial service." The letter then lists the witnesses "of this miracle," *huius miraculi sunt testes*. In addition, it concludes, over 200 men and women were present, who had seen the boy resuscitated from death. "As perpetual memorial of the miracle the bishop and abbot append their seals to this writing, along with seals of the knights, clerics, and priests [all named in the letter]. Dated at Conway, 7 September in the year aforesaid."

This letter, written in the church on the very morning of the reputed miracle, is at odds with sworn testimony presented four years later. How to account for such variance? Since the bishop and abbot were the senior ecclesiastics present, we may assume that they were responsible for most of its content. Knowing how miracles are supposed to be described, they created their own interpretation of events: they emphasize the hardness of the rock; the more elaborate signing by Syward; the cure happening "in the blink of an eye," a topos in descriptions of miracles attributed to countless other saints; the lack of wounds; and Roger's immediate recovery and return to health. No witness of 1307 made such claims; even the vicar, a party to the letter of 1303, did not claim instantaneity of cure in 1307. In this instance, then, documentary "evidence," composed immediately following the accident, provides an abbreviated and skewed account when compared with later testimony. Here the mid-thirteenth century dictum of Innocent IV rings true: it was unnatural "to trust the skin of a dead animal more than the voice of a living man."[38]

Dionysia's Negligence?

John de Griffin, the first finder, was expected to provide sureties, which is the normal routine; but Gervase also was also asked to do so. This suggests that negligence may have been imputed to the father, though if anyone was negligent, it was Dionysia. A cloud of contradictory testimony surrounds her. To begin with, she had cared for the woman in her last illness whose vigils were being observed, so it may be assumed that her desire to participate in the nightlong service was particularly strong. When Gervase told her that Roger was missing, she replied that she was not going to leave the church that night; and Gervase took up the search without her assistance. In fact, she seems to have conflated his first search and his second, when he took a candle with him. In the morning she claimed to have been so saddened by her son's disappearance and by the exhaustive vigils, that she went to sleep. When the news was brought to her, she collapsed, seems to have become suicidal, and was restrained by neighbors; she never did go to the site of her son's accident. The first time she saw him that day, he was brought in either to the mercer's house or to her own. In any case, she does not seem to have gone looking for him that morning, as the vicar stated; and one wonders how she raised a hue and cry as the juror claimed.

Dionysia's house was left unlocked when she and her friend went to church; presumably, she couldn't expect her sleeping children to bar the door from the inside, and the church was only a "stone's throw" away— no need to worry. And yet, when Griffin took her the news in the morning, he presented it in an accusatory manner: not "your son is dead," but "where is your son?"—Griffin knowing full well where Roger was. And the constable's comment to Gervase is also revealing: Roger's father had "vigilled badly as to taking care of his son" who lay dead in a ditch. Nicholas the priest also commented that the child had been left "without any[one] watching" him.

Perhaps the most ominous suggestion of negligence that might have led to the real death of Roger was Syward's accusation that Dionysia was drunk; so much so, apparently, that she didn't notice her son wandering out the door. Vigils were notorious occasions for unchurchly behavior even before St. Augustine's complaints about them. If she were inebriated, her desire to sleep it off at dawn is understandable; her reaction is unusual unless she truly believed that her son was being cared for in a neighbor's house. Syward also claimed that she went looking for Roger that night but could not find him, but if as she claimed she remained in church all night, this was impossible. If, on the other hand, Roger had slipped out of the house before she went to church, she may have lied about leaving him in his cradle. She would be the only one to know this, as Gervase had already left. The only other person who would know, her friend Wenthliana, did not testify at Hereford, although she was still living at that time.

Plenty of evidence shows that most medieval parents were much like modern ones when it came to loving and caring for their children, but as is the case today, sometimes children were victims of parental abuse, such as the boy, aged ten, who was whipped to death by his enraged mother; or the widow whose neighbors prevented her suicide, after which she went home and murdered her two sons and daughter; or the woman who killed her two-year-old daughter with a knife, then forced another daughter (age four) to sit in the flames of the hearth.[39] Apart from such extreme cases, parental negligence also arose, often—as in Roger's case—because of absent parents: when the parents and household went to church leaving behind their two-year-old, he toddled out the door and down a well, in spite of an older sister who was supposed to be watching him; while Edith attended morning services, her infant daughter died in her cradle, a victim of fire; and while another set of parents were away at church one evening, an infant was burned in the hearth.[40]

The chronicler of this last case reported other examples of parental negligence, remedied through the intercession of the defunct King Henry VI. For instance, the parents of the child just mentioned, who fell backwards onto the hearth, had left him alone, "negligently"; another infant, not yet two, was "neglected," while his mother went out to bleach her linen in the sun; he fell into the family cess pit. A Kent girl was flattened when run over by a cart "negligently" operated; and another infant, "neglected" by his watchers, fell down a well.[41] Prefacing another such story, the writer waxes rhetorical: "Where anything negligent is done regarding infants, much adverse fortune will follow; permitting an infant to have its freedom so often turns laughter into tears. . ." and so on.[42]

Suggestions of parental negligence in Roger's case, and especially his mother's, came pointedly from the "castle" folk: the constable and gatekeeper told them of the accident with overtones of accusation; and fellow-townsman Syward's claim that Dionysia was drunk was a seriously damning charge. The two clerics Simon and Richard tended not to impute negligence so clearly, though Richard did note that the child was untended. What is more interesting is the reluctance of the papal commissioners to probe more deeply into the accusation of drunkenness; they seem deliberately to have skirted this issue, believing perhaps that this might have negative implications for Cantilupe's canonization. Another peculiarity is the original suppression of any mention of the miraculous powers of the Holy Cross of Conway church, which (Syward's testimony apart) one would have expected vicar Simon and priest Richard eagerly to have espoused; the miraculous object was, after all, in their own church. Yet they did not, and only revealed this competing supernatural power under direct questioning by the pope's judges. Perhaps they were reluctant to buck what appears to have been the consensus of a community to which they ministered. Whatever the reasons, the two clerics did not at first fulfill their oaths (taken by all the witnesses) to tell "the whole truth."

The Conway case demonstrates once again the fragility and mutability of human perception and memory. Though their reasons for testifying as they did may be out of reach, certainly the witnesses' variant readings of a not so distant past emphasize the limits of historians' use of trial testimony. This is in addition to the now widely recognized scripting of testimony via interrogatories, as well as the barrier of notarial translation of nuanced vernaculars into blunted, formulaic, clerical Latin. Roger's case also presents overtones of collusion between witnesses (vicar and priest, father and mother) in testimony, another de-"objectifying" mechanism.[43] This too limits our reconstruction of a single past, transposing events into multiple pasts. The apparently calm, rational atmosphere of the judicial tribunal where truths are supposed to be revealed is an inviting, useful but unstable forum for the exercise of micro-history, a genre which attracts pointed and often appropriate criticism.[44]

Roger landed literally and figuratively in the overlap of two spheres of contemporary life, church and castle; when his parents, being pulled into church activities, left him alone he was drawn into that other context with which he was familiar, the castle. Dying in the latter context, he came fully to life in the former. Moreover, the hierarchies of each sphere are present in this narration: mayor/constable, seneschal, coroners, jurors, and bailiffs examining potential breaches of the law; and in the other sphere, we have seen supernatural forces expressed through a would-be saint, Thomas Cantilupe; a miracle-working object, the Holy Cross in the town's church; and the imputed powers of a bishop whose touch roused Roger fully and finally to life. Community bonds are also manifested in the expectation that "neighbors" would take in a toddler wandering through town at night; perhaps the women who witnessed Roger walking toward the castle that evening didn't hinder him because of this expectation—someone, surely, would care for him before he harmed himself. In the end, as we have seen, church, community and castle came together in celebrating the child's revival, a miracle attested in a letter composed in St. Mary's church and sealed by representatives of the secular and ecclesiastical hierarchies.

As for the results of this jumble of mixed memories and conflicting statements elicited in 1307, the papal commission's transcripts, boiled down to manageable size at the papal curia, ended up under further scrutiny between 1318 and 1320.[45] In this reexamination, only two issues were raised about Roger's miracle: why the body wasn't totally mangled after the fall (because of its departure from a perpendicular line of descent and its lightness of weight—good Aristotelian thinking). The fact that witnesses disagreed about the softness or otherwise of the ditch bottom didn't vitiate the miracle "as to the substance of the thing that happened" *quantum ad substanciam facti quod evenit*.[46] Second, if the body was unmarked, what killed him? (Internal injuries; and perhaps movement of the wind and fear while falling). These points having been satisfactorily addressed, the matter then passed into papal hands. The case suggests what probably lies behind many other miracles that ended up as a few lines in papal canonization bulls. John XXII's bull of April 1320, in a brief statement about Roger's miracle, notes that the boy was revived after being measured; there is no mention of coin-bending.[47]

In the midst of so much confusing testimony, perhaps the last word should come from the victim himself, whose post-miracle career can be traced for at least a few more years.[48] On October 23, 1307 Roger was brought before the papal commissioners and was asked, without an oath— on account of his tender age, as he was under seven—whether he knew anything about his case, his death, or the miracle. He said no; nevertheless, he added that he no longer wanted to go up to the bridge.[49]

Notes

1. The process is found in Vatican MS Vat Lat 4015, fols. 188r–203v collated with MS Vat Lat 4017; the letter on fols. 188v–89r, and Oxford MS, Exeter

College 158 fol. 38v. Unless specified otherwise, all folio references below are to MS 4015.

2. MS 4015 was used by Robert Bartlett in examining another of Cantilupe's purported miracles in *The Hanged Man: A Story of Miracle, Memory and Colonialism in the Middle Ages* (Princeton: Princeton University Press, 2004). The papal committee and their fates post-1307 on pp. 126–38. Michael Goodich also discusses the Hereford miracles in the present publication.

3. Ian Soulsby, *The Towns of Medieval Wales* (Chichester, UK: Phillimore, 1983), p. 114.

4. Griffin was witness number 6, fols. 198v–200r. Perhaps Griffin specified "English" leagues to distinguish them from "local" leagues, or the notaries, their documents destined for the papal curia, thought it a helpful qualification. The commissioners also asked Griffin how long he believed that Roger had been dead, thus distinguishing the time he *saw* the boy dead, from the total time that Griffin believed he'd been dead. In reply Griffin explained how (he assumed) Roger fell into the ditch the night before.

5. William de Cycon (Cicon) was one of Edward I's Savoyard household knights, Michael Prestwich, *Edward I* (London: Methuen, 1988), p. 209, 215. Vicar Simon's testimony in MS Vat Lat 4015, fols. 189r–91v; he was the first witness to give testimony.

6. Valerie J. Flint discusses the Cantilupe miracles, coroners, and this case in "The Saint and the Operation of the Law: Reflections upon the Miracles of St. Thomas Cantilupe" in *Belief and Culture in the Middle Ages*, ed. Richard Gameson and Henrietta Leyser (Oxford: Oxford University Press, 2001), pp. 342–57. Errors in detail—the ditch never was intended to be a water-filled moat; Syward vowed Roger to make a pilgrimage, not himself; the coroner's name given as Ganvy is probably something like Gannowe—are perhaps due to the faulty *Acta Sanctorum* printed version.

7. On "first finders" see Ronald Finucane, *The Rescue of the Innocents: Endangered Children in Medieval Miracles* (1997; repr. New York: St. Martin's Press, 2000), p. 119.

8. MS Vat Lat 4015, Fol. 191r.

9. He was the third of the eight witnesses to be examined, MS Vat Lat 4015, fols. 192v–94r and 196r–v.

10. As we have seen, the constable also sent the first finder, John de Griffin, on this mission; Griffin and Syward would presumably have had to seek out the coroners and jury living at various places in Conway.

11. MS Vat Lat 4015, fols. 197r–98v.

12. MS Vat Lat 4015, fols. 201v–203v; she was the eighth and final witness.

13. MS Vat Lat 4015, fols. 191v–92v; this passage is lacking in Vat Lat 4017; he was witness number 2.

14. For the chamberlain of the Prince of Wales at Chester, and other details of local administration and personnel, see Thomas F. Tout, *Chapters in the Administrative History of Mediaeval England*, vol. II (Manchester: Manchester University Press, 1937–67), pp. 169–73. Edward I appointed Havering justiciar for north and south Wales following the Welsh wars (1280s), and overseer of military matters in Merionethshire in the revolt of the 1290s,

during which Conway often served as the king's headquarters; David Walker, *Medieval Wales* (Cambridge: Cambridge University Press, 1990), pp. 150, 154–56. He was the first layman listed (after the bishop and abbot) in the 1303 letter taken to Hereford.

15. John of St. John had died the year before; he was a trusted lieutenant of Edward I in Gascony and Scotland.

16. Another version of Nicholas's message was merely that he'd heard a child's cry that evening; now, he is reported as saying that a child was lying dead in the ditch.

17. MS Vat Lat 4015, fols. 200r–201v, 203c. Gervase was witness number 7, recalled after his wife testified.

18. MS Vat Lat 4015, fol. 200v, MS Vat Lat 4017, fol. 75v: *respondit quod non exiret ecclesiam de tota nocte.*

19. MS Vat Lat 4015, fols. 200c–201r, *male vigilaverat circa custodiam dicti Rogeri filii sui. . .*

20. MS Vat Lat 4015, fols. 201v–203v; parents assign them different ages.

21. MS Vat Lat 4015, fol. 202r: *et cum propter predictam esset dolore nimio et propter vigilias precedents sompno gravata dormivit usque ad diem claram. . .*

22. Arnold J. Taylor, *Conwy Castle* (Cadw: Welsh Historic Monuments, rev. ed. 1986), pp. 2–4, 14.

23. MS Vat Lat 4015, fol. 189v.

24. Bending and dedicating a particular coin to a saint was a very common curative practice; Ronald Finucane, *Miracles and pilgrims: Popular Beliefs in Medieval England* (London: Dent & Sons, 1977, repr. New York: St. Martin's Press, 1995, 2004), pp. 94–95.

25. Fol. 193v, *fecerunt in dicta ecclesia scriberi quamdam litteram. . .in attestationem. . .*However, there is no evidence that the bishop or the abbot witnessed Roger's "dead" state.

26. MS Vat Lat 4015, fol. 190v.

27. MS Vat Lat 4015, fols. 194r–96r, on October 25, 1307; Boys was witness number 4.

28. MS Vat Lat 4015, 194v, 4017, 67v, a reference presumably to the elongated footwear of fashionable dandies.

29. Evidently Boys took Roger from Dionysia, carried out de Havering's instructions, and then returned the child to his mother.

30. On the "measuring" technique see Finucane, *Miracles and Pilgrims*, pp. 95–96.

31. It also suggests that even in an urban environment, and under the very eyes of the mayor, manipulation of a presumably dead body could take place; one would expect this in a rural setting where coroners might take days or longer to reach such victims.

32. MS Vat Lat 4015, fol. 198r.

33. For William of Blyborough, keeper of the Prince's wardrobe then chancellor, see Tout, *Chapters* II, 166–68, 170–71. He is not mentioned in the letter or elsewhere in the process; he, Thomas of Cambridge, and John de Havering were named local auditors in Wales on May 1, 1303 and were at work from June 24 to September 4; three days later, all three were in Conway church when Roger was brought in: Tout, *Chapters*, II, 179.

34. For Hugh of Leominster, see Tout, *Chapters*, IV, 71, VI, 61. Edward I died July 7, 1307.

35. David's seal may still have read "Aberconway" although Edward I had already in 1284 shifted the site of this Cistercian abbey from Conway to Maenan; the letter's text, identifying him as abbot of Maenan, is more "accurate" than its seal.

36. John de Havering, William de Sutton, and William de Cicon. The clerics were Thomas of Cambridge, Hugh of Leominster, and Thomas of Esthall; see Tout, *Chapters* vol. II, p. 171: "Altogether there were fourteen clerks acting [for the Prince of Wales] at one time."

37. Richard of Newcastle, Roger of Bruges, and Thomas of Dinbey, all residents of Conway.

38. Quoted in James A. Brundage, *Medieval Canon Law* (London: Longman, 1995), p. 133.

39. Barbara Hanawalt, *Crime and Conflict in English Communities, 1300–1348* (Cambridge, MA: Harvard University Press, 1979), pp. 124, 147–48.

40. Nicholas Orme, *Medieval Children* (New Haven and London: Yale University Press, 2001), pp. 209–211.

41. Paul Grosjean, ed., *Henrici VI Angliae Regis Miracula Postuma* (Société des Bollandistes: Brussels, 1935), pp. 157, 194, 200, 215.

42. Translation in Finucane, *Rescue of the Innocents*, p. 39, from Grosjean, *Henrici VI*, 260. For further examples of parental negligence, Finucane, *Rescue*, pp. 40, 51, 115, 124–31 (which includes Roger of Conway's case), pp. 134–35, 144, 153.

43. For pertinent comments on these problems see Robert Swanson's essay in the present volume.

44. Elizabeth A. Clark, *History, Theory, Text: Historians and the Linguistic Turn* (Cambridge, MA: Harvard University Press, 2004), pp. 75–80; Georg G. Iggers, *Historiography in the Twentieth Century* (Hanover, NH: Wesleyan University Press, 1977), pp. 101–17; Sigurdur Gylfi Magnússon, "The Singularization of History: Social History and Microhistory Within the Postmodern State of Knowledge," *Journal of Social History* 36.3 (2003): pp. 701–35.

45. André Vauchez, *Sainthood in the Later Middle Ages*, trans. Jean Birrell (Cambridge, UK: Cambridge University Press, 1997), pp. 640–41, from BN MS 5373A; Bartlett, *Hanged Man*, pp. 121–22.

46. Exeter College MS 158, fols. 54v–55r; nor did confusion about Roger's lying on his right or left side affect the substance of the miracle.

47. Giusto Fontanini, *Codex constitutionum quas summi pontifices ediderunt in solemni canonizatione sanctorum a Johanne XV ad Benedictum XIII* (Rome: Ex typographia reverendae camerae apostolicae, 1729), p. 133.

48. See Finucane, *Miracles and Pilgrims*, p. 70 and *Rescue of the Innocents*, pp. 137–38; Bartlett, *Hanged Man*, p. 134.

49. Exeter College MS 158, fols. 191r–91v.

CHAPTER 6

A CASE OF DEMONIC POSSESSION IN FIFTEENTH-CENTURY BRITTANY: PERRIN HERVÉ AND THE NASCENT CULT OF VINCENT FERRER

Laura Ackerman Smoller

In the fall of 1453 in a small town in Brittany, a panel of three papal commissioners opened an inquest into the sanctity of Vincent Ferrer. Born in Valencia in 1350, the celebrated Dominican had devoted the final two decades of his life to a preaching tour that took him throughout most of western Europe, culminating in his death in the Breton city of Vannes in 1419.[1] His burial in the cathedral in Vannes touched off a wave of miraculous activity, leading to the opening of the canonization process in 1453. Among the 313 witnesses who testified in Brittany, more than a dozen told the story of the miraculous cure of a Vannes citizen named Perrin Hervé, nicknamed "Fatty" (*Grasset*). The gist of their tale was this: Several years after Vincent's death, Perrin had experienced what might today be called a psychotic break. To many observers in the fifteenth century, however, it appeared to be a case of demonic possession. One morning Perrin had gone out of his senses and had become violently agitated and verbally abusive to the point that it was necessary to physically restrain him. Nonetheless, after he was taken to Vincent Ferrer's tomb, where he quieted and rested a while, Perrin returned to his old self and never again suffered a similar episode. The cathedral clergy rang the bells as a sign of the miracle, and all who had seen what happened said Perrin had been cured miraculously through the intercession of Vincent Ferrer.

As Robert Bartlett has most recently and eloquently demonstrated, the materials generated at canonization inquests, such as that of Hereford Bishop Thomas de Cantilupe, can shed light not just on the deeds and virtues of the candidate for sainthood, but also on the lives and concerns of those persons who testified at the local inquest. In Bartlett's case study, nine witnesses told the story of the miraculous resurrection after hanging of one William Cragh, notorious criminal or hero of Welsh resistance, depending on one's perspective. Their words illuminate the political, social, legal, religious, and even medical milieu of the rough-and-tumble English-Welsh frontier in the early fourteenth century, even as they recount a miracle that helped to underscore the late bishop's reputation for sanctity.[2] What makes the case of William Cragh so compelling to Bartlett (and to numerous historians who have worked on this material)[3] is not simply the connection of the players involved to the grand events of Welsh resistance to English "colonialism," but rather that in this case one has nine witnesses to the same event. Through inconsistencies and cracks in their testimony, one begins to hear the voices and glimpse the preoccupations of persons who might ordinarily leave little or no trace in the written record.[4]

In the case of Vincent Ferrer's miraculous cure of Perrin Hervé, we have not nine but fourteen witnesses giving their version of the tale (figure 6.1). As with Bartlett's case of the hanged man, their stories—and the significant differences between their tales—open a window to the world of fifteenth-century Brittany. In particular, Perrin's tale reveals a complex web of social relationships in the ducal city of Vannes, giving voice, in some instances, to individuals passed over in other written records, and in other cases, putting human faces to the names of men who made a career overseeing the duchy's finances. In addition, the testimony about Perrin's healing points to the political capital to be gained by association with the holy, as well as to the efforts made by the fifteenth-century dukes of Brittany to add to their rule an aura of sacred legitimacy through their ties to Vincent Ferrer and other religious figures. The narratives of Perrin's cure also shed light on the shadowy period between the saint's death and his canonization, offering valuable insight into the ways in which miracles and their publication helped to bolster the nascent cult of Vincent Ferrer.[5] The promoters of Vincent's canonization clearly envisioned Perrin's miracle as playing a major role in that process. Their choice appears to be related as much to the fact that Perrin was well connected to ducal circles as it was to the striking and highly public nature of his infirmity. If, as Michael Goodich has suggested, canonization records frequently reveal a miraculous liberation from demonic possession at the start of a new cult, Perrin Hervé's cure appears to have marked that moment in the early veneration of Vincent Ferrer in Brittany.[6] Or, to speak more precisely, in

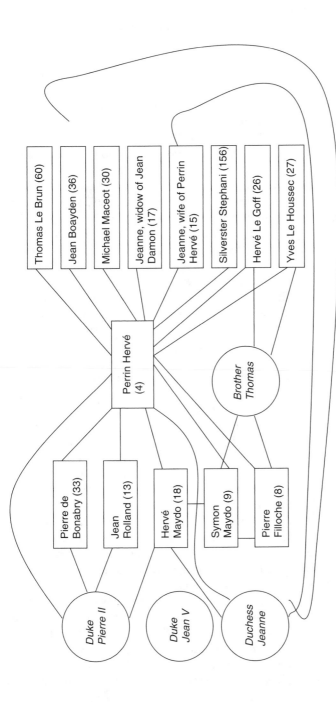

Figure 6.1 Names in rectangles are witnesses, followed by witness numbers. Names in circles and in italics are mentioned in the testimony but are not witnesses. Lines indicate connections mentioned in the testimony.

Perrin's case, the testimony reveals the organizers of the Brittany inquest attempting to position Perrin's cure as just that spectacular cult-starting miracle.

The story

As was only fitting, the commissioners at the Brittany inquest heard the story first from Perrin Hervé himself. Perrin's tale began, as he recalled it, around twenty-eight years ago, that is, some half a dozen years after the death of Vincent Ferrer. Like most witnesses, Perrin's sense of the passage of time was a little hazy; he gave his age as "fifty-seven or thereabouts," a figure more precise than many of those who testified could supply, preferring round multiples of five and ten. The time of year was more fixed in Perrin's mind, as were the day of the week and hour of the day. It was a Saturday, around Easter, and it was around eleven in the morning. Perrin was in the home of Pierre Filloche (Petrus Floch), of whom he was a dependent of sorts (*famulabatur*). Suddenly, there came over him "a certain infirmity in the head and other parts of his body" that immediately "rendered him out of his mind." Perrin began to run through the streets of the little town of Vannes as if he was in a fury, and it became "necessary to bind his hands with iron chains." It was the next day, Sunday, around the hour of vespers in Perrin's recollection, when "his wife, neighbors, and familiars" made a vow to Vincent Ferrer and brought Perrin to his tomb in the Vannes cathedral. There, he was placed on the holy preacher's tomb, with his head wrapped in Vincent's cape.

On Vincent's tomb, Perrin quieted and fell asleep, and in a dream he saw Vincent Ferrer standing before him. Speaking in the vernacular—an unusual concession for a man who preached always in his native Catalan and relied on the apostolic gift of tongues to make his sermons comprehensible to his audience—, Vincent told Perrin, "My son, you will soon be in good health." The notaries at the inquest made a point of rendering these words exactly as Perrin reported them, only afterwards offering a Latin translation. That was an unusual move also, since their standard practice was to translate everything each witness said into a third person, Latin reporting of the testimony. Like their witness, the notaries must have attached special significance to the saint's very words, delivered in Perrin's own French. Awaking from his sleep, Perrin found himself cured, and in a sign of thanksgiving for the miracle he had received, he left the iron chains and shackles that had bound his hands and feet there in the cathedral.[7]

Given the nature of Perrin's trouble, it was only reasonable to expect that other witnesses might be able to provide a fuller version of the story than the crazed and demented Perrin could supply. Such detail came first from Perrin's sometime patron Pierre Filloche. No more certain than Perrin Hervé himself about the date of the events he described, Pierre nonetheless painted a vivid portrait of Perrin, "lying on a pallet near the fire in the house where [Pierre Filloche] lived, tied up with ropes and towels, and invoking the demon and blaspheming God and the saints." Furthermore, Pierre added an incident to which Perrin Hervé had made no reference whatsoever. Namely, Pierre related that Perrin was first led to the Carmelite church of Our Lady of Bondon, near Vannes, where Perrin's behavior took a decided turn for the worse. At Bondon, Perrin "cried out horribly and more horribly." When Perrin was sprinkled with holy water, things disintegrated even more, and Perrin "spit at the image of the Blessed Mary and could not [stand to] hear anything said about God." Finally, one of the friars, whom Pierre Filloche believed was called Brother Thomas, told Perrin's handlers to take him to the tomb of Vincent Ferrer, where he was carried, bound in iron chains.

Again, Perrin slept at the tomb, although Pierre Filloche made no mention of the relic of Vincent's cape. Again, Perrin woke up cured, apparently, unaware of what had happened to him, for he asked bystanders "why he was thus tied and who had brought him there." Insisting that he had been healed through the merits of Master Vincent, Perrin asked the crowd, whose amazement surely now was growing, "Didn't you see Master Vincent talking with me just now?" And at that, Perrin left the cathedral in good health and never had a relapse of his problem, while the cathedral clergy rang the bells as a sign of the miracle.[8]

A third witness, Symon Maydo, also remembered the trip to the Carmelite church of Bondon and the efforts of the unfortunate Brother Thomas. As Symon told it, when Brother Thomas sprinkled Perrin with holy water—and here in the manuscript are five little v-like shapes, as if to indicate Symon's pantomiming of the friar's action—, Perrin again worsened significantly, now invoking the devil, spitting on the image of the Virgin, "and calling her a whore." Again, Thomas recommended a trip to Vincent's tomb, and, again, Perrin grew quiet and fell asleep when placed on the tomb. Just as before, Symon recalled Perrin's confused questions on his awakening and his assertion that he had seen and talked with Master Vincent. Like Pierre Filloche, Symon stressed that Perrin had never had a relapse and that the clergy had signified the miracle by a ringing of the cathedral bells.[9]

Other witnesses told essentially the same story, with some minor variations and elaborations. Jean Rolland, another witness of whom Perrin Hervé had once been a dependent (*familiaris*), was most struck by the violent nature of Perrin's "break." He remembered well seeing Perrin "invoking the demon, blaspheming God and the saints, trying to bite and hit everyone and to run everywhere." Although he did not mention the trip to the Carmelite church, Jean did remember Perrin's incubation and healing at Vincent's tomb. And he noted that this miracle had a wide currency in the city of Vannes.[10]

The testimony of Hervé Le Goff underscored Jean Rolland's sense of how violently out of control Perrin had become that memorable day. Hervé had been among the group who helped lead Perrin to the Carmelite church of Bondon and witnessed at first hand Perrin's extreme reaction to Brother Thomas's attempts to calm him. As Hervé recalled it, when holy water was sprinkled on Perrin, "he tried to bite. . .Brother Thomas." Hervé also emphasized the force it took to get Perrin at last to the tomb of Vincent Ferrer, noting that before his incubation in the Vannes cathedral, Perrin "scarcely could be detained by the witness speaking and the others who detained him." Finally, Hervé escorted the grateful *miraculé* back to Perrin's own house in the Vannes suburb of Notre-Dame du Mené (Beata Maria de Monte), where Perrin, perhaps fearing a repeat of the previous day's incidents, "made the sign of the cross."[11]

The testimony of Jeanne, Perrin Hervé's wife, gives us only the tiniest of glimpses into that home. She well remembered Perrin's break and the way in which "for that day and the following night he was kept by friends and neighbors, with iron shackles." (Given the violent outburst described by other witnesses, one wonders if the neighbors feared for Jeanne's safety.) Like her husband, Jeanne made no mention of the Brother Thomas incident, although she did know that the following day around vespers Perrin was led to the cathedral in Vannes, slept on Vincent's tomb, and awoke healed. She, too, reported on Perrin's vision, noting that the holy Dominican had appeared to him "in the guise in which he preached." But when asked what exactly Perrin said about his vision, she could not respond and was forced to admit that she had not even been present at the church, although at least one other woman, a witness named Jeanne, the widow of Jean Damon, was there. "But she knows well that she sent him from this house. . .sick, and thence he came home healthy."[12]

Several witnesses' testimony gives the impression that the spectacle that drew a crowd was Perrin's ranting and thrashing about; once he quieted down and fell asleep on Vincent's tomb, a number of eyewitnesses appear to have found something better to do. Thus Hervé Maydo (witness Symon Maydo's brother) was able to testify that he had seen Perrin "led, bound, to the tomb of said Master Vincent" and that Perrin "there was cured," but he did not supply any of the details about Perrin's incubation and vision.[13] Pierre de Bonabry recalled well seeing Perrin "bound with cords, invoking the demon, and in a loud voice crying out" and "brought by those who were guarding him to the place of the aforesaid Master Vincent's tomb."

However, when it came to describing Perrin's quieting down, sleeping, vision, and cure, Pierre could only aver that "he heard it commonly said" that those things had happened. Hearing the church bells ring, which Pierre *did* recall distinctly, was proof enough of the miracle.[14] Similarly, Silvester Stephani had seen Perrin bound and demented, "lying on the tomb of said Master Vincent," but evidently had not stayed around to see what would happen next. Rather, like Pierre de Bonabry, "he *heard it said* that the same Perrin 'Fatty' at once afterwards got up from said tomb and appeared totally healthy."[15]

All fourteen witnesses agreed, then, that Perrin Hervé had gone out of his mind and had been healed miraculously at the tomb of Vincent Ferrer. The major difference apparent in the various accounts of the miracle is the presence or absence of the Brother Thomas episode. Four of the witnesses described the trip to the Carmelite church, while no such mention occurs in the testimony of any of the other witnesses, including, most glaringly Perrin Hervé and his wife.[16] Other points of disagreement were more minor. For example, most witnesses described Perrin as being led around by his handlers during his infirmity and not all were sure that his feet had been tied or shackled. Jeanne, Perrin's wife, explained that Perrin's legs had been tied together with a large towel, so that he could walk a little, and one imagines him hobbling along in his undershirt (*camisia*), hands shackled, and ranting away.[17] Pierre Filloche could not remember if Perrin's legs had been tied up or not, but he was adamant that "it was necessary to carry him; otherwise he could in no way have gone."[18] Witnesses also were not entirely clear *when* the events they described had happened, agreeing only that it was some time after the death of Vincent Ferrer. The only other main issue on which witnesses did not agree was the question of what exactly was wrong with Perrin, a point to which I will return later. All in all, however, the stories were abundant and remarkably consistent, a fact which may begin to explain why the organizers of the Brittany inquest chose Perrin Hervé's healing as the first miracle about which testimony was presented at the canonization inquest.[19]

The Characters

That so many people had witnessed and could agree on the essentials of such a striking miracle must, however, have been only part of the reason why the promoters of Vincent's canonization in Brittany decided to highlight the miracle worked on Perrin Hervé. Surely the connection of Perrin and most of the other witnesses to the former and current Dukes of Brittany must have played a key role in that choice as well, for the ducal family had a keen interest in seeing Vincent canonized and may have made much of a miracle involving one well known to them. Through the testimony of Perrin and the other witnesses to his healing, one glimpses not simply the strategies employed by those Bretons interested in Vincent's canonization, but also the network of connections between the powerful and the less powerful in a small fifteenth-century town.

Who was Perrin Hervé? He is identified in the canonization inquest as a dependent (*cliens*) of Pierre II, the reigning duke of Brittany, of around fifty-seven years of age. We learn there also that Perrin was a native of Guillac, in the diocese of St. Malo, and that he had been living in the city of Vannes for forty years. He would have been around seventeen years of age when he came to Vannes and around twenty-three when Vincent Ferrer died and was buried there. Certainly he remembered Vincent's sermons well, as well as the attendance at those events of the then duke and duchess, Jean V and Jeanne de France. It is possible that Perrin had come to Vannes as some sort of servant to Pierre Filloche, of whom he was a dependent at the time of his miraculous healing.[20] If so, it is nice to think that well-connected relatives had helped the young Perrin get close to the powerful in the duchy, for Pierre was an important man in the financial administration of Brittany.[21]

Perrin may well have had several kinsfolk in Vannes who helped him gain access to those in power. For example, Pierre Filloche mentions a neighbor named Alain Hervé, who was in Vannes at the time Vincent Ferrer was there in 1418–19, just a few years after Perrin himself had arrived in town.[22] Perhaps Alain was kin to our Perrin and brokered Perrin's service with his neighbor Pierre Filloche. Furthermore, Yves Gluidic, archpriest of the cathedral in Vannes, in his testimony at the canonization inquest made reference to a "Master Hervé," eleemosynary to Duke Jean, possibly another well-connected relative of Perrin's.[23] Finally, in the years after Perrin's miracle, a man named Mathelin Hervé would come to serve Duke Jean V in a variety of posts, including that of treasurer general.[24] If he, too, were a relative of Perrin's, Mathelin could have served as yet another point of entrée for Perrin into the ducal court.

Whether or not he had help from his relatives, Perrin must have made good use of the connections he did make to ingratiate himself with the powerful men in Vannes who controlled the duchy's finances. (Although Vannes was one of three important ducal cities in the early fifteenth century and would eventually be superceded by Nantes as a sort of "capital" in the latter half of the century, it remained the site of an important ducal residence as well as of the *Chambre des Comptes*, the body in charge of all that concerned Brittany's finances, as well as a major source of advice and counsel for the dukes.)[25] Around the time Perrin had come to Vannes, his patron Pierre Filloche was a ducal secretary, as well as the controller of the

Hôtel in charge of Duke Jean V's household expenditures. From 1424 to 1426, that is, roughly around the time of Perrin's miraculous healing, Pierre Filloche held the office of purveyor general for the ducal *Hôtel*, and he appears again in 1430–32 as treasurer and receiver general for Jean's son François (who would rule as duke from 1442–50).[26] By the time of his miraculous healing, Pierre Filloche's valet was not unknown to the ducal family, for, as Perrin himself proudly related in his testimony, Duchess Jeanne herself had sent Vincent Ferrer's cape to be wrapped around his head during his incubation at the saint's tomb.[27]

Furthermore, Perrin seems to have been able to use his connections to bolster his own career, climbing a ladder that led ever closer to the center of power in the duchy. So, we learn in the canonization inquest that he had at one point been a dependent (*familiaris*) of Jean Rolland, identified there as "counselor and auditor of accounts" for the duke of Brittany.[28] Jean's career was in fact even more glittering than Pierre Filloche's, for he began his path as purveyor general around 1430 and then spent nearly a quarter of a century as a member of the prestigious *Chambre des Comptes*, eventually serving as its president.[29] It is likely that Perrin progressed from his affiliation with Pierre Filloche to his post with the more powerful Jean Rolland, since Perrin had been in Vannes only a few years at the time of his miracle, at which point he was still in Pierre's service. Perrin may have next profited from Jean Rolland's patronage to approach directly Duke Pierre II, who would tap Jean to conduct a financial survey in Vannes in 1455.[30] By the time of Perrin's testimony at the canonization inquest in 1453–some twenty-eight years after his miraculous cure—, he would be identified as a *cliens* of Duke Pierre.[31] It would not be the first time that a member of the duke's financial circle had taken advantage of his position to promote the career of a protégé. Pierre de Bonabry, another longtime member of the *Chambre des Comptes* and one of the other witnesses to Perrin Hervé's miracle, was able to secure a place in the *Chambre des Comptes* for his valet and servant, Geffroy Deline.[32]

While Perrin Hervé used his string of connections to take up a position in the ducal household, he became well known to those men who controlled the duchy's finances. For example, Symon Maydo, who was wealthy enough to promise an annual offering of 20 *solidi* when Vincent's intercession healed his own son, also had a career in ducal finances and held the position of auditor in the *Chambre des Comptes* in 1446.[33] Symon's brother Hervé Maydo, even though he would have been a young lad at the time, was among the privileged group admitted to Vincent's bedchamber as he lay dying in Vannes in the spring of 1419, along with the Duchess Jeanne and other notable ladies, including Jeanne, who became Perrin Hervé's wife.[34] Hervé Maydo also saw distinguished service in the duchy's financial administration under the wing of Jean V's son François. He succeeded Pierre Filloche as treasurer and receiver general for the young François before he was duke, then served Duke François as "*valet de Chambre et de Garde Robe*," treasurer and receiver general, and auditor in the *Chambre des Comptes*.[35]

Besides Pierre Filloche, Jean Rolland, and the Maydo brothers, witness Pierre de Bonabry also was a major player in the duchy's finances. Identified in the 1453 canonization testimony as "counselor to the Duke and auditor in the *Chambre des Comptes*," Pierre de Bonabry was in fact a long-standing member of the *Chambre des Comptes*, serving under three dukes, as well as holding the posts of treasurer general and auditor of the *Chambre*.[36] In addition, Pierre Filloche and Symon Maydo both mentioned that one of the bystanders present for Perrin's healing was a man named Jean Gibon, also a powerful member of the *Chambre des Comptes*, one whose name frequently appears together with Jean Rolland's in administrative records.[37] As Hervé Maydo could so knowingly put it, Perrin's spectacular cure "was in the ducal court. . .reputed to be a miracle."[38]

Furthermore, many of the witnesses who had no connection to ducal financial circles nonetheless show some other sign of status linking them to ducal or other prominent families in and around Vannes. So, for example, a witness named Thomas le Brun, an advocate in the secular court in Vannes, also happened to be the nephew of one Margareta, in whose house near the *Chambre des Comptes* and the ducal castle *l'Hermine* Vincent Ferrer had spent his last days.[39] Her husband, Pierre Drulin, also held some minor posts in the ducal *Hôtel*.[40] Jean Boayden, another witness to Perrin's cure, was, like Hervé Maydo, among the lucky ones admitted to watch Vincent's death in the Drulin home.[41] Silvester Stephani, another witness to the miracle, was connected enough to those who had gotten close to the holy preacher to be able to borrow, when he was in need of the saint's intercession himself, the hard pallet (*materacium satis durum*) on which Vincent Ferrer had slept.[42] Perrin's story was thus well known to the powerful in Vannes.

More than simply suggesting their high status, however, the testimony of the witnesses to Perrin Hervé's healing also points to networks of friendship and patronage that might otherwise go undetected in the written records. Predictably enough, the men who were involved in ducal finances were well acquainted with one another, naming each other when asked for the names of other eyewitnesses to the miracle.[43] Yet their testimony shows that professional ties (and social status) were not the only connections that bound people to one another in fifteenth-century Vannes. Neighbors and the parish were important, as well. So, for example, Perrin Hervé himself recalled that it was his "wife, neighbors, and familiars [*notos*]" who brought him to Vincent's tomb.[44] And among those who led Perrin to the Carmelite house of Bondon was a parchment-maker from the parish of Notre-Dame du Mené in which Pierre Filloche also lived, a man named Hervé Le Goff. Hervé recalled also that he had walked Perrin home after his cure, an evident sign of friendship or at least of neighborly concern.[45] Perrin also had ties to the butcher Yves le Houssec, who could affirm the persistence of Perrin's cure by saying that he "knew him [then] and knows him still to now to be healthy."[46] Seeking supernatural assistance was something that friends did for friends and patrons did for their dependents. Just as Pierre Filloche had brought his dependent Perrin Hervé first to Brother Thomas and then to the tomb of Vincent Ferrer, so, too, Pierre recalled that his neighbor Alain Hervé had brought a serving girl to Vincent Ferrer to be healed when the preacher made the sign of the cross over her.[47]

Politics and Sainthood

Not simply was Perrin Hervé's miracle well known to men and women in power, but the tales of his healing told at the canonization inquest helped to reinforce the close connection between Vincent Ferrer and the dukes of Brittany. The Montfort family who ruled the duchy in the fifteenth century had come to power only in 1364, at the end of a protracted and bitter civil war. To the dismay of the new Montfort dukes, the losing candidate for the ducal throne, Charles of Blois, became the object of a popular religious cult after his death on the battlefield in 1364 and was nearly canonized in the 1370s.[48] Meanwhile, the Montfort dukes of Brittany went about asserting a sovereignty independent of (and yet modeled on) that of their titular overlords, the kings of France.[49]

Central both to Montfort self-representation as sovereigns and to their countering of the cult of Charles of Blois was a careful cultivation of religious figures, particularly Vincent Ferrer. It was Duke Jean V (a Montfort) who had first invited the holy Dominican to preach in the duchy.[50] Both Duke Jean and Duchess Jeanne were avid attendees at Vincent's sermons, and when Vincent fell sick with his final illness, he was borne to Vannes in the duchess's own litter.[51] The duchess was a constant presence in Vincent's death chamber (a room whose occupants constituted a virtual who's who of Breton noble and religious life). After the holy man's final breath, Duchess Jeanne washed and prepared his body for burial.[52] Petitions from Duke Jean's son Pierre II were crucial in the eventual opening of Vincent's canonization process, and when Pope Calixtus III finally enrolled Vincent in the company of the saints in 1455, Pierre contributed 2000 gold pieces to the costs of the canonization ceremonies.[53]

Given the interest of the Montfort family in seeing the canonization of the preacher on whom they had lavished their devotion, it is perhaps not surprising, then, that the ducal family looms in the background of the stories told about Perrin Hervé's healing. Not simply did the miracle benefit a *cliens* of Duke Pierre II himself and enjoy a wide notoriety "in the ducal court" (as Hervé Maydo put it), but small details in the various narratives helped to underscore the close relationship between the Montfort family and Vincent Ferrer.

Take, for example, Symon Maydo's version of Perrin's tale. Like several other witnesses, Symon had recalled Perrin's incubation and healing at Vincent's tomb, as well as that Vincent had appeared to Perrin in a vision there and had spoken to him. Unlike any of the other witnesses, however, Symon remembered Perrin saying that Vincent had "commanded him to tell the Duke [Jean V] that he should get Master Vincent canonized."[54] By the time he related his story for the canonization inquest late in 1453, Symon must have known well that the Montfort dukes had indeed worked hard to carry out just that task. Indeed, Vincent's charge as reported by Symon begins to sound a bit like an after-the-fact prophecy that worked to the glory of both the candidate for sainthood and the zealous Montfort promoters of his cause. Jean V had, in fact, petitioned both Martin V and Eugenius IV to open canonization proceedings in the case of Vincent Ferrer; his son's repeat of the same request led to the inquest in Brittany, in the end fulfilling Vincent's charge to Perrin.[55]

If Perrin's vision truly did include Vincent commanding him to "tell the Duke to get [him] canonized," it was an interesting request indeed. First of all, Vincent's words implied that the preacher, so humble in his lifetime, now appeared to crave the recognition and cult that canonization would bring him. True, a more generous interpretation might view the holy Dominican simply wanting God to receive all glory due to him through his saints, so that his request would be less self-interested than pious, as it were. Nonetheless, the ultimate recipient of Vincent's message was a strange choice for a request for canonization: not the pope in Rome, but the duke of Brittany. Symon's memory (or telling) of the tale thus underscored the ties between Vincent and the Montfort dukes of Brittany by putting the holy preacher in the position of asking the duke for a favor. The duke of Brittany appeared not simply as protector of the church, but as patron of the saints as well. If, indeed, Perrin's story was well known in the ducal court, one can well imagine that the sovereign particularly enjoyed hearing Symon's version of the tale.

Perrin's own account of his healing also contained details that suggested cooperation between the saint and the ducal family in the operation of the miracle. Although Perrin's story had some obvious gaps in it—he did not recall, for example, the Brother Thomas incident—, he supplied one detail that none of the other witnesses mentioned. Namely, Perrin remembered his use of a relic, Vincent Ferrer's cape, which was wrapped around his head as he slept on the holy tomb.[56] Like Symon's memory of Vincent's command to the duke, Perrin's recollection of this detail also pointed to the ties between Vincent Ferrer and the Montfort family. As many witnesses at the canonization inquest recalled, Jean V's wife had displayed a particular devotion to Vincent Ferrer, particularly in the days leading up to the holy preacher's death in Vannes. Witnesses also recalled that, as she prepared Vincent's body for burial, Duchess Jeanne had kept Vincent's cape as a relic, substituting that of her own Dominican confessor in its place.[57] This cape was the very relic that, as Perrin recalled, the duchess herself had sent to be used in his infirmity. If Symon's story had the Breton duke serving as intermediary in the matter of Vincent's canonization, Perrin's tale made the duchess, through her loan of the preacher's cape, a participant in Vincent's miraculous restoration of Perrin to his right mind. Like the donor portraits in painted altarpieces, these small details in Symon's and Perrin's testimony subtly made their point. Even as painted donors appear kneeling, beseeching the saint's intercession, their presence in the composition shows their role as patron of the saint's cult. So, too, the Montfort family emerged as both beneficiaries of and impresarios of the nascent cult of Vincent Ferrer.

Finally, the story of Perrin and Brother Thomas the Carmelite, related by only four of the fourteen witnesses to Perrin's miracle, may also have served as political theater. The incident could well have been an embarrassment for Jean V, however. Jean had supported many religious figures during his long reign, not simply Vincent Ferrer. In particular, in the years after Vincent's 1419 death, the ducal family had lavished patronage on the Carmelite order, with Jean V founding new houses at Bondon and, later, at Rennes.[58] According to Symon Maydo's testimony, Brother Thomas had been brought to Bondon specifically to found the new Carmelite convent there.[59] Whether it was his newness on the spiritual scene or whether Thomas indeed did radiate an aura of holiness, the fact remains that Perrin Hervé's handlers had turned first to Brother Thomas. An air of expectation is apparent in the testimony. As Symon Maydo put it, when Perrin was led to the Carmelite house of Bondon, "many followed so that they might see if a miracle would be worked through the merits of said Brother Thomas."[60] In bringing his servant to Bondon, Pierre Filloche may well have hoped to give the duke's newest spiritual protégé a leg up in the form of a highly public miracle: just the thing to bring the faithful rushing to the new Carmelite house. Bondon, about a kilometer north of Vannes, was if anything a little further from Pierre's house in the suburb of Notre-Dame du Mené than was the Vannes cathedral. If a miraculous boost for Bondon was Pierre's hope, Perrin's subsequent behavior would have been a severe disappointment.

The embarrassment of Brother Thomas's failure must have been doubly great if, as Hervé Martin has hypothesized, this "Brother Thomas" was the celebrated preacher Thomas Cornette (or Conecte).[61] Cornette was evidently an impassioned and effective preacher. In one 1430 sermon, he persuaded children in the audience to go out and attack local women for their extravagant hairstyles.[62] He also thundered against the abuses of a lax and greedy clergy, earning him the praise of later Protestants and the ire of the ecclesiastical hierarchy. In 1434, at the instigation of his enemies, he was tried, condemned, and burned at the stake.[63] In 1448, despite Cornette's condemnation for heresy, Pope Nicholas V confirmed the concession from Pope Martin V that had allowed Brother Thomas to take up two new foundations in Brittany.[64] Nor was Cornette the only Carmelite to come under suspicion in late medieval Brittany. The Carmelites in Leon preached sermons whose contents leaned toward the Wycliffite, and when, in 1365 the Carmelites in Nantes had claimed that a child had miraculously been resurrected in their convent, a number of local citizens suspected fraud instead.[65]

In the case of Perrin Hervé, the absence of the Carmelite episode in the testimony of so many of the witnesses who were tied to the ducal family may well reflect a studied forgetting of an unpleasant detail.[66] But by the time of the 1453 inquest on behalf of Vincent Ferrer, those close to the Montfort family must have been delighted by the fact that the Brother Thomas fiasco did not spell the end of Perrin Hervé's story. For if the tale included one more embarrassment on the part of the Carmelites in Brittany so favored by Jean V, it also exalted another source of spiritual assistance even dearer to the Breton dukes: Vincent Ferrer.

What was Wrong with Perrin Hervé?

If witnesses were not consistent in their accounts of the dating of Perrin's cure or in their recollection of his detour through the Carmelite house of Bondon, they were similarly equivocal about the exact nature of Perrin's infirmity. In short, witnesses were torn between positing a natural and a supernatural cause for Perrin's disorder.[67] Their various diagnoses of the cause of Perrin's erratic behavior reveal much about the layperson's understanding of mental disorders in the later Middle Ages, as well as the penetration of a relatively new learned discourse about the discernment of spirits. Nonetheless, the commissioners at the canonization inquest allowed witnesses to maintain a certain imprecision about the exact cause of Perrin's break. That imprecision and equivocation left wide open the probability that his was a case of demonic possession.

The most benign interpretations of Perrin's condition came from his wife and from Perrin himself, to whom the state of being possessed by a demon appeared to be somewhat embarrassing. Perrin began, after all, simply by stating that "a certain infirmity" had come over his "head and other parts of his body." The major symptom of the infirmity was that he was rendered "out of his mind" (*demens*) "as if in a fury" (*furiosus*). Although he described his condition with the language of illness (*infirmitas*), Perrin's analysis of the cause of the disorder was that it was supernatural, for he told the commissioners that "he believes that he was vexed by a demon."[68] Perrin's wife Jeanne maintained simply that her husband had been "taken in the head" (*mente captus*), although she did not assign any supernatural cause to his mental breakdown or designate what spirit or force had "taken" Perrin. A demon featured in her testimony, but only as part of her list of Perrin's bizarre actions: "he invoked the demon and blasphemed God and the saints."[69] This description may be Jeanne's oblique nod to what she had heard of Perrin's embarrassing behavior at the Carmelite church, or it may just simply reflect the nature of Perrin's ranting throughout his "infirmity." Neither Perrin nor his wife explicitly stated that he had actually been physically possessed by a demon, as in the case of the spectacular exorcism worked by Jesus in Mark 5. In that assessment they were supported by only one other witness, Symon Maydo, who described Perrin only as "out of his senses" (*extra sensum positus*) and "out of his mind" (*demens*). Nonetheless, demons lurked behind their testimony, in the wife's recollection that Perrin had invoked a demon, and his own sense that he had been vexed by one.[70]

For many other witnesses, the case was more clear-cut: Perrin Hervé had been possessed by a demon (*demoniacus*). The demonic possession explained both his crazed behavior and accounted for his infirmity. Thus, Jean Rolland described Perrin as "out of his mind and possessed by a demon," but could also refer to him as "sick and possessed by a demon" (*infirmus et demoniacus*).[71] Hervé Maydo, too, spoke of "said infirmity," but called Perrin *dementem et demoniacum*.[72] For the parchment-maker Hervé Le Goff and the butcher Yvo Le Houssec, Perrin was simply a "demoniac," although each of them also could affirm that he no longer suffered from that "infirmity."[73] Witness Silvester Stephani concurred in the diagnosis of demonic possession, while Michael Maceot spoke of Perrin as "in the fury of one possessed by a demon" (*demoniaca furiositate*).[74] The most colorful analysis of Perrin's state came from the mouth of Jean Boayden, who related how he had "seen the same Perrin possessed by a demon, invoking demons and saying that all the demons in hell were enclosed in his body."[75] No wonder he did not behave well.

Even those who equivocated about the exact cause of Perrin's behavior left open the likelihood that demonic possession lay at its root. Thus, although Pierre Filloche offered no diagnosis of his own, he recalled that when Perrin asked the crowd in the cathedral why he had been tied up, he was told that "he had been out of his mind or possessed by a demon."[76] Similarly, Jeanne, widow of Johannes Damon, as well as Thomas le Brun described Perrin as being "out of his mind *or* possessed by a demon."[77] And Pierre de Bonabry remembered seeing Perrin "invoking the demon and crying out in a loud voice *like one possessed or vexed by a demon.*"[78] To nearly everyone but the most interested of parties, then, it looked as if Perrin had been possessed by a demon.

Perrin indeed exhibited a number of characteristics that would lead observers to conclude that he was possessed. In theory and in practice, however, it was difficult to make the call.[79] On the one hand, his frenzied behavior, his appearance of being "out of his mind," his thrashing about, shouting, and violent behavior, and the necessity of binding him with ropes and chains all were indications of spirit possession. On the other hand, as Thomas Aquinas would comment about states of "abstraction," such trances could have three causes: a bodily cause, "as is clear from those who through some *infirmity* are out of their minds;" the work of demons, as in the case of possession; or divine power, as in spiritual ecstasy.[80] Indeed, intellectuals in the late fourteenth and fifteenth centuries were tortured by the problem of "discerning spirits," that is, determining whether an individual exhibiting such frenzied behaviors was possessed by a demon or by the Holy Spirit.[81] The inconsistent diagnoses of Perrin Hervé's state reflect not simple ignorance on the part of our witnesses, but rather the sorts of ambiguities that troubled contemporary theologians as well.

While in some instances, observers might disagree as to whether a natural cause, a demon, or the Holy Spirit was the agent at work behind what apparently appeared as possessed behaviors, in the case of Perrin Hervé, witnesses' tales contained a number of clues pointing specifically to demonic possession. First of all, there was Perrin's behavior itself. While the authors of treatises on discernment worried a lot about the possibility of false or feigned *sanctity*, no one was particularly concerned about its opposite. The devil would and could be expected to deceive by taking on the outward guise of holiness, but no one worried that God or the saints would "put on" un-Godly behavior. So, when Perrin blasphemed God and the saints and spit on the image of the Virgin, an observer might suspect some natural infirmity, but could safely retire the supposition that he had been possessed by the Holy Spirit. Indeed, Perrin's antics looked much like those described in the exorcists' manuals that circulated widely in the fifteenth century, a time in which saintly exorcisms of demoniacs along the lines of Perrin's cure were, according to one study, declining sharply.[82]

It may well be that the actions of Brother Thomas described by Pierre Filloche and Symon Maydo—as well as Perrin's subsequent reactions—show Brother Thomas trying to confirm that Perrin indeed was possessed along the lines suggested in fifteenth-century exorcists' manuals. Such manuals directed the would-be exorcist secretly to place a consecrated host on the victim's head; to say to him or her, "You have relinquished the God who made you;" or to show the victim a picture of Saint Jerome. If the victim's reaction to any of the above was to go into a fury, one could be assured that this was indeed a case of demonic possession. A sprinkling of holy water, too, could be part of the ritual of conjuring a spirit and determining its nature.[83] If Brother Thomas was indeed attempting to diagnose Perrin's malady, "Fatty's" violent reactions to Thomas's tests pointed to clear demonic involvement: Perrin "spit at the image of the Blessed Mary, nor could he [bear to] hear anything said about God."[84] Far from trying to work a miracle, as the crowd may have anticipated, Brother Thomas may simply have been carrying out instructions from a new-fangled exorcist's manual when he sprinkled Perrin with holy water and found him "not able to bear the said water."[85] Where the liturgical performance of exorcism appeared to fail, however, it was evidently better to return to tried and true remedies: the incubation on Vincent Ferrer's tomb.[86]

A final piece of evidence about contemporaries' understanding of Perrin's ailment comes in the form of Perrin's own rather curious statement that his infirmity came over him "on an empty stomach."[87] Medieval authors often expressed a fear of the devil entering the body through the mouth, while demonic possession was believed to be localized, physiologically, in the stomach or intestines.[88] Since some demoniacs were reported to have ingested a demon along with food or drink, Perrin's assertion might indicate that he was trying to distance himself somewhat from the conclusion that he was demonically possessed.[89] He hadn't eaten any food; he couldn't have swallowed a demon. Given Perrin's nickname ("Fatty"), contemporaries may well have viewed him as a sinful glutton whose eating was likely to get him into trouble at some point, and his statement may have taken aim at such sentiments. On the other hand, Perrin's insistence that his infirmity began "on an empty stomach" could just as easily point to demonic possession as the cause. With no food in his stomach, there was all the more room for a demon to enter it; further, the possibility that noxious vapors from something Perrin had eaten were the cause of his infirmity became virtually nil.[90]

The commissioners who ran the Brittany inquest were apparently willing to leave the exact nature of Perrin's problem up in the air, however. Although they did not hesitate to interrupt other witnesses to ask for clarification about an illness miraculously cured or a death miraculously reversed,

the commissioners posed no such questions about Perrin's ailment.[91]
It may well be that such learned men of the church knew that the question of spirit possession was a tricky one, difficult even for men of the
cloth, and that a lay witness could and should not be expected to make
that call. Or it may be that, with the authors of treatises on the discernment of spirits, they fell back on the gospel injunction: "Ye shall know
them by their fruits" (Matt. 7:16).[92] If so, the fruits of Perrin's possession
clearly fell from a demonic tree. But in addition, the promoters of
Vincent Ferrer's canonization in Brittany may well have prepared the
commissioners to view Perrin's case as a clear instance of demonic possession. It was Guillermus Coetmur, member of the Vannes cathedral
chapter and procurer for the canonization inquest, whose job it was to
call and line up the witnesses on behalf of Vincent Ferrer.[93] And
Coetmur, along with those who advised him, chose to present Perrin's
cure as the first miracle of the inquest. In that choice, Coetmur may have
been shaping his case to fit a known pattern in the development of new
saints' cults in the later Middle Ages.

The Inauguration of a Cult

Michael Goodich has recently argued that, for a number of thirteen-and
fourteenth-century saints, the decisive moment in the inauguration of the cult
was a public exorcism, which became the new saint's "premier miracle."[94]
In Goodich's examples, drawn from the miracles of Thomas Cantilupe and
Joachim Piccolomini, such a miracle occurred near or on a major feast
day, the *miraculé* specifically identified the new (or proposed) saint as the
intercessor responsible for the miracle, and the clergy present did not
follow traditional procedures for exorcising demons. Furthermore, this
"premier miracle" was typically *not* the first posthumous miracle attributed
to the candidate for sainthood, although it occurred relatively soon after
the putative saint's death. But it did play a crucial role in the new cult.
Goodich speculates that it took "such a dramatic, ritualized public miracle"
as an exorcism that dramatized the age-old conflict between God and
Satan, to initiate "the enthusiasm which enabled a large number of
thaumaturgical miracles at the site of the tomb."[95]

At first glance, Perrin Hervé's miraculous cure would appear to be one
more example in support of Goodich's case. A dramatic, highly public
event, Perrin's liberation from demonic possession at Vincent Ferrer's
tomb took place, by his and his wife's testimony, around the major feast of
Easter. His cure scarcely involved the cathedral clergy, save their role in
ringing the bells in thanksgiving after his cure. As for the unhappy side-trip

to Brother Thomas's Carmelite friary, it served only to underscore the power of Vincent's intercession. The episode's appearance in the canonization inquest as the first miracle there described (either *in vita* or *post mortem*) gives the impression that Perrin's exorcism was indeed that cult-inaugurating "premier" miracle of Goodich's paradigm. That impression finds confirmation in the testimony of those witnesses who place the miracle vaguely "after the death" of Vincent Ferrer or "around two years or so after the death of this Master Vincent."[96] Other evidence situates the miracle somewhat later, however. Perrin Hervé and his wife both dated the miracle to twenty-eight years previously, that is, in 1425, six years after the holy Dominican's death.[97] Jean Boayden recalled that the miracle had occurred "long after the death of the aforementioned Master Vincent," while Silvester Stephani placed the miracle as late as "a decade after the time of said Master Vincent's death," that is, around 1429.[98] Furthermore, according to Symon Maydo and the others who testified about Brother Thomas, the miracle would have to postdate the founding of the Carmelite house of Bondon in 1425.[99] Perrin's healing must have taken place at least six years after Vincent's death, then. Nor could it have been the first of a wave of miracles worked at the tomb, for a number of witnesses at the canonization inquest described a swell of miracles in the first few years after Vincent's death, which had subsequently died down.[100] If witnesses were correct in their sense that pilgrimages to Vincent's tomb had dwindled after five or six years, Perrin's exorcism would have come toward the end of the initial burst of enthusiasm toward Vincent Ferrer, not at its beginning.

If Perrin's spectacular public cure did not function to stimulate a wave of healings at Vincent's tomb and inaugurate his cult, it may nonetheless have served an important role in *rekindling* the flames of devotion to the popular preacher in the run-up to his canonization. Witnesses also testified that pilgrimages to Vincent's tomb had increased in the several years leading up to the canonization inquest, or, perhaps, roughly from the time that Duke Pierre II began petitioning Pope Nicholas V to canonize Vincent. It is clear from the canonization inquest that the dramatic cure of Pierre II's *cliens*, Perrin Hervé, was well known in the ducal court. It seems likely, too, that, as Duke Pierre and his representatives met with the papal curia and the Dominican hierarchy (as they did in Nantes at the Dominican chapter general of 1453), they shared with the pope and the Order of Preachers such a spectacular example of their hoped-for saint's intercession.[101] As witnesses made clear, in the years leading up to the canonization inquest, Brittany preachers broadcast Vincent's miracles from their pulpits on Sundays, at major feasts, and at sales of indulgences.[102] One can easily imagine Perrin's story gaining notoriety through such sermons.

The orchestrators of the Brittany canonization inquest, then, may well have chosen to foreground Perrin Hervé's miraculous cure not because it was the miracle that had inaugurated the Breton cult of Vincent Ferrer, but rather because it looked like the sort of spectacular public exorcism described as initiating other saints' cults. Its numerous witnesses were largely the sort of high status individuals whose word carried weight in courts of law, and its setting (at the saint's tomb), plus the apparition of Vincent in Perrin's dream, confirmed that the miracle was indeed due to Vincent's intercession. And if Perrin's healing in all likelihood had not touched off the wave of miraculous healings in the years after Vincent's death, it had not been without its effects in the duchy. The fourteen witnesses who testified to Perrin's cure offered evidence about nearly twice as many miracles as did the average Brittany witness. After witnessing Perrin's cure, many of them had gone on to invoke the saint's intercession for themselves or their family or friends.[103]

As for Perrin's story, its impact seems to have been the greatest in the duchy of Brittany itself, where it had such a wide currency. While the tale may well have helped convince Calixtus III and his cardinals to canonize Vincent Ferrer in 1455, Perrin Hervé's cure appears not at all in the brief listing of miracles in the first *Vita* of the new saint, penned by Dominican Pietro Ranzano.[104] The miracle does, however, show up in a collection of posthumous miracles compiled by Francisco Castiglione in 1470, but Perrin there is not identified by name. And although the miracle is the first one in Castiglione's list, Perrin is described simply as crazed and frenzied, without a hint of his demonic possession, and without any suggestion that his healing helped inaugurate the new cult.[105] But the notion of a miraculous exorcism sparking devotion to the saint must have remained a powerful one. When, in 1615, Martin de Bellassise, bishop of Vannes, wished once again to revivify the cult of Vincent Ferrer, he commissioned a large tapestry devoted to the saint's life and miracles. The first miracle depicted on the tapestry was the healing of the demoniac Perrin Hervé.[106]

Notes

1. The standard accounts of Vincent's life are *Acta Sanctorum. Ed. novissima* (Paris: V. Palmé, 1863–), April, vol. 1, pp. 476–527 (Hereinafter *AASS*); Henri Fages, *Histoire de Saint Vincent Ferrier*, 4 vols. (Paris: Picard, and Louvain: Uystpruyst, 1901–04); Matthieu Maxime Gorce, *Saint Vincent Ferrier (1350–1419)* (Paris: Plan-Nourrit, [c1924]); Sadoc M. Bertucci, "Vincenzo Ferrer, santo," in *Bibliotheca Sanctorum*, 12 vols. (Rome: Instituto Giovanni XXIII, 1969–80), 12: 1168–76; S. Spanò, "Vincenzo Ferrer," in *Il grande libro dei santi: dizionario enciclopedico* (Turin: San Paolo, 1998),

3:1936–39; Fr. José M. de Garganta, O.P. and Fr. Vicente Forcada, O.P., intro. and ed., *Biografía y escritos de San Vicente Ferrer* (Madrid: Biblioteca de Autores Cristianos, 1956). See also P. Sigismund Brettle, *San Vicente Ferrer und sein literarischer Nachlass*, Vorreformationsgeschichtliche Forschungen, 10 (Münster: Aschendorff, 1924). See *Bibliotheca hagiographica latina* (Brussels: Society of Bollandists, 1898–99), numbers 8656–69. The canonization inquests have been edited and slightly abridged as vol. 3 of Fages, *Histoire*. Although the records of the canonization process no longer exist in Rome, lost since at least the mid-sixteenth century, the fifteenth-century local copy of the Brittany inquest, together with accompanying letters from the commissioners who conducted the inquest, survives in Vannes, Archives Départementales du Morbihan, MS 87 G 11. (Hereinafter ADM MS 87 G 11.) In addition, there is a sixteenth-century copy of three of the four local inquests (made from a rather well-worn exemplar in Palermo): Valencia, Universidad de Valencia, Biblioteca, G.C. 1869, M. 690, "Proceso de la canonizacion de San Vicente Ferrer, 9 del junio 1590." To avoid the plague that was raging in Brittany at the time, the papal commissioners opened the inquest into Vincent's sanctity in the town of Malestroit, about 35 kilometers from Vannes, the site of Vincent's tomb. As the plague abated enough for them to feel safe, they journeyed to Vannes to inspect the tomb in the cathedral, but continued to examine witnesses in the Priory of Sanctis Albis near Vannes (although later they traveled to other towns in the duchy to examine witnesses). This information appears in letters written to the cardinals who charged them with their duties by the sub-commissioners who carried out the inquest, in ADM MS 87 G 11, at signature 8, pages numbered, in a later hand, pp. 15, 16, 19, 23 {this signature, pages [1]-29, is mis-leaved between witnesses numbers 239 and 240, as it appears also in my microfilm of the MS (1 Mi 1)}, and in Fages, *Histoire*, 4:391, 394, 396, 397, 399. [On this MS, see also Thomas Wetzstein, "*Virtus morum et virtus signorum?* Zur Bedeutung der Mirakel in den Kanonisationsprozessen des 15. Jahrhunderts," in *Mirakel im Mittelalter: Konzeption, Erscheinungsformen, Deutungen, Beiträge zur Hagiographie*, 3, ed., Martin Heinzelmann, Klaus Herbers, and Dieter R. Bauer (Stuttgart: Franz Steiner Verlag, 2002), p. 353, n. 6].

2. Robert Bartlett, *The Hanged Man: A Story of Miracle, Memory, and Colonialism in the Middle Ages* (Princeton, NJ: Princeton University Press, 2004). For other examples of ordinary lives glimpsed through canonization proceedings, see Sharon Farmer, *Surviving Poverty in Medieval Paris: Gender, Ideology and Daily Lives of the Poor* (Ithaca: Cornell University Press, 2002); Ronald Finucane, *The Rescue of the Innocents: Endangered Children in Medieval Miracles* (New York: St. Martin's, 1997); Michael Goodich, *Violence and Miracle in the Fourteenth Century: Private Grief and Public Salvation* (Chicago: University of Chicago Press, 1995).

3. E.g., Michael Richter, Michael Goodich, Jussi Hanska: see Bartlett, *Hanged Man*, p. 143. Cantilupe's dossier also is treated in the contributions to this volume by Michael Goodich ("The Multiple Miseries of Dulcia of

St. Chartier (1266) and Cristina of Wellington (1294)") and Ronald Finucane ("The Toddler in the Ditch: A Case of Parental Neglect?").

4. A method I have followed in my own "Miracle, Memory, and Meaning in the Canonization of Vincent Ferrer, 1453–54," *Speculum* 73 (1998): 429–54.

5. For the role of miracle stories in another new cult around the same time, see also Jean-Michel Matz, "Rumeur publique et diffusion d'un nouveau culte à la fin du Moyen Age: les miracles de Jean Michel, Evêque d'Angers (1439–1447)," *Revue d'histoire de l'Église de France* 77, no. 198 (1991): 83–99.

6. Michael Goodich, "Liturgy and the Foundation of Cults in the Thirteenth and Fourteenth Centuries," in '*De Sion exibet lex et verbum domini de Hierusalem'. Essays on Medieval Law, Liturgy, and Literature in Honour of Amnon Linder*, ed. Yitzhak Hen, Cultural Encounters in Late Antiquity and the Middle Ages, 1 (Turnhout: Brepols, 2001), pp. 145–57.

7. ADM MS 87 G 11, witness number 4 (Perrin Hervei alias Grasset). The manuscript is not consistently foliated or paginated throughout (and is bound out of order), and I cite witnesses' testimony by witness number rather than by folio. Fages abridges the testimony throughout his edition of the canonization inquests; the manuscript is therefore preferable.

8. ADM MS 87 G 11, witness number 8 (Petrus Floch).

9. ADM MS 87 G 11, witness number 9 (Symon Maydo).

10. ADM MS 87 G 11, witness number 13 (Johannes Rolandi).

11. ADM MS 87 G 11, witness number 26 (Herveus Le Goff).

12. ADM MS 87 G 11, witness number 15 (Johanna, uxor Perrini Hervei alias Grasset); witness number 17 (Johanna, relicta Johannis Damon).

13. ADM MS 87 G 11, witness number 18 (Herveus Maydo).

14. ADM MS 87 G 11, witness number 33 (Petrus de Bonabri).

15. ADM MS 87 G 11, witness number 156 (Silvester Stephani). My emphasis.

16. ADM MS 87 G 11, witnesses numbers 8 (Petrus Floch=Pierre Filloche), 9 (Symon Maydo), 26 (Herveus Le Goff), and 27 (Yvo Le Houssec). It is possible that Michael Maceot (witness number 30) also testified to (or agreed in the memory of) the Brother Thomas episode; that is, he is reported to have "testified about the miracle done in the person of Perrin Hervei, also known as Fatty, concerning his demoniac fury, as Petrus Floch, a previous witness." On such summarizing of witnesses' testimony in English ecclesiastical courts, see R. N. Swanson's contribution to this volume: " '. . .et examinatus dicit. . .': Oral and Personal History in the Records of English Ecclesiastical Courts," p. 206 of his typescript.

17. ADM MS 87 G 11, witness number 15 (Johanna uxor Perrini Hervei alias Grasset).

18. ADM MS 87 G 11, witness number 8 (Petrus Floch).

19. The first three witnesses give testimony only about Vincent's life. It is perhaps also significant that Perrin was placed among the first four witnesses, because one of the three commissioners, Johannes, Bishop of St. Malo, left the inquest after hearing only the first five depositions: ADM MS 87 G 11, signature 8, p. 22.

20. All from Perrin's own testimony, ADM MS 89 G 11 (witness number 4).

21. Jean Kerhervé, *L'État Breton aux 14e et 15e siècles: Les Ducs, l'Argent, et les Hommes*, 2 vols. (Paris: Maloine, 1987), 1:237: in 1416 (i.e., within 3 years perhaps of Perrin Hervé's arrival in Vannes), Pierre Filloche was ducal secretary and controller of the ducal residence in Vannes (i.e., a financial officer in charge of domestic expenses); see also 1:227, 247; 2:707, 766.

22. ADM MS 87 G 11, witness number 8 (Petrus Floc'h).

23. ADM MS 87 G 11, witness number 1 (Dominus Yvo Gluidic).

24. Kerhervé, *L'État Breton*, 1:241, 245, 247, 251, 275, 289; 2:802, 835.

25. Jean Kerhervé, "Nantes. Capitale des Ducs de Bretagne?," in *Nantes et la Bretagne*, ed. Jean Guiffan (Morlaix: Editions Skol Vreich, 1996), pp. 63–78; Michael Jones, " 'En son habit royal': le duc de Bretagne et son image vers la fin du Moyen Âge," in Jones, *Between France and England: Politics, Power and Society in Late Medieval Brittany*, Variorum Collected Studies Series, CS769 (Aldershot, UK, and Burlington, VT: Ashgate, 2003), p. 179 (dukes had "joyous entries" in Nantes, Rennes, and Vannes). On the Chambre des Comptes and its role, see Kerhervé, *L'État Breton*, 1:341–405.

26. Kerhervé, *L'État Breton*, 1:237 (ducal secretary and controller of the Hotel), 247 (purveyor general), and 227 (personal treasurer for the young François).

27. ADM MS 87 G 11, witness number 4 (Perrinus Hervei alias Grasset).

28. ADM MS 87 G 11, witness number 13 (Johannes Rolandi "scutifer Dominus de Kaerdelan consiliarius et auditor computorum Domini Ducis Britannie").

29. Kerhervé, *L'État Breton*, 1:245, 247 (purveyor general); 290, 354 (president in 1456), 361 (president and auditor in 1446–68), 362 (presided over redacting of a *rentier* for Vannes in 1455); 2:792 (service of 23 years in the *Chambre des Comptes* in 1456). Rolland's name also appears on a list of witnesses in a letter describing the opening ceremonies of the Brittany canonization inquest: ADM MS 87 G 11 (in signature 8, p. 19), and edited in Fages, *Histoire*, 4:399.

30. Pierre Filloche may have been out of ducal service by 1453, the date of the canonization inquest. He seems to have been most closely connected to Jean V and particularly to François I, who died in 1450; in the inquest, he is identified only as a citizen of Vannes (*civis venetensis*). Kerhervé, *L'État Breton*, 1:227, 237, 247; 2:707, 766; ADM MS 87 G 11, witness number 8 (Petrus Floch).

31. ADM MS 87 G 11, witness number 4 (Perrinus Hervei alias Grasset).

32. Kerhervé, *L'État Breton*, 1:368; 2:768. Pierre de Bonabry got his start as a clerk of a man named Auffroy Guinot, who would eventually serve as the duchy's treasurer general: Kerhervé, *L'État Breton*, 2:765 (clerk to Guinot), 792 (25 years in the *Chambre* in 1468), 839 (more than 30 years in the ducal court).

33. ADM MS 87 G 11, witness number 9 (Symon Maydo) (he also named among the miracles of Vincent Ferrer the recovery of a silver cup that he himself had lost); Kerhervé, *L'État Breton*, 1:364.

34. ADM MS 87 G 11, witness number 18 (Herveus Maydo): he says he's forty-six years old in 1453, which would have made him twelve in 1419; he mentions the presence of the Duchess at Vincent's death; witness number 9 (Symon Maydo) also mentions the presence of his brother Hervé Maydo at Vincent's death; witness number 15 (Johanna uxor Perrini Hervei alias Grasset) mentions her own presence at Vincent's death chamber, although she did not have very distinct recollections of it, in part because she was so young at the time.

35. Kerhervé, *L'État Breton*, 1:227, 252, 281, 288, 290, 353; 2:767.

36. ADM MS 87 G 11, witness number 33 (Petrus de Bonabri); Kerhervé, *L'État Breton*, 1:353 (auditor of Chambre in 1448), 354 (and in 1456 and 1468), 364 (and in 1443); 2:765 (auditor for 32 years).

37. ADM MS 87 G 11, witness number 8 (Petrus Floch) and witness number 9 (Symon Maydo); on Jean Gibon, see Kerhervé, *L'État Breton*, 1:353, 361, 366, 372, 386.

38. ADM MS 87 G 11, witness number 18 (Herveus Maydo).

39. ADM MS 87 G 11, witness number 69 (Thomas le Brun).

40. Kerhervé, *L'État Breton*, 2:868 (*lieutenant du contrôleur et ancien receveur de Rhuys*).

41. ADM MS 87 G 11, witness number 36 (Johannes Boayden).

42. ADM MS 87 G 11, witness number 156 (Silvester Stephani), although he is probably not of extremely high status, not being in the "stacked" first 30–60 witnesses, who are almost overwhelmingly of high status.

43. As were witness number 8 (Petrus Floch), who when "asked who was present," named "Simon Maydo, Johannes Gibon, and many innumerable others"; and witness number 9 (Symon Maydo), who named "Yvo Bugaut, Johannes Gibon, Perrotus Floch, the witness just preceding, and others about whom he doesn't recall." (It may be that Yvo Bugaut was related to Éon Bugaut, who was a receiver for Auray and owned five houses in Vannes listed in a 1455 *rentier*: Kerhervé, *L'État Breton*, 2:868.)

44. ADM MS 87 G 11, witness number 4 (Perrinus Hervei alias Grasset).

45. ADM MS 87 G 11, witness number 26 (Herveus Le Goff).

46. ADM MS 87 G 11, witness number 27 (Yvo Le Houssec).

47. ADM MS 87 G 11, witness number 8 (Petrus Floch).

48. Jean-Pierre Leguay and Hervé Martin, *Fastes et malheurs de la Bretagne ducale 1213–1532* (Rennes: Ouest France, 1982), pp. 131–40; Patrick Galliou and Michael Jones, *The Bretons, The Peoples of Europe* (Oxford, UK, and Cambridge, MA: Blackwell, 1991), pp. 214–27; André Vauchez, "Canonisation et politique au XIVe siècle. Documents inédits des Archives du Vatican relatifs au procès de canonisation de Charles de Blois, duc de Bretagne (†1364)," in *Miscellanea in onore di Monsignor Martini Giusti*, 2 vols., Collectanea Archivi Vaticani, 5–6 (Vatican City: Archivio Vaticano, 1978), 2:381–404; Michael Jones, "Politics, Sanctity and the Breton State: The Case of the Blessed Charles de Blois, Duke of Brittany (d. 1364)," in *The Medieval State: Essays Presented to James Campbell*, ed. J.R. Maddicott and

D.M. Palliser (London and Rio Grande: Hambledon Press, 2000), pp. 215–32, reprinted in Michael Jones, *Between France and England: Politics, Power and Society in Late Medieval Brittany*, Variorum Collected Studies Series, CS769 (Aldershot, UK, and Burlington, VT: Ashgate, 2003).

49. See especially Michael Jones, *The Creation of Brittany: A Late Medieval State* (London and Ronceverte: Hambledon Press, 1988), chapter 1 ("The Duchy of Brittany in the Middle Ages"), pp. 8–11, and chapter 5 ("The Chancery of Brittany from Peter Mauclerc to Duchess Anne, 1213–1514"), pp. 121–23; Jones, " 'En son habit royal,' "; Galliou and Jones, *Bretons*, pp. 237–46.

50. ADM MS 87 G 11, witness numbers 3 (Henricus du Val) and 32 (Johannes Bernier).

51. ADM MS 87 G 11, witness number 10 (Alieta uxor Perroti Alanou).

52. ADM MS 87 G 11, for e.g., witness numbers 6 (Oliverius Le Bourdiec presbiter) and 7 (Perrina de Bazvalen).

53. According to the eyewitness account by Pietro Ranzano, in a letter written to fellow Dominican Giovanni da Pistoia, in Rome, Biblioteca Casanatense, MS 112, fol. 63v (hereinafter Bibl. Cas. MS 112).

54. ADM MS 87 G 11, witness number 9 (Symon Maydo).

55. Petitions by Jean V and his children were recalled by Pietro Ranzano in Bibl. Cas. MS 112, fols. 61r, 62r.

56. ADM MS 87 G 11, witness number 4 (Perrin Herveus alias Grasset).

57. ADM MS 87 G 11, witness numbers 4 (Perrinus Hervei alias Grasset), 6 (Oliverius Le Bourdiec presbiter), and 7 (Perrina de Bazvalen).

58. Hervé Martin, *Les ordres mendiants en Bretagne vers 1230-vers 1530. Pauvreté volontaire et predication à la fin du Moyen-Âge* (Paris: C. Kincksieck, 1975), pp. 67–68. (Martin gives the foundation dates as 1425 for Bondon and 1448 for Rennes.) A missal from the Carmelite house in Nantes contains portraits of the ducal family, including a depiction of Jean V having himself weighed, part of his fulfillment of a vow of his weight in gold to be given to the Carmelites in Nantes should he be delivered from his 1420 captivity by his Penthièvre cousins: Jones, " 'En son habit royal,' " p. 259; Jones, *Creation of Brittany*, chapter 16 ("Les manuscrits d'Anne de Bretagne, Reine de France, Duchesse de Bretagne"), p. 378 (The MS is now in Princeton, NJ: Robert Garrett Collection, MS 40).

59. ADM MS 87 G 11, witness number 9 (Symon Maydo).

60. ADM MS 87 G 11, witness number 9 (Symon Maydo).

61. Martin, *Ordres mendiants*, p. 68.

62. Leguay and Martin, *Fastes et malheurs*, p. 358. See also Prosper-Jean Levot, *Biographie Bretonne*, 2 vols. (Vannes, 1852–57; repr., Geneva: Slatkine, 1971), 1:437–39 [Conecte ou Connecte (Thomas)].

63. Levot, *Biographie Bretonne*, 1:438.

64. E.-R. Vaucelle, *Catalogue des lettres de Nicolas V concernant la province ecclésiastique de Tours d'après les registres des Archives Vaticanes* (Paris: Picard, 1908), no. 397, p. 83: "11 octobre 1448. Au général des Carmes et aux prieurs de

la province de Tours. –Confirme la concession faite par Martin V [1417–1431] à Thomas Connette, condamné par hérésie, de recevoir dans le duché de Bretagne deux endroits pour y bâtir des couvents."

65. Carmelites in Leon: Leguay and Martin, *Fastes et malheurs*, p. 358; the suspicion about the "miracle" in Nantes: Martin, *Ordres mendiants*, p. 371.

66. Amongst those connected to the ducal family, only Symon Maydo and Pierre Filloche mention the trip to Brother Thomas; it does not form part of the story told by Perrin Hervé, Jean Rolland, Perrin's wife, Hervé Maydo, or Pierre de Bonabry, all of whom had connections to the ducal family.

67. Although Nancy Caciola has recently argued that, in discussions of the discernment of spirits in the fifteenth century, it is impossible to draw such distinctions: "Spiritual Physiologies I: Naturalizing the Discernment of Spirits in the Later Middle Ages," paper delivered at the workshop "Miracles as Epistemic Things" held at the Max Planck Institute for the History of Science, Berlin, October 30, 2004. See also her *Discerning Spirits: Divine and Demonic Possession in the Middle Ages* (Ithaca and London: Cornell University Press, 2004), esp. pp. 207–15.

68. ADM MS 87 G 11, witness number 4 (Perrinus Herveus alias Grasset).

69. ADM MS 87 G 11, witness number 15 (Johanna, uxor Perrini Hervei alias Grasset)

70. Caciola, *Discerning Spirits*, p. 41, offers a list of terms for possessed females drawn from exorcists' manuals that includes the notion of being "vexed" by a demon: *daemoniaca, vexata, obsessa, energumena, famula Dei*. In other instances, vexation by demons is something clearly different from possession, as when demons vex and torture a saint beloved of God. Along the lines of Perrin's distinction between being vexed and possessed, Caciola also quotes Vincent of Beauvais's attempt "to systematize the vocabulary of demonic interference" in the *Speculum naturalis*: "Energumens [i.e., demoniacs], properly speaking, are people whom demons harass interiorly [i.e., as opposed to exterior "vexing"]." (Caciola, *Discerning Spirits*, p. 214).

71. ADM MS 87 G 11, witness number 13 (Johannes Rolandi).

72. ADM MS 87 G 11, witness number 18 (Herveus Maydo).

73. ADM MS 87 G 11, witness numbers 26 (Herveus Le Goff) and 27 (Yvo Le Houssec).

74. ADM MS 87 G 11, witness numbers 30 (Michael Maceot) and 156 (Silvester Stephani).

75. ADM MS 87 G 11, witness number 36 (Johannes Boayden).

76. ADM MS 87 G 11, witness number 8 (Petrus Floch).

77. ADM MS 87 G 11, witness numbers 17 (Johanna, relicta Johannis Damon) and 60 (Thomas Le Brun).

78. ADM MS 87 G 11, witness number 33 (Petrus de Bonabri).

79. Caciola, *Discerning Spirits*, esp. pp. 31–78.

80. Thomas Aquinas, *Summa theologiae*, 2a 2ae, quaest. 175, reply art. 1, quoted in Caciola, *Discerning Spirits*, p. 33. (emphasis added.)

81. Caciola, *Discerning Spirits,* esp. chapter 6. A major thrust of Caciola's argument is that the debate came to center on *women's* behavior in particular and that the focus on the discernment of spirits was, in the end, a way of controlling and disciplining women's spirituality into less ecstatic, more controllable forms. The case of Perrin Hervé offers an important counter example; not *all* late medieval demoniacs were women.

82. André Goddu, "The Failure of Exorcism in the Middle Ages," quoted in Caciola, *Discerning Spirits,* pp. 235–36. Caciola notes, however, that if exorcisms connected to saints were on the decline, the proliferation of exorcists' manuals in small, portable format, indicates the flourishing of exorcism as liturgical performance.

83. Caciola, *Discerning Spirits,* pp. 241, 244–45, 249.

84. ADM MS 87 G 11, witness number 8 (Petrus Floch).

85. ADM MS 87 G 11, witness number 9 (Symon Maydo).

86. Interestingly enough, one manual of exorcism directed that the victim be wrapped in a clerical stole, not unlike Perrin, who slept on Vincent's tomb with his head wrapped in the preacher's cape. Caciola, *Discerning Spirits,* p. 242.

87. ADM MS 87 G 11, witness number 4 (Perrinus Hervei alias Grasset), who describes himself as *jejuno stomacho.*

88. Caciola, *Discerning Spirits,* pp. 42–43 (demons entering through mouth); 189–207 (physiology of possession).

89. Caciola, *Discerning Spirits,* pp. 41–42 (Gregory the Great's anecdote about a nun who ingested a demon along with a cabbage eaten without making the sign of the cross over it; a demon drunk in with some milk that suddenly turned black).

90. For e.g., Marsilio Ficino, *Three Books on Life,* ed. and trans., Carol V. Kaske and John R. Clark (Binghamton, NY: Medieval and Renaissance Texts and Studies, in conjunction with the Renaissance Society of America, 1989), I.vii (p. 125): "And excessive food recalls all the power of nature first of all to the stomach to digest it. This renders nature unable to exert itself at the same time in the head and for reflection. In the next place, food badly digested dulls the sharpness of the mind with many dense vapors and with humors. But even if the food is sufficiently digested, nevertheless, as Galen says, 'the mind that is choked up with fat and blood cannot perceive anything heavenly.' "

91. Laura Smoller, "Defining the Boundaries of the Natural in the Fifteenth Century: The Inquest into the Miracles of St. Vincent Ferrer (d. 1419)," *Viator* 28 (1997): 333–59.

92. For e.g., Jean Gerson and Pierre d'Ailly, as quoted in Caciola, *Discerning Spirits,* p. 290; see also Laura Smoller, *History, Prophecy, and the Stars: The Christian Astrology of Pierre d'Ailly, 1350–1420* (Princeton, NJ: Princeton University Press, 1994), pp. 100–101 (d'Ailly's two treatises *De falsis prophetis*).

93. For Coetmur's appointment as procurer: ADM MS 87 G 11 (signature 8, pp. 20–21) and Fages, *Histoire*, pp. 390–391.

94. Goodich, "Liturgy and the Foundation of Cults," p. 146.

95. Goodich, "Liturgy and the Foundation of Cults," p. 157.

96. "After the death": ADM MS 87 G 11, witnesses numbers 8 (Petrus Floch) and 17 (Johanna relicta Johannis Damon); "around two years or so after. . .": witness number 33 (Petrus de Bonabri).

97. ADM MS 87 G 11, witness numbers 4 (Perrinus Hervei alias Grasset) and 15 (Johanna uxor Perrini Hervei alias Grasset).

98. ADM MS 87 G 11, witness numbers 36 (Johannes Boayden) and 156 (Silvester Stephani). They may have both been asked specifically about the time of the miracle, since in the testimony of both witnesses, there is a phrase stating that the witness "does not remember otherwise about the time."

99. ADM MS 87 G 11, witness numbers 9 (Symon Maydo), 8 (Petrus Floch), 26 (Herveus Le Goff), and 27 (Yvo le Houssec).

100. For e.g., ADM MS 87 G 11, witness numbers 6 (Oliverius Le Bourdiec presbiter), 8 (Petrus Floch), 39 (Egidius Maletaille), 111 (Johannes Bourdin), and 239 (Yvo Natal).

101. Ranzano, Bibl. Cas. MS 112, fol. 62v; Fages, *Histoire*, 2:315, 322.

102. For example, ADM MS 87 G 11, witness numbers 1 (Yvo Gluidic), 5 (Alanus Philippot), 28 (Johannes Jegot), 38 (Johanna, wife of Johannis Baut), 58 (Johanna uxor Guillermi Bourdon), 122 (Oliverius Danoual), and 281 (Johannes Avice).

103. As did Perrin Hervé, Symon Maydo, Jean Rolland, Hervé Maydo, Yvo Le Houssec, Jean Boayden, and Silvester Stephani. On an average, Brittany witnesses testified to 1.44 miracles each; the witnesses to Perrin Hervé's miracle testified, on an average, to 2.57 miracles each.

104. Ranzano's *vita* appears in *AASS*, April, vol. 5, pp. 481–510; his brief listing of miracles *post mortem* is at pp. 509–510; it includes none of the miracles from the Brittany inquest.

105. Castiglione's list of miracles can be found in *AASS*, April, vol. 5, pp. 510–512, as well as in Vincent Ferrer, *Sermones de tempore et de sanctis* (Venice: Jacobus Pentius de Leuco, for Lazarus de Soardis), fol. [a3]v (exemplar from Bridwell Library Special Collections, Perkins School of Theology, Southern Methodist University, call number Bridwell 06298).

106. Fages, *Histoire*, 2: 282–83. Only the section of the tapestry with Vincent's posthumous miracles survives and still hangs in the cathedral in Vannes.

CHAPTER 7

SINGLE WOMEN, WORK, AND FAMILY: THE CHANCERY DISPUTE OF JANE WYNDE AND MARGARET CLERK

Cordelia Beattie

the same Margarete then or yet havyng no childe of her owne feithfully promysed to take the seid Jane your seid Oratrice [female petitioner] as her daughter and childe and do to her as she wold to her doughter or childe yf she had eny of her owne.[1]

> [Petition of Thomas Wynde and his wife, Jane]

for the favour and godewille she [Margaret] bare to the same Jane on a tyme when she was sike she then by her wille bequested to the same Jane dyverse parcelles of hir gods and if she had thenne died she shuld have had theym and afterward the same Jane departed unkyndly from hir ayenst hir plesur wherfor she withdrewe her favour from hir.[2]

> [Margaret Clerk's Answer]

The above two extracts are taken from the records of a dispute heard in the English Court of chancery at the end of the fifteenth century. Thomas Wynde and his wife, Jane, submitted a petition asking for a writ of *sub pena* to force Jane's former employer, Margaret Clerk, to appear before the Chancellor. Thomas, while cited as a co-petitioner, is only invoked at the beginning and end of the petition. The petition claims that Margaret owed Jane some recompense for a term of service that lasted more than six years. Margaret Clerk, in turn, submitted a written response to their allegations, which would help the court decide what action to take next. As was conventional in chancery, these documents were written in the third person. Since chancery was not a court of record, how this case ended is not known. The survival of Clerk's answer, in addition to the original petition, makes this case relatively unusual for a minor dispute.

Legal battles, by their nature, focus on the moment at which a relationship breaks down. In this case, though, to support their respective stories each side offered an account of the relationship between the two women prior to the dispute. Both women were then unmarried but there were clearly disparities in their age, wealth, and power. Margaret Clerk was engaged in brewing and was wealthy enough to hire a chantry priest.[3] This would probably associate her with what can be called an urban bourgeoisie.[4] The location of the household is not given but Margaret is said to be "of Ramsey," which was a small town in Huntingdonshire.[5] The Wyndes' petition is endorsed with the name of a surety from London but sureties could be found once the bill was brought to chancery.[6] The petition also states—as can be seen in the first extract—that Margaret had no children of her own but it is unclear whether she was widowed or never married. Her wealth might suggest the former, although she could have inherited property from her parents rather than a husband.[7]

The two documents give different accounts of the circumstances of Jane's employment and subsequent service, although there are a couple of points on which they agree. First, that Jane was a servant in Margaret's house until she left to marry Thomas. Second, Margaret did have Jane written into her testament at one point. However, what were primarily under dispute in this case were the terms of Jane's employment and her claim to the disputed bequest. In order to make the argument for economic compensation, Jane's petition not only emphasizes the women's working relationship but alleges that Margaret had promised to treat her "as her daughter and childe." Margaret's answer downplays both aspects and argues that she owed Jane nothing. The historian need not position herself with the chancellor and adjudicate whose story should be believed.[8] Edward Muir and Guido Ruggiero suggest that "lies can often tell more about the past than apparent truths. . .Not just any lie will do in testifying about a crime. Usually lies must have the ring of credibility."[9] In this case, both documents were presumably intended to offer plausible accounts. As such they allow one to move beyond the alleged truths of the dispute itself on to broader cultural attitudes, about—for example—employment practices and kinship. Aspects of Jane and Margaret's accounts will be compared with what was stated in other chancery petitions. It must be borne in mind, though, that the stories told would have been affected by the court to which they were being presented. The documents that survive—in this case, the written petition and answer—were determined just as much, if not more, by the legal requirements of chancery as by actual events.[10] For this reason, the nature of the court, its procedure, and the sources will be discussed first.

The Court of Chancery

This essay is concerned with what is known as the "English" side of chancery, the chancellor's jurisdiction to deal with bills of complaint, so-called because the records are predominantly in English.[11] The key aspect of the "English" side is that it did not operate according to the principles of common law. Although some scholars prefer to call the late medieval chancery a "court of conscience" rather than an equity court, the important point is that the chancellor decided cases according to some notion of what was fair or just.[12] As the chancellor was not bound by legal precedent, there was no need for chancery to be a court of record. This perhaps explains why we rarely get to know the final judgment on a case before 1544, and not all the supporting material survives.[13] In order for a case to fall under the remit of the "English" side, the petitioner had to claim that he or she would not get justice in a common law court, for example, because the case was not actionable under common law, the petitioner was too poor to afford legal counsel, or the opponent was so powerful that the trial would be unfair.

The Wyndes do not fall into the "too poor" or "too powerless" categories, and do not make those claims. The case essentially revolves around a breach of trust. According to the petition, Margaret had promised to treat Jane as if she were her daughter and child and this was the understanding under which she had performed over six years of service. The Wyndes had no documentary evidence on which they could take this claim to a common law court. There was no written agreement and, indeed, no specific oral agreement as to what Jane should get for her service. Margaret had made a testament in which she had promised her various goods, but, as she was still alive, she had a right to change it. By appealing to the chancellor, the Wyndes presumably hoped that this would either force Margaret to offer a settlement or that the chancellor would make Margaret act on the initial promise.[14] Chancery differed from a common law court in that it could not only award damages but also order the performance of an agreement.[15]

It has been argued that courts like chancery, which operated on some principle of "equity," were more attractive to women because they circumvented the restrictions of common law, such as married women's coverture.[16] Tim Stretton is more circumspect and argues that just as the common law could be used to women's advantage, so too could equity be used against them.[17] It should be remembered that the petition under discussion was brought in joint names. Thomas Wynde clearly had a vested interest in Margaret Clerk being made to hand over some compensation to his wife, Jane, as—under the law of coverture—it would become his legal property.

Compared with common law procedure, bringing a case to chancery was a less formal process. Chancery was always open and could sit anywhere.[18] A case was begun by a bill of complaint, rather than by purchasing a command that a court deal with a case (known as an original writ).[19] This meant that the process could be swifter and cheaper than that of a common law court. The complaint to chancery could be made orally but it is difficult to estimate how many cases began in that way.[20] The petitions, which are our main source for what happened in chancery, are the bills that were handed in to the court by lawyers.[21] Although these were commonly written in English from the reign of Henry VI (1422–61),[22] it is not the case—as one social historian has claimed—that they "were written (or dictated) fairly informally by local people. . .using whatever arguments and forms of expression they thought would be most convincing."[23] Chancery petitions are very formulaic, both in terms of their structure and the language used. The petitions, therefore, do not offer an unmediated petitioner's "voice" but, then, neither does any source. Before returning to the specific case of the Wyndes and Margaret Clerk, I shall argue that there are ways in which the chancery documents can be understood as belonging to the parties in dispute, but it is important that the constraining factors are also recognized.

Haskett has identified the existence of eleven distinct sections in a chancery petition, each of which served a particular function. A petition begins with an address to the chancellor, the feature that has allowed petitions to be approximately dated. The next four sections together constitute the description of the case (what should have happened, what has prompted the bill, and the effects of the problem). The petition ends with a prayer to the chancellor (a formal request for help), itself divided into six sections.[24] The language used is also often formulaic—for example, claims that the problem had led to the "utter undoing" of the petitioner—but there is more diversity in the description of the case.[25] While both the format and the language of the petitions suggest the involvement of lawyers, this does not rule out the importance of the petitioner.[26] Haskett's analysis of bill pairs—petitions pertaining to the same problem but from different petitioners—led to his argument that the distinct canon of form was used by lawyers "in a very active and creative manner" to better suit an individual petitioner.[27] This enables one to think about the creation of a petition as interplay between a lawyer and a petitioner. The petitioner would tell her story to the lawyer, not necessarily unprompted. The lawyer would structure and reword certain aspects of the story to fit the formula of a chancery petition but ensure that it was tailored to the individual petitioner.

Both petitioner and lawyer would have wanted to present a case that was going to have the greatest chance of success in chancery, but they would not have had free reign to concoct a fiction. There are also examples of petitions that failed due to errors of fact and had to be resubmitted.[28] The intention of a chancery petition was not to tell a compelling story but to get the case accepted into this venue. A brief discussion of the procedure of a chancery case will substantiate this point.

After a petition was handed in to chancery, if its case was appropriately set out a writ would be issued. Most petitions request a writ of some sort, usually to have either the opponent brought into chancery or the petitioner if he or she could not afford bail or was being denied it due to a powerful opponent.[29] The Wyndes' petition requested a writ of *sub pena* to require Margaret Clerk to appear in chancery. The next stage would have been for the opponent to answer the charges made, under oath. This differed from the common law system where the rule against self-incrimination prevented the use of oaths.[30] It is likely that the opponent would have had to do this in person.[31] The petitioner then had the option of submitting a replication, responding to the opponent's answer, which might in turn produce a rejoinder from the defendant, and so on, until the allegations of the bill had been whittled down to a set of agreed points at issue.[32] These were then used for the next stage, the gathering of evidence. Witnesses could be examined and depositions produced. By the mid-fifteenth century, it seems that all these elements were presented to the chancellor in written form.[33] Margaret's answer was evidently submitted in this way as it concludes by asserting that she was willing to prove her case in chancery, if required. The chancellor could then make a decision on the evidence that was before him, order a search for further evidence, or examine further any of the parties involved. It is likely that not all cases lasted the distance, with some being dismissed, and others lapsing due to lack of funds or because the defendants had settled out of court.[34]

In many ways what was presented in the written documents was crucial for both parties as their day in court—if it came—was far along the process. In the Elizabethan Court of Requests, which had a virtually indistinguishable process from chancery at that date, attorneys appeared at this hearing, with or without the parties they represented.[35] According to Stretton, in this court "judges were asked to choose between two or more conflicting representations of the truth, rather than to attempt to reconstitute the truth itself, as they might under an inquisitorial system. They relied on the arguments and evidence presented by each party, and rarely cross-examined witnesses to establish points not already raised by counsel. In short, they. . .restricted themselves to deciding which of the versions offered to them by competing lawyers was more compelling."[36] It has been argued that procedure was less formal before the sixteenth century, but it is still likely that from the mid-fifteenth century the written documents were the main means by which petitioners and their opponents could communicate their version of events, although both needed to ensure that they could defend in person whatever was alleged therein.[37] In this sense, then, the surviving texts can be seen as representing the respective voices of Jane and Margaret.

The Dispute

According to Jane's petition, when she was a single woman, aged eighteen, she and some of her "frendes" (kin) came to an agreement with Margaret Clerk that Jane should serve Margaret "in the occupacioun of brewing." No covenant was made between them as to the length of service, nor regarding money or other reward for the work. However, Margaret promised to treat Jane as if she was her daughter, as she had no children of her own. Jane came to Margaret with clothing, provided by her kin, and thirty ells of linen cloth.[38] The petition then relates that Margaret became ill and, at the point of death, made her testament and bequeathed to Jane some clothing, various household goods including brewing equipment, and first option to buy Margaret's house, and the rest of the brewing vessels. Jane served Margaret for around six and a half years and left to get married. She took neither wages nor apparel from Margaret.

Margaret, in her response to the petition, counters this story in a number of ways, first, as regards the initial agreement for Jane's service. According to Margaret's answer, a long time prior to taking in Jane, she had retained the service of a priest, Sir William Conyngton, to sing mass and pray for her and the souls of her parents and other relatives. Subsequently, he asked Margaret to take in his niece, Jane, offering to pay for her meat and drink and all other charges as she would do service for him too. Second, the answer challenges Jane's claim that she had brought with her cloth paid for by her own kin. It argues that Margaret had paid for the flax "and other stuffe" to make yarn, which she set Jane to spin "at the coste and charge of the same Margaret." This made thirty ells of cloth which she gave to Jane, along with "many other thynges. . .while she was yn hir service." Third, the answer disputes that the testamentary bequests which the petition had referred to were recompense for service and instead claims that they arose from "the favour and godewille" which Margaret then had toward Jane. As far as Margaret was concerned, there was no breach of promise as if she had died at that point Jane would have received the goods. However, Margaret's right to change her own will, which she did when Jane left her service "ayenst hir pleasur," is also asserted.

Both sides anticipated that their stories were credible and would help their case in chancery. At the heart of this dispute was Jane's work. Was she employed by Margaret or by her uncle? Who should have provided for her? Was she owed anything for the work performed? Jane's petition alleges that she was employed by Margaret in the trade of brewing, her kin would continue to provide her with clothing but Margaret would treat Jane as if her own daughter and, at the end of the period of service, she would be rewarded materially for her work. Margaret's answer is very clear that Jane was employed to wait on her uncle, a chantry priest, and providing for her was his responsibility. As such, this case can be used to think about women and work, in particular the overlapping spheres of service, apprenticeship, and family.

As P.J.P. Goldberg has put it, "Any relationship between master or mistress might technically be seen as one of service."[39] In this dispute, we have two very different but plausible accounts of a service relationship. In one, the young woman was employed in a trade and expected recompense. In the other, she undertook a variety of chores in return for bed and board. One school of thought sees both forms of work as offering young women various opportunities. Historians such as Smith, Goldberg, and Poos have made the case for the prevalence of "life-cycle service" in medieval England from at least the late fourteenth century. Young people, between the ages of twelve and thirty, would leave home and reside in an employer's household, usually serving for contractually limited periods, until they left to marry or work independently.[40] As such, service has a significant place in any discussion of women's work. Goldberg has most forcefully argued the positive aspects of service. For example, it "allowed them greater opportunity to find and even reject prospective marriage partners. . . It permitted them a degree of independence that young girls living at home with their parents could not have enjoyed," and could also offer "a craft or commercial training that might be valuable subsequently."[41] However, most recently, Kim Phillips has argued—from the evidence of low wage rates and that some women worked for food, lodging, and clothes only—that "it is difficult to see how such harsh working conditions could have in general held a high degree of economic and emotional independence for young women."[42] The two different accounts that Jane's petition and Margaret's answer offer will not resolve this debate. They do suggest, though, that the issue of what young women could expect from service was also contested in the late fifteenth century. I shall use the details of this case alongside other evidence, particularly from additional chancery petitions, to say more about both types of service relationship. Key areas which will be discussed are the age of servants, the links between service and marriage, remuneration, the nature and status of work performed, the involvement of others in setting up service positions, and the relationship between servant and employer.

Jane's petition can be used to think about the age of entering and leaving service in late fifteenth-century England. However, as some of the data is presented in an approximate or contradictory way in this petition, attention should first be paid to how precisely time was recollected. The petition states that Jane was "xviij yeres and more" when she went to work for Margaret Clerk. Does this mean a few months beyond age eighteen or does this suggest that Jane did not know her precise age? It is possible that the latter was the case as there was no official system for recording births until the sixteenth century. In other courts there were inquiries into the exact age of individuals, which relied on witness testimony about when a birth took place and how they recalled this.[43] Goldberg, in his study of fourteenth and fifteenth century deposition evidence from the diocese of York, found that "age is recorded fairly consistently for witnesses from the late fourteenth century onwards. . .In the case of younger witnesses. . .precise ages are indeed frequently given and these may be regarded with some real measure of confidence. But for most older age groups. . .ages are frequently rounded up to the nearest decennial. Such ages are often qualified as approximate (*circiter*) or a minimum *(et amplius)*." He gives the example of one man who was said to be twenty "or more" when he first testified early in 1394, but to be age thirty when he deposed five months later.[44] The arguments concerning whether one Alice de Rouclif was eleven or twelve at the time she allegedly consummated her disputed marriage, though, suggest that even the ages of younger individuals could be approximations.[45] Jane's petition also relates that she worked for Margaret for "vj yeres and a half," although no agreement had been made at the outset as to length of service. However, further on in the petition there is a reference to "the seid terme of vj yeres." The discrepancy might be because no fixed term had been agreed and Jane's leaving came about because she was getting married, rather than the end of a specific term. The petition recounts that Jane served "unto the tyme your seid Oratrice was married." Margaret's answer alleges that "Jane departed unkindly from hir ayenst hir pleasur," which suggests an unexpected departure. The periods of service stated, therefore, might both be approximations.[46]

We might accept, then, that Jane was not much older than eighteen when she entered Margaret's service and that she worked for just over six years. Goldberg's study of ecclesiastical court depositions found no servant below the age of twelve and rarely beyond about twenty-seven or twenty-eight.[47] Jane therefore seems to fit the profile of a life-cycle servant. I discuss what other petitions suggest about the age of servants, though, as later I make use of a petition relating to a female servant of the age of seven.

An Italian visitor to London around 1500 commented that males and females were commonly put into service at the age of seven or nine, but the scholarly consensus seems to be that this was the view of a stranger, based chiefly in London, and primarily concerning apprentices.[48] Chancery petitions, even when relating to service disputes, only occasionally give information about the age of the servants. Besides Jane's petition, all other references to the age of servants denote younger persons. For example, one John Brown's petition complains that his master sold his lands in Welle, Norfolk, while he was "within age of xiiij yere. . .tender of age and in his dayly service and rule."[49] The petition of John Langrake, a citizen of London, tells how he had been unfairly accused of having raped a servant "being of the age of xii yere which is of right wanton disposicion."[50] That of John Elyngham, keeper of the King's pavilions, recounts how Alison, wife of Roger Benyngton, had abducted his "daughter and servant" to look after her sick husband. The girl is called a "child" but said to be aged twelve.[51] In another petition, there is a reference to a "child" being employed to wait on a boarder but no age is given.[52] So far, all these cases fit with the minimum suggested by Goldberg, but a late fifteenth century petition relates how Katherine Cole agreed to let her daughter "being within vij yere of age"[53] live with the widow Elizabeth Broun for the latter's "ease in her age." Barbara Hanawalt found evidence that service might start as young as seven, but argues that twelve was considered a more suitable age for a servant.[54] Nicholas Orme notes examples of female servants of the ages of seven and nine, but suggests that it was more common for regular work to start from the ages of twelve and fourteen.[55] It might well be that, whereas cause papers might under-represent the young as testimony below the age of puberty was forbidden, age was most often emphasized in chancery petitions when the servant was young, presumably in order to add an extra dimension to the disputes.[56]

The information given in Jane's petition suggests that she married around the age of twenty-four or twenty-five. Those who argue for the prevalence of life-cycle service see this and late age of marriage for both sexes (mid to late twenties) as demonstrations that late medieval England followed what has been termed a northwest European marriage pattern.[57] Jane's move from service to marriage is one replicated in other petitions. For example, the petition of Alice, widow of Robert Chamberleyn, relates to when she was in service for her now deceased brother, "in her youthe afore the tyme of her marige." Cross-referencing with other sources has established the brother as a member of York's mercantile elite. The impression given is that Alice went into service with the expectation that she would leave to marry and that the employment would help increase her marriage portion. The petition claims that during this time—first stated as eight years—Alice delivered to her brother more than five marks, various household goods, and a decorated girdle, and that the money "was gevyn unto her by her frendys towards her marige." Her brother subsequently promised her forty marks on her marriage in recompense for the money, the goods, and her service, now stated as twenty-two years.[58] There are other petitions which suggest that employers might promise a marriage portion for successful service, although they originate in the counties and probably relate to noble service.[59] While some employers did make generous bequests to former servants, Goldberg's study of testamentary bequests to servants in York suggests that legacies of clothing, beds and bedding, chests and pots and pans (which might also be useful toward setting up a marital household) were more commonplace.[60] This is more in line with what Jane was offered, stated as Margaret's "best furred gowne, 1 maser, 1 hernes gyrdeyll, diverse bedding and napry, dyvers utensils with many and divers thynges of her household to a grete value and also certen' bruyng vessels and certen' malte to the value by estimatioun of vj. or vij. marc' or above." Presumably Thomas Wynde is cited as co-petitioner in this case because any property his wife then received would legally be seen as his.[61]

Employers might have viewed the eligibility of servants as a potential problem. The nature of life-cycle service—with the single servant moving into the employer's household—meant that marriage effectively signaled its end with the former servant and spouse moving into a household of their own.[62] Margaret Clerk's answer makes reference to Jane leaving "ayenst hir pleasur." This perspective is evidenced in other petitions. That of three men, one a notary, claims that John Olney had taken a suit of trespass against them for witnessing a contract of marriage between Richard and Alice Bonyfey, saying "they had taken out of his service the seid Alice." Richard's status is less clear, although he was said to be also living in Olney's house.[63] Thomas Shiplode's petition relates how, when he was an apprentice with John Leycestre of Bristol, he contracted marriage with Joan Kerver, also Leycestre's servant. Leycestre then imprisoned him in his house until Shiplode signed a bond saying that he owed his master eleven pounds. The result was that he was not in a position to sue Joan regarding the contract of marriage, despite his confessor's advice to do so.[64] We get a picture from the petitions, then, of service as enabling marriage for the servant—financially and through contact with potential spouses in the household—and as incompatible with it, in that it would cause the servant to leave.

Jane Wynde apparently stayed with the same employer for more than six years. Goldberg and Poos have suggested that it was common for servants to change employers annually, although both found cases where servants stayed in a particular household for a length of time.[65] Chancery petitions suggest that such different practices entailed different pay arrangements. There are generally two types of chancery petition from female servants: those relating to a contractual wrangling which had led the women to be pursued in common law courts, often on other grounds such as debt or theft, and those pursuing the payment of a bequest after the death of a former employer. The contractual disputes concern agreed terms and wage rates. The bequest ones seem to offer a more immediate parallel to this dispute, in that they stem from those who had stayed with one employer for a significant amount of time, sometimes for agreed recompense at the end, sometimes on a less specific understanding, as was alleged in Jane's petition. For example, the petition of William Kyrkeby and his wife, Elizabeth, claims that no wages were ever agreed for Elizabeth's service with William Plummer, her cousin, but that he did promise payment for her service of twelve years. In this case her father seems to have been the intermediary and perhaps the kin connection led to the lack of detail in the original agreement.[66] The petition of John Nyman and his wife, Edith, does suggest a more specific arrangement with her former master, Walter Rawlys. It claims that Edith was "contynually in service" with him for nine years "and more" which meant he owed her four pounds and sixteen shillings, which he kept promising to pay before he died. The petition attempts to make Eve Rawlys, his widow and executrix, pay up.[67] However, that of Henry Archer and his wife, Joan, suggests that such bequests might not be fixed at the start but reflect the servant's contribution during the period of service. It alleges that Joan's master, John Welles, wanted to bequeath to her twenty pounds for the "grete and contynuell labour and attendaunce that she had with hym yn his sekeness," and the Archers were pursuing Welles' executor, William Clif, for that amount. From the surviving testament it can be seen that Welles did leave a servant called Joan twenty pounds, while other female servants were allocated forty shillings.[68] Margaret Clerk's answer claims that she made the favorable bequest to Jane "for the favour and godewille she bare to the same Jane, on a tyme when she was sike."

It is possible that individuals might stay in a particular household for a substantial period of time if they were learning a trade, one of the benefits posited for life-cycle service. Indeed, Jane's petition constructs a picture of a service relationship in which she would learn a particular occupation and eventually take over her mistress's business. While it does not go as far as arguing a formal apprenticeship, there are elements to the account which suggest a not dissimilar situation. According to the petition, Jane "was put to serve with the seid Margaret Clerk in the occupacioun of brewing." This statement associates the petition with ones which relate to apprenticeship agreements, rather than those from other female servants which rarely mention what specific tasks the women performed.[69] For example, the petition of Edmund Crosse, a London dyer, tells how Margaret Westhouse was put with his wife Agnes "to lerne the crafte and *occupacioun* of Shepstry."[70] The petition of John Jonson of Exeter and his wife, Anastase, relates how Katherine Raddon was brought to them by her relative, Thomas Raddon, to be "taught the crafte of a sylkwoman" but, when he saw that Katherine was "well and perfectely instructe and lernyed in her seid *occupacion*," he removed her and refused to pay for the three years. In this petition, Katherine's period of instruction is also referred to as "service."[71]

The petition of Emma Wyngar suggests the existence of a practice that shared some similarities with a formal apprenticeship but also with a more general service arrangement. Emma's petition asserts that when she was put in service with William Rippyngale and Margery, his wife, it was agreed that Margery would teach the girl "the crafte and misterie of a silkewoman and sewing." Emma's mother was to pay yearly twenty shillings for the teaching and the girl was to do other service in return for meat and drink. Emma only stayed with them for two years, whereas an apprenticeship would usually last seven years.[72] Also, the petition claims that she did indeed do other work for the couple.[73] We do not know how widespread such arrangements were, but cases involving male apprentices not only show that some felt they should not have to perform other unskilled tasks but that employers might expect this.[74] Phillips' contribution to the historiographical argument about how prevalent female apprenticeships were in late medieval England also supports the case for less formal arrangements. She argues that "the substantial numbers of mistresses and masters of girls appearing before the mayor's court [of London] to answer why they had not properly enrolled them suggests that female apprenticeship was more common and *ad hoc* than available records indicate, and many girls may have served for only a short time, providing craft households with useful and financially attractive labour."[75] It is perhaps also telling that most of the references to female apprentices come from a limited range of trades (usually textile ones).[76] While the London craft fraternity of the Brewers provided for the good treatment of apprentices who were the sons and *daughters* of members in 1388, Judith Bennett found little evidence of any apprenticeships—male or female—in the London brewing trade before the sixteenth century.[77]

The crucial difference between Jane's petition and the apprenticeship ones is that there is no suggestion that Margaret was being paid to train her. Indeed, if she was, surely Jane should not have expected any recompense. In the case of Katherine Raddon, her kinsman was meant to pay five marks for her learning and forty shillings annually for her bed and board. Another petition relates how William Balard found a position for his cousin's daughter, Elyn, to "lerne shepstrywerke" with Hugh Sande and his wife, Joan. The girl's father, John Usher, was to pay forty shillings and find clothing for her.[78] In the above cases, someone—usually a relative—was still providing for the worker. The closest Jane's petition comes to this is the suggestion that her kin provided her with clothing. In service relationships the master or mistress would have provided clothing, as well as food and accommodation.[79] This detail was presumably to add to the claim that Jane was not working for merely bed, board, and clothing, but expected material recompense at the end.

The reference to a specific trade in Jane's petition was perhaps intended to elevate her position above that of a mere domestic servant. Brewers' servants could command decent wages, differentiated by skill, because they were essential to many brewers. However, Bennett has found that by the early fifteenth century such servants were overwhelmingly male and, by the late fifteenth century, single women were employed for only the least skilled and desirable tasks.[80] Another possible reason for the petition's specific reference to brewing is that it associated her further with the contested bequest. The petition relates how Margaret had bequeathed to Jane, amongst some other goods, certain brewing vessels and malt to the value of at least six or seven marks, and gave Jane first option to purchase her house and the rest of the brewing vessels. The overall impression given by the petition, then, is that Jane was being trained to take over Margaret's business. While female servants might have been increasingly pushed to the unskilled aspects of the brewing trade after the Black Death, women continued to run brewhouses, although this obviously required capital to invest in premises, equipment, and labor. As a result, such women were usually married or widowed.[81] With the backing of her husband, Jane might well have been in a position to buy Margaret's house and the rest of the brewing equipment and so to run such an operation.

It could also be argued that the petition was not just using Jane's service of six or more years to lay claim to recompense, but also the position of pseudo-daughter to declare entitlement to the bequest of clothing, household goods, and brewing equipment, which can be seen as providing for her future. An interesting parallel is offered by the work of Dennis Romano on artisan households in fifteenth-and sixteenth-century Venice.[82] As evidence for his contention that the lines between servants, apprentices, and kin were indistinctly drawn, he cites a widow who gave up her three year old daughter for adoption to a cook, who promised to treat the girl as his own child and marry her off as best he could. The contract between them stipulated that if the girl left the cook's household before this, her mother was to reimburse his expenses.[83] Jane's petition argues that Margaret had promised to treat her "as if her own daughter or child." While it is asserted that employers effectively stood *in loco parentis* to their life-cycle servants,[84] the only other petition I have found which uses similar language seems to refer to a cross between adoption and service. The petition of Robert Cole and his wife, Katherine, relates how Katherine had agreed that her seven year old daughter should live with Elizabeth Broun to help her in her old age on condition that the woman "teche hit in all thyng as hit were her owen doughter of her bodye coming." The case came to chancery after the old woman's death as the mother wanted her daughter back but was being challenged by the woman's son.[85] If the understanding between Jane and Margaret was similar to the one discussed by Romano, it would account for both the lack of payment to Margaret for the alleged training and Jane's belief that she should still have been rewarded for her period of service. Margaret's answer does not respond to Jane's claim about treating her as if her daughter, but it does allege that "Jane departed from her unkindly." Although "unknyndly" could suggest ingratitude or discourtesy, it was also used regarding children who violated natural obligations to their parents; "kinde" suggests inherent qualities.[86] The petition of Robert Cole and his wife refers to "the tendre favoure that your said oratrice oweth unto her said childe as *nature* requireth" [my italics] in order to explain the mother's attempt to get her daughter back. Jane's departure without Margaret's consent might also explain the latter's refusal to honor her side of an earlier agreement, if there was one.[87]

Before considering Margaret's answer further, the prominent involvement of a relative and/or a cleric in finding young women household positions deserves comment. Goldberg concluded, from his study of late medieval York, that service positions were most frequently found through informal networks based on kinship, trade, or locality, although Hanawalt has noted the involvement of clerics in London.[88] Jane's petition relates how her kin negotiated the arrangement with Margaret. From Margaret's answer, it seems that the key party was Jane's uncle, a chantry priest. Earlier I noted the kin involvement in the placing of Elizabeth Kyrkeby, and this was probably the case with Alice Chamberleyn who went into service for her brother.[89] From the cases just discussed, William Balard's petition relates how he placed Elyn because he was better acquainted in London than his cousin, her father, perhaps because he was a chaplain, Katherine Raddon's relative, Thomas Raddon, was a priest, and Margaret Westhouse was placed by Christopher Plomer, the parson of St Michael's in Basingshaw, London. We can also find examples of clerics involved in setting up other service positions. For example, the petition of James Gere, a priest, tells how one Joan Busshe "beyng contre woman and of olde acquayntaunce with your said suppliaunt required him to set her in to service" in London, which he arranged.[90] Clerics were evidently viewed as trusted intermediaries by both sides, particularly in large cities. The petition of

Thomas Lawton complains that the clerk Thomas Beyvyll put one Agnes Todde to board with him in Newport Paynell, Buckinghamshire, saying that she was "of good true and honest disposicoun." However, after she had been in Lawton's house fourteen weeks or more, she stole goods to the value of sixteen pounds.[91] Vouching for someone was clearly a serious matter. The petition of John Twigge, a London haberdasher, claims that a physician, Wolfram Cook, had taken an action against him for having vouched that Agnes Copley was a "trewe woman," as—subsequently employed by Cook as a servant—she stole from him.[92] Margaret's answer gives the impression that she only took Jane in at the request of the young woman's uncle.

Margaret's response has much less to say regarding work performed than Jane's petition but it is at pains to challenge her version as Margaret does not accept that she owes Jane anything. According to Margaret's account, she took Jane in at the request of her chantry priest. The agreement was that he would pay for Jane's food, drink, and all other charges, as she would serve him too. This is plausible. The petition of Alison Taillor, a widow, relates how she employed a "child" to wait on Thomas Webster, a priest, who was boarding with her. The agreement was that she would be fully repaid as he would make her executor of his will.[93] As noted earlier, Margaret also challenges Jane's claim that she had brought with her cloth paid for by her own kin. Her answer counters that she had paid for material to make yarn, which she set Jane to spin, and gave her the cloth which was produced. The reference to Margaret making Jane spin is perhaps also included as it was low status work that any female servant would have been required to do.[94] This and waiting on her uncle are the only tasks mentioned in Margaret's answer. In this version, Jane performed services for Margaret in return, primarily, for lodging and some clothing, and there is no suggestion that Jane learned a trade.

It is here that the second type of chancery petition from female servants becomes relevant. These petitions typically claim that the servants were being falsely sued under the common law, usually for debt or theft, because their employers wanted their labor for free. For example, the petition of Agnes Kyrkeby claims that she was a servant to Robert Brand, a London brewer, for more than six years but he had not paid her so she told him she was leaving his service. He allegedly then initiated various suits against her so that she would work "for nought."[95] The petition of Isabel Estgate contends that John Marchall, a London hatter, had agreed to pay her thirteen shillings and four pence a year. She threatened to leave his service when, after more than half a year, she had only received ten pence. According to the petition, Marchall then began an action of debt against her so that he could have her service without wages.[96] Such petitions suggest a tension between servants, who felt they should be able to hire out their labor freely and be adequately and timely rewarded, and employers, who wanted to retain servants, preferably without paying wages.[97] While the Wyndes initiated this legal dispute, a similar tension between the key parties seems to have existed: Jane felt her service should be materially rewarded and Margaret evidently felt that board and lodging, provided jointly by Jane's uncle and herself, was sufficient recompense.

The claims on both sides in this dispute are commonplace. For example, Maryanne Kowaleski, in a study of late fourteenth century mayor's court records from Exeter, commented: "Servants who wanted to break their service contract normally advanced one of two complaints to show just cause: either their employer's failure to pay their salary or physical abuse. . .Employers frequently sued servants for withdrawal of their services before their term had expired, or for leaving 'without reasonable cause'. Other employers complained about dishonest servants who robbed their masters or cheated them over a period of years."[98] Such allegations have been found in most studies of master-servant relations, regardless of place or period.[99] It is presumably in part about the nature of the relationship, contractual but unequal. In terms of the strategies deployed in the dispute between the Wyndes and Margaret Clerk, though, it is perhaps possible to tie these into a particular historical context.

Goldberg's thesis about the attractiveness of life-cycle service largely pertains to the period from the Black Death to the mid-fifteenth century. He argues that while in the late fourteenth and early fifteenth centuries a high demand for labor led to "excessive" wages, a falling demand in the second third of the fifteenth century meant that by 1500 service was increasingly seen as "menial" and less appropriate for the daughters of urban elites. This view is largely based on his research on York but he does use a cause paper from late fifteenth century London to support this contention.[100] It is likely, though, that demand for servants in the capital remained high and that economic recession did not affect London until the sixteenth century.[101] Others have questioned this hypothesis more generally.[102] Whether there was a shift in how service was viewed in the late fifteenth century or not, it was thought credible at this date for Jane to paint her service as skilled labor which should be materially rewarded and for Margaret to argue in defense that the work itself was not significant enough to discuss or further reward.

The documents of this dispute, then, both give plausible accounts of the relationship between the two women. They have been analyzed for what they suggest of wider cultural understandings of the institution of service and its interconnectedness with other employment practices and familial relationships. It is important, though, that the records are related back to the legal process which produced them. I have argued that the petition and the answer do not allow access to unmediated voices, that the structure and language of the petition and the answer were affected by the involvement of lawyers and the nature of the court. Some scholars who use legal records to discuss subaltern groups argue that it is a matter of isolating the various "veils" or "filters," such as formulaic language, particular legal requirements, or patriarchal conventions, so that we can see past them.[103] Yet to remove such skeins from the records would be to initiate a new form of distortion as people's lives were affected by such factors.[104] Christopher Cannon has argued, regarding common law pleas, that—while we might doubt the stories told of events that supposedly happened outside of court—we cannot doubt the mediated status of the plea: "it is representation in the third person, a report of what a woman said, not her 'complaint' but what 'she complains.' The texts these women had a rightful access to through their legal speaking were, like the stories their speech tells, controlled by the men who wielded legal pen and parchment and who dictated the forms of speech allowable in court."[105] The contention is that legal documents can reveal much about women's lived life at law. While I have sympathy with the project of recovering the lives of ordinary people, recognition of the limitations of the evidence is not to give up on historical subjects but rather a refusal to simplify their lives, which were lived within discursive systems.[106] We need a methodology that respects this point and this essay suggests one of the ways in which social and cultural historians might use chancery records.

Notes

1. The National Archives of the UK (TNA): Public Record Office (PRO), C 1/234/43 (1493–1500). The Petitions are undated but references to specific chancellors in the bills' addresses set date limits in the absence of other information.
2. TNA: PRO, C 1/234/44.
3. The annual cost for a chantry priest was about £6 per annum by the late fifteenth century: Clive Burgess, " 'For the Increase of Divine Service': Chantries in the Parish in Late Medieval Bristol," *Journal of Ecclesiastical History*, 36 (1985): 50 [46–65]. Evidence from Reading and Salisbury confirms the amount: Dr Andrew Brown, personal communication.
4. For the argument that most brewers were not very rich, and that unmarried women would have been amongst the poorest of this group, see Judith M. Bennett, "Women and Men in the Brewers' Gild of London, CA. 1420," in *The Salt of Common Life: Individuality and Choice in the Medieval Town, Countryside, and Church: Essays Presented to J. Ambrose Raftis*, ed. Edwin Brezette DeWindt, SMC 36 (Kalamazoo: Medieval Institute Publications, 1995), pp. 186, 226–28 [181–232].

5. Anne Reiber DeWindt, "The Town of Ramsey: The Question of Economic Development, 1290–1523," in *Salt of Common Life*, pp. 53–116.

6. Margaret E. Avery, "An Evaluation of the Effectiveness of the Court of Chancery Under the Lancastrian Kings," *Law Quarterly Review*, 86 (1970): 96 [84–97].

7. Margaret's answer reveals the chantry priest was "to synge masse and praie for hir and the soules of hir fader and moder and other of hir frendys." This suggests that her parents were deceased but also does not mention a former husband.

8. For discussion of the problematic role of the historian discussing the subaltern from legal records, see John H. Arnold, *Inquisition and Power: Catharism and the Confessing Subject in Medieval Languedoc* (Philadelphia: University of Pennsylvania Press, 2001), pp. 1–15. See also Edward Muir and Guido Ruggiero, "Introduction: The Crime of History," in *History from Crime*, ed. Edward Muir and Guido Ruggiero, trans. Corrado Biazzo Curry, Margaret A. Gallucci, and Mary M. Gallucci (Baltimore: John Hopkins University Press, 1994), pp. vii–x [vii–xviii].

9. Edward Muir and Guido Ruggiero, "Afterword: Crime and the Writing of History," in *History from Crime*, p. 230 [226–36].

10. For a similar argument regarding ecclesiastical court records, see P.J.P. Goldberg, "Fiction in the Archives: The York Cause Papers as a Source for Later Medieval Social History," *Continuity and Change*, 12 (1997): 438 [425–45]. Regarding the records of canonization inquests, see Laura A. Smoller, "Miracle, Memory, and Meaning in the Canonization of Vincent Ferrer, 1453–1454," *Speculum*, 73 (1998): 430–31 [429–54].

11. J.H. Baker, *An Introduction to English Legal History*, 3rd edn. (London: Butterworths, 1990), pp. 117–18.

12. For a summary of the debate see Timothy S. Haskett, "The Medieval English Court of Chancery," *Law and History Review*, 14 (1996): 249–80 [245–313]. See also P. Tucker, "The Early History of the Court of Chancery: A Comparative Study," *English Historical Review*, 115 (2000): 795 [791–811].

13. See Timothy S. Haskett, "The Curteys Women in Chancery: The Legacy of Henry and Rye Brown," in *Women, Marriage, and Family in Medieval Christendom: Essays in Memory of Michael M. Sheehan, C.S.B.*, ed. Constance M. Rousseau and Joel T. Rosenthal, SMC 37 (Kalamazoo: Medieval Institute Publications, 1998), p. 379 n37 [349–98].

14. Stretton found that for many cases in the Elizabethan Court of Requests, which dealt with similar cases to the medieval court of chancery, settlement and arbitration were commonplace: Stretton, *Women Waging Law in Elizabethan England* (Cambridge, UK: Cambridge University Press, 1998), pp. 82–83.

15 Alan Harding, *The Law Courts of Medieval England, Historical Problems: Studies and Documents*, 18 (London: George Allen & Unwin Ltd, 1973), p. 102.

16. Emma Hawkes, " '[S]he will. . .protect and defend her rights boldly by law and reason. . .': Women's Knowledge of Common Law and Equity Courts

in Late-Medieval England," in *Medieval Women and the Law*, ed. Noël James Menuge (Woodbridge: Boydell Press, 2000), pp. 151–56, 160–161 [145–61]; Maria L. Cioni, "The Elizabethan Chancery and Women's Rights," in *Tudor Rule and Revolution: Essays for G.R. Elton from his American friends*, ed. Delloyd J. Guth and John W. McKenna (Cambridge, UK: Cambridge University Press, 1982), pp. 159–82. On coverture, see Caroline M. Barron, "The 'Golden Age' of Women in Medieval London," *Reading Medieval Studies*, 15 (1989): 35–37 [35–58].

17. Tim Stretton, *Women Waging Law*, pp. 28, 33. Butler has also demonstrated how both husbands and wives could make shrewd use of chancery to work around the rules of coverture: Sara M. Butler, "The Law as a Weapon in Marital Disputes: Evidence from the Late Medieval Court of Chancery, 1424–1529," *Journal of British Studies*, 43 (2004): 291–316.

18. Baker, *Introduction to English Legal History*, p. 119.

19. Tucker, "Early History," p. 791.

20. On the debate, see Tucker, "Early History," pp. 793–94.

21. Angus McIntosh, M.L. Samuels, Michael Benskin, eds., with the assistance of Michael Laing and Keith Williams, *A Linguistic Atlas of Late Mediaeval English*, 4 vols. (Aberdeen: Aberdeen University Press, 1986), 1:49. Petitions not in a chancery hand seem to be the originals submitted to chancery which were then copied by chancery clerks before being presented officially: John H. Fisher, Malcolm Richardson, and Jane L. Fisher, eds., *An Anthology of Chancery English* (Knoxville: University of Tennessee Press, 1984), p. 21.

22. Previously they were written in French, with a few in Latin. See John H. Fisher, *The Emergence of Standard English* (Lexington: University Press of Kentucky, 1996), p. 54.

23. Marjorie Keniston McIntosh, *Controlling Misbehavior in England, 1370–1600* (Cambridge, UK: Cambridge University Press, 1998), p. 119.

24. For a fuller discussion of the format, with examples, see Timothy S. Haskett, "The Presentation of Cases in Medieval Chancery Bills," in *Legal History in the Making: Proceedings of the Ninth British Legal History Conference, Glasgow, 1989*, ed. William M. Gordon and T.D. Fergus (London: Hambledon Press, 1991), pp. 12–13, 22–28 [11–28].

25. For e.g. on the language used in discussions of marital violence, see Butler, "Law as a Weapon," p. 296.

26. As many petitions are not in what is known as Chancery Standard English, this suggests the involvement of county lawyers: Timothy S. Haskett, "County Lawyers?: The Composers of English Chancery Bills," in *The Life of the Law: Proceedings of the Tenth British Legal History Conference, Oxford, 1991*, ed. Peter Birks (London: Hambledon Press, 1993), pp. 9–23. In terms of dialect, it has been found that it did not necessarily cohere with the regional characteristics of the petitioner: McIntosh, Samuels, and Benskin, eds., *Linguistic Atlas of Late Mediaeval English*, 1:49–50.

27. Haskett, "County Lawyers," p. 11; Haskett, "Presentation of Cases."

28. Haskett, "Presentation of Cases," pp. 17–21.

29. See Tucker, "Early History," pp. 798, 800–801.

30. Stretton, *Women Waging Law*, p. 80. The examination of the defendant under oath has led to comparisons being drawn with how ecclesiastical courts dealt with suspected heretics. See Haskett, "Medieval English Court of Chancery," p. 256.

31. Stretton, *Women Waging Law*, pp. 79–80.

32. Avery, "Evaluation," p. 91.

33. Haskett "Medieval English Court of Chancery," p. 278. This is the period from which it is commonly said that other documents, besides the initial bill, start to survive. See also Avery, "Evaluation," p. 90.

34. Stretton *Women Waging Law*, p. 82.

35. Stretton, *Women Waging Law*, p. 81.

36. Stretton, *Women Waging Law*, p. 14.

37. Avery, "Evaluation," pp. 86–90. On the employment of attorneys see her p. 86 and Fisher, *Emergence of Standard English*, pp. 54, 162 n41.

38. An ell was a measure of length, used in particular for measuring cloth, fixed in medieval England by various acts of Parliament at forty-five inches.

39. P.J.P. Goldberg, *Women, Work, and Life Cycle in a Medieval Economy: Women in York and Yorkshire c.1300–1520* (Oxford: Clarendon Press, 1992), p. 158. Cf. Sarah C. Maza, *Servants and Masters in Eighteenth-Century France* (Princeton: Princeton University Press, 1983), p. 6: "domestic service is first and foremost a relationship."

40. Richard M. Smith, "Geographical Diversity in the Resort to Marriage in Late Medieval Europe: Work, Reputation, and Unmarried Females in the Household Formation Systems of Northern and Southern Europe," in *Woman is a Worthy Wight: Women in English Society c. 1200–1500*, ed. P.J.P. Goldberg (Stroud: Sutton Publishing Limited, 1992; repr. as *Women in Medieval English Society*, 1997), pp. 29–31, 35–45 [16–59]; Goldberg, *Women, Work, and Life Cycle*, pp. 158–202, 225–32; L.R. Poos, *A Rural Society after the Black Death: Essex 1350–1525* (Cambridge, UK: Cambridge University Press, 1991), pp. 183–206, 225.

41. P.J.P. Goldberg, "Female Labour, Service and Marriage in the Late Medieval Urban North," *Northern History*, 22 (1986), pp. 26, 24 [18–38].

42 Kim M. Phillips, *Medieval Maidens: Young Women and Gender in England, 1270–1540* (Manchester: Manchester University Press, 2003), p. 131. See also Mavis E. Mate, *Women in Medieval English Society* (Cambridge, UK: Cambridge University Press, 1999), p. 57. Maza concluded, regarding service in eighteenth-century France, that it opened up possibilities for some but exposed many to "great dangers": Maza, *Servants and Masters*, p. 105.

43. See S.S. Walker, "Proof of Age of Feudal Heirs in Medieval England," *Mediaeval Studies*, 35 (1973): 306–323; J. Bedell, "Memory and Proof of Age in England 1272–1327," *Past and Present*, 162 (1999): 3–27.

44. Goldberg, *Women, Work, and Life Cycle*, p. 222.

45. P.J.P. Goldberg, trans. and ed., *Women in England c.1275–1525* (Manchester: Manchester University Press, 1995), pp. 58–79. A study in Ghana in the 1960s found that with children from the age of one, families

would only approximate their ages. John C. Caldwell, "Study of Age Misstatement among Young Children in Ghana," *Demography*, 3 (1966): 486 [477–90].

46. Le Roy Ladurie observed how peasants in early fourteenth century Montaillou were vague in their descriptions of time, for example, "three or four years ago." Emmanuel Le Roy Ladurie, *Montaillou: The World-famous Portrait of Life in a Medieval Village* (1978; repr. London: Penguin, 1990), p. 280. An example from Margaret Clerk's answer is that she "long tyme before" had engaged Jane's uncle as a chantry priest.

47. Goldberg, *Women, Work, and Life Cycle*, pp. 168–72. See also Poos, *Rural Society*, pp. 192–95.

48. Charlotte Augusta Sneyd, ed., *A Relation, or Rather a True Account, of the Island of England*, Camden Society, 37 (London: Camden Society, 1847), pp. 24–25. Nicholas Orme, *Medieval Children* (New Haven: Yale University Press, 2001), pp. 309–310; Goldberg, *Women, Work, and Life Cycle*. Cf. Ian Blanchard, "Reviews," *Economic History Review*, 2nd ser. 37 (1984): 118 [115–20].

49. TNA: PRO, C 1/22/67 (1452–54 or possibly 1494–1501).

50. TNA: PRO, C 1/64/1158 (1475–80 or 1483–85). This case is discussed in Barbara A. Hanawalt, *Growing Up in Medieval London: The Experience of Childhood in History* (New York: Oxford University Press, 1993), pp. 183–84.

51. TNA: PRO, C 1/1500/2 (1386–1558).

52. TNA: PRO, C 1/169/5 (1486–93 or 1504–1515).

53. TNA: PRO, C 1/64/731 (1475–80 or 1483–85). Further discussed below.

54. Hanawalt, *Growing Up*, pp. 114, 179.

55. Orme, *Medieval Children*, pp. 308–309. Seven, twelve and fourteen were all thought to be significant ages, denoting the age of reason and age of consent for females and males respectively. See Orme, *Medieval Children*, pp. 68, 336, or Phillips, *Medieval Maidens*, pp. 23, 27, 31.

56. Richard H. Helmholz, *Marriage Litigation in Medieval England* (London: Cambridge University Press, 1974), pp. 155. On the under-representation of the young in cause papers see Frederick Pedersen, "Demography in the Archives: Social and Geographical Factors in Fourteenth-century York Cause Paper Marriage Litigation," *Continuity and Change*, 10 (1995): 420 [405–36]. Goldberg's evidence, though, does include older witnesses who assert how many years it was since they first entered service which gives him their approximate age at entry: Goldberg, *Women, Work, and Life Cycle*, pp. 168–72.

57. Smith, "Geographical Diversity," pp. 25–27, 35–43; Goldberg, *Women, Work, and Life Cycle*, pp. 225–32, 325–29; Poos, *Rural Society*, pp. 141, 147–58. Cf. Mate, *Women in Medieval English Society*, p. 60.

58. TNA: PRO, C 1/126/26 (1506–1515). The damaged petition only names the brother as Thomas F [. . .], a York merchant, but tells how he left his wife, Margaret, as his executrix. She then died so the petition was directed against her executors, William Whytlam, a priest, and George Smyth, a

merchant. The brother can therefore be identified as Thomas Fonyby, a citizen and alderman of York, who died in 1504, leaving his wife, Margaret, as his executrix. Margaret's will of 1506 names her executors as William Whitlame, priest, and George Smyth, merchant. This allowed me to date the petition more narrowly. I acknowledge here the help of Charlotte Carpenter and her database of York's civic elite, 1476–1525. C 1/205/35 (1493–1500) is also an example of a relative, here the girl's father, making annual payments to her master to be kept toward her marriage.

59. E.g. TNA: PRO, C 1/28/179 (1459–66), C 1/61/269 (1480–83), C1/50/94 (1475–80 or 1480–85). On noble service, see Phillips, *Medieval Maidens*, pp. 109–120.

60. Goldberg, *Women, Work, and Life Cycle*, p. 182 and see P.J.P. Goldberg, "What Was a Servant?" in *Concepts and Patterns of Service in the Later Middle Ages*, ed. Anne Curry and Elizabeth Matthew (Woodbridge: Boydell Press, 2000), p. 18 [1–20].

61. For other examples of husbands and wives co-petitioning about what was owed to the wife, see discussion of the Kyrkebys, Nymans and Archers below. There are also similar cases where the husband petitions in his name only. For example, TNA: PRO, C 1/50/94 (1475–80 or 1480–85), C 1/61/269 (1480–83), C 1/187/13 (1493–1500).

62. See Poos, *Rural Society*, pp. 188–92.

63. TNA: PRO, C 1/22/122 (probably 1453–54 but perhaps 1495–1501).

64. TNA: PRO, C 1/75/83 (fourteenth to fifteenth century). From a different perspective, the petition of William Gerardson claims that John Evan tried to force him to marry one of John's servants, who was "not of no virtuse condition": C 1/64/299 (1475–80 or 1483–85). Similar cases are discussed in P.J.P. Goldberg, "Masters and Men in Later Medieval England," in *Masculinity in Medieval Europe*, ed. D.M. Hadley (London: Longman, 1999), pp. 58–61 [56–70]; Shannon McSheffrey, "Men and Masculinity in Late Medieval London Civic Culture: Governance, Patriarchy and Reputation," in *Conflicted Identities and Multiple Masculinities: Men in the Medieval West*, ed. by Jacqueline Murray (New York: Garland Publishing Inc., 1999), p. 250 [243–78].

65. Goldberg, *Women, Work, and Life Cycle*, pp. 174–77; Poos, *Rural Society*, pp. 195–97, 201–204.

66. TNA: PRO, C 1/329/48 (1504–1515). See also the case of Alice Chamberleyn above.

67. TNA: PRO, C 1/151/116 (1486–93 or 1504–1515).

68. TNA: PRO, C 1/28/519 (1459–66); E.F. Jacob with the assistance of H.C. Johnson, eds., *The Register of Henry Chichele, Archbishop of Canterbury, 1414–1443*, 4 vols., Canterbury and York Society, 42, 45–47 (Oxford: Clarendon Press, 1937–47), 2:615–20. This is one of a small number of cases that I have managed to cross-reference with other sources. Usually this relies on a named party being a prominent member of a civic elite. In this example, the master, John Welles, was described in the petition as a London alderman and further information about him can be found in

Sylvia L. Thrupp, *The Merchant Class of Medieval London* (1948; repr. Ann Arbor: University of Michigan Press, 1989), p. 373. The testament reveals that Henry Archer had also been a servant for John Welles, which is presumably how he met his wife.

69. Exceptions include the petition of Joan Bryges which claims that when she was in the service of Richard Thomson she "hade the charge of brede and aylle and other vataylles in his hows" and that of the widow Agnes Elsworth who was hired to look after her master's child: TNA: PRO, C 1/285/24 (1504–1515), C 1/261/33 (1502–1503). On the lack of evidence concerning the specific work of servants see Goldberg, "What Was a Servant?" p. 11, and Poos, *Rural Society*, p. 204.

70. TNA: PRO, C 1/296/70 (1504–1515) [my italics]. A shepster was a seamstress or tailor.

71. TNA: PRO, C 1/327/2 (1504–1155) [my italics]. Joan Wolbarowe's petition which tells how "xiiij yeres past she stode prentice with Katherine Dore of London silkthrowster" also refers to her as a "servant": C 1/75/106 (fourteenth to fifteenth century); it can be dated more precisely to 1459–66 by the survival of related documents, C 1/27/482 and C 1/28/83. For "servant" as a term that was applied to apprentices see Elaine Clark, "Medieval Labor Law and the English Local Courts," *American Journal of Legal History*, 27 (1983): 337 [330–53].

72. Phillips argues that there was no impetus for girls to serve a full term if they would not receive the freedom of the City at the end of it: Phillips, *Medieval Maidens*, p. 134. See also Hanawalt, *Growing Up*, pp. 142–43.

73. TNA: PRO, C 1/274/12 (1502–1503).

74. See Goldberg, "Masters and Men," p. 61.

75. Phillips, *Medieval Maidens*, p. 134. This supports the argument of Caroline M. Barron, "The Education and Training of Girls in Fifteenth-Century London," in *Courts, Counties and the Capital in the Later Middle Ages*, ed. Diana E.S. Dunn (Stroud: Sutton, 1996), pp. 144–46 [139–153]. Cf. Judith M. Bennett, "Medieval Women, Modern Women: Across the Great Divide," in *Culture and History 1350–1600: Essays on English Communities, Identities, and Writing*, ed. David Aers (New York: Harvester Wheatsheaf, 1992), p. 159 [147–75].

76. Barron, "Education and Training," p. 144.

77. Barron, "Education and Training," p. 145; Bennett, "Women and Men in the Brewers' Gild," pp. 196–97.

78. TNA: PRO, C 1/258/6 (1502–1503). Elyn stayed until she married. Shepstry was presumably the wife's craft as the husband is referred to a "brigge," a bridgekeeper. Hans Kurath and Sherman M. Kuhn, eds., *The Middle English Dictionary* (Ann Arbor: University of Michigan Press, 1956–2001; hereafter cited as *MED*), briggere (n.).

79. Clark, "Medieval Labor Law," p. 347; Goldberg, "What Was a Servant?" pp. 7, 16–17.

80. Judith M. Bennett, *Ale, Beer, and Brewsters in England: Women's Work in a Changing World, 1300–1600* (New York: Oxford University Press, 1996), pp. 49, 54–57.

81. Bennett, *Ale, Beer, and Brewsters*, pp. 52–56, 75. As discussed above, Margaret's marital status is unknown. There are earlier examples of never married women being left brewhouses to run: Bennett, "Women and Men in the Brewers' Gild," p. 204.

82. Dennis Romano, *Housecraft and Statecraft: Domestic Service in Renaissance Venice, 1400–1600* (Baltimore: John Hopkins University Press, 1996), pp. 99–105. Smith and Goldberg have argued that in the fifteenth century Italian service was very different to that in northwestern Europe, as suggested by the work of Klapisch-Zuber: Smith, "Geographical Diversity," pp. 27–35, 39–45; Goldberg, *Women, Work, and Life Cycle*, pp. 324–61, esp. 343–45; Christiane Klapisch-Zuber, "Female Celibacy and Service in Florence in the Fifteenth Century," in her *Women, Family and Ritual in Renaissance Italy*, trans. Lydia Cochrane (Chicago, University of Chicago Press, 1985), pp. 165–77; Christiane Klapisch-Zuber, "Women Servants in Florence during the Fourteenth and Fifteenth Centuries," in *Women and Work in Preindustrial Europe*, ed. Barbara A. Hanawalt (Bloomington: Indiana University Press, 1986), pp. 56–80.

83. Romano, *Housecraft and Statecraft*, p. 99. For European examples of assertions that servants or apprentices were to be treated as if the master's child, see Ruth Mazo Karras, *From Boys to Men: Formations of Masculinity in Late Medieval Europe* (Philadelphia: University of Pennsylvania Press, 2003), p. 121; J.E. Shaw, *The Justice of Venice: Authorities and Liberties in the Urban Economy, 1550–1700*, British Academy Postdoctoral Fellowship Monograph (Oxford: Oxford University Press, 2006), chapter 6.

84. Goldberg, "Masters and Men," p. 57; Clark, "Medieval Labor Law," p. 343.

85. TNA: PRO, C 1/64/731 (1475–80 or 1483–85).

86. *MED*, unkindeli (adv.), 3 (a), 4, 5 (a); kinde (n.), 1 (a), 2 (a), (c), 5b (a).

87. Cf. Klapisch-Zuber, "Women Servants," p. 68; Maza, *Servants and Masters*, pp. 171–72.

88. Goldberg, *Women, Work, and Life Cycle*, pp. 177–80; see also his "What Was a Servant?" pp. 13–14. Hanawalt, *Growing Up*, pp. 175–76; see also her p. 133 for examples of an abbot and a recluse performing similar functions.

89. See also TNA: PRO, C 1/46/86 (1467–72 or possibly 1433–43) and C 1/20/13–14 (probably 1425–53; possibly 1465–83).

90. TNA: PRO, C 1/77/44 (1485–86).

91. TNA: PRO, C 1/100/22 (1486–93).

92. TNA: PRO, C 1/31/493 (1465–71 or possibly 1480–83). Hanawalt dates this case to 1483: Hanawalt, *Growing Up*, p. 176.

93. TNA: PRO, C 1/169/5 (cited above).

94. Barbara A. Hanawalt, '*Of Good and Ill Repute': Gender and Social Control in Medieval England* (New York: Oxford University Press, 1998), p. 99; P.J.P. Goldberg, "Coventry's 'Lollard' Programme of 1492 and the Making of Utopia," in *Utopians and Idealists in the Later Middle Ages*, ed. Rosemary Horrox and Sarah Rees Jones (Cambridge, UK: Cambridge University Press, 2001), p. 99 [97–116].

95. TNA: PRO, C 1/66/390 (1475–80 or 1483–85).

96. TNA: PRO, C 1/31/77 (1465–71 or possibly 1480–83). Estgate probably should not have expected any wages before the end of the year: Clark, "Medieval Labor Law," p. 340. See also C 1/66/368 (1475–80 or 1483–85), and C 1/61/377 (1480–83).

97. Some such chancery cases are discussed in Madonna J. Hettinger, "Defining the Servant: Legal and Extra-legal Terms of Employment in Fifteenth-century England," in *The Work of Work: Servitude, Slavery, and Labor in Medieval England*, ed. Allen J. Frantzen and Douglas Moffat (Glasgow: Cruithne Press, 1994), pp. 206–228; I am grateful to Caroline Barron for drawing this article to my attention.

98. Maryanne Kowaleski, "Women's Work in a Market Town: Exeter in the Late Fourteenth Century," in *Women and Work in Preindustrial Europe*, p. 154 [145–64]. See also Clark, "Medieval Labor Law," pp. 335–36, 41.

99. For e.g. see Merry E. Wiesner, *Working Women in Renaissance Germany* (New Brunswick: Rutgers University Press, 1986), pp. 89–90; Monica Chojnacka, *Working Women of Early Modern Venice* (Baltimore: John Hopkins University Press, 2001), pp. 121–22; Maza, *Servants and Masters*, pp. 98–100; Cissie Fairchilds, "Masters and Servants in Eighteenth Century Toulouse," *Journal of Social History*, 12 (1978), 373–74 [368–93].

100. Goldberg, *Women, Work, and Life Cycle*, pp. 194–202; Goldberg, "What Was a Servant?" pp. 19–20.

101. Barron, "Golden Age," p. 48.

102. Mate argues that "there is no proof one way or the other": Mate, *Women in Medieval English Society*, p. 60. Goldberg cites as supporting evidence the work of Brodsky on late sixteenth century London but Ben Amos's research on sixteenth-century Bristol suggests that such changes might not have happened *until* the late sixteenth century: Goldberg, *Women, Work, and Life Cycle*, p. 201; Ilana Krausman Ben-Amos, "Women Apprentices in the Trades and Crafts of Early Modern Bristol," *Continuity and Change*, 6 (1991), 247 [227–52]. Bennett has cautioned that historians might be guilty of accepting the paradigm of "a great divide" between the medieval and the early modern periods and, in particular, she is not persuaded by Barron's account of a fall in female apprentices from the late fifteenth to the late sixteenth centuries, again based on Brodsky's evidence: Bennett, "Medieval Women, Modern Women," pp. 150, 159, 172 n53; Barron, "Golden Age," p. 48.

103. For such approaches see, for example, Sara Heller Mendelson, " 'To shift for a cloak': Disorderly Women in the Church Courts," in *Women and History: Voices of Early Modern England*, ed. Valerie Frith (Toronto: Coach House, 1995), p. 6 [3–17]; Sharon Farmer, "Down and Out and Female in Thirteenth-Century Paris," *American Historical Review*, 103 (1998): 370, 372 [345–72]; Caterina Bruschi, " 'Magna diligenti est habenda per inquisitorem': Precautions before Reading Doat 21–26," in *Texts and the Repression of Heresy*, 4, ed. Caterina Bruschi and Peter Biller, York Studies in Medieval Theology (Woodbridge: York Medieval Press, 2003), pp. 81–110.

104. As noted in Valerie Frith, "Introduction," in *Women and History*, ed. Frith, p. xix [ix–xxiii] and Christopher Cannon, "The Rights of Medieval English Women: Crime and the Issue of Representation," in *Medieval Crime and Social Control*, ed. Barbara A. Hanawalt and David Wallace (Minneapolis: University of Minnesota Press, 1999), p. 168 [156–85]. See also Arnold, *Inquisition and Power*, p. 7.

105. Cannon, "Rights of Medieval English Women," p. 166.

106. For similar stances, see Sheila Fisher and Janet E. Halley, "Introduction. The Lady Vanishes: The Problem of Women's Absence in Late Medieval and Renaissance Texts," in *Seeking the Woman in Late Medieval and Renaissance Writings: Essays in Feminist Contextual Criticism*, ed. Sheila Fisher and Janet E. Halley (Knoxville: University of Tennessee Press, 1989), p. 13 [1–17]; Steven Justice, *Writing and Rebellion: England in 1381* (Berkeley: University of California Press, 1994), pp. 9, 260–61; Arnold, *Inquisition and Power*, pp. 1–15.

CHAPTER 8

"...ET EXAMINATUS DICIT...": ORAL AND PERSONAL HISTORY IN THE RECORDS OF ENGLISH ECCLESIASTICAL COURTS

Robert N. Swanson

"**F**alse horeson, thou shall not commande me to make any heges or gappis, nor thy maister. And if thou dar tare me, thow shall abye." So the chaplain Nicholas Kendall was alleged to have addressed John Lentwhit in a dispute which, in 1528, found its way before an ecclesiastical court at York. The violent words were allegedly followed by violent deeds, as Kendall then threw a hatchet at Lentwhit and drew blood, and also struck him with a "long pyked staffe."[1] The truth of the record cannot be guaranteed—witnesses confirmed the deeds, but not the words—but the words were certainly what Lentwhit wanted on record as having been said. This is only one of numerous oral snippets documented in the surviving records of the pre-Reformation English church courts, although they are not all so forceful in their expression, or so violent in their contexts (even if in this case the precise background remains unclear).

Such recording offers significant opportunities to hear otherwise silenced voices, and through their words gain insights into the lives of people from all ranks of society.[2] The Romano-canonical documentary procedures used in the church courts give access to voices in ways not possible through the common law and customary processes of the English secular courts. Particularly important are the witnesses' statements offered during a case, where they survive. Although the record is often indirect—especially if surviving only in Latin, and therefore affected by the complexities of translation—this is perhaps the closest it is possible to get to medieval

English oral history. Such documents throw light on all aspects of life, and are vital for the reconstruction of communities and individual lives. They show the tensions and normalities which are usually unrecorded, even though they are fundamental aspects of human social life, and may well be overlooked simply because their very ordinariness means that historians take them for granted. It is impossible here to present an adequate survey; all that can be offered is a selective—almost random—discussion of a few individual cases, to provide a taste of the material.

Before considering those cases, however, something must be said about the material, and the context of its production.

★   ★   ★

A major legacy of the growth of the "papal monarchy" over the Catholic Church in the twelfth and thirteenth centuries was the extension across Europe of a basically uniform system of canon law, backed up by its own array of law courts and legal processes.[3] The structure was not entirely uniform, with the strength of custom validating important differences in local arrangements, and sometimes competences. England was fully part of this structure,[4] with sparring between the claims of canon and common law a constant feature of the late medieval centuries.[5] Even though the balance gradually tipped in favor of the common law courts, the church courts dealt with a large amount of business through to the Reformation.

The full pattern of courts was complex, with a series of layers within England which might deal with any particular case, and above them all the ultimate authority of the central papal courts. At all levels, the courts acted to discipline those who were accused of breaking the moral and behavioral regulations of the Christian life, and to provide a forum for resolution of interpersonal disputes linked to the areas over which the church claimed jurisdiction.[6] One important consideration is that the regular jurisdictional pyramid was repeatedly disrupted by the existence of numerous enclaves of varying geographical extent and jurisdictional competence (the "peculiar jurisdictions") which removed a large number of parishes (and their parishioners) from the "normal" arrangements, and which had their own courts.[7]

The complexity of the jurisdictional aspirations and administrative arrangements of the medieval English church created many fora in which voices might be recorded. Two of the more specialized must be set aside for now. There is no room here to discuss the voices and narratives of heretics as revealed in records of their trials.[8] Nor is there space to hear the voices of members of religious houses as they respond to the inquiries made at visitations of those houses.[9] The concern here is with the testimony offered by "ordinary people"—laity and secular clerics—in the customary pattern of ecclesiastical courts. A distinction perhaps needs to be made between two different types of such activity, which both potentially offer access to voices, but to different types of voice. The formal pattern of courts was only part of the structure, recording cases summoned or submitted for judgment. The church's disciplinary and supervisory concerns also created a pattern of irregular tours of inspection of parishes (mainly by bishops and archdeacons, or where appropriate by those exercising peculiar jurisdiction). As people commented on and complained about the state of affairs within the parish, reports which might well lead to more overtly court-centered proceedings in the follow-up, the voice which is heard is not so much individual as collective, recording the uncertainty of community gossip about sexual misdemeanors and doubtful liaisons, the exasperation of priests and parishioners as they finally decided that long-standing disputes were beyond resolution by negotiation or cajolery, and the sense of hurt as relations between priests and people collapsed into bickering and mutual accusations of breach of duty and responsibility. In the latter case, the voice of the priest may sound more individually than the voice of any single parishioner, but the priest was not always on his own when stating his case.[10] Individual voices are perhaps more audible in the records of subsequent court action, where this occurred. In general, the procedural record is bald and impersonal, but occasionally more personal testimony breaks through the shell and shows something of the lives behind the records.

★ ★ ★

The problem of the impersonality of the official record of visitations also affects the documents which survive from the main church courts (usually those of the bishop's consistory). Records of sittings are often formulaic, and provide little concrete information about the parties. Summary proceedings—as in London—offer little opportunity to penetrate the screen, although the few details recorded can be revealing, especially when agglomerated into a social history.[11]

Even with lengthy cases the court books serve as a screen, the official record of process and outcome (if an outcome is in fact recorded). Only occasionally does the mask slip. In general the court books are the formal distillation of a much more complex documentary process, little of which survives.[12] Yet files of ancillary documents do sometimes give access to the voices of those involved in the actions, recording the formal testimony of witnesses summoned for plaintiffs and defendants as they sought to make their case. Such survivals are, unfortunately, limited. The best known tranche exists at York, with a long series of these "cause papers" surviving from the early 1300s for centuries thereafter.[13] Equivalent series must have existed elsewhere, notably for the Canterbury province's Court of Arches, but that court's central archive has long been lost.[14] Sometimes the testimony was formally recorded in special registers, like the deposition books from Norwich.[15] Examples of such material also survive scattered in archives across England, retained by the parties among their muniments. While the records of the main courts have largely been identified and listed, such strays are often unrecorded.[16]

★　★　★

The voices transcribed in this material offer anything from a few words to extensive commentaries; in any one case they may vary in number from one or two to dozens. However, these are not wholly free and unedited voices; necessarily they are mediated, by the legal process which required their words, and by the administrative process which noted down their answers to the questions. The latter has most obvious impact on the format of the documents. It affects the basic record: many of the words survive only in Latin translation, and therefore necessarily as edited statements—although English is increasingly embedded among the Latin legal formulae in the fifteenth and sixteenth centuries. More importantly, the words are pared down to the essentials. These are not stenographic transcripts, but edited highlights. Negative responses are baldly recorded as negatives: ignorance did not have to be explained and detailed, no matter how long-winded the witness actually was in saying "nescit" ("does not know") or "nescit deponere" ("does not know how to depose")—maybe the most frequent responses of all. Paring down also affects positive responses, especially when reduced to a note that one witness confirmed or agreed with another. Yet here the need to substantiate a statement often gives access to the voice, detailing time, place, fellow witnesses, informants, and events. The record may be that of a somewhat summarized, muted voice; but it is still a personal statement.

The context of legal proceedings also affects the reliability of the records. Despite the disclaimers in almost every statement, these are not impartial and disinterested pronouncements. The witnesses had been called to support a case; even if they were in fact unconcerned about which side won, they had been chosen because of their particular memorized version of events. The resulting records have rightly been described as "a collection of narratives, highly organized to fit specific circumstances and suitable to further the argument of the litigant for whose position they were produced."[17] The witnesses' memories and narratives may be factual, but they are memories of a particular combination and understanding of facts—which were not matched by the memories of the witnesses for the opposing side.

Where a file contains the testimony for only one party's witnesses, this undermines its acceptability; even where both sides have their say, it will usually be impossible to test which is actually the more truthful (no matter how plausible), and the absence of other documents may hide the eventual outcome. Among all the recorded detail, which sometimes suggests coherent and extensive local social memory, the possibilities of prompting and coaching, or downright subornation, cannot be discounted.[18]

The narrative role of this testimony also needs some comment, for few of the voices tell complete tales. That, usually, is neither their role nor their function, and excessive expectations will soon be dashed.[19] For the cases the protagonists provide rival skeletal narratives, their own voices mediated by lawyers and the demands of legal process. The witnesses were needed to confirm, and as appropriate enhance or embellish, that basic outline. Their contributions are episodic and fragmentary, often adding details to only some points in the story, and unable to comment on the rest. Yet, when combined, they usually do add up to a narrative, using personal and collective memory to support a conclusion. While adding to the narrative of the case, the witnesses also provide narratives of themselves, to varying degrees. It may be no more than a statement of age and place of residence, but can extend to information about stages in their careers; memories of movement; or statements of family relationships. Such secondary narratives cannot be investigated here, but their existence, and the utility of the court records as sources on the witnesses' own lives, and not just for the cases in which they appear, should be recognized.

All of the evidence is anecdotal. It is also all conflictive, and often conflicting. Much turns on specific incidents, on their ambiguities or deliberately different interpretations. Often there are resonances which make a single event part of a greater pattern. One such is Thomas Grysetwhaite's tale of his experience when he went to pronounce a summons to court in Slaidburn church.[20] He entered the church during mass, the time when numerous parishioners could be expected to be present to witness his actions. However, his appearance and reading of the summons provoked a violent response, and he had to take refuge with the priest at the altar. His safety was so threatened that he needed an escort for the first mile of his return journey, while his opponents encouraged the local youths to pelt him with stones. His experience was not unique: other summoners and apparitors encountered similar or more violent hostility.[21]

How Grysetwhaite's opponents explained away his experience—as they presumably tried to do—is not recorded: this is one of the cases where only the allegations survive (here further mediated by being formulated as an ex officio prosecution), with no witness statements. This does not invalidate Grysthwaite's reconstructed narrative as a personal memory, any more than autobiography is necessarily undermined by being a personal record; but it must be treated appropriately—the narrative may well involve storytelling. A final issue must be raised about the context in which the hearings occurred. The counter-narratives offered by the opposing parties did not exist in isolation; in theory individual witnesses were not partisan, but people whose role was to report facts which were widely known. They might be able to add specific knowledge and details from personal experience, but it was also important that their narrative was a generally accepted one, a tale which was the *publica fama* in a region whose dimensions varied with the demands of each specific case. Each individual witness was therefore expected to confirm that his or her narrative conformed to that *publica fama*, that "common knowledge about a set of events or a legal situation, which was often more stable than rumor, and often more depersonalized than reputation."[22] This *fama* had to be attested, but also witnessed: "the first element of the *fama* nexus was performance, from which the act of observing was of course inextricable. In the legal sphere, observed actions [and, it can be added, heard, and overheard words] had practical, real-world consequences, for they created in viewers' minds certain presumptions regarding status and ownership."[23] Witnesses might recount personal knowledge, but it is usually not private information.

Fama in the social circumstances behind most of these court cases is necessarily oral: most of these testimonies are tales of matters heard and talked about—essentially hearsay evidence. (This is not to discount the eye-witness element, but the appeal to *fama* means that that eyewitness account has already—allegedly—been orally circulated and gained credence within a community; because of this *fama* became a legal weapon.)[24] Some of the evidence may be mere gossip, or the matter for gossip, but in many cases the world recorded is one of more structured talk rather than gossip:[25] conversations which passed on specific information, sometimes with the suggestion of a deliberate oral transmission of long-term memory; reports of oral pronouncements in courts; meetings to clarify the reliability of common rumor. The last element is important, for *fama* ultimately had to be reliable. Witnesses were constantly asked for qualitative and quantitative evaluations of the sources of their information: the decision on the relative validity of the counter-narratives which their evidence constructed to some extent depended on an assessment of the worth of those sources, and indeed of the witnesses' own personal reliability. Many witnesses were precise in identifying their informants, and in asserting their reliability (and, where long-term memory mattered, their age); again thereby emphasizing the importance of talk in the social dynamics. But the rivalry of the narratives also meant that the reliability of witnesses could be—perhaps had to be— impugned, a tactic formalized in the offering of challenges to their testimony on grounds of their links with the parties, or their own moral failings. At the same time, it was also important to stress the common report, which sometimes led witnesses to suggest just how common it was. Master John Neuton, for instance, said that he had his knowledge of the common talk in Holderness about the kinship between John and Katherine Hildyard from "a hundred and more" informants—a total which makes it unsurprising that he could not recall their names.[26]

* * *

While many caveats affect the analysis of these witness statements, they cannot be allowed to overwhelm the general fact of their utility. Their value has already been amply demonstrated in discussions of marriage;[27] their potential as sources for social and economic history has also been recognized.[28] Sometimes a single case provides enough material for an extensive narrative about individuals—as, for example, in the York marriage case which has come to be known as "the Romeo and Juliet of Stonegate."[29] More often, the information is agglomerative, there to be weighed in the balance as reflections of communal or family responses to a dispute. It is, often, as a reflection of community opinion that the testimony really comes into its own. Here it is impossible to deal with many cases in detail, so one each will be taken from the York cause papers to indicate narratives based on individual conflict, family dispute, and communal discord. The selection is governed by the need to choose cases capable of demonstrating a point; the overall aim is to demonstrate just how the voices resonate, in harmony and discord.

* * *

The first example of conflicting narratives derives from a purely personal dispute between two individuals. In 1526 William Preston brought a case at York against John Hall for allegedly impeding the execution of the will of Joan Gaythay (Preston being her executor).[30] According to the chaplain Humphrey Spawnton, who wrote her will for her in April 1524, Gaythay bequeathed a few pieces of silverware and jewelry, and a cow, then held by Hall. The cow was left to serve as her mortuary, while Preston as executor was to dispose of the rest to benefit her soul. All turned on whether what Gaythay bequeathed was still hers to dispose of. Thomas Hobson said that he had seen and heard Gaythay voluntarily give full possession of the goods to Hall, but says nothing of the cow. The essence of this account (again without the cow) was confirmed by Rowland Eden, another eyewitness, although he admitted that he had never afterwards heard Gaythay confirm the gift. A third eyewitness, William Wilson, did include the cow in his report. For Preston, Nicholas Bell said that he, acting for Gaythay, had handed the cow and its calf to Hall some three years before Gaythay's death; Hall was to care for them while receiving the milk. Bell had also handed the other things to Hall as security for a loan, to hold until it was repaid. William Anderson expanded on the terms of the will, saying that the pledged items were to be redeemed by Preston and sold to pay debts, implement the will, and finally benefit Gathay's soul. The outcome does not appear in the file, but the return of the goods had evidently been discussed before the case was brought. Hall had refused to return the pledges, but had seemingly handed over the cow as the mortuary (the calf's fate is not mentioned). Whether he was greedy, whether there was misunderstanding, whether Gaythay had not repaid the loan and used words which (possibly unintentionally) led Hall to believe that she was relinquishing her claims, is impossible to determine.

★   ★   ★

Disputes within families could be equally partisan and discordant. Here, marriage cases offer the clearest examples, but the category of "marriage cases" is extensive. The status of a marriage often had to be decided as the prelude to another judgment, especially if a decision that the marriage was valid would sink a claim to an inheritance based on a charge of bastardy, or would undermine attempts to deny a widow her rights of dower.

A case in which the depositions date from June 1370 provides a good illustration of these issues.[31] It originated in a dispute in the royal courts, when Peter Hildyard challenged the rights to dower claimed by Katherine Hildyard, his father's second wife and widow. Peter denied that the marriage had been valid, arguing that his father and stepmother were related within the prohibited degrees and had not procured a dispensation for their marriage (John was in the third and Katherine the fourth generation of descent from a common ancestor, making them kin in the third and fourth degrees). As the validity of marriages was a matter under the jurisdiction of the church courts, Peter's move immediately (but temporarily) halted the secular case, pending the verdict in the ecclesiastical court. The surviving file is the bulkiest of the three being discussed here, but the main concern must be with the witness statements, and their contrasting narratives. The case involved a gentry family, and supplementary documents survive to flesh out the context.

Katherine's witnesses perhaps had the more difficult task, and simply from the tone of their testimony present the weaker case.[32] Faced with the charge that Katherine had married when fully aware of the impediment of consanguinity, they were in the unenviable position of having to plead her ignorance, without being able to prove it conclusively. Their testimony often therefore stresses her character: she simply would not have married John if she had known of the impediment (not even for a thousand pounds in gold, according to John de Colnvill). One witness conceded that she had referred to John Hildyard as her kinsman, but that was only because they shared a surname. Another (John de Colnvill again) said that the prospective marriage had been rumored for a year beforehand, and no one had suggested consanguinity as an impediment. Ivo de Riston (also known as Ivo Lardeman), the chaplain who solemnized the marriage, said that he had made both parties swear an oath on the gospels that they knew of no obstacles before he proceeded to the nuptial mass, and that before the wedding Katherine had sought advice from Sir Thomas de Sutton. At the same time, the motivations of Katherine's opponents had to be made suspect. John de Colnvill offered a touching vignette of John and Katherine Hildyard as the former lay on his deathbed. A weeping Katherine bemoaned her future widowhood, the fact that she would be alone and would have to deal with hostile (step)children. In response, John placed a curse on any of his children who should threaten her.[33] It is impossible to tell whether this scene actually happened, or is mere "artistic verisimilitude." It bears comparison with other examples of reportedly direct speech which served multiple purposes, most significantly (in this case) Thomas Hildyard's allegedly verbatim recollection of John Hildyard's words as he commissioned an envoy to go to the papal court to procure a dispensation. John not only set out what the dispensation was for, but supposedly also admitted that he and Katherine were fully aware of their consanguinity when they married.

Katherine's witnesses also had to construct a narrative of the marriage ceremony and the couple's subsequent married life which contradicted that advanced by her stepson. Accordingly, the marriage was reported as taking place after the publication of banns (although admitting that they were pronounced only once, immediately before the solemnization), and after daybreak. Moreover, the couple had been generally taken as legitimately married, and lived together as true husband and wife.[34] There was the complication of the rumor (of which some of Katherine's witnesses denied any knowledge) that John and Katherine had sent the chaplain John de Estthorpe to the papal curia to procure a dispensation. Eleanor de Barton (Katherine's maternal half-sister) sought to rebut the rumor by saying that she had discussed the matter with Estthorpe at Hull after his return, and he had vigorously denied that that had been the purpose of his journey. Her story was backed up by Ivo de Riston, who said that he had several times heard Estthorpe declare that he had never been asked to seek a dispensation. The treatment here seems to reflect the need to construct a personal and purposeful narrative within the constraints of existing *publica fama*. The fact of Estthorpe's journey to the papal court could not be ignored; but stories about the purpose of the journey could be refuted by a plausible denial based on supposed conversations with him. Ivo de Riston also acknowledged that John Hildyard was said to have been cited before the archbishop of York, but said that he did not know the grounds for the citation (that was again something which other witnesses denied having heard of).

Unfortunately, however, not all of Katherine's witnesses were fully informed. One (rendered nameless by damage to the document) was obviously caught unprepared, and said that the first he had heard of any proclamation of the banns was when he came to be examined. Moreover, although he said that there had been no talk of consanguinity before the marriage, later it was commonly said that John and Katherine were related in the third and fourth degrees.

The weaknesses of Katherine's case are only made more glaring by the weight of her opponent's evidence. It is unsurprising that Peter Hildyard called assorted kinsmen to his aid (two of Katherine's seven recorded supporters had also been relatives, but women). The key issue was of course the consanguinity, and on Peter's side witness after witness recited a family tree which clearly demonstrated that John and Katherine were related— and, moreover, asserted that they had been well aware of the fact before the marriage, and had treated each other as relatives. The only haziness and disagreements in these recitals relate to the distant past, and to uncertainties about the family's place of origin before it moved to Yorkshire in the thirteenth century. The precision of the pedigree is impressive; but the tales of its transmission perhaps cannot all be accepted without question. Possibly the family's social rank made its genealogy common knowledge, but it is worth noting that in another case of alleged consanguinity, from 1519, several witnesses agreed that there was kinship, but did not know the details; while others confirmed a pedigree presented as a written family tree.[35] In 1370 John Helwysson's report suggests that he had the Hildyard pedigree drummed into him by the concerted efforts of three people (two of them fellow witnesses) about a decade before the trial, but it does not quite ring true. Peter Hildyard's supporters were at pains to stress the age and probity of their informants, some of whom were allegedly centenarians, but they may be declaring something more than common knowledge. It is certainly odd that John Helwysson said he learnt the pedigree from John de Sprottelay senior, but John de Sprottelay junior apparently only heard of it in the year before the case—and not from his father.[36]

In constructing their narrative of the marriage ceremony and the postmarital events, Peter's witnesses naturally aimed to produce a very different picture from that offered by the other side. The marriage itself became a furtive ceremony, being performed without any banns, and taking on an almost Gothic character. Several witnesses insisted that it was held long before dawn—some said three hours before, others that it would have been possible to walk ten miles before the sun rose. The scene is most elaborately sketched in the testimony of Thomas Hildyard, Peter's brother: the marriage had been solemnized "in the shadows of night, before the dawning of the day by the space of ten English miles, with the door of the chapel closed, and with the windows of the chapel obscured by sheets and surplices hanging over them, lest the light of the candles rising up should be seen from the outside." The summons before the archbishop and John de Estthorpe's mission to the curia also became central issues. John de Veer of Sproatley said that he had heard the couple admit the summons, and that Estthorpe had several times told him of his journey.

The case before the archbishop of York (John Thoresby) is referred to only sketchily. It occurred in 1367, probably at the palace at Bishopthorpe, which suggests that it was held in the archbishop's court of audience. The reports strongly suggest Thoresby's personal involvement, but this could be for effect. The outcome was allegedly (and, in all likelihood, actually) a decree that the couple should henceforth abstain from sex, and live as brother and sister. John Helwysson of Sproatley backed up his comments on this by saying that he had actually seen that John and Katherine slept in separate beds, in separate rooms, and so believed that they did treat each other as brother and sister. Thomas Hildyard also reported the use of separate beds. By implication this was in response to the archbishop's decree, but as Helwysson could only testify for the six months before John Hildyard's death, a long illness might account for the separation (and so in fact support the testimony advanced for Katherine by Matilda de Allerton). William de Hornsee appears as a central but shadowy figure in giving details of the 1367 case; he is frequently mentioned, but died before the hearings in 1370.

Following the archbishop's decree, the search began for a papal dispensation—or, more likely, a dispensation from the papal penitentiary. In fact there may have been two attempts to procure this: John Hildyard is the only witness to mention a first mission by William de Setrington (with whom he had allegedly discussed the matter) before that by John de Estthorpe. Needless to say, the mission(s) failed, with the dispensation being denied. Two witnesses were particularly significant here. One was none other than John de Estthorpe himself—whose appearance must have demolished the hearsay testimony supposedly derived from him which had been presented by Katherine's witnesses. Estthorpe reported that he had been asked to obtain the dispensation, and had been sent with a schedule setting out the kinship. He had been promised an annuity of 6 marks for life if he succeeded in his task (he would also have had to fulfill chantry obligations). As if Estthorpe's contribution was not enough, Peter Hildyard's witnesses also included Master John de Neuton, a notary who deposed that he had met Estthorpe at the curia and seen the schedule brought by him. If Estthorpe's testimony was not damaging enough, Thomas Hildyard made the mission seem as incriminating as possible. As already noted, he gave an allegedly verbatim statement of his father's words to Estthorpe, requiring him to obtain the dispensation from the consanguinity, but going further and declaring that both he and Katherine had been fully aware of the impediment before they married.

A novel element introduced by Peter's witnesses to challenge the marriage—and to undermine Ivo de Riston's evidence for Katherine—was the allegation that Riston had been formally suspended from his priestly functions by archbishop Thoresby for solemnizing the marriage.[37] Eye-witnesses said that they had seen him abstaining from his duties, John de Veer adding that Ivo had explained that he was being punished for his role in the wedding. John de Sprottelay junior claimed that John de Estthorpe had said that Ivo de Riston wanted him to obtain a dispensation for him against the irregularity incurred by celebrating while suspended.

In all this, it is hard to construct a convincing single narrative of the events. Only Ivo de Riston gives a rough date for the marriage, shortly before the feast of St. Martin, seven years before the hearing—so it probably took place in 1363. Doubts were perhaps soon raised: John Hildyard (Peter's brother) said that the marriage was denounced to the archbishop by John de Bildeston, then rector of Routh, who left that post in July 1366.[38] However, the matter was not tried until 1367, with a note of the proceedings appearing in the file. The suggestion that there were two attempts to procure a dispensation only complicates matters. If it is right, one could have preceded the case of 1367, the other certainly followed it. (More precisely, it was part of that process: the issue was put on hold to allow a dispensation to be obtained.) Estthorpe said that he was approached only at Pentecost, 1368, and both attempts could have followed the 1367 case. Estthorpe went to Rome itself, during the period of Urban V's return to the city, rather than to Avignon; the Hildyards may not have known of his failure until early 1369. The failure to obtain the dispensation was probably fatal to Katherine's case. No formal sentence appears in the file, but a document of 1371 indicates that her marriage to John was no longer officially recognized.[39]

★   ★   ★

A third category of contrasting narratives which appears in the cause papers is perhaps more truly "social," in that it explicitly claims to reflect the perceptions of communities. Here rival versions of *fama* were in open conflict, rather than *publica fama* being treated as a supporting force in personal or familial disputes. The parties were whole villages (or those who claimed to be their representatives or mouthpieces), acting in defense of claims which are allegedly threatened by another community. Such clashes of communal memories tend to occur most forcefully in cases which concern the identity of a subsidiary settlement within a parish. These were often provoked by disputes over the responsibility for providing and paying a priest in a chapel there, or because the subsidiary settlement was hoping to change its status, and to gain recognition as a separate parish. Memories necessarily conflicted when, in cases of the second type, the claim was that the subsidiary chapel had long enjoyed the effective rights of a parish church, and rather than claiming a novel status was in fact resisting oppression.

Such struggles for autonomy were not uncommon in late medieval England; they constitute a clear genre of cases which has already attracted some attention.[40] Slightly different—but perhaps no less fiercely fought— were cases where the subsidiary settlement sought not a complete break, but a more nuanced status within the parish. Records of a case of this kind survive among the York cause papers of 1393, centering on the payment of a priest at the chapel of Stoke Bardolph in the parish of Gedling, in Nottinghamshire.[41] Stoke's inhabitants claimed that this was the formal responsibility of the rector of one mediety of Gedling (Ralph de Kellom, in post from 1379), a claim which he denied. (The other mediety was appropriated to the prior and convent of Shelford, and was a vicarage; a similar arrangement probably prevailed there, but was not contentious. Indeed, one witness, Richard Mayster, stated that while the rector did not celebrate or provide a chaplain, the vicar had carried on with the arrangements.)[42]

The inhabitants claimed that Kellom had withdrawn the chaplain for the past four years. The issue had been judged by the church authorities at least once before this case: supporting documents submitted by Stoke's inhabitants include a transcript supposedly from the register of archbishop Thomas Arundel stating that the villagers had claimed that they were accustomed to have a chaplain on Sunday, Wednesday, and Friday, but no longer had one through the fault of the rector and vicar. They had proved their case except for Sundays and feast days when they had to go to the mother church. The declaration did have a saving clause, for the rights of the proprietors, and for fuller defense by the rector and vicar.[43] In 1393 the submission of this transcript produced a vehement response from Kellom, who challenged its validity as evidence.

Numerous witnesses were called on each side. While there is considerable agreement on many points—notably the difficulty of access from Stoke to

Gedling church because of floods—the arrangements with regard to the chaplain were recalled in many different ways, some of which must reflect partisan leanings.

The most obvious people to question were previous chaplains. Several clerical witnesses had indeed celebrated in the parish. Thomas Dey, at the time of examination vicar of Muskham, had previously been vicar at Gedling (for the priory mediety).[44] Aged over sixty, he said that he lived in Gedling and neighboring places for all of his life. He declared that the inhabitants of Stoke were obliged to receive their sacraments and sacramentals at Gedling. This, however, was a point which they did not formally deny: they only sought a chaplain on Wednesdays, Fridays, and Sundays (and probably not every Sunday, although the statements are somewhat unclear on this point). Dey himself said that the chaplain had celebrated on Wednesdays and Fridays, and that if the rectorial chaplain and the vicar alternated the Sunday services, they each received 40d. yearly from the inhabitants. Interrogated on the supply and payment of the chaplains, he was surprisingly vague on details; but agreed that the rectors had provided and paid them. He recalled the names of only two rectorial chaplains: Richard de Claresburgh, whose name suggests kinship with a former rector John de Claresburgh (1349–62), and Ralph de Stoke. The latter was perhaps from Stoke Bardolph: Dey reported that Richard had lived at Gedling, and so must have journeyed to Stoke to conduct the services. Ralph lived at Gedling for two years, but thereafter at Stoke. The chaplains had journeyed between the two sites by various routes, listed by Dey as "sometimes through the woods, sometimes by the common way, sometimes by the foss called *Carletondyk*, sometimes along the furlongs in the manner of hunters."

A second clerical witness, William de Askham (also aged over sixty) had been parochial chaplain at Gedling when Master John Howden was rector (1369–79), and administered the sacraments and sacramentals to the parishioners in alternate weeks. Presumably he had served at Stoke in the other weeks, but he is oddly silent on his direct activity there. (Other witnesses say he served the chapel, he never explicitly admits it. He does say that he had been in peril of death in the floods, and that the chaplains residing at Gedling did not go to Stoke when there was flooding.) Askham confirmed that the chaplain was meant to celebrate on Wednesday, Friday, and Sunday, at the cost of the rector. In contrast John de Dorem, a chaplain at Newark in 1393, said that he had served at Gedling for a year under Kellom, and for half a year under his predecessor, and then the rectors had never provided a chaplain at Stoke; moreover, the inhabitants had never asked them to provide one.

One batch of witnesses for Kellom was fairly abrupt in its statements, simply denying that he had any obligation to provide a chaplain. Possibly the most convincing of these was John, rector of Arnold, who had been parochial chaplain at Gedling in the time of Thomas Leverington (d.1369) for three-quarters of a year (when aged twenty-six), and at twenty-eight was hired as a chaplain to celebrate for someone's soul during the rectorship of John Howden.[45] Richard Basage tempered his statement by saying that the rectors he had known had sent chaplains to celebrate at Stoke, "out of courtesy and not by obligation"—"*ex curialitate et non ex debito.*" He perhaps hints at changes since the Black Death, for he said that he could not comment on the pre-plague arrangements.[46] He also nuances his assessment of *publica fama* when, in commenting on the final article, he said that it was considered true at Gedling and Carlton, but the opposite was asserted in Stoke.[47]

Like Richard Basage, other witnesses for the rector conceded a customary arrangement for the chaplains to serve Stoke on Wednesdays and Fridays (with additional service on Sundays for which they received separate payment), while declaring that it was not the rector's obligation to provide them. John de Longford, the vicar of Gedling since 1369, declared himself ignorant of any rectorial obligation to provide a chaplain at Stoke, but said that he had seen William de Askham celebrating there, and that chaplains of the present rector "often" celebrated at Stoke, but "not by [the rector's] command or desire" ("*non ex precepto vel voluntate*"). He knew nothing of earlier arrangements. Some of the witnesses were more specific about the circumstances under which chaplains had served at Stoke. Ralph Roo said that while Kellom was away studying at Cambridge his chaplains had sometimes celebrated at Stoke at the request of the inhabitants and others, but not by his will or order.[48] Roo's report was repeated by William Deken, who said that Kellom had known what was going on, but insisted that the chaplains were not acting in accordance with his will or orders. William Clerk, denying any rectorial obligation to provide a chaplain, nevertheless agreed that chaplains had gone to Stoke in two periods: once when John de Burton, knight, was farmer of the manor of Stoke Bardolph, and the inhabitants paid the chaplains 6s. 8d. for their labor; and again, with a similar arrangement, when John Bryes was farmer of the manor. John Ridale denied any formal obligation, but reported hearsay evidence from Roger Schephirde of Stoke that the rector's chaplain had sometimes gone to Stoke to celebrate, and had been paid 6s. 8d. John Wylowes said that he actually seen the current rector celebrate at Stoke, and reported that he (Kellom) had also hired Robert Basage (not the witness who appears in the case) to celebrate there for a year.

The discrepancies between the witnesses are striking, with memory being either selective or incomplete. Some witnesses recalled the provision of a chaplain going back to before the Black Death. William Kirketon, aged sixty and more, declared that the arrangement for the chaplains had existed at least ten years before the plague, and had continued unchanged until the present row. The rector and vicar served the parish church in alternate weeks, and in between served the chapel on the declared days at their own expense, although Stoke's inhabitants gave 6s. 8d. annually to the celebrants as a courtesy ("*ex curialitate*"). Richard Tascar was more circumspect. He recalled the custom being in force "before the first plague," naming three chaplains (Ivo de Fresby, Robert de Lek, and Robert de Crumbwell) who had acted in the time of John de Glaston (rector from 1330 to 1349: John Wright said he had died in the plague). However, when asked about the public fame of the arrangements he temporized: they were known before the Black Death, but whether they were now public knowledge he could not say ("*de fama nunc laborante nescit deponere*").

Part of the issue may have been whether the rector of Gedling could actually afford to pay for a chaplain, with witnesses being asked about the value of the rectory as a whole, and of Stoke Bardolph as parcel of it. The responses on this point varied. John Kirketon and Robert de Stanebrigge gave the highest value for the rectory at forty marks (£26 13s. 4d.). Kirketon set Stoke at only 13s. 4d. Thomas Dey gave possibly the most reliable response, for he had held the priory mediety at farm, and its income and burdens matched those of the rectory. The rectory was currently worth more than in the past, and he valued it at £20, with Stoke's contribution amounting to 100s. William de Askham agreed on the rectory's value, but put the Stoke income at nine marks (£6). John Wylowes gave the lowest valuation for the rectory, at just twenty marks (£13 6s. 8d.).[49] Several respondents said that it was impossible to put a value on the Stoke components, because they were not actually accounted for separately. Thomas Dey noted that the rectory resources included lands at Stoke which were to fund a chaplain if the rector chose to appoint one. These lands were mentioned by other witnesses, although their precise value was not given. Richard de Mernam (incidentally the one witness in the case identified as a serf) gave the name of these lands as *Chapelland*.

Amid all the confusion of these reports, exactly what was happening at Stoke is left very unclear. From the evidence given by Richard de Mernam, it appears that the vicar, or the vicar's chaplain, was continuing to serve at Stoke, and may indeed have stepped into the breech when Kellom proved recalcitrant. On the other hand, John Roo said that Kellom did not provide a chaplain at Stoke because the inhabitants had hired a certain Ralph to celebrate daily there (possibly the Ralph de Stoke mentioned by

Thomas Dey), who lived at Stoke, and therefore they had not insisted that a chaplain be provided while he remained. The row may have erupted when that hired chaplain left, and Stoke's inhabitants sought a return to the earlier (and, probably, cheaper) arrangements.

Precisely which memories were most reliable in this affair is impossible to say. Reading through the evidence, the claims of Stoke seem most convincing, but they clearly did not convince the judge. The final sentence decided for the rector, leaving his opponents with a legal bill of at least £10 8s. 6d.

★   ★   ★

A few cases can only suggest the potential wealth of memories and narratives to be culled from the records of the medieval English church courts. To some extent, all of the examples used here have been cherry-picked—not every case leaves witness statements; not all witness statements are informative. Yet this material does merit wider consideration and exploitation. The search for memory, or for memories, is a complex task, with its own methodological issues: "Do we hunt it [memory] with a questionnaire, or are we supposed to use a butterfly net?"[50] Arguably, the witness statements of the medieval church courts use both approaches. The penetration of the questionnaire marks the search for responses to specific issues put to the witnesses, while the butterfly net both seeks the generalization of *publica fama* and, having caught specific witnesses, aims to pin down their responses for future research and examination.

The conflicting testimonies also reveal the conflict of memories—or, to be precise, the conflict of reports which their articulators declare to be memories. They support, and go beyond, the claim that "The social meaning of memory. . .is little affected by its truth; all that matters is that it be believed, at least at some level."[51] These memories are not merely of the past, in the present; they are for the future. In the context of their recording, they mark a battle for acceptance as truth, and to become definitive for the future. They are, however, trapped by being personal memories which claim to be social: each witness must offer personal recollections which can plausibly fit into a wider context, by arguing that his or her statement conforms to a widely and publicly accepted version of events, to the *publica fama*. Of necessity, where there is conflict between narratives, there are rival social memories—although for the purposes of a court case the existence of that rivalry cannot usually be acknowledged. (However, it sometimes is, as in the recognition of different views at Gedling and Stoke Bardolph.) The cases seek to resolve specific disputes, and in doing so to control and direct the wider social memory. This is most apparent in the fate of

Katherine Hildyard: she reverted to being the widow of her former husband, Peter Nuthill.[52] Control over the future was harder to establish where communal memories clashed over identities and histories. Appeals and tenacity might eventually subvert a victory, or at least force a compromise. The Stoke Bardolph case reran an earlier dispute; elsewhere, in Warwickshire, Ditchford Frary's struggle for parochial autonomy was played out over some forty years.[53]

Until recently, many medieval voices remained unheard because historians were not listening, did not have their ears properly attuned. Those who shouted attracted attention; more muted voices, recorded only in odd snatches, were ignored. As the hearing becomes more sensitive, more voices become audible. The records of the medieval English church courts are a significant source to allow the hitherto unheard to speak, and in the process evoke the day-to-day lives and concerns of "ordinary" people.

Notes

1. York, Borthwick Institute of Historical Research [hereafter BIHR], CP.G137.

2. Most surviving major records are surveyed in Charles Donahue, Jr, ed., *The Records of the Medieval Ecclesiastical Courts*, 2 vols. Comparative Studies in Continental and Anglo-American Legal History/Vergleichende Untersuchungen zur kontinentaleuropäischen und anglo-amerikanischen Rechtsgechichte, 6–7 (Berlin: Duncker and Humblot, 1994), vol. 2.

3. In general, James A. Brundage, *Medieval Canon Law* (London and New York: Longman, 1995). An incomplete and summary survey of medieval continental church court records is provided in Donahue, *Records*, vol. 4. This indicates that material similar to that under consideration here for England survives widely scattered across European archives, even if "A great variety of procedures are encompassed under the broad heading 'Romano-canonic procedure' " (p. 24, among general comparative comments at pp. 23–25, 28–30). An admittedly cursory search for comparative secondary material suggests that while much scholarship has discussed and analysed the administration and formal processes of canon law, the records have been little exploited for their contribution to social and economic history. For one instance of such use (structured of course by the specific nature and context of the documents and the local jurisdictional patterns), see Chris Wickham, *Courts and Conflict in Twelfth-Century Tuscany* (Oxford: Oxford University Press, 2003), chapter 6.

4. See Richard H. Helmholz, *The Oxford History of the Laws of England, volume I: The Canon Law and Ecclesiastical Jurisdiction from 597 to the 1640s* (Oxford: Oxford University Press, 2004).

5. Robert N. Swanson, *Church and Society in Late Medieval England* (1989; rev. Oxford: Basil Blackwell, 1993), chapter 4.

6. The pioneering analysis is Brian L. Woodcock, *Medieval Ecclesiastical Courts in the Diocese of Canterbury* (London: Oxford University Press, 1952).

7. Swanson, *Church and Society*, pp. 18–19; for a regional discussion, Robert N. Swanson, "Peculiar Practices: The Jurisdictional Geography of the Pre-Reformation Church," *Midland History*, 26 (2001): 69–95. For editions of court records of such jurisdictions, see Lawrence R. Poos, ed., *Lower Ecclesiastical Jurisdiction in Late-Medieval England: The Courts of the Dean and Chapter of Lincoln, 1336–1349, and the Deanery of Wisbech, 1458–1484*, Records of Social and Economic History, n.s. 32 (Oxford: Oxford University Press, for the British Academy, 2001); John S. Purvis, *A Mediaeval Act Book, with some Account of Ecclesiastical Jurisdiction at York* (York: Herald Printing Works, 1943); Alice M. Cooke, ed., *Act Book of the Ecclesiastical Court of Whalley, 1510–1538*, Remains, Historical and Literary, Connected with the Palatine Counties of Lancaster and Chester [Chetham Society Publications], n.s. 44 (Manchester: Chetham Society, 1901).

8. See e.g., Norman P. Tanner, ed., *Heresy Trials in the Diocese of Norwich, 1428–31*, Camden Society, 4th series, 20 (London: Royal Historical Society, 1977); Norman Tanner, ed., *Kent Heresy Trials, 1511–12*, Kent Records, 27 (Maidstone: Kent Archaeological Society, 1997); Shannon McSheffrey and Norman Tanner, eds., *Lollards of Coventry, 1486–1522*, Camden Society Publications, 5th series, 23 (Cambridge, UK: Cambridge University Press, 2003).

9. E.g. Peter Heath, ed., *Bishop Geoffrey Blythe's Visitations, c.1515–1525*, Collections for a History of Staffordshire, 4th series, 7 (n.p.: Staffordshire Record Society, 1973); A. Hamilton Thompson, ed., *Visitations of Religious Houses in the Diocese of Lincoln*, Canterbury and York Society, 17, 21, 33 (London: Canterbury and York Society, 1915–27).

10. Arthur T. Bannister, "Visitation Returns of the Diocese of Hereford in 1397," *English Historical Review*, 44 (1929): 279–89, 444–53, 45 (1930): 92–101, 444–63; Katherine L. Wood-Legh, ed., *Kentish Visitations of Archbishop William Warham and his Deputies, 1511–1512*, Kent Records, 24 (Maidstone: Kent Archaeological Society, 1984); A. Hamilton Thompson, ed., *Visitations of the Diocese of Lincoln, 1517–1531*, Lincoln Record Society, 33, 35, 37 (Lincoln: Lincoln Record Society, 1940–47); T.C.B. Timmins, ed., *The Register of John Waltham, Bishop of Salisbury, 1388–1395*, Canterbury and York Society, 80 (Woodbridge: The Boydell Press, 1994), pp. 113–68; T.C.B. Timmins, *The Register of John Chandler, Dean of Salisbury, 1404–17*, Wiltshire Record Society, 39 (Gloucester: Alan Sutton Publishing, 1984), pp. 1–129.

11. For the late medieval London material, Richard M. Wunderli, *London Church Courts and Society on the Eve of the Reformation*, Speculum Anniversary Monographs, 7 (Cambridge, MA: Medieval Academy of America, 1981).

12. Richard Helmholz, *Marriage Litigation in Medieval England* (Cambridge, UK: Cambridge University Press, 1974), pp. 7–11. As far as I know, no "normal" consistory court book has been published in full. Records of

episcopal courts of audience are in A. Hamilton Thompson, *The English Clergy and Their Organisation in the Later Middle Ages* (Oxford: Clarendon Press, 1947), pp. 206–46; Margaret Bowker, ed., *An Episcopal Court Book for the Diocese of Lincoln, 1514–1520*, Lincoln Record Society, 61 (Lincoln: Lincoln Record Society, 1967). For an archidiaconal court book, Elizabeth M. Elvey, ed., *The Courts of the Archdeaconry of Buckingham, 1483–1523*, Buckinghamshire Record Society, 19 (Welwyn Garden City: Buckinghamshire Record Society, 1975).

13. Helmholz, *Marriage Litigation*, pp. 11–22. For the York files, David M. Smith, *A Guide to the Archive Collections in the Borthwick Institute of Historical Research*, Borthwick Texts and Calendars: Records of the Northern Province, 1 (York: University of York, 1973), p. 57; David M. Smith, ed., *Ecclesiastical Cause Papers at York: The Court of York, 1301–1399*, Borthwick Texts and Calendars: Records of the Northern Province, 14 (York: University of York, 1988); David M. Smith, ed., *The Court of York, 1400–1499: A Handlist of the Cause Papers and an Index to the Archiepiscopal Court Books*, Borthwick Texts and Calendars: Records of the Northern Province, 29 (York: University of York, 2003); Katherine M. Longley, ed., *Ecclesiastical Cause Papers at York: Dean and Chapter's Court, 1350–1843*, Borthwick Texts and Calendars: Records of the Northern Province, 6 (York: University of York, 1980), pp. 1–11.

14. For surviving material, Norma Adams and Charles Donahue, Jr., eds., *Select Cases from the Ecclesiastical Courts of the Province of Canterbury, c.1200–1301*, Selden Society Publications, 95 (London: Selden Society, 1981).

15. Edward D. Stone and Basil Cozens-Hardy, eds., *Norwich Consistory Court Depositions, 1499–1512 and 1518–1530*, Norfolk Record Society, 10 (n.p.: Norfolk Record Society, 1938).

16. For strays, Dorothy M. Owen, *The Medieval Canon Law: Teaching, Literature and Transmission* (Cambridge, UK: Cambridge University Press, 1990), pp. 27–28; Annie Cottam, "An Altcar Tithes Dispute in the Fourteenth Century," *Transactions of the Historic Society of Lancashire and Cheshire*, 82 (1930): 136–62; Richard W. Hunt, "The Abbot and Convent of Merevale v. the Rector of Halsale: A Tuitorial Appeal in the Fourteenth Century before the Court of Arches," *Transactions of the Historic Society of Lancashire and Cheshire*, 101 (1949): 47–61; Robert N. Swanson, "Parochialism and Particularism: The Disputed Status of Ditchford Frary, Warwickshire, in the Early Fifteenth Century," in *Medieval Ecclesiastical Studies in Honour of Dorothy M. Owen*, ed. Michael J. Franklin and Christopher Harper-Bill (Woodbridge: The Boydell Press, 1995), pp. 241–57.

17. Frederik Pedersen, *Marriage Disputes in Medieval England* (London and New York: Hambledon and London, 2000), p. viii.

18. The charge appears in challenges to witnesses, as in Stafford, Staffordshire Record Office, D.603/A/Add/1933. Witnesses in a case concerning the immunities of the provostship of Beverley (York, BIHR, CP.E222) cited the endowment by King Athelstan, saying that they had received their information from the then provost.

19. ". . .hopes that they might provide a miniature study emulating *Montaillou* have vanished": Dorothy M. Owen, "White Annays and Others," in *Medieval Women*, ed. Derek Baker, Studies in Church History Subsidia, 1 (Oxford: Basil Blackwell, 1978), p. 334 [331–46].

20. York, BIHR, CP.F312.

21. Thomas Hahn and Richard W. Kaeuper, "Text and Context: Chaucer's *Friar's Tale*," *Studies in the Age of Chaucer*, 5 (1983): 85–86 [67–101]; G.R. Elton, *Star Chamber Stories* (London: Methuen & Co., 1958), pp. 195–97.

22. Chris Wickham, "*Fama* and the Law in Twelfth-Century Tuscany," in *Fama. The Politics of Talk and Reputation in Medieval Europe*, ed. Thelma Fenster and Daniel Lord Smail (Ithaca, NY, and London: Cornell University Press, 2003), p. 16, with the concept discussed at greater length in the article as a whole. See also Thelma Fenster and Daniel Lord Smail, "Introduction," in Fenster and Smail, *Fama*, p. 2.

23. Thelma Fenster and Daniel Lord Smail, "Conclusion," in Fenster and Smail, *Fama*, p. 210; words in [ ] are my interpolation.

24. See Phillipp R. Schofield, "Peasants and the Manor Court: Gossip and Litigation in a Suffolk Village at the Close of the Thirteenth Century," *Past and Present*, 159 (May 1998): 29–37 [3–42].

25. Chris Wickham, "Gossip and Resistance among the Medieval Peasantry," *Past and Present*, 160 (August 1998): 3–24; but see the dissatisfaction with "gossip" in Fenster and Smail, "Introduction," in *Fama*, pp. 8–10.

26. York, BIHR, CP.E108. John de Sprottelay junior also mentioned a hundred unnamed informants.

27. Pederson, *Marriage Disputes*; Helmholz, *Marriage Litigation*; Owen, "White Annays," in *Medieval Women*.

28. P.J.P. Goldberg, *Women, Work and Life Cycle in a Medieval Economy: Women in York and Yorkshire, c.1300–1520* (Oxford: Clarendon Press, 1992), esp. pp. 217–66 (again emphasizing marriage evidence), 295–303.

29. Pedersen, *Marriage Disputes*, chapter 2; Frederik Pedersen, "*Romeo and Juliet of Stonegate*": A Medieval Marriage in Crisis, Borthwick Papers, 87 (York: University of York, 1995).

30. York, BIHR, CP.G958.

31. York, BIHR, CP.E108. Briefly discussed (not fully reliably) in Pedersen, *Marriage Disputes*, pp. 166–69.

32. The end of the record is damaged, and although it ended with a date of the examination (now incomplete), the damage makes it impossible to tell whether further membranes are missing.

33. "eadem Katerina stetit iuxta lectum in quo idem Johannem iacebit, et flevit ac dixit: 'Ego unius sepe fui vidua, et habui plures filios ingratos.' Et ad illa verba prefatus Johannes respondit, elevatis manibus de lecto, et dixit: 'Si aliqui de filiis meis faciant tibi umquam, ego do eis ita plene maledic-cionem meam sicut eos generavi.'" ["Katherine stood by the bed in which that same John was lying, and wept and said: 'I shall often be on my own as a widow, and have many hostile sons.' And the aforesaid John responded to those words, with his hands raised from the bed, and said: 'If any of my sons

does anything to you, I give them my curse as fully as I fathered them.' "]
Author's translation.

34. Matilda de Allerton said that they lived "ut veri coniuges in thoro et mensa,
nisi quando supervenit aliqua infirmitas." ["like true married people in bed
and board, except when some sickness intervened."] The legalism of "in
thoro et mensa" was presumably to counter suggestions of a formal judicial
separation, while accepting the appearance of such separation in living
arrangements during times of illness (possibly with particular reference to
John Hildyard's final illness: see below). Peter Hildyard's witnesses stress a
legal separation imposed by the archbishop after a court case (see below),
yet such a separation did not actually deny the marriage, and recognized the
vows as still in force (Helmholz, *Marriage Litigation*, p. 100). Despite the
contention that consanguinity cases always resulted in formal dissolution
(Helmholz, *Marriage Litigation*, pp. 71–72), here the evidence (see below)
suggests that the separation was imposed pending resolution of the canonical impediment by papal dispensation. For a comparable case, see York,
York Minster Library, L2(3)c, fol. 51r. In 1367 John and Katherine received
a grant of lands as husband and wife, Beverley, East Riding Archives,
DDHI/Winestead Leiger, pp. 86–89.

35. York, BIHR, CP.G46.

36. Although he declared himself kin in the second degree to Peter, and in the
fourth to Katherine, presumably on the basis of this genealogy.

37. On the penalty, Michael M. Sheehan, "Marriage Theory and Practice in
the Conciliar Legislation and Diocesan Statutes of Medieval England,"
Mediaeval Studies, 40 (1978): 437–39 [408–460].

38. York, BIHR, Reg. 11, fol. 218r.

39. Bradford, West Yorkshire Archive Service, SpSt4/11/82/30.

40. Swanson, "Parochialism and Particularism," in *Medieval Ecclesiastical Studies*,
pp. 242–45, 257.

41. York, BIHR, CP.E208.

42. For the succession to the two moieties of Gedling at this point, see
Keith S.S. Train, *List of the Clergy of Central Nottinghamshire, Part I*,
Thoroton Society Record Series, 15 (Nottingham: Thoroton Society,
1953), pp. 53–54, 56.

43. The transcript, dated at Nottingham, September 16, 1392, is said to be from
the archbishop's register, and to follow from the comperta of a visitation.
No equivalent entry is in Arundel's surviving register, which records only
acta of the vicars general during his absence from the see (York, BIHR,
Reg. 14). "Register" may be generic rather than specific, with the entry in
fact being from a visitation record, or the subsequent court book.

44. No Thomas Dey appears in Train's list of Gedling vicars (*List*, p. 56), but he
is probably the Thomas de Saxundale who exchanged for North Muskham
in 1364.

45. Not included in the incomplete list of rectors of Arnold in Train, *List*, p. 5.

46. "quod factum fuit. . .ante magnam pestilenciam nescit deponere."

47. The rector of Arnold likewise confirmed opinion in Gedling and Carlton, but "de locis tamen vicinis nescit deponere."

48. This comment adds to the information about Kellom's university connections in Alfred B. Emden, *A Biographical Register of the University of Cambridge to 1500* (Cambridge, UK: Cambridge University Press, 1963), p. 338.

49. The rectory mediety was valued at twenty marks for clerical taxations: *Taxatio ecclesiastica Angliæ et Walliæ, auctoritate P. Nicholai IV, circa A.D. 1291* (London: [Records Commission], 1802), p. 310. In 1535 it was formally valued at £14 5s. 11d.: *Valor ecclesiasticus temp. Henr. VIII. auctoritate regia institutus*, 6 vols. (London: [Records Commission], 1810–34), 5:161.

50. James Fentress and Chris Wickham, *Social Memory* (Oxford: Blackwell, 1992), p. 2. To be fair, the question as worded is somewhat ambiguous: in context it concerns "memory" as an abstract more than "memories" as specific recollections.

51. Fentress and Wickham, *Social Memory*, p. xi.

52. In 1371 Peter Hildyard, as John's son and heir, granted an annuity to Katherine as the late wife of Peter de Nuthill: Bradford, West Yorkshire Archive Service, SpSt4/11/82/30 (see also 31–33, from 1379).

53. Swanson, "Parochialism and Particularism," in *Medieval Ecclesiastical Studies*, pp. 247–56.

CHAPTER 9

WITNESS PROGRAMS IN MEDIEVAL MARSEILLE

Daniel Lord Smail

Between the late thirteenth and early fifteenth centuries, numerous patrons commissioned lavishly illustrated manuscripts of the *Grandes Chroniques de France*.[1] Ranging in size from ornate capitals to full-page spreads, the illustrations in this chronicle attest to the truth of the political claims made in the text. In the language of the Roman-canon legal system that was beginning to penetrate northern French legal thought at this time, they can be thought of as witnesses providing proofs based on sight. The facts to which they attested reinforced the claims made by the written modes of proof offered in this as in other late medieval chronicles, including copies of important documents and extracts of supposedly direct speech. Valois' claims to kingship, for example, were argued in the text of fourteenth-century redactions of the *Grandes Chroniques*, and then proven both by the texts of treaties and speeches and by the illustration program that associated Valois kings with their Capetian, Carolingian, or Merovingian forebears. Hearing, another mode of proof discussed by Roman-canon jurists, was naturally more difficult to represent. Even so, artists solved the conundrum via the age-old method of having scrolls issue from the mouths of speakers, giving the reader the comforting illusion of having heard direct speech.[2] Seen in this way, one can imagine a manuscript of the *Grandes Chroniques de France* as the transcript of an enormous lawsuit or legal argument. The text of the chronicle played the role of the plaintiff's argument, the story set out in the plea or *libellus*.[3] Proof of the argument lay in the copies of documents, in the transcripts of direct speech, and, especially for the casual reader, in the illustrations.

As Anne Hedeman has pointed out, many of the images found in the extant manuscripts of the *Grandes Chroniques de France* consist of stock workshop scenes, reused and slightly adapted to fit the demands of the patrons. The practice was common in all medieval manuscript art. If the principal figures in the illustrations were distinguished at all, the distinction was achieved by means of symbols or clothing or, in many cases, captions or other textual references. Apart from these markers, there is a remarkable sameness to the images, a sameness of composition, background, facial expression, and posture. To the modern reader, the generic nature of the illustrations offends our notion of verisimilitude. It is difficult to consider a drawing a "true" illustration of Philip of Valois if it looks exactly the same as an illustration of Louis IX or Clovis. Yet to a late medieval reader, Philip's identity did not reside so much in his appearance or in the depiction of an accurate historical context as in his symbology. The sameness of the illustration acted as a comforting proof of Philip's royal status.

The generic quality of late medieval manuscript illustration bears more than a passing resemblance to the generic quality of witness testimony in fourteenth-century court cases. Consider the following extracts of testimony drawn from a lawsuit heard in August 1340 in the city of Marseille. The testimony was given by five men and one woman on behalf of some plaintiffs who were attempting to evict a quarrelsome woman, Dousa d'Esparron, from their neighborhood. Dousa was said to be the concubine of a shoemaker named Antoni d'Ays, the defendant. Each of the extracts below comes from roughly the same point in the depositions.[4]

(Testimony of Bernart de Baro) He saw and knew that Dousa was a garrulous, quarrelsome woman, overflowing with great wickedness and garrulousness. During the time that Dousa lived on the street in the house of Antoni d'Ays, Dousa incessantly brought forth many taunts and insults and defamations and affronts against the ladies and wives of certain good men of Negrel street.

(Testimony of Peire Raos) On numerous occasions, on various days and at various times of day, he saw Dousa quarreling with the good and honest ladies of Negrel street, using insulting and defamatory words, and especially with mistress Biatris de Podio, with Elis Alfanta, wife of Gilet Alfans, with Jauma de Sant Marcel, and with the wife of Gavot the shoemaker, and with various other ladies and people of the said street, with whom Dousa had various insulting and defamatory words.

(Testimony of Peire de Trets) On various days and at various times he had heard Dousa quarreling with the good and honest ladies of Negrel street, using defamatory and insulting words, to which ladies, Dousa, in the audacity of her boldness, kept saying to the dishonor of the ladies various vituperative, insulting, and defamatory words, with many and various people of the street listening.

(Testimony of Peire Bermon) Asked if at any time he saw Dousa quarrelling and using insulting words with the ladies of the street, he said no, that his house is a long way from the house of Antoni; however, he heard it said by the ladies of the street and by all of Antoni's neighbors that Dousa was garrulous and combative and overflowing in all wickedness and garrulousness.

(Testimony of Aycelena d'Aubagne) She knew Dousa at that time to be a garrulous and combative woman, overflowing in all wickedness and garrulousness, on account of certain defamatory words which she heard were said by Dousa about the honest ladies of Negrel street. Asked if she heard Dousa quarrelling and using insulting words with the ladies of the street, she said no.

(Testimony of Jacme Bermon) Dousa was a combative and garrulous woman, overflowing in all wickedness and garrulousness, and while she lived in Negrel street in the house of Antoni d'Ays the shoemaker, before having been ejected by the royal court from the said street and separated from the house of Antoni, she incessantly used to bring forth many taunts, insults, and defamations against the good and honest ladies of Negrel street.

There are differences here. Two of the witnesses didn't actually hear the insults. Some name names; others don't. Certain witnesses mention details that are not mentioned by others, such as the fact that Dousa had previously been evicted from Negrel street. One witness, Peire de Trets, went out of his way to note that the quarreling took place in the street, with others listening. From clues like these we can get a hint of the witnesses as individuals, in much the same way that we can tell one artist from another even when they borrow a stock workshop scene. All the same, the testimony is relatively homogenous, a homogeneity all the more striking because the witnesses were male and female, near-neighbors and strangers to Negrel, and, as we learn elsewhere, shoemakers and workers in unrelated trades: in short, a varied lot. The homogeneity was embedded both in what one might call the syntax of the deposition, the basic order in which points were addressed, and in the repetition of key nouns or adjectives and their other grammatical forms: *locax, rixosa, iniuria, diffamatio, malicia*. With the exception of *diffamatio*, all these words appear in the articles of proof offered by the plaintiffs and were simply parroted in the depositions. The resulting echoes serve to link the depositions together as a programmatic series. Similar echoing devices, according to Hedeman, linked the individual illustrations of the *Grandes Chroniques* into an organic whole.[5] Art historians describe devices like this as forming part of an illustration program, the goal of which is to build a series of stylistically similar images. The images do not convey truth claims so much as they gradually build up, over the course of the reader's perusal, a representation of a set of truth claims. In a similar way, the witnesses recruited by late medieval litigants can be said to form a witness program, a sequence of depositions designed to build up an image or an aesthetic of truth.

In studying medieval court records, it is tempting to privilege idiosyncratic or anomalous witnesses and the wonderful insights they sometimes provide on everyday life and customs. But we risk much if we lose sight of the sameness that underlies most medieval witness depositions, often right alongside the bizarre and the wonderful. Conformity was an expectation on the part of readers and listeners. It was the aesthetic means whereby medieval observers interpreted and evaluated truth claims of all kinds, those made in witness depositions as well as those found in chronicles and any other documents that made truth claims.

The aesthetic that emerges in many witness programs was designed to carry a powerful moral statement. In the case of Antoni d'Ays, the moral aesthetic painted Dousa as a gossip and a shrew. No one could possibly have any sympathy for such a person. To illustrate the point, plaintiffs and their legal teams found ways to recruit sympathetic witnesses and occasionally yielded to the temptation to coach them on what to say. But with or without coaching, sympathetic witnesses naturally participated in the truth regime of their own culture, and implicitly understood the need to follow the script laid out for them in the plaintiff's articles. This is why the witnesses in the case of Antoni d'Ays recounted much the same story, with only slight variations. In considering the resulting depositions, notice how the "facts" of the case, the actual words Dousa supposedly uttered, were of little importance:

> (Testimony of Bernart de Baro) Interrogated about the words Dousa said to the ladies to their dishonor, he said he did not remember at present.
>
> (Testimony of Peire Raos) Asked what words Dousa had with the ladies, he said that at present he does not recall, so he says.
>
> (Testimony of Peire de Trets) Asked what sort of verbal battles and fights Dousa had with the ladies, he said that he does not remember at present, so he says. . .Asked about the year, month, week, day, and hour, he said that he does not remember, so he says.
>
> (Testimony of Aycelena d'Aubagne) Asked if she heard Dousa quarrelling and using insulting words with the ladies of the street, she said no.
>
> (Testimony of Jacme Bermon) Asked what sort of verbal battles and fights, wickednesses, insults, and defamations Dousa had with the honest ladies of the street, he said that he does not remember, so he says.

So profound is the reluctance to utter the actual insults that one is tempted to erect hypotheses: the witnesses were lying; they were squeamish about repeating foul language; they did not understand the need for facts. Yet the very fact that *all* these witnesses responded in the same way suggests the powerful homogenizing effect of the witness program. It is possible, even likely, that memory of the insults was disclaimed lest any discrepancies be used to invalidate the truth of the testimony. Contrary to what Roman-canon jurists claimed, it was impressions that mattered in witness programs, not facts.

To illustrate these arguments I discuss a typical case from the civil court records of late medieval Marseille.[6] The case is a dotal retrocession, an attempt on the part of a wife, or in this case the woman's father, to recover a dowry from the insolvent estate of her husband or father-in-law. Dowry suits were very common in fourteenth-century Marseille, constituting 11 percent of all secular civil lawsuits. Most, so far as we can tell, were successful. The case of Laurens Giraut, heard in the summer of 1334, is interesting in part because it is one of the few where the plaintiff and his legal team failed. The spirited defense offered by Bertran Vital, the bride's father-in-law, holder of the dowry, and hence chief defendant in the suit, managed to dissolve the moral aesthetic of the witness program arrayed against him. The attempt made by Laurens and his legal team to frame Bertran's actions in a moralizing template came back to haunt the plaintiff, and by the end of the trial Laurens was exposed as a sour and litigious man who had tried to exploit the courts in pursuit of a private vendetta, possibly alienating his own daughter in the process. The case is revealing not only because Laurens attempted to build a conventional witness program, following a style that was normally quite successful, but also because his own witnesses, goaded by Bertran, ultimately balked at Laurens's attempt to mold the moral contours of their testimony to suit the prevailing aesthetic of dotal retrocessions.

★   ★   ★

The plaintiff, Laurens Giraut, was a relatively low status though respectable resident of a suburb of Marseille known as Syon. We don't know when he was born but he had surely lived through some interesting times: the Sicilian Vespers of 1282, which marked the turn of the wheel of fortune for the Angevin kingdom of Naples, Marseille's overlord; the fall of Acre in 1291, an event that hastened the collapse of Marseille's once-great Mediterranean trading network; the great famine of the late 1310s; and the burning of four Spiritual Franciscans in 1318.[7] But this was the stuff of high politics, and Laurens was just an ordinary man, concerned with domestic things like establishing a household with his wife, Laura, and marrying off their daughter Secilieta. Fourteenth-century records can only provide tantalizing glimpses into the lives of relatively low-status individuals, and we don't actually know when Secilieta got married, though clues suggest that the wedding took place in the late 1320s. Her husband was a young man named Jaumet Vital, who lived in the neighboring suburb of Moriers.

Laurens gave his daughter a substantial dowry of one hundred royal pounds.[8] Since Jaumet was still in the paternal control of his father, Bertran Vital, Secilieta's dowry came into Bertran's possession. Bertran reciprocated with a counter-dowry of forty pounds in clothing and goods. By 1334, Secilieta had given birth to two children.

Bertran Vital and his son Jaumet were described in records as *laboratores*. Though one is tempted to describe them as laborers or tillers of the soil, and although Bertran, by his own account, did in fact work hard for a living, he was also a landowner, householder, and small-time speculator in property. Like many so-called *laboratores* or urban peasants in the city of Marseille at this time, he lived in the suburbs close by the city walls and made his way out to his fields by day to work.[9] Laurens, too, was also described in places as a *laborator*, as were many of the witnesses heard in the trial.

By the early 1330s, worrisome rumors, called *fama* in contemporary sources, had come to the ears of Laurens: Bertran Vital was selling off property at a great rate. *Fama* was not the sort of idle or spiteful gossip attributed to Dousa d'Esparron. It was honest gossip with a purpose, essential to the proper functioning of networks of credit and trust.[10] *Fama* also reported that Bertran was so deeply indebted to the Jewish banker Bondavin de Draguignan that he had been forced to repay him by means of a donation of all his worldly goods.[11] According to this rumor, Bertran no longer owned his home in the suburb of Moriers, and was instead renting it from Bondavin for a large annual sum of ten pounds. Contributing to Laurens's discomfort was the possibility, indeed the likelihood, that Secilieta's dowry of one hundred pounds had been bundled into the large dowry of one hundred and seventy-five pounds that Bertran had given to his daughter, Johana, when she got married early in the 1330s.

We cannot know if Laurens tried to resolve the issue through a careful word in Bertran's ear or through private arbitration, the usual sort of thing. All we can know is that relations between the two family patriarchs had deteriorated by the late spring of 1334, and in June, Laurens formally sued Bertran for return of Secilieta's dowry. A suit like this was a hostile gesture. Reading hundreds of similar cases from fourteenth-century Marseille, it has become clear to me that few people viewed a lawsuit as a dispassionate device for recovering goods or rights.[12] Instead, the emotions that motivated both plaintiffs and defendants in a lawsuit were identical to those characteristic of the culture of vengeance. The entire course of the ten-month lawsuit setting Laurens against Bertran bears all the hallmarks of vengeful litigation.

Originally lodged in one of Marseille's lesser courts, the suit was transferred on July 12, to the palace court, the major court of first instance in Marseille. A few days later, witnesses were interrogated on the list of articles, the *tenor positionum*, that Laurens and his legal advisers had put together. The *tenor* ran as follows:[13]

1. First, for Secilieta's dowry, Laurens gave to Bertran and Jaumet his son a total of one hundred pounds, consisting of appraised lands and money.
2. Next, Bertran Vital and his son are heading toward insolvency, owing to a multitude of creditors who have seized and are seizing practically all their goods.
3. Next, Bertran has many creditors. If they are all paid, nothing or little will be left to him.
4. Next, Secilieta and her husband and their two infants are living in the house of Laurens, her father, without Bertran providing any expenses.
5. All this is public talk and *fama*.

With the exception of point 4, which is slightly unusual, this list of arguments is quite similar to those found in most dotal retrocessions from Marseille. This is not necessarily because Laurens was legally astute. Instead, the sameness almost certainly derives from the fact that Laurens, like most other litigants, made use of the services of procurators and lawyers (*advocati*) who knew the ropes. In particular, Laurens relied heavily on a procurator or expert pleader named Bernat Raymon, a familiar figure at court during the 1320s and 1330s and an expert in pleading dotal retrocessions. Far more than Laurens, Bernat would have understood the legal template most appropriate in cases such as this one.

The standard template made it hardly necessary to do more than demonstrate the size of the dowry and prove the suspicion of insolvency. Just a few months earlier, for example, Bernat had pleaded a retrocession on behalf of a woman named Nicolaua Chaberta, who was suing her husband, Guilhem. In their articles, Nicolaua and her procurator: 1) noted the existence of a 250 pound dowry, and 2) observed that the husband was heading toward insolvency.[14] Other dotal retrocessions show variants on this theme. When Moneta Maleta sued her husband in August 1334, the problem was not insolvency per se. Instead, he had been condemned by the criminal court for some unspecified deed and all his goods had been seized by the court. Moneta—assisted, once again, by Bernat Raymon—successfully sued the court for return of her dowry, pointing out that her claims as first creditor on the estate took priority over the court's criminal claim.[15] The principle in both kinds of dotal suits, however, was the same: when a dowry was threatened by a husband's action or inaction, the wife was empowered to extract it from the estate.

Dotal retrocessions were not contested very often by insolvent or criminous husbands. Giraut Malet certainly had little incentive to defend his estate from his wife Moneta, since a successful defense would only see the money go into the coffers of the Angevin crown. Perhaps we might have expected that Guilhem Chabert would put up more of a fight, but he didn't, and Nicolaua's case ended after a few pages, most likely in her favor. As this and many other cases suggest, husbands may have been in collusion with their wives in defending the conjugal estate through the wives' dotal rights. In other words, many dotal retrocessions are exceptions to the rule that lawsuits were emotionally equivalent to acts of vengeance. Some, however, were truly nasty, clearly products of failing marriages—they include accusations of spousal abuse, among other things—and husbands in such cases did contest the suits lodged against them. In such cases, a parade of witnesses came before the court to attest to the husbands' financial improprieties. Such was the case with Bertran Vital.

Bertran's responses to Laurens's accusations reveal that he chose not to contest point 1, the existence of the dowry. Advised by his own lawyer, he did contest points 2 and 3 and rejected the legality of point 4, observing that the claim was not pertinent to a dotal retrocession. Since the judge ruled in his favor no testimony was actually taken on this point, and the resulting depositions addressed only points 2, 3, and 5, namely, Bertran's supposed insolvency, his inability to pay his creditors, and the question of whether all this was *fama*.

Interrogations in Marseille were usually led by a notary of the court. No rules governed the space of interrogation: some took place indoors, in private homes; others outdoors, in the central plaza of Accoules where the court itself convened; still others in foreign cities, with the resulting transcripts then sent to Marseille to be included in court records. After each witness was sworn in, the contested points were read out in the vernacular and the witness was asked if she or he knew anything about the matter. Responses to particular points often began with one of three stock formulas: "the witness knows nothing" (*respondit quod se nichil scire*); "the witness knows little other than" (*nichil aliud scire nisi quod* or *nichil nec quod*), followed by a relatively short observation; and "the witness knows a great deal" (*tantum scire*), a response that usually inaugurated testimony that was rather damaging to a defendant.

To prove their points, Laurens and his procurator did not in fact get their witnesses to offer the court a careful accounting of Bertran's estate, in much the same way that Dousa d'Esparron's adversaries never bothered to list her insults. Instead, the witness program they put together was designed only to illustrate the prevailing *fama* in the suburbs of Syon and Moriers: that Bertran was on the path to insolvency. Consider these extracts from the depositions taken on point 2:[16]

(Testimony of Guilhem Restesin, *laborator*) He has heard it said by many persons, neighbors and acquaintances of Bertran Vital, whose names he does not remember at present, that Bondavin de Draguignan, Jew of Marseille, received in payment from Bertran his whole house with all goods and appurtenances, in which there is a certain well, by reason of a debt that Bertran owed to Bondavin. He also heard it said that Bertran then rented the house and its appurtenances from Bondavin for ten pounds per year.

(Testimony of Guilhem Hunier, *laborator*) He has heard it said by Peire Asami, pawnbroker, and many others, acquaintances of Bertran Vitalis and his son, whose names he does not remember at present, that Bondavin de Draguignan, Jew of Marseille, received from Bertran a house in payment for a certain debt that Bertran owed to Bondavin.

(Testimony of Peire Asami, pawnbroker) He heard it said that Bondavin de Draguignon, Jew of Marseille, received from Bertran a house with all its appurtenances for a twenty-four pound debt in which Bertran was obligated to Bondavin, that is to say the house in which there is a certain well. The notary Paul Giraut made the instrument.

(Testimony of Ricart de Massilie, *laborator*) He heard it said by many of Bertran Vital's neighbors living together in the street of Moriers that a certain Jew, whose name was not made known to the witness, received from Bertran a house in which there is a certain well in payment for a debt that Bertran owed to the Jew.

(Testimony of Johan Blanc, *laborator*) He heard it from Jacme Bonacros and many other neighbors of Bertran Vital that Bondavin de Draguignan, Jew, received from Bertran a house in which there is a certain well in exchange for a debt.

Laurens and his legal advisers also went to the trouble to find notaries who had drawn up or witnessed acts whereby Bertran sold off properties, evidently a practice characteristic of men who were headed toward insolvency. A series of notaries came before the court to attest to the existence of contracts of sale:[17]

(Testimony of Peire Mayin, notary) On 2 January 1330, in a certain house of Jacme Martin who lives in the street of the Jerusalem, in the presence of Guilhem Gayrart, Aycart Porcel, Bermon Filho, and the witness himself, Bertran Vital received forty-five pounds from Raymona Filhola in exchange for a house located in the street of Prat Auquier. . .which he sold to Raymona.

(Testimony of Johan de Gompina, notary) On 4 calends of April, the eleventh indiction, 1328. . . he wrote in one of his cartularies . that Bertran Vital, a *laborator* and citizen of Marseille, sold to Ugo Martin, a *laborator*. . . a parcel of vineyard.

> (Testimony of Paul Giraut, notary) On 12 February 1329 he wrote in a
> certain protocol of his that Bertran Vital sold to the late Johan de Alto, mer-
> chant and citizen of Marseille, a certain garden.

Curiously, neither these nor the other two notaries who served as witnesses
found it necessary to offer written acts to the judge.

None of this hearsay seems particularly convincing. Even the depositions
of the notaries cannot be taken to prove insolvency, as Bertran himself
would argue later. However, Laurens's legal team was developing his argument in the context of a well-established custom in Marseille according to
which the *fama* of insolvency alone sufficed as proof in cases of dotal retrocessions. While serving once again as procurator in a dotal retrocession, this
one heard in 1337, Bernat Raymon put it to the judge in this way: "when
a woman is petitioning for her dowry, because her husband is verging on
insolvency, the *fama* of the neighbors alone is sufficient (*quando mulier petit
dotem suam quia maritus vergit ad inopiam sufficit sola fama vicinorum*)."[18]

The suspicion of insolvency may not appear to be a valid justification for
a dotal retrocession. Yet it was, as Bernat well knew. To appreciate why, one
has to understand that no rules governed the nature of credit in fourteenth-
century Marseille. Creditors were perfectly free to withdraw credit for no
other reason than bad *fama*, regardless of the debtor's "real" financial condition. But consider the effect of Laurens's suit on Bertran's fama. The courts
in Marseille met outdoors, in public view, and the rumor of any given suit
rapidly made its way to the ears of interested parties. The mere act of
initiating a dotal retrocession on the grounds of bad *fama*, therefore, was a
self-fulfilling prophesy. Witness depositions did not merely reflect an existing reality. Where *fama* is concerned—and most suits in Marseille involved
some degree of testimony on *fama*—they actively reshaped or even created
that reality. An effective witness program was, indeed, an art form.

The importance of *fama* helps explain why the notaries who served as
witnesses did not bother to bring in their cartularies or even instruments of
sale. Laurens and his legal advisers were not asking them to attest to the
existence of the contracts. What he wanted was their opinion about *why*
Bertran was selling off so much property. Two notaries saw fit to provide
such an opinion:[19]

> (Testimony of Peire Mayin, notary) A great *fama* is working against Bertran
> (*magna fama viget contra predictum Bertrandum*) since he sold and alienated the
> said properties; for that reason he does not believe Bertran Vital has the
> money or other goods sufficient to secure the dowry.
>
> (Testimony of Paul Giraut, notary) On account of the sales, he believes
> Bertran was failing rather than holding his own and was badly managing his
> goods.

These suggestions offer a hint at the argument that Laurens would later develop at length, namely, that Bertran could not be trusted to manage his own estate and the dowry embedded in it. The witness program developed by Laurens and his legal advisers had two distinct components. The first, promoted primarily by urban peasants who moved in the same neighborhoods or social circles as the two principals, was designed to establish the *fama* of Bertran's indebtedness to Bondavin de Draguignan. As in the case of Antoni d'Ays, there are slight variations among the depositions, but in general they conform to a single story line. The syntax (except in Ricart's case) took the following basic form: "The witness had heard it said by *name* that Bondavin received a house from Bertran." One interesting fact is that the debt to Bondavin was not specifically mentioned in the original titles presented by Laurens. That four out of the five witnesses mention the Jewish banker by name suggests either that the *fama* concerning Bondavin was very strong or that the witnesses had been very carefully coached, or, as one might suspect, a little bit of both. The other programmatic echo is provided by the reference to the well. The fact that Bertran's house contained a well was not mentioned in the titles, and it is in fact a highly unusual device for identifying a piece of property (most were located in space by naming the abutting property-owners). Here, it is particularly difficult to believe that the witnesses were not coached. But whereas the echo might appear suspicious to a modern reader, it carried quite the opposite aesthetic in the legal culture of fourteenth-century Marseille.

We shouldn't discount the possibility that the syntactical homogeneity found in the depositions was a product of the conventions of transcription and translation. All interrogations followed a scripted format. Furthermore, one presumes that the notaries who actually wrote out depositions were working from notes taken during the interrogation. Perhaps they were inclined to supply sense and syntax to those parts of the testimony where their notes were lacking. Court notaries, moreover, were not excellent Latinists. In the depositions taken in the case of Antoni d'Ays, perhaps the word *locax* appears so often simply because that was the only way this notary knew how to translate the many Provençal words that could have been used to denote a gossipy, garrulous, tale-bearing, tongue-wagging rumormonger. In the case of Laurens Giraut, a major stylistic echo, apart from the name of Bondavin and the reference to the well, was the expression "he heard it said" (*audivit dici*), which was a formula and not something that every witness said in exactly that way. Notarial practices therefore were partly responsible for flattening out witness idiosyncrasies and imposing a dull sameness throughout depositions. Here, though, it is important to bear in mind that the notary responsible for interrogating witnesses and writing out the transcripts of depositions was technically in the employ of the plaintiff. The court paid for none of these expenses. Perhaps on some level, notaries simply identified with plaintiffs and, on their behalf, tailored depositions to the prevailing aesthetic of truth.

There is greater difference in the depositions of the notaries, since they described separate acts of sale. Even here, though, the basic syntax (date, seller, buyer, property) is quite similar. Once again, this particular argument was not listed in the articles, and it is very likely that the notaries had been coached by the plaintiff. There is a suspicious sameness to the conclusions that two of the notaries drew from the sales: the rate at which properties were being sold off suggests insolvency. It is, after all, a curious claim. Property sales of various kinds were not uncommon in mid-fourteenth-century Marseille. The 900 or more extant notarized property transactions from the years 1337 to 1362 account for close to 14 percent of all notarial transactions from those years, or as many as 350 per year in a city of around 25,000 people, most of whom did not own property. Surely notaries did not assume that each and every sale contained a hint of insolvency. As Peire Mayin suggested, his interpretation of Bertran's activity was affected by the existing *fama* concerning Bertran. But it is also likely that the notaries' sense of Bertran's impending insolvency was heightened when, recruited as witnesses to Laurens's witness program, they became aware of the number of transactions enacted by their fellow notaries. In other words, the very act of assembling a body of notaries to serve as witnesses may have created or promoted the very *fama* that the notaries were supposed to be reporting on. Here again, we see how the act of building witness programs did not result in a passive set of facts that reflected reality. The programs themselves created or shaped reality.

The witness program developed by Laurens was typical of those found in other cases, reflecting the involvement of the expert pleader Bernat Raymon on his legal team. In other dotal retrocessions, the suit might well have ended at this point, with the husband putting up just enough of a fight to satisfy the judge that there was no collusion but otherwise happy enough that his wife's rights should be acknowledged before those of his creditors. What makes this case unusual is that the principal defendant was the husband's father, not the husband. Husbands, in Marseille, usually had control of their wives' dowries, either because their own fathers were dead or else because they had been emancipated from paternal control. Jaumet, as the diminutive ending to his name indicates, was still a young man when he got married, still in *patriapotestas*. If the issue had been Jaumet's insolvency, perhaps he would have abandoned any defense while continuing to live with Secilieta. Bertran had no such incentive, and fought the accusation of growing insolvency with great vigor. Resistance was tantamount to a claim of creditworthiness, and carried with it the implication that the suit was initiated in the spirit of vengeance, not for dispassionate pecuniary motives. In his defense, Bertran was joined by Ugo de Sant Peire, a procurator who figures frequently in litigation during the 1320s. Together, they put together a defense whose chief arguments ran like this:[20]

1. First, Bertran Vital is a laborious and industrious man who by the grace of God and by his own industry has acquired for himself all the goods he possesses.
2. Next, Bertran Vital bought from Bertomieu Bonvin and Esteve de Fonte and their brothers a certain property located next to the garden of the Franciscans which cost him 300 pounds. He still owns this property today and it is worth more than 300 pounds.
3. Next, Bertran has a certain vineyard at Peras, four *quarteriatas* in size, worth eight pounds.
4. Next, Bertran has a certain house in the suburb of Moriers which, with its appurtenances, is worth 150 pounds.
5. Next, he leases nine *quarteriatas* of garden and vineyard belonging to the heirs of the late Ugo Auriol of which Bertran's share of the proceeds is worth more than 40 pounds.
6. Next, among acquaintances and neighbors and in the city of Marseille, Bertran is reputed to be rich and of good standing.
7. Next, he has six *quarteriatas* of vineyard in the close of lord Bertomieu Bonvin, half of which comes to him; Bertran's share of the proceeds is worth twenty-five or thirty pounds.
8. Next, if it is found that Bertran has alienated any properties, he bought and alienated these properties for the purpose of making money (*causa lucrandi*).
9. Next, if he alienated anything, he gave it in dowry for his daughter to the son of Raymon Castagne, 175 pounds in cash, which dowry Bertran stipulated ought to be restored to him if there was any reason to restore it.
10. Next, Bertran bought clothing and utensils worth forty pounds for his daughter-in-law, which the daughter-in-law, wife of his son, now holds.

Various witnesses came to attest to Bertran's diligence, industry, and good standing. With a few exceptions, the six depositions are more or less interchangeable; once again, the rule of conformity was upheld. All six, for example, began with minor variations on the following boilerplate: "He has known Bertran Vital for X years as a good and worthy and laborious man." More particular elements do enter into the testimony. By way of example, Jacme Bonacros, a merchant who lived in Moriers, introduced some interesting particulars, telling the interrogating notary that just fifteen days earlier, he had been at Bertran's house, where he saw no small amount of goods, utensils, clothing, and other things, all symbols of financial stability.[21] Yet these were just minor variations on the theme.

The competing witness programs put together by Laurens, Bertran, and their legal teams have several interesting features. As is common in many witness groups assembled by plaintiffs and defendants in fourteenth-century Marseille, they include a mixture of near-neighbors and rather more distant acquaintances. In the case of Laurens, his first group of witnesses were chiefly urban peasants, presumably friends or close acquaintances. But Laurens was able to corroborate their possibly biased testimony with the testimony of a pawnbroker, Peire Asami, and a number of presumably impartial notaries. Bertran countered with his own fellow urban peasants and added to them the depositions of two rather more significant individuals. One was the merchant, Jacme Bonacros, elevated enough to have served on the city council in 1339. The second was Nicolau Bonvin, an urban notable who lived within the city walls, not in the suburbs, and therefore did not offer testimony out of neighborly interest.

The second interesting feature of the two witness groups, or at least the urban peasants in each, derives from their neighborhood of residence. In Laurens's group, the two urban peasants whose residences I have been able to track in other sources lived in the suburb of Syon, where Laurens himself lived. By contrast, three of Bertran's four urban peasants are known to have lived in Moriers, Bertran's neighborhood of residence. There is at least a hint here that what was *fama* among the residents of Syon was not the *fama* in Moriers, among the neighbors who knew Bertran best.

Finally, the witness groups included no women. This is a little unusual, since women figure as witnesses in roughly a fifth of all witness groups in fourteenth- and early fifteenth-century court records. But other records show that women testified relatively infrequently in cases of male insolvency. The *fama* concerning insolvency in Marseille was a *fama* that circulated primarily among men.

Following Bertran's rebuttal, things were evidently looking good for the defense, and it was at this point in the trial that Laurens shifted to more nasty techniques. He and his procurator began by offering a second set of articles to justify his claim of Bertran's growing insolvency. Tellingly, he protested as he did so that he had no intention of injuring anyone but merely wanted to preserve his rights—a hollow claim, as the slanderous nature of the accusations make clear:[22]

1. First, Bertran visits wine taverns, drinking and eating shamefully (*inhoneste*).
2. Next, Bertran uses prostitutes, spending his goods (*bona*) shamefully.
3. Next, Bertran manages his estate (*substancia*) badly.
4. This is public talk and *fama*.

In making these claims, Laurens was not just aiming at proving a set of facts. He was also seeking to show how Bertran was not living up to certain standards of behavior that were well entrenched in fourteenth-century moral discourse. Medieval historians have made much of the arguments of Norbert Elias and others to the effect that the civilizing process involved a growing sense of the virtues of self-restraint.[23] Whether this is an accurate depiction of the trend in moral norms in medieval and early modern European is open to debate, but there is little doubting the values of self-restraint and control when it comes to management of the household. Court records from late medieval Marseille contain powerful statements that condemned men who wasted their worldly goods, their *bona* or *substancia*, and by extension the dowries and inheritances of their wives, daughters, daughters-in-law, and sons. Related accusations of drinking and consorting with lowlifes crop up from time to time in other contexts in proof programs and witness depositions in the judicial records of late medieval Marseille. In an appellate case heard in 1352, for example, a woman named Jacme Augeleria tried to impugn the reputation of several witnesses who had testified against her, and did so by accusing them of being tavern-goers and gamblers. Several witnesses on her behalf responded circumspectly to the accusation but three upheld it, one of them commenting that the men were frequent tavern-goers and gamblers at dice, another describing one of the adversary witnesses as a gambler, tavern-goer, and habitual liar.[24] In a similar case heard in 1354, two men were described as the sort of men who hang about in the taverns of the poor, described as hopeless taverns of low status and dishonest way-of-life.[25] This is exactly the sort of impression Laurens hoped to convey.

That Laurens and his procurator were not making wild accusations in the hopes that *something* would stick is suggested by the fact that they didn't accuse Bertran of gambling, a common accusation, though the other three accusations—excessive drinking, sex with prostitutes, and bad management—were bad enough. In developing a new witness program, Laurens recruited four new witnesses to join with a single holdover, Peire Asami, from the first group. He almost certainly expected his charges to be upheld by his witnesses, and he certainly had precedence on his side: in other examples of this kind of character assassination witnesses almost always fell in lockstep with the plaintiff. But here, something went wrong for Laurens.

That something begins with the fact that defendants in Marseille's courts were always given a chance to guide the interrogation process. Though all witnesses were asked to comment on the contested points, defendants, advised by advocates, were also allowed to draw up their own list of additional interrogations. A number of such lists have survived, including Bertran's interrogatories in this case.[26] Even in cases where the list itself has been lost, however, we can detect the presence of interrogatories because the depositions are systematically punctuated by questions beginning "*Interrogatus est*. . ." (The witness was asked. . .) followed by a probing question. In some cases it is possible that the interrogator was responsible for devising the question, but most derive from the defendants' interrogatories.

Some of the interrogatories were global: Are you related to the plaintiff? Do you hold the defendant in enmity? Others were linked to specific articles. In this case, for example, if witnesses had responded positively to point 2— they didn't, in the event—they would have been asked the following interrogatories: Which prostitutes did he consort with? In which place and what year, month, week, day, and hour? How much *bona* did he spend on the prostitutes? Was it gold or silver and how much of it? If he spent other *bona*, what was it? In cases where both lists of interrogatories and depositions have survived it is clear that notaries or judges did not ask all the defendants question. Some interrogatories were clearly designed to waste time or to harass witnesses unnecessarily. In this case, we can tell that Bertran's list of interrogatories was followed scrupulously by the interrogating notary. As a result of Bertran's clever goading, the witness program so carefully assembled by Laurens fragmented into a series of depositions that broke sharply with the moral aesthetic he was aiming for, with results that solidly supported Bertran's defense.

Point 1 was a very common accusation in Marseille's courts, and in responding to it witnesses often used the invitation to describe the defendant as a drunkard who wastes his money in taverns and associates with lowlifes (men described as *inhonesti* or *homines male conversationis*). Four of the witnesses on this point responded with the expression *tantum inde scire*, and all proved their intimate knowledge in great detail:[27]

> (Testimony of Bertomieu Blanc, *laborator*) He knows a great deal. A year ago in August, on a certain day he doesn't remember, around dinnertime, the witness was going to the house of the Gasquetz where Miramas the taverner

sold red wine for twenty-four shillings per *milhayrola*. There he found a certain man whose name he doesn't remember at present with whom he did business for the purpose of selling the witness's wine. In the tavern the witness says he found Bertran eating tripes and figs and drinking, and the witness himself ate tripes and figs and drank in the same tavern. The witness was asked who was present at this eating and drinking, and he answered Peire Gramond, Miramas the taverner, and Michael the gardener. The witness added that he had seen Bertran Vital drinking in many different houses where wine was sold.

(Testimony of Guilhem Rogier, *laborator*) He knows a great deal. A year ago, the witness saw that Bertran, together with the witness himself and two men, drank and ate in the house of the lady Beguines (*in domo dominarum Beguinarum*) living next to the house of Raolin Vivaut where red wine was sold. Asked about the day and hour the witness says he doesn't remember. The witness also said that a year ago, on a day and time he doesn't remember, the witness saw that Bertran was drinking with the witness in the house of Bertran Gayrier where white wine was once sold.

(Testimony of Aycart Finaut, weaver) He knows a great deal. Two years ago, on days and times that the witness doesn't remember at present, the witness saw Bertran Vital drinking both in the house of Jacme Bonacros and in the house of Raymon Enneat, his neighbors; the witness himself drank with him in the said houses where there were taverns and where red wine was legitimately sold in public (*ubi vinum rubeum venele publice vendebatur*).

(Testimony of Ugo Morlans, *laborator*) He knows a great deal. During the Lord's birthday just past, on a day he doesn't remember, before dinnertime, the witness saw Bertran Vital drinking in Raolet's house, which is situated in front of the Bertran's own house, in which place Raolet sells sweet wine and wafers (*nectar et nebule*).[28] Of this sweet wine and wafers, Bertran, the witness, Bertomieu Blanc, Johan Garin, and Ugo Odol all drank and ate together. Bertran and the witness bet six pennyworth of sweet wine at dice.

(Testimony of Peire Asami, *laborator*[29]) He knows little other than that this year, on days and times which he doesn't remember at present, the witness saw Bertran drinking in the taverns written below. First, the tavern of Ugo Faysonerie where Miramas the taverner sold wine. Next, in the house of Guilhem Gasquet on another occasion. Next, in the house of Jacme Bonacros on another occasion. Next, in the house of Peire Vital on another occasion. Asked how he knows this, he answered that while he was passing along the streets of the said taverns he saw Bertran drinking in the taverns, which is not to say that the witness himself entered or drank in those taverns.

The success of the strategy depended on the plaintiff's ability to evoke the strands of high Christian moral discourse that inveighed against drunkenness and associated sins like sloth or *luxuria* as well as the vernacular moral discourse that placed high value on a man's ability to manage the family patrimony.

But Laurent and his procurator were never able to get their witnesses to subscribe fully to this moral claim. From this point onward in the testimony, the interrogator switched to the list of interrogatories that Bertran's lawyers had come up with. These were the key questions: In which taverns did Bertran shamefully drink wine and eat? Who was present? And the vital question that exposed Laurens's hypocrisy: Do other upstanding men in Marseille's suburbs, including those who manage their estates well, visit the taverns of their neighbors and friends in a similar way?[30]

In responding to these interrogatories, the witnesses shrugged off the crudely Puritan framework that Laurens's legal team had tried to foist on them and pointed out the obvious:[31]

> (Testimony of Bertomieu Blanc, *laborator*) Other upstanding men of the suburbs are accustomed to drink with their neighbors in their neighbors' taverns just as is customary to choose carefully (*solociare*) among one's neighbors and friends. The witness himself, together with Bertran Vital and Andrivet Bastier, once partook of sweet wine in the house of Raolet who was then selling sweet wine.
>
> (Testimony of Guilhem Rogier, *laborator*) Asked if Bertran is used to drinking and eating shamefully in taverns, answered that Bertran well and honestly (*bene et honeste*) drank and ate in the said taverns just as a good man ought to drink and eat. . .It is the custom among men of the suburbs to drink in the taverns of their neighbors and friends in this way.
>
> (Testimony of Aycart Finaut, weaver) Asked if he saw Bertran patronizing other taverns in places where there are taverns, drinking and eating shamefully, he answered that at no time had he ever seen Bertran drinking and eating in other taverns. . .Asked if other upstanding men in Marseille's suburbs, including those who manage their estates well, visit the taverns of their neighbors and friends in a similar way, he answered yes.
>
> (Testimony of Ugo Morlans, *laborator*) Asked if in Raolet's house he had seen Bertran drinking sweet wine and eating wafers in a shameful way, he answered no, rather, he chose carefully where they drank and ate (*ymo solociando ubi potebant et comedebant*).
>
> (Testimony of Peire Asami, *laborator*) From one neighborhood to another, the custom is to drink as they did, though not within the city walls. Asked if Bertran drank shamefully, he said no, nor did he see him drunk.

Some of the sameness in these depositions derives from the fact that the witnesses (or at least their statements, as recorded by the notary) sometimes parroted the words of the interrogation. But even so, all these depositions show more variation than did the depositions given in Laurens's first witness program. The type of wine that was drunk varies from one witness to the next, as does the food. The taverns vary. Unusual or ad hoc comments find their way into the depositions: one witness mentions the price charged for the wine and talks about drinking customs; another played dice; a third snoops in tavern doors to see who's drinking. We finally get the sense that we are meeting real people with different experiences. But this failure of conformity is a telling clue that Laurens and Bernat had been unable to craft an aesthetically uniform witness program.

The resistance is palpable. Embedded in Peire's testimony, for example, is a suggestion that seems to run through the other four responses: the idea that fancy lawyers just don't know how drinking customs work in the suburbs. It is true that the plaintiff, Laurens Giraut, was himself a *laborator* who lived in the suburbs. But surely it was the procurator who had come up with this strategy. In this light, the witness revolt looks very much like an act designed to preserve the moral autonomy of suburban behavior from a moral/legal discourse generated for a different sort of world, the wealthier, more "bourgeois" lifestyle of the intramural city.

No witness proved willing to respond to points 2 and 3, the accusation of consorting with prostitutes and running an estate badly—here, it appears that Laurens's legal team had stumbled badly. On both these points, the responses consist either of "he knows nothing" or something inconsequential. On the last point, the question of *fama*, the witnesses completely reversed the relatively bad *fama* portrayed by Laurens's first witness program, saying things like "Bertran has good *fama*"; "Bertran well and diligently does his business, working his garden, and the witness believes that because of his hard work he has acquired a great deal of profit"; and "he's a good man, upright (*legale*); he doesn't fight."

Staring defeat in the face, Laurens and his legal team played their last card, initiating a lawyerly tactic known as a witness exception procedure that was designed to impugn the standing of some of the witnesses who had testified for Bertran.[32] The articles claimed that one was a public usurer; a second was related to Bertran through marriage and spiritual kinship; a third was not only a spiritual kinsman but also a low-life and a drunkard who shared food and wine with Bertran, a sign of close friendship; and the fourth was publicly defamed as a murderer. Had they stuck, all four accusations would have negated their testimony and placed Bernat's case in jeopardy.

The procedure was only partially successful. All six witnesses were women, a normal feature of cases involving a determination of bonds of friendship or kinship. Female testimony was a little more unusual as far as a reputation for homicide goes, and in point of fact each of the six women disclaimed all knowledge of point 4. Perhaps Laurens, at this point in his long dispute with Bertran, found it impossible to recruit any men as witnesses. Several of the women confirmed Johan Borgonho's reputation as a usurer. The most interesting depositions concern point 3, the accusation that Peire Taleta was not only a kinsman but also Bertran's housemate (*familiaris, domesticus*), eating and drinking with Bertran, as well as "a man of vile way-of-life, drinking and hanging about dishonestly and publicly in taverns." Two witnesses departed markedly from the story line prescribed by Laurens:[33]

> (Testimony of Raymona de Gauta) Bertran and Peire Taleta mutually call one another cousin and hold each other as spiritual kin; they converse together in Bertran's house and while they are eating and drinking. But she does not firmly remember whether Peire Taleta has a vile way-of-life nor whether she has seen him drinking in taverns.
>
> (Testimony of Jacma Uverna) Peire and Bertran are often conversing together with honest speech (*conversantes conversatione honesta*) and not in taverns or in other dishonest drinking spots. They are called and hold one another as spiritual kinsmen.

The case ended almost immediately after the hearing of the witness exception procedure. On March 24, 1335, more than eight months after the start of the trial, Bertran lodged a formal complaint over the heavy expenses and efforts occasioned in the suit against him and requested a judgment. Judgment was duly given the following week. As in most trial transcripts, the judgment itself was not included in the register. Two clues, however, let us know that Laurens's suit had failed. First, Bertran was allowed to present the judge with a list of expenses to be assigned to Laurens. The expenses came to twenty-five pounds fifteen shillings and included not only the usual fees paid to lawyers and notaries but also six pounds for sixty days lost labor. Second, Laurens's procurator formally lodged a request to appeal the judgment to the court of first appeals. No record of this appeal is extant.

Within two and a half years of this judgment Laurens was dead. We learn this from a notarized act of arbitration that provides an interesting coda to the case.[34] The arbitration was the outcome of a dispute between Laurens's widow, Laura Girauda, and her daughter Secilieta. It seems to have arisen because, upon Laurens's death, Secilieta had become her father's universal heir, but had been unwilling to repay her own mother's dowry out of the estate. In all likelihood, Laura had initiated (or threatened to initiate) her own dotal retrocession against Secilieta, thereby levering Secilieta into a compromise. The act took place within the church of Notre Dame des Accoules, a symbolic peacemaking site. In arbitrations, it would have been typical for each party to name one of the two arbitrators. One of these was Nicolau Bonvin, the notable who had supported Bertran Vital, and it seems very likely that he had been chosen by Secilieta and/or her father-in-law. On this reading, it may be that Secilieta had always identified with her husband's family, and was resentful toward the efforts of her own father and mother to break up her marriage. Bertran, for his part, managed to outlive his adversary though he eventually succumbed to the plague in 1348. His widow, Resens, took on the role of family matriarch. An act from 1353 shows her exercising guardianship over her granddaughter, Mabilieta Castagne. Immediately afterward, we find her leasing property to her son, now old enough to be called Jaume, and to her grandson Nicolau.[35]

* * *

The case of Laurens Giraut is typical of thousands of similar cases found in the judicial archives of the city of Marseille in the fourteenth and fifteenth centuries. It has none of the exciting or titillating detail found in some cases heard before ecclesiastical inquisitions or criminal trials in late medieval Europe. Its interest lies in its very banality. For most people who encountered the law in late medieval Europe—and at times it seems as if this included a fair spectrum of the population—this was their rather humdrum experience. The case does contain some delightful details about the rhythms of everyday drinking habits among urban peasants in the suburbs of fourteenth-century Marseille: taverns classified according to the color of wine they sold; the custom of eating fruit and wafers while drinking; the idea of the Beguines earning a little income by running a little wine tavern for peasants; the careful distinction that men drew between drinking in the taverns of friends and drinking in more impersonal settings. On this last point, one wonders whether Peire Asami shrank from entering those taverns not because he was a killjoy but because he was from Syon, and not among friends in the suburb of Moriers.

The case also shows how both *fama* and moral values shaped the ways in which ordinary litigants built witness programs. Truth, in Marseille's courts, was not something that people readily distinguished from common belief and opinion. Truth lay uncomfortably in the realm of what we might call appearances: if Bertran was *thought* to be insolvent, then he *was* insolvent, for all intents and purposes. The rapid withdrawal of credit from someone reputed to be verging on insolvency would, in any event, transform the impression into a reality soon enough. To convey this truth, litigants strove to present their case as common opinion, something that everyone knows, and, moreover, something that everyone knows in much the same way. Homogeneity was valued as an aesthetic of truth: a claim simply seemed more truthful to contemporary observers if opinions regarding it were relatively uniform, and if elements of subsequent depositions echoed each other in their syntax and vocabulary. Sympathetic witnesses aimed at making sense with a discursive framework. As a corollary to this, the "facts" of a case were subordinate to the discourse they sought to represent. When Laurens's witnesses rebelled against his attempt to stigmatize Bertran's actions, they framed their claims within a commonsense moral discourse, namely, that men can drink honestly and well in the taverns of neighbors and friends. On this point, there was unanimity of opinion.

The forces that promoted the homogenization of witness testimony in medieval court cases looks like an obstacle that prevents us from getting at the "real" voices of witnesses. Yet one should be reluctant to see this as yet another failure of medieval documentation. Yes, it is tempting to pursue the voices of individuals. In cases of litigation from late medieval Marseille, there are plenty of instances where one feels that the voice of the individual has managed to escape the forces of homogeneity. Like the other contributors to this volume, I find these voices captivating and even persuasive. But even so, I don't believe that we need to lament or try to get around the fact of homogeneity. If we admit that the homogeneity of witness depositions is not just the product of procedures; if we acknowledge that the everyday epistemology of the later Middle Ages valued conformity and discouraged individuality and located truth in appearances rather than incidental clues; then we can view witness depositions as situated uses of a larger moral values and expectations that are interesting in their own right.

Notes

1. See Anne D. Hedeman, *The Royal Image: Illustrations of the Grandes Chroniques de France, 1274–1422* (Berkeley: University of California Press, 1991).
2. See Michael Camille, "Seeing and Reading: Some Visual Implications of Medieval Literacy and Illiteracy," *Art History*, 8 (1985): 29 [26–49]. My thanks to Heidi Gearhart for directing me to this article.
3. The characterization of pleading as storytelling exists in contemporary court cases. In cases from Marseille's Roman-canon law courts, for example, it was conventional to describe the things told in the *libellus* as a *narratio* or *narrata*, a "story" or "things told." A defendant who chose to contest a suit would "deny the things told as they are told in the *libellus* (*negat narrata prout narrantur in dicto libello*)." For an example see France, Archives Départementales des Bouches-du-Rhône (hereafter ADBR) 3B 853, fol. 78r, case opened on February 26, 1401 on fol. 61r.
4. ADBR 3B 41, between fols. 166r and 170v, case opened on August 16, 1340 on fol. 164r.
5. Hedeman, *Royal Image*, p. 176.
6. The entire case can be found in ADBR 3B 29, fols. 29r–70v, opened July 12, 1334, and is entitled "Causa Bernardi Raymundi procuratoris Laurensii Giraudi contra Bertrandi Vitalis."

7. In general see Victor-L. Bourrilly, *Essai sur l'histoire politique de Marseille des origines à 1264* (Aix-en-Provence: A. Dragon, 1925); Régine Pernoud, *Essai sur l'histoire du port de Marseille des origines à la fin du XIIIeme siècle* (Marseille: A. Ged, 1935); Georges Lesage, *Marseille angevine: recherches sur son évolutions administrative, économique et urbaine de la victoire de Charles d'Anjou à l'arrivée de Jeanne 1re (1264–1348)* (Paris: Boccard, 1950); Édouard Baratier, Histoire de Marseille (Toulouse: Privat, 1973); Raoul Busquet, *Histoire de Marseille*, ed. Pierre Guiral (Paris: Éditions Robert Laffont, 1978).

8. In fourteenth-century Marseille, the standard unit of currency was the royal pound, at twenty shillings per pound and twelve pennies per shilling (see Henri Rolland, *Monnaies des comtes de Provence, XIIe-XVe s. Histoire monétaire, économique, corporative. Description raisonnée* [Paris, 1956]). Apprentices and agricultural laborers generally earned two to four shillings per day and a house might cost as little as ten pounds and as much as several hundred.

9. On Mareille's urban peasants, see Francine Michaud, "The Peasant Citizens of Marseille at the Turn of the Fourteenth Century," in *Urban and Rural Communities in Medieval France: Provence and Languedoc, 1000–1500*, ed. Kathryn Reyerson and John Drendel (Leiden: Brill, 1998), pp. 275–89.

10. The subject of and literature on *fama* is surveyed in Thelma Fenster and Daniel Lord Smail, *Fama: The Politics of Talk and Reputation in Medieval Europe* (Ithaca: Cornell University Press, 2003).

11. It was a plausible rumor: this kind of notarial contract (*donatio omnium bonorum or a datio insolutum*) was relatively common in Marseille and was typically used in just these circumstances.

12. See my *The Consumption of Justice: Emotions, Publicity, and Legal Culture in Marseille, 1264–1423* (Ithaca: Cornell University Press, 2003).

13. ADBR 3B 29, fol. 37r.

14. ADBR 3B 29, fols. 1r–3r, case opened on May 24, 1334.

15. ADBR 3B 29, fols. 128r–29r, case opened on August 18, 1334.

16. ADBR 3B 29, fols. 38r–40v

17. ADBR 3B 29, fols. 41r–43v.

18. ADBR 3B 31, loose sheet between fols. 105–106, case opened on February 25, 1337 on fol. 96r. Since judicial offices rotated every year, new judges were occasionally unaware of Marseille's court customs, and arguments like this are not unusual. It is true that the custom was disputed in this case and the outcome is not known; nevertheless, the custom is amply attested in cases like Laurens's where *fama* alone did serve as the sole form of proof.

19. ADBR 3B 29, fols. 41v, 43v.

20. The articles can be found on fols. 34v–35v and are repeated, with minor changes, on fols. 49r–50r.

21. ADBR 3B 29, fols. 51v–52r.

22. ADBR 3B 29, fol. 57r.

23. See, among others, C. Stephen Jaeger, *The Origins of Courtliness: Civilizing Trends and the Formation of Courtly Ideals, 939–1210* (Philadelphia: University of Pennsylvania Press, 1985); Pieter Spierenburg, ed., *Men and*

Violence: Gender, Honor, and Rituals in Modern Europe and America (Columbus, OH: Ohio State University Press, 1998).

24. ADBR 3B 812, fols. 31r, 32v, 35v, cased opened on June 1, 1352 on fol. 26r.

25. ADBR 3B 54, fol. 32v, case opened on July 19, 1354 on fol. 6r.

26. See ADBR 3B 29, loose sheet sewn between fols. 59–60. In general, interrogatories first took form on separate sheets of paper, called *cedulae*, that were handed over to the court by the defendant or his procurator. Some were subsequently copied into the record. In other cases, as in this one, the *cedula* was simply folded and stuck into the binding of the register. In cases where the *cedula* was actually sewn into the binding it stood a good chance of survival. Loose *cedulae*, however, were frequently lost, which accounts for the relatively poor survival rate.

27. ADBR 3B 29, fols. 57v–62v.

28. My thanks to Richard Gyug for assistance with translations here and elsewhere.

29. Earlier, Peire Asami had been described as a pawnbroker, and this change of professional labels is unusual though not unprecedented. "Asami" was a very unusual surname in Marseille; it is extremely unlikely that this is a different Peire Asami.

30. ADBR 3B 29, loose sheet sewn between fols. 59–60, fol. 1r.

31. ADBR 3B 29, fols. 57v–62v.

32. ADBR 3B 29, fols. 63r.

33. ADBR 3B 29, fols. 65v, 66r.

34. ADBR 381E 384, fols. 254r–55r, December 30, 1337.

35. ADBR 381E 64bis, fols. 6r–v and 7r, November 10, 1352.

CHAPTER 10

A RAPE TRIAL IN SAINT ELOI: SEX, SEDUCTION,
AND JUSTICE IN THE SEIGNEURIAL COURTS OF
MEDIEVAL PARIS

Edna Ruth Yahil

L ate medieval French customary law was, in theory, quite strict about
rape, and medieval customary texts prescribed severe punishments for
forcible sexual intercourse.[1] Unsurprisingly, the few surviving court
records from the period demonstrate a very different reality: rape was a
crime that was rarely prosecuted and even less frequently punished in both
ecclesiastical and secular tribunals.[2] The few cases that did go to trial were
usually dismissed, settled out of court, or resulted in an acquittal. To make
matters even more complicated for the historian, court records for rape
cases tend to be poorly documented, with only hints about the complex
stories that lie behind the accusation or about the lives of the plaintiffs and
victims.[3] As a result, scholars have tended to write composite histories
about rape prosecution or legal procedure, rather than focus on the lives of
individuals accused of such crimes.

It is for this reason that the case of a twenty-eight-year-old Parisian
dressmaker named Jehan Feuchre is so remarkable.[4] Arrested by three
sergeants from the seigneurie of Saint Eloi on October 30, 1464, Jehan was
accused of rape and also of the more serious charge of "deflowering" a local
girl name Denise. He was jailed for almost a fortnight, during which time
he was interrogated twice. Ordinarily in a seigneurial court such as Saint
Eloi, a criminal confession would have been written on loose sheets of
paper used by the court and then lost to posterity, with only a brief record
of the imprisonment, payment of bail, or judge's decision noted in an

official court register.[5] In this instance, however, Jehan's (sometimes conflicting) confessions were scrupulously copied by the scribe in the register of Saint Eloi. In the course of responding to his interrogators, Jehan detailed his background and his interactions with Denise and in doing so spoke volumes about the society in which he lived. His personal story can serve as a case study about life in late medieval Paris.

This article is a multilevel reading of Jehan Feuchre's confessions that begins with the text itself and slowly radiates outwards to consider the individual, the construction of his narrative, and the society in which he lived.[6] It begins at the simplest level by examining the source in which Jehan's story is found. It then moves to the level of the individual, that is, to biography, yet as Jehan tells his personal account, he also recounts a collective biography of his small social circle as well as that of the society in which he lives. The third level is to read Jehan's narrative as a construction of the confessing subject. His words serve as a first-hand account of his experience which can then be placed within the larger context of Parisian youth culture. Jehan describes in vivid details his flirtatious behavior and eventual seduction of Denise and, in doing so, speaks volumes about sex and social norms in his society. At the same time, his narrative must be read in light of its genre, that of a legal document. Jehan constructs his narrative within the framework of a criminal trial, responding to his interrogators and protecting his own self-interests. In doing so, he demonstrates a highly sophisticated knowledge of medieval law and legal institutions. Finally, this case is contextualized within the larger framework of law and society by examining the motives that plaintiffs had for pursuing a futile case in court, and the reasons why the legal officers of Saint Eloi may have found a case involving a rather marginal member of society particularly interesting. Overall, this article demonstrates the richness of seigneurial court records—a source that has been all but ignored by historians—for writing the history of late medieval Paris.[7]

Level One: The Source

It is by virtue of geographic happenstance that we can learn Jehan's story. Although the rue Percié where both Jehan and Denise lived was located *intra-muros*, this neighborhood was not in the part of the city that was under the control of the Provost of Paris (and hence the King of France), but rather in an independent territory, a small judicial jurisdiction that had been ceded to the priory of Saint Eloi in 1280.[8] By virtue of domicile of the defendant and plaintiff, this case was heard by the *maire* of Saint Eloi in a small local court rather than by the Provost of Paris at his seat at the Châtelet. There are very few extant records from the Châtelet,[9] however, a few fifteenth-century registers recording the activities of Saint Eloi and three other similar courts have survived and are housed today in the *Archives Nationales* in Paris.[10] The five extant registers from Saint Eloi cover the seigneurial court's activity from 1447–1500 (with a lacuna from 1471–1487, presumably the result of a lost register or two).

The priory of Saint Eloi acted in much the same way that a secular lord would by administering, controlling, and policing its seigneurie. However, unlike many other seigneurial lords at the time, who had little real power, the priory was extremely influential in that it held the right to both high and low justice within its tiny territory. The *maire* controlled a court that not only settled small disputes amongst local inhabitants but also heard more serious cases including theft, murder, rape, and homicide. Furthermore, the court's judges were allowed to exact corporal and even capital punishment, hanging prisoners on the gibbets of the abbey of Saint Maur.[11] A royal privilege issued at the end of the fourteenth century further expanded the priory's rights by permitting the *maire* to hear appeals in specially convened assizes.

Jehan's imprisonment and interrogation followed the general procedure for criminal cases under customary law.[12] Denise's father and godfather denounced him to the judge, who then arrested and imprisoned Jehan as well as Denise's father after an automatic counteraccusation. Jehan was interrogated on two separate occasions, the first time on October 30 by a subordinate judge, most likely the lieutenant of the *maire*. On Sunday, November 4, a second interrogation was held and this time it was Jehan Longue, the *maire* who also worked as a lawyer at the Châtelet, who presided over the interrogation in the presence of two procurers from the Châtelet. Longue began by reading the written transcript from the first trial aloud and asked Jehan whether the contents were correct. He then proceeded to further examine the prisoner. At the conclusion of the second interrogation, Longue asked Jehan if he would be willing to marry Denise, to which the exhausted prisoner agreed. The following day, Denise's parents and godparents came before the court and agreed to pay an enormous *caution* (bail) of 6 *écus* on behalf of Jehan and the judge ordered that he be released the following Sunday. The scribe noted briefly in a register entry dated November 11, that "on this day Jehan Feuchre is a freed prisoner." Missing from the register is any reference to witness testimony and the report of a matron who would have examined Denise.

Jehan's words as recorded by the *greffier* (scribe) are, therefore, the only records that survive from this case. Extreme caution must be used however when reading this confession. Almost thirty years ago, Emmanuel Le Roy Ladurie claimed that the confessions found in the Jacques Fournier registers could "be considered the direct testimony of peasants," which could be used to reconstruct the world of Montaillou.[13] Since then, critics such as Father Leonard Boyle, Renate Rosaldo, and John Arnold have demonstrated that a more nuanced approach must be used to read court records.[14]

As a historian, I have deliberately chosen to use the word "confession" to describe Jehan's speech, for that is the term that contemporaries applied to his act. The *greffier* made a marginal note, that is, the word "*confession*" next to the entries for October 30 and November 4.[15] Yet "confession" is a bit of a misnomer: it should not be forgotten that Jehan was being *interrogated*. His words cannot be considered as direct speech, but rather as controlled, mediated responses to two interrogators: an unnamed interrogator on October 30, and Jehan Longue on November 4. His words were further mediated by the *greffier* who intentionally or not altered their meaning by recording them on paper. For example, in the first interrogation, the *greffier* only indicated twice (always at the conclusion of the confession) that Jehan was responding to specific questions by using the formula "he was asked if he" (*interrogue se il*), all the other paragraphs begin with the phrase "he further stated" (*dit oultre que*), implying that Jehan was speaking continually and on his own volition. Thus the text flows from one response to the next, providing a more aesthetically pleasing and free-flowing narrative, but one that is less true to Jehan's actual experience. The scribe indicates the questions four times in the second confession, but since this is done only at the very beginning and at the end of the confession, the final result is similar.

Judges and scribes are not the only figures tampering with the voices of the past. Historians who fail to tread carefully also can be guilty of further distorting the past. Indeed, Edward Muir and Guido Ruggiero have likened the historian to the criminal, referring to his or her scholarship as a "crime," like that of gravedigger.[16] They provide only a partial solution for those arrogant enough to attempt to still write history, arguing that while the historian cannot escape from disturbing the dead, he can still treat his subject respectfully. Thus we shall humbly delve into the life and times of Jehan Feuchre, always remaining respectful and keeping in mind the limits of the original source.

Level Two: Ordinary People, Ordinary Lives?

History is, by its very nature, a collective account of the stories of individuals. The historian is forced to generalize, to use the few sources available to create an overall image of an ancient way of life. These sweeping generalizations are necessary, but often the experiences of the very people who make up the fabric of society get lost in the process. The Jehan Feuchre case allows the historian to rectify this injustice by reconstructing a momentous event in the life of a fifteenth-century individual while at the same time illuminating some of the daily conflicts, struggles, and compromises that made up late medieval urban life. A close reading of Jehan's confessions enables us to discover how a young Parisian dressmaker flirted with, seduced, and eventually impregnated a fourteen-year-old girl. Her parents then chose to have him prosecuted in a local court, not in order to punish him—although passing two weeks in the cold, dank jail of Saint Eloi could not have been a pleasant experience—but rather to force him to marry their daughter.

All criminal *confessions* began with a brief biography of the accused. Like so many who had come before him, Jehan was asked to state name, age, occupation, and domicile at the beginning of his interrogation.[17] Yet even more can be learned by a close reading of Jehan's confessions: he speaks in detail not only about his background but also about other trial participants, including Denise, her parents and godparents, the other maid Gervaise, and other members of his community. Thus, in constructing an intensely personal narrative, he speaks at the same time to a larger collective experience.

Jehan's background was similar to that of many marginal youths who spent time in the dark, dank prisons of Paris. A native of the town of Crebin near Besançon, Jehan spent a peripatetic youth seeking employment opportunities. At the age of 19, after several failed attempts at finding stable work first in Langres and then Bar sur Aube, he finally arrived in Paris where he moved from workshop to workshop. At the time of his arrest, he was working as a dressmaker and living in a room rented from a man named Pierre le Chaussetier on the rue Percié, in the parish of Saint Paul on the right bank of Paris.

Jehan Feuchre fit in well economically and socially with the other inhabitants of his neighborhood. This neighborhood was one in which many individuals involved in the clothing industry—dressmakers, dyers, weavers, pressers—clustered. In comparison to other Parisian neighborhoods, the population was relatively humble and not very dense, with just over half the population classified as laboring or non-laboring poor.[18]

His social position should be clarified in terms of the "typical" profile of an itinerant, struggling youth who passed through the judicial systems of medieval Paris.[19] As Flandrin has pointed out, young men in urban centers tended to be servants, apprentices, or journeymen who "were struggling against married men who monopolized social and political power and who did not want the unmarried to have sexual intercourse with their wives, their daughters, and their maids."[20] Jehan may have been sexually repressed, but unlike servants or apprentices, he did have the right to marry. Whether he would have been considered a "good catch" is another question. As a member of the dressmaking guild, Jehan was better off than the majority of Parisians who worked as day laborers, but the clothing business was not particularly well remunerated and his métier—*cousturier*—was less lucrative than that of a tailor, who not only sewed but also had the right to cut cloth as well.[21] He was therefore neither at the top nor the bottom of the social scale.

Denise also lived a fairly typical life. She worked as a servant like many young Parisian woman.[22] Her parents lived nearby on the rue de Seville. At the time of the trial, she was fourteen or fifteen years old and living and working as a servant in the home of her godfather, Guillot du Fay, whose home was so close to Jean's house that he "would pass by and then pass by again on numerous occasions."[23] She shared a room and spent much time with another servant named Gervaise, who was twenty-six years old.

Jehan and Denise were ordinary Parisians living ordinary lives. Were it not for the fact that Jehan was arrested, their memory would have died many hundreds of years ago. Instead, as a result of an extraordinary event, Jehan spoke about their relationship before a tribunal and his words were recorded by a local court scribe in a register that happened to survive for hundreds of years. Thus the lives of two ordinary folk have been passed down to posterity.

Level Three: Constructing a Narrative

Confession, testimony, response—no matter which label is placed on Jehan's words, he was playing a constructed role—that of confessing subject—as he spoke to his interrogators. He was not only recounting his autobiographical past, but also (re)constructing a narrative of the events that eventually led to his imprisonment. It is essential to consider the factors that may have influenced Jehan's retelling of this story, such as memory, pleasing his interrogators, and avoiding punishment:

- *Memory.* Jehan's memory of the events was unique to him. It is highly probable that his perception of his interactions with Denise differed from hers or those of her parents:
- *Pleasing his interrogators.* The jailhouse confession is constructed in such a way that the subject is "invited to confess" before his interrogators, a process that is facilitated by the format of the confession, i.e., the use of probing questions.[24] In recounting his story, Jehan was at a certain level trying to provide his interrogators with the responses that he believed they wanted to hear.
- *Avoiding punishment.* Torture and capital punishment, while practiced less frequently in the fifteenth than in the thirteenth or fourteenth centuries, were not unknown in the seigneurial courts of Paris.[25] Jehan's

local knowledge enabled him to construct his confessions in a way that would reduce his punishment, demonstrating a wide-ranging popular understanding of judicial systems.

In an attempt to analyze Jehan's confessions, we cannot but help pass judgment on his narrative. It is simply not possible to let Jehan's words speak for themselves without questioning their veracity or their deeper meaning. Some of Jehan's confessions can probably be accepted at face value. In the course of his confessions, Jehan recalls his interactions with Denise in the days and weeks prior to any formal sexual act. These recollections are illustrative in that they demonstrate normal patterns of flirtation and seduction that must have been commonplace in medieval Paris. Jehan's description of youthful flirtation, chance encounters in the streets, attempts at seduction, and attempts to elude the watchful eyes of suspicious chaperones sounds entirely plausible. His description of the sex act itself, however, should probably be read with a bit more suspicion, keeping in mind Jehan's strategies.

Jehan Feuchre moved to the rue Percé on Saint Magdelene's day (July 22, 1464) and must have come across his neighbor Denise shortly thereafter. In his first confession,[26] Jehan relates that whenever he would walk by Guillaume du Fay's house, Denise and an older maid with whom she worked named Gervaise would often make obvious signs of love, and their forwardness surprised him since he would not respond. Sometimes, the two girls would stop him in the road carrying flowers and pins in their hands and they would make small bouquets that they would attach to his hat. Eventually, Jehan succumbed to Denise's flirtatious advances. He fell in love with the young girl and wanted to follow her into the du Fay house, but he was only willing to do so when du Fay and his wife were not home. Since neither he nor the girls knew ahead of time when the du Fays would be gone nor when they might return, he was never able to find an opportunity to enter the house.

Things progressed rapidly and passions became more heated. On August 10, the day of the festival of Saint Lawrence, Denise once again stopped Jehan in the street. He recalled their conversation as follows:

> Denise asked whether I[27] was going to the Saint Lawrence festival and whether I was going there to seek a wife. When I responded, "yes," she said that she would accompany me. She then said that it was time that I marry a girl about fourteen or fifteen years old and that she was that age. She continued saying that I was handsome and that she truly liked me.

Jehan was so taken by Denise's beauty and her words that an even deeper love for Denise swelled within him. Nevertheless he set off to the festivities without her. Upon returning later that day, he found the other maid Gervaise standing with Madame du Fay in front of the Porte Baudoix. Gervaise began to flirt with Jehan when her mistress and their other companions were not looking:

> I found du Fay's other maid [Gervaise] by the Porte Badouix standing behind her mistress. This maid threw a pear down towards where I was standing and I received this pear without the mistress or anyone else being aware.

Was this a sign of indifference on Mme. du Fay's part or were Jehan and Gervaise merely pulling the wool over their elder's eyes as youth are so often wont to do? Continuing on his way home, he found Denise once again standing in front of the du Fay house and she too threw him a pear, but he insisted to his interrogators that this flirtation occurred "without any promise of marriage."

Up to this point, Jehan Feuchre was testifying to fairly typical behavior. Flirtation, even that which took place secretly without the knowledge of ever-present neighbors and chaperones, could hardly be considered abnormal, and there must have been plenty of other Parisian youths engaged in similar behavior. Unfortunately, there is no way to know what question the interrogator posed next, but the entire tone of Jehan's confession changed with the next paragraph, which begins with the innocuous "he further stated that."

Two or three weeks later, Jehan passed once again in front of the du Fay house. It was around the time of day when the windows and doors of the house were opened. Jehan was able to see the girls inside and speak to them. He asked them whether they might come to his room, and the two responded that they did not know when they might be able to get away and suggested instead that perhaps he might come to their house when they would find themselves alone.

About half an hour later, Jehan saw the two girls standing on the street, indicating that they were now unchaperoned. While Gervaise stood by observing, Jehan grabbed Denise by the hand and without any resistance led her into a kitchen that was attached to the room facing the street. Jehan stated:

> I took Denise and lay her on the floor. She put up no resistance except to tell me that I should wait until another time and that the other maid could tell on them. Yet when I saw that she was no longer putting up any resistance, I climbed on her, took hold of my penis, and tried to enter her. But I was not able to because I *threw my semen* [ejaculated outside her body]. Therefore I cannot have deflowered her as I am accused.

Jehan's accusers clearly pushed him on this point. He continued his confession by stating that he returned to the house on three or four occasions when he knew that the du Fays were either sleeping or out of the house. The couple would go to the room where Denise and Gervaise slept; one time Denise led the way, the other time it was Jehan who initiated. Denise would lie down on the floor and then he would climb on top of her. But he insisted that he couldn't have deflowered her because he was always careful to "throw his semen." He added for good measure, "if [the matrons working for the court discover that] she is not a virgin, then it must have been someone else's fault!"

It is in these last paragraphs that Jehan's legal strategy become apparent. From the very beginning, he details a reciprocal flirtation. He demonstrates to his interrogators that he knew both chambermaids and saw and communicated with them frequently. He states outright that all parties, including the hapless spinster Gervaise, gladly participated. Yet in this stage of his confession he begins to hint at stronger accusations. Certain tropes, such as the seduction scene in the kitchen—which would have been in the front of the house—would have been clearly read by contemporaries as the activities of prostitutes.

The counter accusation of prostitution was not a far stretch. As Jehan and his interrogators knew well, the line between the chambermaid and prostitute was often quite fine. Neither profession required formal training and criminal records from other Parisian courts testify to the fact that chambermaids occasionally supplemented their earnings through paid sexual activity either on their own initiative or at the behest of their family or employers.[28] The key phrase in his confession was that Gervaise had been aware of what was going on: Jehan testified that everything had happened in front of the older maid (*tout devant et tout au veu et sceu*). Jehan did not actually come out and *explicitly* accuse the girls of prostitution, but the implication of his words was very clear: Gervaise was acting as a procuress, a *maquerelle*.

Why did Jehan Feuchre hesitate to state outright that Denise was a prostitute? His contemporaries often came before local courts with various, quite explicit accusations: that someone was a prostitute, a *paillarde*, a *fille de joie*, a *fille amoureuse*; that someone was a procuress, a *maquerelle*; that men and women were constantly going in and out of someone's house, that the chambermaid claimed to be a niece, but her stomach was suddenly swelling, or that there were frequent fights happening outside a house. Furthermore, medieval society would not have frowned upon a young, unmarried man visiting a prostitute. Nonetheless, Jehan resisted the urge to explicitly accuse Denise of prostitution.

The interrogator clearly understood Jehan's implication. The final question posed at the first interrogation was so crucial that the scribe actually wrote it down: "He [Jehan Feuchre] was asked whether he gave any gifts to Denise in order to deceive her?" Jehan responded to the interrogators that indeed he had given Denise a small gold-plated rod and a little mirror. He insisted, however, that this was not done to deceive Denise but rather because she had first given him a gift and he was merely initiating in kind. Jehan then went on to say that he gave a second mirror to Gervaise because he knew full well that Gervaise was aware of everything that had happened between him and Denise. Once again, his words had a double meaning. Could he be implying that he had paid the two girls for sex, but couching his accusation in a description of a mutual exchange of gifts?

Jehan's second strategy was to deny that he and Denise actually consummated their relationship. For a rape conviction, the plaintiff had to prove that full penetration had occurred, a task that was not very easy in the Middle Ages.[29] Intromission, in and of itself, did not constitute defloration. Jehan did not deny that he and Denise had shared some intimacy; he merely insisted that true consummation never occurred. His knowledge of medieval customary law was sophisticated enough to shape his confession in a way that would enable him to avoid serious punishment.

Five days later, Jehan was interrogated once more, but this time the *maire* of Saint Eloi came to his cell to serve as the interrogator.[30] Following custom, Jehan Longue began by reading the written confession of October 30 to Jehan Feuchre and asking him if everything that he had read was correct, to which Jehan replied affirmatively. Longue then asked him whether he knew Guillaume du Fay and his wife, to which Jehan replied: "They are good folk who live a good life, are honest, and highly regarded."

Longue followed up by questioning how well Jehan and Denise had known each other and presenting details that he must have obtained by speaking to Denise or perhaps Gervaise. It is at this point that Jehan proceeded to change slightly the story that he had told during his first interrogation. He began by recounting the events that took place on Saint Lawrence Day when he passed by the du Fay house and saw Denise:

> Last Saint Lawrence day, I spoke to Denise and asked her if she wanted to go to the festival with me. After we had spoken many words together, Denise asked me if I wanted to have a drink with her and whether I would come into the house, to which I responded that I didn't want a drink. Denise then said to me that she thought I was a handsome boy (*beau filz*) and that I pleased her a lot. I responded that she seemed beautiful to me and was also pleasing.

Jehan then changed his original confession further. On a different day, a time that he hadn't mentioned in his first confession, and perhaps on one other occasion Gervaise and Denise came to his bedroom around ten o'clock in the morning and made the bed. He said that:

> I took Denise and asked her if she would like to be my paramour (*estre sa dame par amours*). She said that she would be happy to, but she didn't want Gervaise to know and promised to return alone to my room later, but in the end she did not.

Instead, on that very same day he returned to du Fay's house and found Gervaise and Denise standing outside. He mentions that he spoke to Denise at length, but doesn't specify the topic of conversation (*apres plusieurs parolles eues entre luy et ladicte Denise*). He then told his inquisitors:

> I took her by the arms and took her into the kitchen of [the] house, lay her on the ground, took her and climbed on top of her. And I affirm by oath that I could not have deflowered Denise because I controlled myself and threw my semen. My organ never entered inside Denise. And furthermore, on several occasions I came to visit and speak with Denise—perhaps four or five times—but hardly anything happened. And I thought she was a virgin (unless someone other than me has deflowered her) and that is what she told me.

Longue's two final questions were extremely serious. First, he asked whether Denise had given Jehan anything in the name of marriage (in other words, if the couple had been secretly wed). When Jehan replied in the negative, Jehan Longue concluded with the final, pivotal question: "He was asked if he would be willing to take and marry [the] said Denise." And Jehan agreed, providing that her parents would increase their support.

The tone of the second confession is radically different from the first. The presence of Jehan Longue and other important officials added an extra level of *gravitas* to the situation. Jehan realized that resistance was futile at this point and reshaped his testimony in order to please his interrogators. He praised Denise's family and no longer alluded to her *mauvaise vie*. However, he still needed to protect himself from serious punishment and therefore focused on the argument that he hadn't deflowered Denise. Longue asked deliberative, probing questions and slowly built up to the desired outcome of the court—that Jehan agree to marry Denise—and the prisoner had no choice but to agree. Yet Longue did not follow the usual practice in seigneurial courts and free Jehan immediately. Instead, he ordered the prisoner to be freed only the following Sunday, letting him suffer a few more days in the gruesome jail of Saint Eloi. In the end, the outcome of this simple tale of youthful misadventure ended as such tales of sex and seduction usually did, with the seducer agreeing to marry his teenage victim. Yet most couples wed without the threat of legal proceedings: Jehan and Denise's path to the wedding aisle was unique merely because of the extreme measures taken by Denise's family and the officers of the court of Saint Eloi.

Level Four: The Rape Accusation

While the term *rape* has a very specific meaning in the twenty-first century, it was not always defined as sexual violence in earlier eras. In the Middle Ages, the crime of *raptus* technically referred to the abduction—sometimes willing—of an individual, who need not necessarily have been a woman.[31] Annick Porteau-Bitker has surveyed the records of a wide range of secular French courts and determined that abduction was more frequently prosecuted than sexual violence in the late Middle Ages.[32] It is not surprising; therefore, that very few rape (as defined by sexual violence) cases were heard in the seigneurial courts of Paris. In the fourteenth-century court of Saint Martin des Champs, only six cases of rape were recorded in a twenty-five year period.[33] Of these, only one resulted in a death conviction, the other perpetrators either disappeared from the court records or were absolved. In my research on the seigneurial court of Saint Germain des Prés, I have come across fewer than ten rapes over the course of almost one hundred years. All but two of the Saint Germain cases involved the rapes of extremely young girls and there was only one conviction, but with a drastically reduced punishment.[34]

The Saint Eloi record leaves no doubt that the crime being prosecuted was sexual violence: in recording Jehan Feuchre's imprisonment, the *greffier* wrote that "Feuchre had violated and deflowered Denise." The final reading level looks at the Jehan Feuchre case on an institutional and societal level and poses perhaps the most puzzling question of all: Why was Jehan Feuchre prosecuted for rape at all? The probable answer is that Jehan happened to have been in the wrong place at the wrong time. Denise's parents were keen on forcing him to marry their daughter at the very moment that the officials of the court of Saint Eloi were eager to prove their jurisdictional authority.

Denise's parents and godparents are mere shadows on the page of the Saint Eloi register in which only their names and addresses is written. The little that we know about Denise's parents and godparents is primarily implicit and can be deduced only by reading between the lines of Jehan's confession. The scribe records that they instigated the initial arrest and that Guillot Bonnot was willing to be imprisoned on behalf of his daughter. The legal procedure is in and of itself proof that neither the du Fays nor the Bonnots were indifferent guardians. Their motive for going to court was clearly a restoration of honor, not only of Denise's honor, but also that of the family.

The reason for their anguish is not hard to imagine: Denise was clearly pregnant. Flirting was considered normal behavior and even youthful sexual exploration could be overlooked in the world in which Jehan and Denise lived, but somehow there was an invisible moral line concerning illegitimate pregnancy that once crossed caused great cultural distress.[35] Although Denise's pregnancy was not stated explicitly in the Saint Eloi register, there are several factors that support this interpretation. The first is Denise's young age. While she was older than the pre-adolescent rape victims who came before the court of Saint Germain, she was still considerably younger than the typical medieval bride (and was below the legal canonical age for marriage). The timeframe of the events as described by Jehan are also highly suspicious. Jehan met Denise in July, the alleged sexual activity took place in late August, and two months later Jehan found himself in the prison of Saint Eloi. Finally, Jehan repeatedly insisted that penetration had not taken place, and that if she was not a virgin someone else was to blame.

If an illegitimate pregnancy brought disgrace to the family, then honor had to somehow be restored. Launching a rape procedure served a dual purpose for the du Fays and Bonnots. First, regardless of the certain futility of seeking a conviction, the simple step of beginning proceedings against an accused rapist was enough to restore dignity to the victim's family. Neither the du Fays nor the Bonnots ever expected that Jehan Feuchre would hang for his crime. Families who began rape proceedings in the various courts of Paris were not interested in conviction but rather in the act of bringing forth the claim before a legal tribunal. Publicly accusing the perpetrator of rape was all that was needed to restore honor to the victim and her family, afterwards other forms of judicial or extrajudicial negotiations and compromise could be reached.[36] In this case, the motive of the du Fays and the Bonnots is clear: they were interested in restoring honor to the family and forcing Jehan Feuchre to marry their pregnant fourteen-year-old daughter. Young men frequently impregnated young girls in the Middle Ages, and usually the families were able to persuade them to marry their daughters without taking such drastic steps. Jehan Feuchre was simply more stubborn, more reluctant than most to fulfill his societal obligations. The question of why he was so adamant about not marrying Denise, unfortunately, will never be answered.

Institutional questions surrounding this case are much more complicated: What was the priory of Saint Eloi's interest in the case of Jehan Feuchre? Why was the *greffier* compelled to copy Jehan Feuchre's confession into the register? The answer lies in the complex political maneuvering that was taking place in Paris in the period following the end of the Hundred Years' War.

Late fifteenth-century Paris was not a unified city, but rather a patch-work of land and people overseen by multiple judicial powers including royal, municipal, seigneurial, and ecclesiastical authorities. These jurisdictions were not clearly defined, and they often squabbled with one another over overlapping territories and rights. Rape and murder cases were especially significant in cases of jurisdictional conflict, for they demonstrated that the *seigneurie* in question had the right to high justice. It is for this reason that one finds a significant if not particularly large number of rape cases in the registers of the *Parlement*. In such cases, the *Parlement* was hearing appeals *involving* rape cases where the issue at stake was not the powerless and insignificant victim, but rather which lord had the power to try rape in a certain jurisdiction.[37]

The priory of Saint Eloi happened to control the small sliver of *intra-muros* Paris in which Jehan Feuchre and Denise Bonnot lived. Despite the immense privileges accorded to the priory of Saint Eloi, the court was not particularly active in the 1460s. Jehan's case takes up approximately two pages in a single register in which was noted all the "sentences, condemnations, acts, appointments, defaults, memoirs, reports and other activities of said jurisdiction and *seigneuries* of Saint Eloi" for the period from April 21, 1462 to May 8, 1468. The reason that this case was so carefully recorded in the Saint Eloi register probably had nothing at all to do with Denise or Jehan, but rather the nature of the case and the political situation in Paris. From the fourteenth century, the monarchy attempted to have rape trials heard by royal judges even in jurisdictions where the right to hear rape trials had been conceded years before. Most likely, the publicity of this trial was part of a political ploy on behalf of the *maire* Jehan Longue who wished to promote his own career or to reinforce the right of Saint Eloi to high justice in defense of the ever-present pretensions of the Provost of Paris.[38]

The social historian might fear that a seemingly insignificant story about an ordinary Parisian would get swept away into the well-known, general narrative about the attempts of the French kings to assert judicial and political control at the end of the Middle Ages. Yet this is not the case. (Re)telling Jehan's story gives modern readers a better understanding of the life of ordinary medieval folk as they came to terms with the manifestations of the emergence of the modern state. Furthermore, Jehan's actions in constructing his narrative demonstrate that non-elites, even those living on the margins of society, had a better understanding of legal culture than has previously been suggested and thus a far more wide-ranging recourse to courts and legal procedures. In the end, Jehan Feuchre's voice—even if it is muted by judges, scribes, and historians—helps challenge current historians' ideas about the increasing centralization of royal authority and the monopoly of an elite over judicial institutions and practices at the end of the fifteenth century.

Notes

1. For example, "Quiconques est pris en cas de crime et atains du cas, si comme de murtre, ou de traïson, ou d'homicide, ou de fame esforcier, il doit estre trainés et pendus et si mesfet auanqu'il a vaillant, et vient la forfeture au seigneur dessous qui li siens est trouvés et en chascuns sires ce qui en est trouvé en sa seigneurie." For translation see F.R.P. Akehurst, trans. and ed., *The Coutumes de Beauvaisis of Philippe de Beaumanoir* (Philadelphia: University of Pennsylvania Press, 1992), n. 824, pp. 302–3: "Whoever is arrested for a serious crime and convicted, for example for murder, or treason, or homicide, or rape, should be drawn and hanged, and he forfeits all his wealth to the lord, and to the lord on whose lands his possessions are situated, and each lord takes what is situated in the area under his control." Philippe de Beaumanoir, *Coutumes du Beauvoisis*, 2 vols. (1899–90; repr. Paris: A. and J. Picard, 1970), n. 824. I would like to thank Stéfan Gouzouguec for his valuable assistance with the Saint Eloi source material and Kathryn Norberg for her comments and suggestions on an earlier draft of this essay.

2. This is true throughout Medieval Europe, see: James Brundage, "Rape and Seduction in the Medieval Canon Law," in *Sexual Practices and the Medieval Church*, ed. Vern L. Bullough and James Brundage (Buffalo: Prometheus Book, 1982), pp. 141–48; James Brundage, *Law, Sex, and Christian Society in Medieval Europe* (Chicago and London: University of Chicago Press, 1987); Kathryn Gravdal, *Ravishing Maidens: Writing Rape in Medieval French Literature and Law* (Philadelphia: University of Pennsylvania Press, 1991); Barbara Hanawalt, "Whose Story Was This? Rape Narratives in Medieval English Courts," in *"Of Good and Ill Repute": Gender and Social Control in Medieval England*, ed. Barbara Hanawalt (New York: Oxford University Press, 1998), pp. 124–41; Barbara Hanawalt, *Crime and Conflict in English Communities 1300–1348* (Cambridge, MA: Harvard, 1979); Kim M. Philips, "Written on the Body: Reading Rape from the Twelfth to Fifteenth Centuries," in *Medieval Women and the Law*, ed. Noël James Menuge (Woodbridge, Suffolk, UK: Boydell Press, 2000), 125–44; Annick Porteau-Bitker, "La justice laïque et le viol au Moyen Age," *Revue historique du droit français et étranger*, 66 (1988): 491–526; Guido Ruggiero, *The Boundaries of Eros: Sex Crime and Sexuality in Renaissance Venice* (Oxford: Oxford University Press, 1985).

3. The notable exception is the infamous Le Gris-Carrouges affair, a fourteenth-century rape case that resulted in the last judicial duel of the Middle Ages. This cause célèbre was documented not only in the registers of the *Parlement*, but also in the writings of Froissart, Juvenal des Ursins, Jehan le Coq, and the Chronicler of Saint Denis: L. Bellaguet, *Chronique du Religieux de Saint-Denis (1380–1422)*, 6 vols. (Paris: Crapelet, 1842), 1:462, 464, 466; Jean Juvenal des Ursins, *Histoire de Charles VI, roy de France. . .in Nouvelle Collection des Mémoires pour servir a l'histoire de France depuis le XIIe siècle jusqu'à la fin du XVIIIe*, ed. Michaud and Poujoulat (Paris: Ed. du commentaire analytique du Code Civil, 1836), pp. 371–72; digitalized in 1995, Paris,

Bibliothèque Nationale (hereafter BN), NUMM–30877, available at www.bnf.fr; Leon Mirot and Albert Mirot, eds., *Chroniques de Jean Froissart*, vol. 13 (Paris: C. Klincksieck, 1957), pp. 102–07; Marguerite Boulet, *Questiones Johannis Galli* (Paris: E. de Bocard, 1944), questions 80, 81, 83, 89, and 91. More recent treatments include, Bernard Guenée, "Comment le Religieux de Saint-Denis a-t-il écrit l'histoire? L'exemple du duel de Jean de Carrouges et Jaques Le Gris (1386)," in *Pratiques de la culture écrite en France au XVe siècle: actes du Colloque international du CNRS, Paris, 16–18 mai 1992*, ed. Monique Ornato and Nicole Pons (Louvain-la-Neuve: Fédération internationale des instituts d'etudes médiévales, 1995), pp. 331–43; and Eric Jager, *The Last Duel: A True Story of Crime, Scandal, and Trial by Combat in Medieval France* (New York: Broadway, 2004).

4. Paris, Archives Nationales (hereafter, AN) Z2 3258 (Justice of Saint Eloi), October 30-November 11, 1464.

5. One of the better collections of these loose sheets of paper dating from the end of the fifteenth and early sixteenth centuries can be found in AN Z2 3405 and 3406 (Justice of Saint Germain des Prés), yet these two cartons represent but a fraction of the papers that were issued by this court.

6. This reading strategy is a modified version of the one proposed by the Ottoman historian, Dror Ze'evi for reading Shari'a court records. Ze'evi's model consists of four "circles" or levels of investigation that extend outward from the source record to society at large. Dror Ze'evi, "The Use of Ottoman Shari'a Court Records as a Source for Middle Eastern Social History: A Reappraisal," *Islamic Law and Society* 5 (1998): 35–57.

7. Criminal court records from late medieval royal courts have been utilized before to write the history of medieval Paris, but most historians have used records from the *Parlement* and the Châtelet: Esther Cohen, " 'To Die a Criminal for the Public Good': The Execution Ritual in Late Medieval Paris," in *Law, Custom, and the Social Fabric in Medieval Europe: Essays in Honor of Bryce Lyon*, ed. Bernard S. Bachrach and David Nicholas (Kalamazoo, MI: Medieval Institute Publications, 1990), pp. 285–304; Claude Gauvard, *De grace especial. Crime, état et société en France à la fin du Moyen Age* (Paris: Publications de la Sorbonne, 1991); Bronislaw Geremek, *The Margins of Society in Late Medieval Paris* (Cambridge, New York, Paris: Cambridge University Press and Editions de la maison des sciences de l'homme, 1987); Walter Previnger, "Violence Against Women in a Medieval Metropolis: Paris around 1400," in *Law, Custom, and the Social Fabric*, pp. 263–84.

8. Today this is the *rue Percée*. See, Abbé Lebeuf, *Histoire de la ville de tout le diocèse de Paris*, ed. Cocheris (Paris: Féchez et Letouzey, 1893) 1:328 and 370, n. 9.

9. For an overview of the Châtelet, see Charles Desmazes, *Le Châtelet de Paris, son organization, ses privilèges* (Paris: Didier, 1863); Ernest-Désiré Glasson, *Le Châtelet de Paris et les abus de sa procédure aux XIVe et XVe siècles*, d'après les documents récemment publiés (Paris: A. Picard et fils, 1893); L. Batiffol, "Le Châtelet de Paris vers 1400," *Revue Historique* 61 (1895): 225–64; 62 (1896): 42–53 , 266–83; and 63 (1897): 225–35. There are very few extant medieval

criminal and civil registers for the Châtelet: AN Y 10531 *Registre criminel du Châtelet de Paris* (September 6, 1389–May 18, 1392), repr. and ed. in Henri Duplès-Agier, *Registre criminel du Châtelet de Paris: du 6 septembre 1389 au 18 mai 1392*, 2 vols. (Paris: C. Lahure, 1861); AN Y 5266, *Registre des prisonniers entrés au Châtelet* (June 14, 1488– January 31, 1489); and AN Y 5220–5232 *Registres de la Prévôté de Paris au Châtelet* (1395–1455), partially reprinted in Gustave Fagniez, *Fragment d'un répertoire de jurisprudence parisienne au XVe siècle* (Nogent-le-Rotrou: impr. de Daupeley-Gouverneur, 1891) and François Olivier-Martin, *Sentences Civiles du Châtelet de Paris (1395–1505). Publiées d'après les registres originaux* (Paris: Receuil Sirey, 1914). BN, Collection Clairambault 763 and 764 (1401–1528) has extracts from the registers of the audience of the Châtelet.

10. The Saint Eloi registers are: AN Z2 3257–3261 (Justice of Saint Eloi, covering 1447–1500 with a lacuna from 1471–1487). There are also a few loose documents and parchments pertaining to the Justice of Saint Eloi in AN L 612. There is no secondary work that specifically focuses on the court of Saint Eloi. Fifteenth-century registers also survive from other seigneurial Parisian courts, such as For l'Evêque, Saint Germain des Prés, and Temple, yet only Saint Germain des Prés has been studied extensively. For a general overview of the medieval seigneuries in the thirteenth and fourteenth centuries, see Célestin Louis Tanon, *Histoire des justices des anciennes églises et communautés monastiques de Paris, suivie des registres inédits de Saint-Maur-des-Fossés, Sainte-Geneviève, Saint-Germain-des-Prés, et du registre de Saint-Martin-des-Champs* (Paris: L. Larose et Forcel, 1883), Célestin Louis Tanon, *Registre criminel de la justice de St. Martin des Champs à Paris au XIVe siècle* (Paris: L. Willem, 1877). On the fate of the seigneuries in the Early Modern period, see Pierre Lemercier, "Les justices seigneuriales de la région parisienne de 1580 à 1789" (Paris: Floritan, 1933). On the court of Saint Germain up until 1410, see Françoise Lehoux, *Le bourg Saint-Germain-des-Prés depuis ses origines jusqu'à la fin de la Guerre de cent ans* (Paris: published by the author, 1951), chapter 5; on Saint Germain in the fifteenth and early sixteenth centuries, see Edna Ruth Yahil, "Creating Justice in Late Medieval France: The Seigneurial Court of Saint Germain des Prés" (PhD thesis, University of California, Los Angeles, 2004).

11. For example, the hanging of Simon le Bourguignon, AN Z2 3260 (Justice of Saint Eloi), February 9, 1490–91. For other examples of corporal punishment in Saint Eloi, see Tanon, *Histoire des justices*, p. 196, n37.

12. The classic work on criminal procedure in France is Adhémar Esmein, *Histoire de la procédure criminelle en France et spécialement de la procédure inquisitoire depuis le XIIIème siècle jusqu'à nos jours* (Paris: E. Duchaemin, 1882); an English translation is available, but it is riddled with errors, *A History of Continental Criminal Procedure with a Special Reference to France*, trans. John Simpson (London: John Murray, 1914). On the elaboration of the custom of Paris in the fourteenth and fifteenth centuries, see François Olivier-Martin, *Histoire de la coutume de la prévôté et vicomté de Paris* (Paris: Ernest Leroux, 1922). Recently, Louis de Carbonnières completed an exhaustive

study on procedure used in the criminal *Parlement*, Louis de Carbonnières, *La procédure devant la chambre criminelle du Parlement de Paris au XIVe siècle* (Paris: H. Champion, 2004). There was no single authoritative source of law in fifteenth century France, and procedure varied from court to court, but it appears as though most of the seigneuries of Paris followed a somewhat simplified version of the custom of Paris as used in the Châtelet. On procedure in Saint Eloi and the other seigneuries of Paris, see Tanon, *Histoire des justices*.

13. "Le témoinage sans intermédiaire, que porte le paysans sur lui-même." Emmanuel Le Roy Ladurie, *Montaillou, village occitan de 1294 à 1324* (Paris: Gallimard, 1975), p. 9. The English translation of *Montaillou*—Emmanuel Le Roy Ladurie, *Montaillou: The Promised Land of Error*, trans. Barbara Bray (New York: G. Braziller, 1978)—is a poor substitute for the original.

14. Important critiques of Le Roy Ladurie and his methodology include, Leonard E. Boyle, "Montaillou Revisited: Mentalité and Methodology," in *Pathways to Medieval Peasants*, ed. J.A. Raftis (Toronto: Pontifical Institute of Medieval Studies, 1981), pp. 119–40. Renato Rosaldo, "From the Door of His Tent: The Fieldworker and the Inquisitor," in *Writing Culture: The Poetics and Politics of Ethnography*, ed. James Clifford and George E. Marcus (Berkeley: University of California Press, 1986), pp. 77–97; John H. Arnold, *Inquisition and Power: Catharism and the Confessing Subject in Medieval Languedoc* (Philadelphia: University of Pennsylvania Press, 2001). For an overview of historiographic trends since the publication of Montaillou, see Edna Ruth Yahil, "Revisiting *Montaillou*," *Comitatus*, 33 (2002): 149–64.

15. The only other marginal notes used by the greffier are *emprisonment* on October 30 and *eslargissement* on November 5. On the use of and development of marginal notes, see Edna Ruth Yahil, "Creating Justice in Late Medieval France," Appendix 1.

16. Edward Muir and Guido Ruggiero, "Introduction: The Crime of History" in *History from Crime*: Selections from *Quaderni storici, ed.* Edward Muir and Guido Ruggiero (Baltimore: Johns Hopkins University Press, 1994), pp. i–xviii.

17. This long-standing legal practice would only be formalized in 1539, in the Edict of Villers-Cotterêts. See *Ordonnances royaulx sur le faict de la justice & abbreviation des proces* (Lyon: Thibault Payen, 1539); digitalized in 1999, *Acte royal. 1539–08. Villers-Cotterets*, BN, NUMM–79170, available at www.bnf.fr.

18. 323 of the 618 hearths in this neighborhood listed in the *taille* were classified as *menu peuple*, see Geremek, *Margins of Society*, chapter 3. On poverty in general, see Sharon Farmer, *Surviving Poverty in Medieval Paris: Gender Ideology, and the Daily Lives of the Poor* (Ithaca and London: Cornell University Press, 2002). On the workers of Paris, see Geremek, *Le salariat dans l'artisanat parisien aux XIIIe-XVe siècles. Etude sur le marché de la main d'œuvre en Moyen-âge* (Paris: Ecole des hautes études en sciences sociales, 1992).

19. On profile of criminals see Gauvard, *De grace especial*; Geremek, *Margins of Society*; and Esther Cohen, *Peaceable Domain, Certain Justice* (Hilversum: Verloren, 1996)

20. Jean Louis Flandrin, "Repression and Change in the Sexual Life of Young People in Medieval and Early Modern Times," in *Family and Sexuality in French History*, ed. Robert Wheaton and Tamara K. Hareven (Philadelphia: University of Pennsylvania Press, 1980), p. 31.

21. Statistical information on household income at this period is extremely hard to come by, but a rough estimate based on the 1421 tax imposed by Charles VII on the city of Paris shows that dressmakers were at the bottom of the fiscal hierarchy of professionals. See chart in "Hierarchie fiscale des groupes professionels" in Jean Favier, *Les Contribuables Parisiens à la fin de la guerre de cent ans. Les rôles d'impot de 1421, 1423 et 1438* (Geneva: Droz, 1970), p. 33.

22. On domestic work, see David Herlihy, *Opera Muliebra: Women and Work in Medieval Europe* (Philadelphia: Temple University Press, 1990), David Nichols, *The Domestic Life of a Medieval City: Women, Children and the family in Fourteenth-Century Ghent* (Lincoln: University of Nebraska Press, 1985), David Nichols, "Children and Adolescent Labour in the Late Medieval City: A Flemish Model in Regional Perspective," *English Historical Review* 110 (1995): 1103–1131.

23. For a detailed map of the area, see Armand Brette, *Atlas de la censive de l'archevêché dans Paris* (Paris: Imprimerie nationale, 1906), plate 43. Adrien Friedman describes in details the various censives and other documents that allow us to better understand the geography of this territory and also provides a reconstructed map. Adrien Friedman, *Paris. Ses rues, ses paroisses, du moyen âge à la Revolution* (Paris: Plon, 1962), pp. 15–20.

24. For a much more detailed analysis of the confessing subject, see John H. Arnold, *Inquisition and Power*.

25. An account book from 1487 lists payments made by the abbey of Saint Germain des Prés to a *sergent des questions* who called to torture a reluctant witnesses, AN LL 1112, fols. 328r–45v. Tanon has found evidence of torture in most of the seigneurial courts of Paris in the fourteenth century, as well as references from 1409 to the *questionnaire* (questionario) of For l'Eveque. See Tanon, *St Martin*.

26. AN Z2 3258 (Justice of Saint Eloi), October 30, 1464, fols. 91r–92r.

27. I have taken the liberty of transforming what the *greffier* recorded in the third person back into the first person that Jehan would have used in his oral testimony.

28. AN Z2 3267 (Justice of Saint Germain des Prés) May 17, 1460: Agnes widow of the barber Guillaume Carbonniere was accused of being her niece's *maquerelle*.

29. In 1518, Jehan Las came before the court of Saint Germain to accuse Guillaume Boucault of raping his seven year old daughter. A matron inspected the young girl, found that there had been forced entry and rupture of the girl's hymen, but she could not determine whether penetration had been completed: "Ont trouve qu'il ya on enforcement et def'floration de lentree de la partie inferieure mais que on na point on ne peulte tellement opine y ayt en corruption ammoyen de lad. Fille et ny a on que bien." AN Z2 3290 (Justice of Saint Germain des Prés), April 30, 1518. Under

customary law, incomplete penetration did not constitute rape, and so Boucault was set free.

30. AN Z2 3258 (Justice of Saint Eloi), November 4, 1464, fols. 92r–92v.

31. However, the term most frequently referred to the abduction of women and *capere* was used for men, hence "plures personas ceperunt et occiderunt plures mulieres rapuerunt". AN X2A 5 (Criminal Châtelet) fol. 181, March 11, 1350. Cited in Porteau-Bitker, "La justice laïque," p. 495.

32. Historians make wildly different claims about rape prosecution depending on the type of source that they use and their methodology. Claude Gauvard counts a total of eight rapists in the 1488 *registre d'écrou* from the Châtelet, AN Y 5266A , arguing that this demonstrates the severity of the crime and the "political maturity of the Châtelet judges," Gauvard, *De grace especial*, 2:814 n98. Jacques Rossiaud claims that 80% of rape cases were gang rapes, a figure that may be accurate for medieval Dijon (although Rossiaud is very vague about which sources he used and how he came up with his statistics), but most certainly cannot be applied to France in general. Jacques Rossiaud, "Prostitution, jeunesse et société dans les villes du Sud-Est au XVe siècle," *Annales ESC*, 31 (1976): 281–325, English translation "Prostitution, Sex, and Society in French Towns in the Fifteenth Century," in *Western Sexuality: Practice and Precept in Past and Present Times*, ed. Philippe Aries and André Bénjin (Oxford, Oxford University Press, 1985), pp. 76–94; Jacques Rossiaud, *Medieval Prostitution*, trans. Lydia F. Cochraine (Oxford: Oxford University Press, 1988). Annick Porteau-Bitker's work ("La justice laïque") is by far the best overall survey on the subject of rape in medieval France covering a wide range of courts and geographic regions, and yet it is virtually unknown in English-language historiography which usually cites Rossiaud's statistics as the norm for France without further reflection. Several strong caveats of course must be added to Porteau-Bitker's conclusions: like women today, medieval woman may have been hesitant to seek legal redress at the cost of their reputation or because they were unlikely to win such cases. Another influencing factor may be the paucity of surviving records for local seigneurial or provincial courts that would have heard rape cases of common women. The fact remains, however that there are very few cases in any court in which an individual like Jehan Feuchre was accused of sexual violence without another extenuating circumstance (kidnapping, pillage, etc.).

33. Tanon, *Saint Martin*; Gravdal, *Ravishing* Maidens, chapter 5.

34. AN Z2 3272 (Saint Germain des Prés) June 8 and 9, 1488: Marette Suet, a young woman from Paris accused another Parisian, Estienne Le Maistre, Jehan Bardoin's varlet *tanneur* of rape. That same day, Marette went before the court of Saint Germain and maintained that Estienne took her against her will (*gre et volunte*) to a wheat field near the Pre aux Clercs because he wished to force her to his will (*se force davoir sa compaigne*). She was eventually saved when a sergeant heard her cry. The following day, Etienne confessed that he had found Marrette the previous day around three o'clock in the afternoon near a piece of wheat near the Pre aux Clercs. He took her by the

hands and led her into the piece of wheat to have his way with her (*pour en faire sa volunte*) and when Marrette resisted, he slapped her in the face once or twice, threw her to the ground, and then took her to the piece of wheat. Estienne's punishment was to publicly ask Marette for forgiveness (*myse et acrier mercys et pardon*) and then to pay a fine: he was ordered to pay 8 s. p. to Marette as an amend and another 20 s. p. reduced to 8 s. p. to the court and was held in prison until he paid the sum.

35. Evidence of Parisians' sensibility to illegitimate pregnancy can be found throughout surviving court documents of late medieval France. In a case from Saint Germain, neighbors who knew that a chambermaid was sleeping with her master did not complain to the court until the girl's stomach started to swell. When asked why there was a delay in reporting the illicit sexual activity, one witness feebly replied that "[the chambermaid] had said that he was her uncle," AN Z2 3405 (Justice of Saint Germain des Prés). Additionally, Denise's pregnancy increased the chance of her parents receiving a judgement in their favor: regardless of the type of case or whether they were plaintiffs or defendants, pregnant women always faired better than their non-pregnant counterparts in late medieval Parisian courts to the extent that women would fake pregnancies in order obtain a more favorable judgment (AN Z2 3265 (Justice of Saint Germain des Prés) March 8, 1409–1410. From a practical standpoint, this case would never have come to trial had Denise not been pregnant.

36. AN Z2 3272 (Justice of Saint Germain des Prés) January 17, 1487–88: In another case from Saint Germain, a priest was accused of raping a nine-year-old girl. The father brought a complaint to the court knowing full well that it would be dismissed since priests had the right to be tried in more lenient ecclesiastical courts. Later, the girl's father tried a different tactic: he returned to the court claiming that the girl had been physically (as opposed to sexually) injured and was in danger of dying, a different legal claim than rape, AN Z2 3272 (Justice of Saint Germain des Prés), January 26, 1487–88. In this case as well, the act of publicly accusing the priest in the local court was more important than a conviction.

37. Thus these cases are rarely useful for studying rape and sexual violence—most of the cases focus on reasons for the legal appeal and mention rape only in passing.

38. On royal attempts to strip seigneuries of the right to high justice, see Porteau-Bitker, "La justice laïque," p. 51; Esther Cohen, *The Crossroads of Justice: Law and Culture in Late Medieval France* (Leiden, New York: E.J. Brill, 1993), p. 18.

LIST OF CONTRIBUTORS

CORDELIA BEATTIE is Lecturer in Medieval History at the University of Edinburgh. Dr. Beattie has published various articles on women and work, marriage and the household and coedited a collection titled *The Medieval Household in Christian Europe c.850–c.1550: Managing Power, Wealth, and the Body* (Brepols, 2003). She is currently writing a monograph on ideas of the single woman in late medieval England.

RONALD C. FINUCANE, who received his PhD after his study at Stanford and Oxford, is Professor of History at Oakland University in Rochester, MI. Two of his four books deal with medieval miracles. He is a Fellow of the Royal Historical Society.

JAMES GIVEN is Professor of History at the University of California, Irvine. He received a BA degree from Yale University and MA and PhD degrees from Stanford University. He is the author of *Inquisition and Medieval Society: Power, Discipline and Resistance in Languedoc* (1997), *State and Society in Medieval Europe: Gwynedd and Languedoc under Outside Rule* (1990), and *Society and Homicide in Thirteenth-Century England* (1977). He has taught at the University of Michigan, Dearborn, and Harvard University.

MICHAEL GOODICH is Professor of History at the University of Haifa. His recent works include *Lives and Miracles of the Saints: Studies in Medieval Latin Hagiography* (2004), *Other Middle Ages: Marginal Groups in the Medieval Period* (1998), and *Violence and Miracle in the Fourteenth Century: Private Grief and Public Salvation* (1995). His research focuses on the social and ecclesiastical history of the central Middle Ages, with special emphasis on hagiography.

AMOS MEGGED (PhD, Cambridge) is a Senior Lecturer in the Department of History at the University of Haifa. He specializes in the social and cultural history of early colonial Mexico; his present research deals with the restructuring of memory among indigenous groups in early colonial Mexico as well as with single women's households in seventeenth-century Mexico. His recent publications include *Exporting the Catholic Reformation: Local Religion in Early-Colonial Mexico* (New York: Brill 1996).

RENÉE LEVINE MELAMMED is Associate Professor of Jewish History at the Schechter Institute of Jewish Studies in Jerusalem. Her first book, *Heretics or Daughters of Israel: The Crypto-Jewish Women of Castile* (Oxford University Press,

1999) received two National Jewish Book Awards. Her most recent book is *A Question of Identity: Iberian Conversos in Historical Perspective* (Oxford University Press, 2004).

DANIEL LORD SMAIL is Professor of History at Harvard University and has published numerous articles on law and society in late medieval Marseille. He is a coeditor of *Fama: The Politics of Talk and Reputation in Medieval Europe*, a collection that speaks to many issues discussed in the present volume. His *The Consumption of Justice: Emotions, Publicity, and Legal Culture in Marseille, 1264–1423* (Ithaca: Cornell University Press, 2003) was a co-winner of the 2004 James Willard Hurst Prize of the Law and Society Association.

LAURA ACKERMAN SMOLLER is Associate Professor of History at the University of Arkansas at Little Rock. She is the author of *History, Prophecy, and the Stars: The Christian Astrology of Pierre d'Ailly* (Princeton, 1994), as well as numerous articles on late medieval astrology, eschatology, and miracles. She is currently at work on a book titled *The Saint and the Chopped-Up Baby: The Cult of Vincent Ferrer and the Religious Life of the Later Middle Ages.*

ROBERT N. SWANSON is Professor of Medieval History at the University of Birmingham, England. He has worked extensively on the western church in the late Middle Ages, with particular focus on pre-Reformation England. His books include *Church and Society in Late Medieval England* (1989), *Religion and Devotion in Europe, c.1215–c.1515* (1995), and *The Twelfth Century Renaissance* (1999). He is currently writing a major book on indulgences in England, from ca.1300 to the Reformation.

EDNA RUTH YAHIL recently completed her doctorate at UCLA titled "Creating Justice in Late Medieval France: The Seigneurial Court of Saint Germain des Prés." Her research focuses on lawmaking, legal culture, and popular understanding of judicial institutions in the Middle Ages and early modern period. Currently she is working in the Education Sector at UNESCO.

INDEX

abduction 74, 262,
accidents 127–30
   see also parental negligence
adoption 189–90
adultery 103
Aguilar, Gonzalo de 53, 54
Albigensians *see* Cathars
Alexander IV, Pope 104
Alfonso, María 54
Allerton, Matilda de 213
Alonso, Fernando 56
Alvárez de Vosmediano, Juana 87
Angeles, Isabel de los 78
Anian, Bishop of Bangor 134, 136, 139, 141
Annales school 1
apparitions *see* visions
apprenticeship 9, 185, 187–9
Aquinas, Thomas 106, 164
Archer, Henry 187
Archer, Joan 187
Arcila, Catalina de 88–9
Arevalo, Pedro de 52
arrest
   Cathars 8, 16, 18, 19–20, 21, 34, 35, 36
   Isabel de Montoya 89
   New Christians 48
   Pastoureaux 105
art 227–8, 229
Arundel, Thomas, Archbishop 215
Asami, Peire 235, 240, 241, 243, 244, 245, 247
Askham, William de 216, 217
D'Aubagne, Aycelena 229, 230

Augeleria, Jacme 241
augury 32, 34
Autier, Guillaume 17–18, 20
Autier, Pierre 17–18, 20
autobiography 207–8, 252, 256
D'Ays, Antoni 228, 229, 230, 237

Badajoz, Bartolomé de 59
Balard, William 188, 190
bankruptcy 10, 231, 232, 233, 234–40, 247
Baro, Bernart de 228, 230
Barva, Juan García 55
Basage, Richard 217
Basage, Robert 217
Bastier, Andrivet 244
Bautista, Juana 75
Bélibaste, Guillaume 19–21, 22–5, 26–7, 28, 29, 30, 31–2, 33–5
Bellassise, Martin de 168
Bell, Nicholas 210
Bermon, Jacme 229, 230
Bermon, Peire 229
Beyvyll, Thomas 191
Bilbury, William de 139
Bildeston, John de 214
Blanc, Bertomieu 242–3, 244
Blanc, Johan 235
blasphemy 153, 163, 164, 165, 211
Boayden, Jean 163, 167
Bonabry, Pierre de 154–5, 157, 158, 164
Bonacros, Jacme 235, 240, 243
Bonnot, Denise 251, 252, 255, 256–60, 262–3

Bonnot, Guillot 262–3
Bonvin, Bertomieu 239
Bonvin, Nicolau 240, 246
Bonyfey, Alice 186
Bonyfey, Richard 186
Borgonho, Johan 245
Boys, John de 128, 130, 135–6
Brand, Robert 191
brewers 4, 178, 182, 183, 187,
    188, 189
Brok, John de 132
Broun, Elizabeth 185, 190
Brown, John 185
Brown, Judith 2
Brun, Thomas le 158
Bryes, John 217
bulls, papal
  of canonization 6, 100, 106, 108,
    109, 115, 145
  establishment of Spanish Inquisition
    5, 43
Burton, John de 217
Bushe, Joan 190

Cabesco, Gabriel de 71
Cadahalso, Juana de 53
Cadena, Juana de la 57, 58, 59
Calixtus III, Pope 159, 168
Cambridge, Thomas de 134, 140
canonization 6, 99, 100
  Philip of Bourges 100–1
  Thomas of Hereford 108
  Vincent Ferrer 149, 150, 155–6,
    159–62
canon law 99, 101–2, 204
Caracule, Antonio de 59
Carmelites 161–2, 165, 167
Castellano, Antón Martínez 51
Castiglione, Francisco 168
Cathars 8, 15, 16–22, 27, 36, 101
  Cathar church 23
  Good Men/Good Women (perfecti)
    17, 23
Celestine V, Pope 107–8
Cepudo, Juan Martínez 54

Chabert, Guilhem 233, 234
Chabert, Nicolaua 233, 234
Chamberleyn, Alice 185–6, 190
chancery 3, 4, 9, 177–80, 192–3
  case procedure 181–2
  contractual disputes 187–90
  sections in petition 180–1
Charles of Blois 159
children 143–4
  domestic service 185, 191
Chinchilla, Gómez de 50, 59
Chishulle, Robert de 134
Cicon, William de 128, 129, 130,
    131, 134, 140
circumcision 48
Ciudad, Catalina de 47
Ciudad, Sancho de 47–8
Claresburgh, John de 216
Claresburgh, Richard de 216
Clement IV, Pope 115
Clement VI, Pope 115
Clergue, Pierre 37
clergy 149, 153, 162, 166, 215–16,
    217–19
  and female employment 190–1
clergy as witnesses 51, 53, 56, 100,
    102, 107, 135, 137, 141, 142,
    216–17
Clerk, Margaret 177, 178, 179, 181,
    182–3, 186, 187, 189, 191, 192
Clerk, William 217
Coetmur, Guillermus 166
Cole, Katherine 185, 190
Cole, Robert 190
Colnvill, John de 211
common law, English 179, 193, 203,
    204
community 2, 132–3, 209
compurgatory witnesses 46, 59, 60
concubinage 70, 71, 72, 74, 75, 84,
    228
confession 22, 56, 57, 85, 90, 92,
    110, 253–4, 255, 256–7, 260–1
Conrad of Marburg 101, 102, 114
consanguinity 9, 209, 210–14

conversos see New Christians
Conyngton, Sir William 182
Cook, Wolfram 191
Copley, Agnes 191
Cornette, Thomas 162
    see also Thomas, Brother
coroner 128, 129, 130, 133, 134,
    135, 138, 139, 141, 145
courts 2–3
courts, ecclesiastical 2, 9, 184, 203,
    204–5, 210, 219, 220, 251
courts, secular 2, 43–4, 102, 158,
    203, 251, 262
courts, seigneurial 10, 251–3, 261,
    262, 264
Cragh, William 113
Cray (or Cragh), Cristina see Cristina
    of Wellington
crime 112, 143
    see also homicide; rape; theft
Cristina of Wellington 7–8, 108,
    109–13, 114
Crosse, Agnes 188
Crosse, Edmund 188
Crumbwell, Robert de 218
Crusades 3, 105
Cruz, Mateo de la 79
Cruz, Monica de la 79
cults 6, 7
    inauguration 7, 166–8
curia, papal 99, 100, 102, 106,
    107–8, 116, 145, 167, 211, 213
cursing see blasphemy

David of Maenan, Abbot 134, 141
Davis, Natalie 2
Daza, Juan González 54–6
decretals 101
defense witnesses (abono) 45, 46, 47,
    60, 61
    Juan González Daza's trial 55–6
    Juan González Pintado's trial 52–3
    María González's trial 50–1
    Marina González's trial 57–8
de Fez, Juan 47, 48, 59

Deken, William 217
Deline, Geoffrey 157
delusions see Devil; visions
demons 16, 104, 113, 153, 163,
    164, 165
    see also Devil; Satan
depression, clinical see melancholia
depression, post-natal 107
d'Esparron, Dousa 228–9, 232, 234
Devil 81–2, 89, 90, 102, 104, 108,
    164, 165
    see also demons; Satan
Dey, Thomas 216, 218
Díaz, María 47, 48–50
diet 48, 49–50, 52–3, 54, 55, 56, 57
Dionysia 127, 129–30, 131–2, 133,
    134, 136, 138, 139–40, 141, 142–5
dispensation 210, 211–12, 213–14
divination 25–6, 32, 78, 89
domestic service see service, domestic
Dominicans 17, 82, 89, 102
Dominic, Saint 107
Donadieu, Martin 114
Dorem, John de 216
dowry 9, 10, 231, 232, 233–4, 236,
    238, 239, 246
Draguignan, Bondavin de 232,
    235, 237
dreams 79, 111, 114, 152
    see also visions
drugs 69, 77, 78, 87, 91
    see also poisoning
Drulin, Pierre 158
drunkenness 7, 33, 131, 132, 140,
    143, 144, 241, 242–6, 247
Du Fay, Guillaume 256, 260, 262, 263
Du Fay, Guillot 256, 262
Dulcia of St. Chartier 7, 102–4, 105,
    106, 108, 114

Eden, Rowland 209
Edward I, King 110, 113, 127,
    132, 141
Elizabeth of Thuringia 101, 102,
    107, 108, 114

Elyngham, John 185
Engelburt of Admont 106
England 3, 112
Enneat, Raymon 243
Erenchun, Tomás López 85
Espina, Gracia de 57, 58, 59
Estgate, Isabel 191
Esthall, Thomas de 134
Estrada, Francisco de 89
Estthorpe, John de 211–12, 213–14
Eugenius IV, Pope 160
excommunication 109
execution see hanging
exorcism 7, 102, 163, 164–5, 166–7, 168
see also possession
ex-votos 112

Falcón, Diego 58
Falcón, Fernán 48, 51, 54, 55, 57, 59
fama 9–10, 101, 208, 211, 212, 215, 217, 219, 232, 233, 234–7, 240, 241, 245, 247
Faysonerie, Ugo 243
feast days, Jewish 49–50
Fernándes, Leonor 58
Ferrandes, Pedro 56
Ferrer, Vincent 6, 149, 152
  canonization 7, 149, 150, 155–6
  inauguration of cult 166–8
  and Montford dukes 159–62
Feuchre, Jehan 251–2
  imprisonment and interrogation 253–4
  rape accusation 262–4
  social position 255–6
Filloche, Pierre 152, 153, 155, 156–7, 161, 164, 165
Finaut, Aycart 243, 244
Floch, Petrus see Filloche, Pierre
folk medicine 4, 91
Fonte, Esteve de 239
Fournier, Jacques, Bishop of Pamiers 8, 15, 16, 28, 29, 30, 35, 36, 253
France 3, 17, 104

Franciscans 17, 73, 77–8, 85, 90, 110
Francis of Assisi, Saint 107
Franco, Luisa 74, 75
Fresby, Ivo de 218
friars see Carmelites; Dominicans; Franciscans

Gamond, Peire 243
Gamowe/Gannowe, Stephen de 128, 130
García, Alonso 51, 52
García, María 56
Gasquet, Guilhem 243
Gaufrid of Bourges 102
Gauta, Raymona de 246
Gayrier, Bertran 243
Gaythay, Joan 209–10
Gayut, William 109
gender studies 1
Gere, James 190
Gervaise 255, 256, 257, 258, 259, 260, 261
Gervase 127, 129, 130–1, 139, 141, 142
Gibon, Jean 158
Ginzburg, Carlo 2
Girauda, Laura 246–7
Giraut, Laurens 231–3, 234–5, 236, 237, 240–2, 244, 245, 246, 247, 248
Giraut, Paul 236
Glaston, John de 218
Goitias, Joseph de 85
Gómez, Antonia 49–50
Gompina, Johan de 235
González, Bartolomé 56
González, Catalina 50
González, Leonor 55
González, María 50–2, 56
González, Marina 56–60
González, Pedro 59
Gregory IX, Pope 101, 115
Griffin, John 128, 132, 138, 143
Grysetwhaite, Thomas 207–8
Guevara, Miguel de 87–8
Guglielm of Milan 109

Guglielmo of Sta. Sabina,
   Cardinal   100
Gui, Bernard   36, 43, 99, 114, 116
Gutierrez, Marina   50

Hall, John   209, 210
hanging   7, 109, 110, 112, 114,
   115, 150
Havering, John de   128, 130, 134,
   136, 139, 140
Havering, Nicholas de   128, 130, 133
healing   69, 71, 78, 85, 87, 89, 90,
   150, 153–5, 156, 166–7
Hedwig of Silesia   106
Helwysson, John   212
Henry VI, King   143, 180
heresy   3, 7, 90, 101, 162
   persistence   6
   punishment   5–6, 36
   see also Cathars; divination;
      inquisition; New Christians;
      magic
Hernández, Luisa   68, 69
Herrera, Alonso de   53
Hervé, Jeanne   154, 155, 163
Hervé, Mathelin   156
Hervé, Perrin   7, 149, 150, 152–5,
   160–1, 166–7
   and ducal financial circle   156–7
   infirmity   162–6
Hildyard, John   209, 211, 212, 213
Hildyard, Katherine   209, 210–14,
   220
Hildyard, Peter   209, 210, 212, 214
Hildyard, Thomas   213
Hobson, Thomas   209
holidays, Christian   50, 51, 57
Holy Land   105, 106
homicide   27, 72, 102, 104, 245
honor   10, 67, 74, 92, 262–3
Honorius III, Pope   99, 101
Hornsee, William de   213
Howden, John   216, 217
Hugh of Leominster   140
Hunier, Guilhem   235
Hurtado, Juan   91

illness   101, 159, 162–3, 164,
   165–6
Inés   74, 75
infants   see children
informants   8, 15, 44, 208
   see also Falcón, Fernán; Sicre,
      Arnaud
Innocent III, Pope   5, 101, 114,
   115, 142
inquisition, as legal procedure   5,
   38, 101
   see also heresy
inquisition, Spanish   4, 5
   anonymity of witnesses   43–4, 46, 61
   defense tactics   45–6
inquisitors   15–16, 36, 91, 101
   of Carcassone and Toulouse
      15–16, 18
insanity   102, 103, 107
insolvency   see bankruptcy
interrogation   232–3, 234, 242,
   244–5, 253
Islam   see Muslims

Jacopo of St. Giorgio   100
James, William   114
Jeanne, Duchess of Brittany   156,
   159, 161
Jean V, Duke of Brittany   156, 159,
   160, 161, 162
Jesuits   82
Jesús, Maria de   88
Jews   5, 8, 44, 106
Johannes of Wolfhagen   114
John XXII, Pope   100, 107–8, 109,
   145
John of Ely, Bishop   113
John of Salerno   106
John, Rector of Arnold   217
Johnson, Anastase   188
Jonson, John   188
Judaism   46, 49
Judaizers   44–6
   trials   47–61
Junac, Raimonde de   22, 23–5, 26,
   28, 32, 35

Kellom, Ralph de   215, 217, 218
Kendall, Nicholas   203
Kerver, Joan   186
kinship   9, 73, 178, 183, 188, 189,
   190, 210, 212
kinship, spiritual   245, 246
Kirketon, John   218
Kirketon, William   218
Kowaleski, Maryanne   192
Kyrkeby, Agnes   191
Kyrkeby, Elizabeth   187, 190
Kyrkeby, William   187

Laboysans, Jeanne   107, 114
Lacy, John de   111
Ladurie, Emmanuel Le Roy   1
Langrake, John   185
larceny   see theft
Lawton, Thomas   191
Le Goff, Hervé   154, 159, 163
Le Houssec, Yves   159, 163
Lek, Robert de   218
Lentwhit, John   203
Leycestre, John   186
Lievana, Juan de   56
litigation   232–3, 239, 240, 247–8
liturgy   73, 81, 82, 87, 165
Longford, John de   217
Longue, Jehan   253, 254, 260,
   261, 264
López, María   51
Louis IX, King   105, 106, 107, 228
Lucius III, Pope   5

Maceot, Michael   163
magic   6, 75, 82, 90, 106, 109
   love magic   76, 77, 87, 92
Magnus, Albertus   106
Malara, Dicho de Lope   51
Maleta, Moneta   233
Malet, Giraut   234
Malet, Moneta   234
Marchall, John   191
Margaret of Hungary   101
marginal groups   1, 73

marranos   see New Christians
marriage   9, 209, 261
   Cathars   24
   Council of Trent's decree   71
   and servants   185–6
   and witchcraft   104
   see also consanguinity; dowry
Marseille   10, 228, 231, 232, 234,
   236, 238, 240, 247
Martin IV, Pope 100
Martin V, Pope   160, 162
Martínez, Alonso   56
Martínez, Antonia   55
Martínez, Diego   92
Martínez, Juan   54
Martínez, Pascuala   56
Martin, Hervé   162
Marzy, Robert de, Bishop of
   Nevers   102
Massilie, Ricart de   235
Maurs, Guillaume   35
Maury, Guillemette   19, 20, 21, 25,
   26, 28, 29–30
Maury, Pierre   21, 22, 23–5, 26, 28,
   29, 30, 31, 32, 33–4, 35
Maydo, Hervé   154, 157–8, 160
Maydo, Symon   153, 157, 161, 163,
   165, 167
Mayin, Peire   235, 236
Mazariegos, Diego de   53
melancholia   104
memory   67, 145, 206–7, 219, 256
memory, collective   4, 9, 67, 140,
   207, 215, 218, 219–20
memory, individual   4, 9, 67–8, 72,
   144, 160, 161, 207, 219
menstruation   77
Merlo, Juan de   49
Mernam, Richard de   218
mestizos   68, 77
metahistory   2
Mexico   8, 9, 67
Mexico City   70–1
Michael the gardener   243
microhistory   2, 3–5, 116, 144

midwifery 4, 67, 69, 73, 78, 85, 86
Minci, Pierre de, Bishop of Chartres
   102
minorities 3
   see also Cathars; Jews; mestizos;
      mulattas
miracles 6, 7, 99, 106, 115, 116, 145
   of Philip of Bourges 100–1, 102,
      106
   of Thomas of Hereford 108–12,
      113, 127, 129, 133–40, 150,
      166
   of Vincent Ferrer 149, 150, 152–5,
      167, 168
   vs virtuous life 107–8
Miramas the taverner 242–3
Miranda, Josepha de 75
Molina, Juan González de 56
Molina, Pedro de 55
Montoya, Ana María de 71, 86
Montoya, Isabel de 6, 8–9, 67, 92
   adherents/apprentices 73, 75–6,
      79–80, 85
   antecedents 68
   clients 86–8, 89
   confiscation of belongings 91–2
   early life 69, 70–2
   living 85
   marriage 72
   punishment 85, 90–1
   relationships in House of Seclusion
      75, 77–8
   religious faith 80–1, 82
   supernatural arts 78–9
   testimony 89–90
Montoya y Guzmán, Diego de 68
Morlans, Ugo 243, 244
mulattas 4, 67, 68–9, 72–3, 75, 77, 92
murder see homicide
Muslims 5

narratives, historical 1, 2–5, 10–11
narratives, witness 6–7, 43, 44, 99,
   100, 203–7, 219
   conflicting narratives 208–9

homogenization 229–31, 237–8,
   239–40, 247–8
utility 209
neighbors 4, 10, 27, 58, 88, 102,
   129, 130–1, 140, 142, 145, 152,
   154, 158–9, 236, 240
Neuton, John 209, 214
New Christians 8, 44–5, 47, 48, 49,
   51, 52, 55
New Spain 4, 6, 8, 67, 68, 70, 71,
   74, 76, 77, 80, 81, 92
Nicholas V, Pope 162, 167
notaries 2, 99, 102, 111, 116, 128,
   131, 152, 235–8, 240
Nuthill, Peter 220
Nyman, Edith 187
Nyman, John 187

Odo of Châteauroux, Cardinal-bishop
   of Tusculum 100, 105–6
Odo of Cluny 106–7
Olney, John 186
otherness 1

Palacios, Francisco de 79
Palacios, Margarita de 79, 84, 85
Palafox, Bishop 82, 84
Palma, Gutierrez de 57
Panpan, Juan González 51–2
Paona, Joseph de 90
papal bulls see bulls, papal
papal curia see curia, papal
parental negligence 142–5
parenthood/parents 129–30, 262–3
Paris 3, 10, 106, 252, 255, 263–4
Paris, Matthew 104
Paris, university of 106
Pastoureaux 104–5
Peckham, John, Archbishop 109
Pedrosa, Juan de 52
Pedrosa, María de 50–1
Peire, Ugo de Sant 239
Peña, Gaspar de la 72
Peter Martyr of Milan 6
Petronius, Richard, Cardinal 108

Philip of Bourges   7, 99–108, 115
Philip of Valois   228
Pierre II, Duke of Brittany   156, 157,
   159, 160, 167
Pierre of St. Chartier   102–3
Pietro of St. Praxed   100
pilgrimage   36, 103, 108, 111, 113,
   115, 127, 133, 140, 167
Pinke, Richard   109
Pintado, Juan González   52–4
Plafox y Mendoza, Juan de   73
pledges   209–10
Plomer, Christopher   190
Plummer, William   187
Poblete, Diego de   51
poisoning   7, 27, 102, 104
Pomiès, Gaillard de   29, 30–1
possession   7, 102, 149, 162–6
   see also exorcism
post-traumatic disorder   72
preaching   105, 106, 149, 162
Preston, William   209, 210
prosecution witnesses   44, 45
   effectiveness   60
   Juan González Daza's trial   54–5
   Juan González Pintado's trial   53–4
   María Díaz's trial   48–9
   María González's trial   51–2
   Marina González's trial   57
   Sancho de Ciudad's trial   47–8
proselytes   77
prostitution   72, 73, 259–60
Puigcercós, Bernard   35
Pungilupo, Ermanno   109
punishment   85, 90–1, 112, 116, 256–7
   for heresy   5–6, 36
   see also hanging

Raddon, Katherine   188, 190
Raddon, Thomas   188, 190
Ranzano, Pietro   168
Raos, Peire   228, 230
rape   5, 10, 185, 251, 260, 262–4
Rawlys, Eve   187
Rawlys, Walter   187
Raymon, Bernat   233, 236, 238

Raymund of Penyafort   101, 102
relics   88, 89, 100, 108, 115, 153, 161
religious orders   see Carmelites;
   clergy; Dominicans; Franciscans
Restesin, Guilhem   235
Richard of Chichester, Bishop   101,
   106
Richard of Newcastle   130, 135, 137,
   138, 144
Ridale, John   217
Rippyngale, Margery   188
Rippyngale, William   188
Riston, Ivo de   210–11, 214
rites, Cathar
   consolamentum   16–17
   melioramentum   17, 21
rites, Christian   80
rites, fertility   76, 77
rites, Jewish   47, 48, 49–50, 53, 54,
   55–6, 57
ritual gifts   75–7
Rivera, María de   75–6, 78, 79, 80–1,
   84, 85
Robécourt, Menet de   37
Rodríguez, Alonso   55
Roger   127, 128–30, 133–40
   community's explanations of
      accident of   132–3
   parent's explanation of accident of
      130–2
Rogier, Guilhem   243, 244
Rolland, Jean   153–4, 157
Roo, John   218
Roo, Ralph   217
Rossel, Robert   130
Rouclif, Alice de   184
Ruiz, Francisca   69–70
Ruíz, María   53
rumor   see fama

saints   80–1, 87, 89–90
   inquisition   101–2
saints, cult of   80, 107, 100–1, 108,
   113, 115–16, 150, 152, 159,
   161, 166–8
Sánchez, Catalina   53

Sánchez, Diego 51, 53
Sánchez, María 53
Sánchez, Mateo 53
Sande, Hugh 188
Satan 16, 82, 114, 166
  see also Devil
Schephirde, Roger 217
Schmitt, Jean-Claude 1
scholasticism 106
seduction, sexual 10, 67, 257–61
Segarelli, Gerardo 109
sermons *see* preaching
Serna, Alonso de la 51
Serrano, Juan 71, 86
servants 256
  age 184–5
  false testimony 45
servants, indentures 187–90
service, domestic 9, 177, 178, 182,
  183–4
  demand 192
  employment terms 187–90
  length of service 186, 187
  wages/compensation 185–6, 191–2
Setrington, William de 213
sexual behavior 241, 242, 252
sexuality, history of 5
Shiplode, Thomas 186
Sicre, Arnaud 8, 15, 16, 18–19,
  20–2, 25–6, 27–31, 33–6, 37–8
Simon of Flint 129, 133, 134, 139
Simon of Watford 128, 130, 133,
  135, 137, 141, 144
slaves 69
  false testimony 45
Sosa, Juana de 78–9, 84, 85
Soto, Juan de 52
Spawnton, Humphrey 209
spells 26, 79, 87–9, 90
Sprottelay, John de, Jr., 212, 214
Sprottelay, John de, Sr., 212
Stanebrigge, Robert de 218
Stanislaus of Cracow 107
Stefaneschi, Gaetano 108
Stephani, Silvester 155, 158, 163, 167
Stephen of Bourbon 104

Stoke, Ralph de 216, 218–19
subaltern classes 1–2, 99, 102, 116
  economic conditions in
    England 112
subterfuge 8
  Cathars 22, 23
supernatural 6, 75–7, 82, 102, 106,
  108, 113, 116, 137–8, 145, 159
  see also miracles; visions
superstition 34, 129, 131
Sutton, Sir Thomas de 210
Sutton, William de 134
syncretism 77, 81–2, 83
Syward, John 129, 130, 132–3,
  133–4, 135–6, 136–7, 139, 141

Taillor, Alison 191
Taleta, Peire 246
Talgar, William 113
Tascar, Richard 218
tavern keepers 242–3
Tellez, Diego 57
Teva, Fernando de 55, 57
theft 4, 109–10, 112–13
Thomas, Brother 153, 154, 155,
  161–2, 165, 167
Thomas of Hereford, Bishop 6, 7,
  99, 108–12, 113, 115, 127, 129,
  133–40, 144, 145, 150
Thoresby, John, Archbishop of York
  213, 214
Todde, Agnes 191
Toledo, Francisco de 57, 58,
  59, 60
Torre, Juan de la 49
Torres, Paris de la 55
torture 47, 59, 85, 256
Trets, Peire de 228, 229, 230
Trujillo, Fernando de (former rabbi)
  44, 48–9
Trujillo, Fernando de (merchant) 75
Twigge, John 191

Urban IV, Pope 100
Urban V, Pope 214
Usher, Elyn 189, 190

Usher, John   189
Uverna, Jacma   246

Veer, John de   213
Velázquez, Isabel   86–7
violence   105, 203, 262
Villa Real, Lope de   47
Virgin Mary, cult of the   113, 114
visions   78, 89, 102, 104, 110–11,
    113, 114–15, 154, 160, 168
Vital, Bertran   231, 232, 246–7
  behavior   241–6
  indebtedness   232–40
Vital, Jaumet   231, 232, 233, 238
Vital, Peire   243
Vital, Secilieta   231–2, 238, 246–7
Vivanco, Isabel de   71
Vivaut, Raolin   243

Wales   7, 110, 111, 113, 150
Webster, Thomas   191
Welles, John   187
Westhouse, Margaret   188, 190
William, Count of Cornwall   113
William of Auvergne   104
William of Bourges   99
William of Nottingham   128
Wilson, William   210
witchcraft   5, 87–9, 90, 92, 102, 104
witnesses   3, 5, 6, 8, 9, 43–4, 60–1, 102
  anonymity   43–4, 46
  collusion   135, 144

exception procedure   245–6
of miracles   102, 108, 109, 127–8,
    133–42, 149, 151
  number   46–7, 151
  reliability   208–9
  significance   60
  tacha lists   46, 47, 54, 58–9,
    60, 61
  see also clergy as witnesses;
    compurgatory witnesses;
    defense witnesses; prosecution
    witnesses
women   1, 4, 116
  crimes/criminality   112, 143
  legal position   9
  lower class and caste women
    73–5
  melancholic nature   104
  witnesses   240, 245
women, single   3, 67, 74, 75
  employment   183, 189, 190–1
  strategies of survival   75–7
Wright, John   218
Wycliffites   162
Wylowes, John   217, 218
Wynde, Jane   177, 178, 179, 181,
    182–3, 184, 186, 187, 192
Wynde, Thomas   177, 178,
    179–80, 186
Wyngar, Emma   188

Zamora, Catalina de   49